Lecture Notes in Computer Science 4531

Commenced Publication in 1973
Founding and Former Series Editors:
Gerhard Goos, Juris Hartmanis, and Jan van Leeuwen

Jadwiga Indulska   Kerry Raymond (Eds.)

Distributed Applications and Interoperable Systems

7th IFIP WG 6.1 International Conference, DAIS 2007
Paphos, Cyprus, June 6-8, 2007
Proceedings

 Springer

Volume Editors

Jadwiga Indulska
School of Information Technology and Electrical Engineering
The University of Queensland
St. Lucia, QLD 4072, Australia
E-mail: jaga@itee.uq.edu.au

Kerry Raymond
Faculty of Information Technology
Queensland University of Technology
126 Margaret Street, Brisbane QLD 4001, Australia
E-mail: k.raymond@qut.edu.au

Library of Congress Control Number: 2007927413

CR Subject Classification (1998): D.2, C.2.4, I.2.11, D.4, H.4

LNCS Sublibrary: SL 3 – Information Systems and Application, incl. Internet/Web
and HCI

ISSN   0302-9743
ISBN-10   3-540-72881-3 Springer Berlin Heidelberg New York
ISBN-13   978-3-540-72881-8 Springer Berlin Heidelberg New York

Springer is a part of Springer Science+Business Media

springer.com

©IFIP International Federation for Information Processing 2007
Printed in Germany

Typesetting: Camera-ready by author, data conversion by Scientific Publishing Services, Chennai, India
Printed on acid-free paper   SPIN: 12072446   06/3180   5 4 3 2 1 0

Preface

This volume contains the proceedings of the Seventh IFIP WG 6.1 International Conference on Distributed Applications and Interoperable Systems (DAIS 2007) held in Paphos, Cyprus, June, 6-8, 2007. Distributed applications and interoperable systems have become an integral part of everyday living, part of the socio-economic ecosystem of our human environment. With such interdependence between society and software, distributed software applications must be sustainable and adaptable in the long term, despite the changes in our environment. Therefore, the theme of DAIS 2007 was "Towards Sustainability" and the papers of DAIS2007 addressed the following questions:

- How do we ensure our distributed applications can make local adaptation to specific circumstances of their deployment?
- How do we make our interoperable systems evolvable in the face of widespread change in their environment?
- How do we integrate distributed software within the wider fabric of computing within our modern world?

The conference program presented research contributions in context-awareness, adaptation, mobility, distributed applications and peer-to-peer computing, all of which relate to the sustainability of distributed applications and integrated systems. This year, the technical program of DAIS drew from 97 submitted papers, accepting 24 papers. Each accepted paper was reviewed (as a full paper) by at least three reviewers, coordinated by our International Program Committee.

The DAIS 2007 conference was again sponsored by IFIP (International Federation for Information Processing) and it was the seventh conference in the DAIS series of events organized by the IFIP Working Group 6.1. DAIS 2007 was part of the federated conference DisCoTec (Distributed Computing Techniques), together with the Ninth International Conference on Coordination Models and Languages (COORDINATION) and the Ninth IFIP International Conference on Formal Methods for Open Object-Based Distributed Systems (FMOODS).

We would like to take this opportunity to thank the numerous people whose work made this conference possible. We wish to express our deepest gratitude to the authors of submitted papers, to all Program Committee members and external reviewers for their participation in the paper review process, to Ricky Robinson for publicity, to the DAIS Steering Committee for their advice, to the University of Cyprus for hosting DisCoTec, and to George Angelos Papadopoulos for acting as General Chair of DisCoTec.

June 2007

Jadwiga Indulska
Kerry Raymond

Conference Committees and Organization

Chairs

Steering Committee	Lea Kutvonen, University of Helsinki, Finland
	Elie Najm, ENST, Paris, France
	Hartmut König, BTU Cottbus, Germany
	Kurt Geihs, University of Kassel, Germany
General Chair	George Angelos Papadopoulos, University of Cyprus
Program Co-chairs	Jadwiga Indulska, University of Queensland, Australia
	Kerry Raymond, Queensland University of Technology, Australia
Publicity Chair	Ricky Robinson, NICTA, Australia

Sponsoring Institutions

University of Cyprus
IFIP WG 6.1

Program Committee

N. Alonistioti	University of Athens, Greece
D. Bakken	Washington State University, USA
Y. Berbers	Katholieke Universiteit Leuven, Belgium
A. Beugnard	ENST-Bretagne, France
G. Blair	Lancaster University, UK
I. Demeure	ENST, France
C. Eckert	TU Darmstadt, Germany
F. Eliassen	University of Oslo, Norway
P. Felber	Université de Neuchâtel, Switzerland
K. Geihs	University of Kassel, Germany
R. Grønmo	SINTEF ICT, Norway
D. Hagimont	INP Toulouse, France
S. Hallsteinsen	SINTEF ICT, Norway
J. Indulska	University of Queensland, Australia
H. König	BTU Cottbus, Germany
R. Kröger	University of Applied Sciences Wiesbaden, Germany
L. Kutvonen	University of Helsinki, Finland
W. Lamersdorf	University of Hamburg, Germany
M. Lawley	Queensland University of Technology, Australia
P. Linington	University of Kent at Canterbury, UK

C. Linnhof-Popien	University of Munich, Germany
K. Lund	Norwegian Defence Research Establishment (FFI), Norway
R. Meier	Trinity College Dublin, Ireland
L. Merakos	University of Athens, Greece
A. Montresor	University of Trento, Italy
E. Najm	ENST, France
R. Oliveira	Universidade do Minho, Portugal
A. Puder	State University San Francisco, USA
K. Raymond	Queensland University of Technology, Australia
R. Robinson	National ICT Australia, Australia
A. Schill	Technical University of Dresden, Germany
T. Senivongse	Chulalongkorn University, Thailand
K. Sere	Abo Akademi University, Finland
J.B. Stefani	INRIA, France
E. Tanter	University Santiago de Chile, Chile
K. Zieliński	AGH University of Science and Technology, Poland

Additional Referees

M. Alia	C.P. Kunze	M. Schiely
S. Arteconi	A. Küpper	M. Schmid
D. Bade	F. Liu	S. Serbu
A. Beloued	R. Löfman	G. Simon
S. Bouchenak	C. Lohr	E. Stav
G. Brataas	N. Lopes	M. Strassberger
L. Braubach	J. Martens	H. Sturzrehm
P.-C. David	L. Martin	J. Sudeikat
F. Degerlund	P.H. Meland	G. Treu
H.H. Duong	P. Moen	R. Vila ca
J. Fabry	J.-C. Moissinac	M. Wagner
J. Floch	M. Morel	T. Weise
P. Floréen	M. Neovius	D. Weiss
C. Funk	A. Opitz	L. Wienhofen
B. Girma	J. Pereira	L. Yan
E. Gjørven	A. Pokahr	M. Zapf
K. Henricksen	D. Preuveneers	S. Zaplata
M.U. Khan	R. Rouvoy	

Table of Contents

Mobility II

The Context-Dependent Role Model

Jorge Vallejos, Peter Ebraert*, Brecht Desmet,
Tom Van Cutsem**, Stijn Mostinckx*, and Pascal Costanza***

Programming Technology Lab – Vrije Universiteit Brussel
Pleinlaan 2 - 1050 Brussels - Belgium
{jvallejo, pebraert, bdesmet, tvcutsem,
smostinc, pascal.costanza}@vub.ac.be

Abstract. Implementing context-dependent behaviour of pervasive computing applications puts a great burden on programmers: Devices need to continuously adapt not only to their own context, but also to the context of other devices they interact with. We present an approach that modularises behavioural adaptations into roles. Role selection takes the context of all the devices involved in an interaction into account, ensures an unambiguous scope of adaptation even in the presence of concurrency, and protects the privacy of the devices. Thus, our context-dependent role (CDR) model facilitates expressing interactions between applications in different, possibly conflicting contexts.

1   Introduction

Context-awareness is commonly defined as the ability of an application to *perceive* and *dynamically adapt* its behaviour to the *surrounding environment* [20]. This definition, however, only seems halfway correct, especially in the presence of distribution. Context-dependent adaptations have particular effects on the interactions between devices, and thus are more difficult to coordinate in pervasive computing systems.

Consider the scenario of the context-aware cellphone, in which a person attending an important meeting does not want to be disturbed by incoming calls. Therefore, his cellphone should, for example, automatically signal incoming calls in a discreet way only. The definition of context-awareness given above suffices for this scenario since the cellphone may adapt its behaviour based on information inferred from its surroundings by means of sensors, like the user's location. However, assume further that this person has a relative who is currently in the hospital, and that he wants to be sure that he does not miss any call from the hospital although he is in an important meeting. The issue here is that he may not know what is the phone number or even the identity of the person who

---

* Author funded by a doctoral scholarship of the Institute for the Promotion of Innovation through Science and Technology in Flanders (IWT-Vlaanderen).
** Research Assistant of the Fund for Scientific Research Flanders, Belgium (F.W.O.).
*** Author funded by the Institute for the Promotion of Innovation through Science and Technology in Flanders (IWT-Vlaanderen).

J. Indulska and K. Raymond (Eds.): DAIS 2007, LNCS 4531, pp. 1–16, 2007.

would call him from the hospital. In this case, his cellphone cannot derive the necessary information to decide the kind of signal required for such a special call. The only information it can actually rely on is found in the context of the calling device, which is the fact that the call originates from the hospital. Conversely, if the adaptation were decided at the calling device, it would not only inhibit the callee's ability to discern the calls he wants to receive. It would probably even conflict with the requirements at the callee's phone, as the caller may not, and probably should not, be aware of the callee's context.

The scenario above reveals the problems of distribution for context-dependent adaptations. First, the behavioural adaptation of a device (i.e. signalling calls loud or discreetly) may not only depend on its own context (i.e. "user is in meeting room") but also on the context of all the participants of an interaction (i.e. "call originates from the hospital"). Second, different interactions require adaptations that do not necessarily fit together, such as the different call signals in the cellphone (i.e. loud and discreet signals cannot be combined). Last but not least, external decisions of adaptations can be more vulnerable to context changes and hamper the privacy of the devices.

We propose a role-based object-oriented programming model, called the *context-dependent role (CDR) model*, to facilitate the development of context-dependent adaptations in mobile distributed systems. In this model, (1) roles represent the different behavioural adaptations a software application can dynamically adopt according to the context, (2) an application autonomously decides on an appropriate role based on the context of all the participants, and (3) an adaptation is strictly delimited by the scope of an interaction.

We validate the CDR model by implementing it as an extension to AmbientTalk [16], a programming language especially designed for pervasive computing applications. We use this extension for implementing the scenario of the context-aware cellphone described above.

2   Context-Dependent Adaptations in Mobile Distributed Systems

We now briefly discuss the main properties of context-dependent adaptations in pervasive computing environments to later introduce the specific requirements of distribution for such adaptations. We derive these requirements from the analysis of the scenario of the context-aware cellphone.

Since we focus on context-dependent adaptations in this paper, we do not explicitly deal with the context acquisition, i.e. the way in which software systems obtain information from their surroundings. We rather assume that every application has the necessary support to derive unambiguous context information from potentially unreliable low-level sensor data, like the Context Toolkit framework [24]. We also require that all participants in a mobile distributed system agree on a common representation of the particular context information of interest, like for example the ontology introduced in [22].

2.1   Context-Dependent Adaptations

A context-aware application has to be able to deal with dynamic changes that often lack any periodicity or predictability. The presence of unexpected context changes may lead us to additionally presume that adaptations have to be applied at arbitrary unanticipated points in time. However, adaptations do not necessarily have to happen right after a context change. The context-aware cellphone, for instance, needs to adapt signalling calls only when receiving an incoming call, not necessarily when the user enters the meeting room. This means that an adaptation has a *delimited scope of action*: The adaptation is only required for a specific operation (e.g. a method execution in an object-oriented system) and thus its impact can be limited to the execution of this operation.

In most cases, a context-dependent adaptation affects only parts of the program. The example of the context-aware cellphone illustrates this partial adaptation of behaviour: The adaptation required in this scenario involves exclusively the signals for incoming calls, but leaves other functionality intact. An important requirement for using partial adaptations is that the resulting behaviour of the application should be a *consistent composition* of its default behaviour and the adaptations.

The dependency of the application behaviour on its context does not imply that the code required to reason about the context should get entangled with the rest of the application program. Reasoning about the context inside of the program would lead to undesirable situations such as scattered context-dependent if-statements, resulting in cluttered code that is hard to maintain [12]. Context-dependent adaptations, as well as the reasoning process that they require, should be *modularised* to avoid their entanglement and scattering in the program.

To summarise, context-dependent adaptations:

- occur **dynamically**, with arbitrary frequency, and within a **delimited scope** of action.
- generally affect only part of the program. In this case a **consistent composition** with the rest of the program should be ensured.
- should be **modularised** in such a way that they do not get entangled with the base program.

2.2   Distribution Conditions for Context-Dependent Adaptations

In this section, we analyse the implications for context-dependent adaptations of the distributed nature of pervasive computing environments.

Multiple Influence of Context. The context is not a monolithic and homogeneous set of information for all the participants of a pervasive computing system. It can vary with time and from one device to another. This variability implies that applications might be interacting with others in completely different contexts. The question concerning our focus on context-dependent adaptations is thus how this context heterogeneity may influence the behavioural adaptations of such applications. In the scenario of the context-aware cellphone, for instance, we observe that the behavioural adaptation on the user's cellphone is not only influenced by its location, but also by the location of the calling device.

Conflicting Adaptations. The problem of conflicting adaptations stems from applications that may be involved in several interactions with different remote applications at the same time. Since presumably these interactions require also different adaptations, there is a high probability that applications end up with adaptations that conflict with each other. The context-aware cellphone, for example, cannot adopt two different call signals at the same time, even if the signals are the appropriate adaptations for two different incoming calls. Part of this problem is directly related to the natural concurrency of the mobile devices. Therefore, adaptations must be circumscribed to a delimited scope of action that is unambiguous even in the presence of concurrent interactions.

Privacy Issues. In a distributed system, the decision whether and how to adapt its components can be made at different physical locations. In pervasive computing systems, however, this condition may raise privacy issues. A context-dependent adaptation decided in a different device from the one affected by the adaptation is neither always possible nor always desirable for the users of mobile devices. In the scenario of the context-aware cellphone, for instance, if the caller could decide that the callee's cellphone should be switched to loud signalling mode, the person at the meeting would lose the possibility to discern the calls he wants to receive.

The same argument can be used to rule out centralised adaptation and decision schemes, developed to coordinate the adaptations of collaborative applications [11,9]. If such a cooperation scheme is required, it should also take into account the privacy of each device involved in a common task. We call this the *non-intrusiveness* principle.

Summary. The distribution requirements for context-dependent adaptations introduced in this section are listed below.

- The behavioural adaptation of an application may depend on **multiple contexts**, especially in the case of interactions with other applications.
- Context-dependent adaptations should be circumscribed to a **delimited scope** of action, in a way that is **consistent with concurrency** to avoid conflicting adaptations.
- Context-dependent adaptations should comply with the **non-intrusiveness** principle to preserve the privacy of mobile applications. This principle is also valid for cooperation schemes of adaptations.

To the best of our knowledge, no existing middleware or programming language offers a solution to deal with all of the properties and which satisfies all distribution requirements for context-dependent adaptations presented in this section. We further discuss the related work in Section 5.

3 The Context-Dependent Role (CDR) Model

To address the requirements discussed in the previous section, we now introduce the *CDR model* for context-dependent adaptations in mobile distributed systems. It extends the actor model [1] of concurrency and distribution with the notion of context-dependent roles. In this section, we describe the semantics for creating, selecting, and adopting context-dependent roles.

We use the context-aware cellphone application identified in this paper to illustrate the different components of our model. We implement this application in AmbientTalk [16], an actor-based programming language especially designed for pervasive computing in which we have developed our model. For the sake of conciseness, we do not present an in-depth discussion of AmbientTalk itself. Instead, we introduce specific features as necessary in the course of this section and refer the reader to dedicated publications [14,15] for more information about this language.

3.1 Flexible Composition of Behavioural Adaptations

In the CDR model, a context-aware application is represented as an actor whose behaviour encapsulates the default functionality of the application and all of its context-dependent adaptations. The default behaviour and the adaptations are modelled as objects and organised in a *delegation* hierarchy. Such a hierarchical delegation structure, originally presented in [21], enables the adaptations to extend the default behaviour of the application – placed at the root of the hierarchy – or any other more general adaptation situated higher up the delegation tree. Figure 1 shows the behaviour of the actor that implements the context-aware cellphone application, specifically its feature to receive incoming calls.

In a delegation hierarchy, an object can either override or share behaviour with its parent. This is especially beneficial for modelling *partial* adaptations. In the context-aware cellphone, for instance, the loud and discreet adaptation objects each have a specialised implementation of the signal method, while they share the behaviour of the call method, which is defined in the default

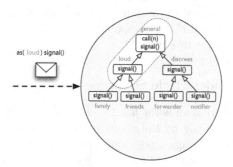

Fig. 1. Context-dependent behaviour of the cellphone actor

behaviour (the **general** object). At the same time, the delegation semantics ensures a consistent interaction between objects that delegate to each other [21]. The following listing presents a definition of the behaviour of the context-aware cellphone actor:

```
contextCellphone: contextActor({
  general: object({
    signal()::{
      playTone("normal-tone")
    };
    playTone(tone)::{...};
    blinkLights()::{...};
    ...
  });
  loud: extend(general,{
    signal()::{
      playTone("noisy-tone");
      blinkLights()}
  });
  discreet: extend(general,{
    signal()::{blinkLights()}
  });
  ...
})
```

Different from normal AmbientTalk actors, whose behaviour is represented by a unique object, actors in our model (created using the dedicated **contextActor** construct) contain multiple behaviour objects. In the code above, the adaptations of the cellphone actor are represented by the **discreet** and **loud** objects which extend the **general** object, overriding the **signal** method.

3.2 Dynamic Adaptation Based on Roles

In the CDR model, the behaviour objects cannot receive messages directly because these objects correspond to the internal state of an actor and, as such, they should only be accessed by the actor. Instead, actors receive messages and respond to them by first selecting the appropriate role and then executing the corresponding method in the adaptation object of that role. The adaptation required by a role-specific message not only involves the object that denotes this role, but also its delegation chain. In the context-aware cellphone, for example, if the **loud** role is specified in an incoming message, the application will respond according to the delegation chain composed of the **loud** and **general** objects (marked by the dotted line in Figure 1).

3.3 Context-Dependent Role Selection

The selection of which role an actor has to adopt to respond to a message is a decision made autonomously by the actor receiving the message but based on the context of both the message sender and receiver. This means that the sender must not indicate the role required for the message execution but rather passes part of its own context information along with the message. The part of the context included in the message is autonomously chosen by the message sending

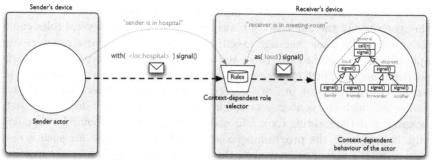

Fig. 2. Context-dependent role selection

actor (discussed later in Section 3.5). Figure 2 illustrates the context-dependent role selection process in the scenario of the context-aware cellphone.

The role selection process is supported by a dedicated entity within the actor, called the *context-dependent role selector*. This role selector is a logic reasoning engine that takes as input the context information of the sender and receiver, together with programmer-defined rules that describe under which conditions a given role can be selected for an incoming message. The output, then, corresponds to the message provided with the role that is most appropriate for the context conditions.

The advantage of designing the role selector as a logic engine is that it offers the developer the expressiveness of the logic programming paradigm. Using a logic programming language, the developer can declaratively specify when a role is applicable, rather than having to specify imperatively when roles become active or inactive by tracking changes in the context.

The rules that the role selector uses to decide on a role have the following structure:

```
role aRole for receiver, message if
    condition1 & ... & conditionN
```

The role selector chooses the role indicated in the head of a rule only if all its conditions are accomplished. The information that these conditions require is retrieved from the logic variables **receiver** and **message**, which are bound to the receiver actor and the message respectively. For instance, we add the following rule to the definition of the context-aware cellphone actor presented in Section 3.1 (by using the **addRule** primitive), indicating that this actor should adopt the **discreet** role when it is at the meeting room:

```
contextCellphone: contextActor({
  general: object({ ... });
  discreet: extend(general,{ ... });
  ...
  // Don't signal calls at the meeting room.
  addRule({role discreet for receiver, message if
          receiver.getContext("location") = "meeting-room"})
})
```

There can be cases where more than one rule matches the context conditions of the receiver and the message that was sent. It means that several roles could be adopted for the same message execution. In our model, however, actors can adopt only one role at the same time, and for this reason, the rules in the context-dependent role selector have a priority order. Only the role that corresponds to the rule with the highest priority is returned as a result. This is the way, for instance, in which the context-aware cellphone application can determine that, although it is in the meeting room, the calls from the hospital should be signalled loudly. In this case, the programmer should add an extra rule for such a new condition with a higher priority than the rule about the receiver in the meeting room described above. The new rule looks as follows:

```
// Signal the calls from the hospital loud.
addRule({role loud for receiver, message if
        message.getContext("location") = "hospital"});
```

In the current implementation of the CDR model, the priority of the rules is determined by the order in which they are defined in the actor, as in the Prolog logic programming language (in Section 4, we propose some alternatives to this basic way of defining priorities). Conversely, it could be that none of the rules matches the current sender's and receiver's context. For this specific case we have defined a default rule without any condition that returns the role corresponding to the default behaviour of the application (the general role).

3.4 Delimited Scope of Adaptations

A behavioural adaptation is delimited by the scope of the execution of a message, which means that an actor adopts the role indicated in a message exclusively to process that message. This delimited scope is ensured by the asynchronous message passing mechanism of actors [2] which explicitly separates the message reception from the message execution by using a message queue. This separation enables the actor to adapt its behaviour to individual messages without the risk of affecting or being affected by the adaptations required for other message executions. This separation also enables actors to include the context-dependent role selection as an extra step between the reception and the execution of a message. Figure 3 illustrates the actor with all its components: the context-dependent behaviour, the context-dependent role selector, and the message queue.

Within the scope of the message execution, we can find other information in addition to the sender and receiver's contexts. The receiver's state and the message itself are also part of the context of the communication and hence they can also be used in the definition of the rules and the methods. For instance, assume that the user in the meeting room wants to send back an explanation about why he is not answering the call to all the callers that have an entry in his address book. We define a caller to be a buddy if the caller corresponds to an entry in the user's address book. So then the rule would also be implemented in terms

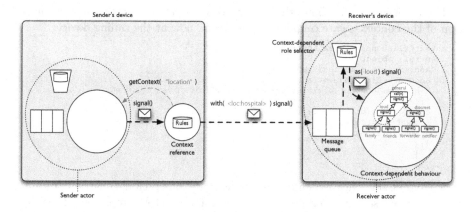

Fig. 3. The implementation of the CDR model in AmbientTalk

of the "inAddressBook" method. The implementation of such a requirement in the actor is as follows:

```
contextCellphone: contextActor({
  ...
  notifier:: extend(discreet,{
    signal()::{
      buddy: getContact(thisMessage.getContext("name"));
      // Send the explanation in a text message.
      buddy<-receiveText("I'm in a meeting until 11:30");
      // Use the signal method defined in the discreet role
      // (the parent of this role).
      super.signal()}
  });

  // Notify only to my buddies that I am in a meeting.
  addRule({role notifier for receiver, message if
           receiver.getContext("location") = "meeting-room" &
           senderName: message.getContext("name") &
           receiver.inAddressBook(senderName)});
  ...
})
```

We benefit from the visibility of the information contained in the message (accessed via the pseudovariable **thisMessage**) in the implementation of the **notifier** role to reply to the message.

3.5 Context Selection

The CDR model preserves the privacy of the receiver actor by allowing it to autonomously decide its adaptations. To also protect the privacy of the message sender we should enable this actor to autonomously select the context that it sends to the message receiver. We introduce *context references* for this purpose. A context reference is a dedicated proxy for a remote actor, whose main responsibility is to get sender's context information and include it in the message sent to the remote actor. Figure 3 illustrates the place of the context reference in the interaction between the two context-aware cellphone applications.

The following listing shows the use of a context reference in the implementation of the context-aware cellphone application, now at the calling device:

```
contextCellphone: contextActor({
  general: object({
    addressBook : makeHashmap();
    addContact(nickname,visibleCtx):: {
      addressBook.put(nickname,makeContextRef(nickname, visibleCtx))
    };
    callContact(nickname):: {
      buddy: getContact(nickname);
      buddy<-signal()
    };
  ... };
... })
```

A context reference is defined using the `makeContextRef` construct. Its definition comprises the identification of the remote actor[1] (represented by the nickname of the cellphone's user in our example), and the context accessible for the reference. Similar to the context-dependent role selector presented in Section 3.3, a context reference enables developers to declaratively specify the part of the context that will be sent to the remote actor. Using the implementation above, for instance, the cellphone's user can add a contact to his address book and reveal his location only during working hours, as follows:

```
contextCellphone<-addContact("Tom",
                   {addRule({send location of sender if
                             time: sender.getContext("time") &
                             time > 8.00 & time < 17.00})})
```

The information that the conditions of the rules for the context reference require, is retrieved from the logic variable **sender** which is bound to the sender actor[2]. These rules are evaluated each time the sender actor sends a message through the context reference. The context reference takes into account the context information indicated in the head of all the rules that accomplish their conditions. If none of the rules succeeds, the context reference does not add any context information to the message.

Another benefit of the context references is that they enable the sender actor to abstract from the passing of the context required in the CDR model. This means that programmers do not have to manually include the context information whenever they send messages (e.g. see the `signal` message sent inside the `call` method). The inclusion of the context information occurs transparently in the context reference. At the same time, a context reference is a central place for configuring what context information to expose to the remote actor.

4   Discussion and Future Work

In summary, in the CDR model: an actor encapsulates a delegation hierarchy composed of a default behaviour and its different context-dependent adaptations,

---

[1] In AmbientTalk such identification corresponds to an intensional description of the service provided by the actor in terms of its properties [16].

[2] We do not consider the receiver for these rules at this stage. In Section 4, we discuss some extensions to this context selection process.

all of them represented as roles; actors respond to messages by first selecting the appropriate role and then executing the corresponding method in the adaptation object of that role; the role required for the execution of a message is autonomously selected by the actor that receives the message, using the context-dependent role selector and based on the context of both the sender and receiver of the message; adaptations have a delimited scope of action which is defined by the execution of a message; and a context reference enables the message sender to be aware of the part of the context exposed to the message receiver.

This model accomplishes the properties of context-dependent adaptations identified in Section 2.1 as follows:

Dynamic adaptations. Dynamic adaptations of behaviour occur transparently for the programmer as a result of the selection of a context-dependent role. This role indicates the behavioural adaptation (object) to which the actor has to address the message.

Delimited scope. Behavioural adaptations are only active within the scope of a message execution. This means that an actor only adopts a certain role to process a single message.

Consistent composition. The composition of behavioural adaptations is defined by the delegation hierarchy. This hierarchy is a flexible structure in which the adaptations can specialise and consistently share behaviour.

Modularisation. Behavioural adaptations in this model are modular since they are encapsulated in objects whose only interaction with the other adaptations is regulated by the semantics of the delegation mechanism. The context reasoning is also concentrated in a single entity called the context-dependent role selector.

The CDR model also copes with the distribution requirements presented in Section 2.2:

Multiple context influence. This model takes the context of all the entities involved in a common task explicitly into account. The execution of a message does not only depend on the application that receives the message (its context and state), but also on the context information of the message sender that is passed along with the message.

Delimited scope and concurrency. Actors communicate by asynchronous message passing which enables them to adapt their behaviour to a message without conflicting with other interactions.

Non-intrusiveness. An actor autonomously decides on the role that it will adopt to process a certain incoming message. This decision is made by its context-dependent role selector. The actor that sends the message also decides autonomously the context information that is passed along with the message.

Although the CDR model can help in tackling some of the challenges for context-dependent adaptations faced in pervasive computing, a number of challenging issues needs to be further explored. For instance, in this model the default behaviour of a context-aware application is represented as a single object. We are currently investigating an extension to this model that enables programmers to also deal with application behaviours composed of multiple objects. The roles of an application, in this case, do not represent the adaptations of one object but rather *modules* of adaptations for several objects. The essence of these modules of adaptation can be found in the notions of class families in CaesarJ [3], class-boxes [6], or layers in ContextL [12]. So far, none of these approaches provide support to deal with pervasive computing systems.

In this paper, we illustrate the benefits of delimiting the scope of an adaptation to the execution of one message. We are currently also investigating how the adaptation scope needs to be propagated in case of having interactions that involve more than one message.

We also propose in this work the use of a delegation hierarchy to model compositions of context-dependent adaptations. In this structure, the adaptations have a predefined location which gives clarity to the behaviour composition, but at the same time restricts the possibilities of adaptations to those denoted by the delegation chains in the hierarchy. A possible alternative to this delegation hierarchy is to have a set of *unwired* behavioural adaptations, similar to mixins [8] or traits [26], which can be dynamically composed whenever they are used.

In the logic reasoning process of context-dependent role selection, we need to ensure that only one role is chosen. For this reason, we establish priorities between the rules that in the current implementation of the CDR model rely on their order of definition. We are currently exploring Choice Logic [29], Ordered Logic [19] and dynamic preferences in Extended Logic programming [10], as more expressive and dynamic ways of defining priorities.

In the CDR model, we define context references as the entities that centralise the context selection process at the message sender's device. A context reference decides the part of the context that is sent to the message receiver based on the sender's context conditions. We are currently working on an extension that also considers the message receiver in the context selection process, e.g. to reason about the context conditions of the receiver or to enable it to prompt the sender for specific pieces of context.

Finally, we are exploring different ways of optimising the logic reasoning process required in the CDR model (context and role selection). We investigate some techniques for caching information [18] and therefore avoiding the recalculation of the role in every message reception.

5   Related Work

Context-Aware Frameworks. There is a huge amount of research on frameworks that support the development and deployment of context-aware systems like WildCAT [13], ContextToolkit [25] or Java Context Awareness Framework [5]. The aim of these frameworks is to provide a generic programming infrastructure that deals with common functionalities like uniform interfaces to access sensor data, event-based system to signal context changes, and reasoning mechanism to aggregate context information. Context-aware frameworks are useful for both pro-active and reactive systems. In the former case, callback methods are used, as part of an event-driven system, to automatically invoke some behaviour in response to relevant context changes. Additionally, framework solutions also provide the ability to query for actual context information such that reactive systems can adopt their behaviour accordingly. Developers have to rely on traditional dispatching constructs like conditional statements or polymorphism to establish the behavioural adaptation. As soon as context-dependent behaviour appears to be the rule rather than the exception, these language constructs become unmanageable. We therefore argue that context-aware frameworks and our role-based model are actually complementary. Whereas the framework solutions provide the required functionalities to develop context-aware systems, our role-based programming model focuses on how context-dependent adaptations can be decently modelled inside of software systems. The synergy between both proposals supports the development of pervasive systems.

The CORTEX [27] is a middleware architecture that exploits the sentient object paradigm: so-called sentient objects receive events as input (from other sentient objects or sensors), process the events by means of an inference engine and generate further events as output. The communication between sentient objects happens asynchronously via an event layer which hides the network and the transformation process of real-world events. Although our model incorporates concepts that also appear in CORTEX, like asynchronous communication and a reasoning system, both approaches address different application domains. The sentient object model of CORTEX is intended for pro-active context-aware systems that autonomously invoke some action in response to relevant context changes. In contrast, our model deals with reactive systems. That is, upon the reception of a message, the behaviour of the most appropriate role is executed.

Actors in Open Distributed and Pervasive Systems. There exists a number of research proposals that extend the actor model to address the software development issues found in open distributed and pervasive environments. Although so far these approaches do not directly deal with context-dependent behavioural adaptations, some of their coordination and adaptation mechanisms may be useful for developing context-aware applications. SALSA [28], for instance, is an actor-based programming language designed for internet and grid computing. This language enables application's adaptation by means of reflection. The basic operations of the actors (communication and message processing) can be freely manipulated at the meta-level of SALSA. These reflective capabilities are mainly used to fulfil a set of default policies like resource profiling, secure communication and coordination, but new policies can also be defined.

ARC [23] is a role-based coordination model for open, distributed and embedded systems. This model also uses a meta-level but in this case to map quality of service (QoS) requirements to coordination constraints. These constraints are transparently imposed to the actors through message manipulation. Unlike roles in the CDR model, roles in the ARC model are totally independent entities (meta-actors) that provide abstractions for actor functional behaviours and that can be shared by multiple actors. The local coordination between actors is conducted by the roles whereas the distributed coordination is conducted by other meta-actors called *coordinators*.

Models of Composition and Conditional Selection of Behaviour. The CDR model also shares a number of properties with some object models of composition and conditional behaviour selection. Split objects [4] is a programming model that uses the delegation mechanism of prototype-based languages for role modelling. Similar to an actor in the CDR model, a split object encapsulates a collection of objects structured in a delegation hierarchy that hold part of the description of the split object (state and behaviour) and represent the different roles the split object can adopt to respond to a message. The difference with the actor is that the split object does require that the messages sent to it indicate a role. This means that the split object cannot autonomously decide its adaptation which contradicts the non-intrusiveness principle defined in Section 2.2.

Composition filters [7] is a composition model that enables programmers to modify the behaviour of object-based components through the manipulation of incoming and outgoing messages. As in the CDR model, object behaviours are fully encapsulated, and the behavioural adaptations are exclusively performed inside the component (by using *filters*).

Predicate dispatching [17] generalises a diversity of method dispatching proposals into a unified theory of dispatch. This is established by permitting arbitrary predicates to control the applicability of methods. The authors paid special attention to static typechecking to ensure that there always exists a single most-specific method. Our model can be regarded as a specific application of predicate dispatch in which predicates are associated with roles.

6   Conclusion

Within the domain of pervasive computing, we focus on the capacity of software applications to adapt to their dynamically reconfigurable environments. We describe a number of properties for context-dependent adaptations and then establish some specific requirements of distribution for such adaptations, derived from the analysis of a concrete scenario of context-aware cellphone applications. We observe that context-dependent adaptations occur dynamically and within a delimited scope of action. In addition, these adaptations should be consistently combined with the default behaviour of the application, and clearly modularised to avoid the entanglement between the adaptations and the application behaviour. To cope with the effects of distribution on context-dependent adaptations, an adaptation should take into account the context of all the applications involved in an interaction, have an unambiguous scope of action even in the presence of concurrent interactions, and finally protect the privacy of the interacting applications.

In this paper, we propose the context-dependent model to deal with the properties and distribution requirements described above. In this model, context-aware applications are represented as actors provided with a set of behavioural adaptations organised in a delegation hierarchy. Each adaptation is represented as a role that an actor can adopt to respond to a message. The actor autonomously selects a role for each message based on the context of the message sender and receiver. The context information of the sender that is used for this selection, is passed along with the message and is also autonomously chosen by the sender.

Currently, we are investigating different extensions of our model, like increasing the units of adaptations, making more flexible composition structures of adaptations, propagating the adaptation scope for multiple-actor interactions, and enhancing the expressiveness and efficiency of the context and role selection process.

References

1. Agha, G.: Actors: a Model of Concurrent Computation in Distributed Systems. MIT Press, Cambridge (1986)
2. Agha, G., Hewitt, C.: Concurrent programming using actors. Object-oriented concurrent programming, pp. 37–53 (1987)
3. Aracic, I., Gasiunas, V., Mezini, M., Ostermann, K.: Overview of caesarj. In: Rashid, A., Aksit, M. (eds.) Transactions on Aspect-Oriented Software Development I. LNCS, vol. 3880, pp. 135–173. Springer, Heidelberg (2006)
4. Bardou, D., Dony, C.: Split objects: a disciplined use of delegation within objects. In: Proceedings of the 11th ACM SIGPLAN conference on Object-oriented programming, systems, languages, and applications, pp. 122–137. ACM Press, New York (1996)
5. Bardram, J.E.: The java context awareness framework (jcaf) - a service infrastructure and programming framework for context-aware applications. In: Pervasive, pp. 98–115 (2005)
6. Bergel, A., Ducasse, S., Nierstrasz, O., Wuyts, R.: Classboxes: controlling visibility of class extensions. Computer Languages, Systems and Structures 31(3-4), pp. 107–126 (2004)
7. Bergmans, L.: The composition filters object model. Technical report, Dept. of Computer Science, University of Twente (1994)
8. Bracha, G., Cook, W.: Mixin-based inheritance. In: Meyrowitz, N. (ed.) Proceedings of the Conference on Object-Oriented Programming: Systems, Languages, and Applications / Proceedings of the European Conference on Object-Oriented Programming, pp. 303–311, ACM Press, Ottawa, Canada (1990)
9. Brewer, E.A., Katz, R.H., Amir, E., Balakrishnan, H., Chawathe, Y., Fox, A., Gribble, S.D., Hodes, T., Nguyen, G., Padmanabhan, V.N., Stemm, M., Seshan,S., Henderson, T.: A network architecture for heterogeneous mobile computing. Personal Communications, IEEE (1998)
10. Brewka, G.: Well-founded semantics for extended logic programs with dynamic preferences. Journal of Artificial Intelligence Research 4, 19 (1996)
11. Correa, C.D., Marsic, I.: A flexible architecture to support awareness in heterogeneous collaborative environments. In: Fourth International Symposium on Collaborative Technologies and Systems (CTS 2003), pp. 109–116 (November 2003)

12. Costanza, P., Hirschfeld, R.: Language constructs for context-oriented programming - An overview of ContextL. In: Dynamic Languages Symposium (2005)
13. David, P.-C., Ledoux, T.: Wildcat: a generic framework for context-aware applications. In: MPAC '05. Proceedings of the 3rd international workshop on Middleware for pervasive and ad-hoc computing, pp. 1–7. ACM Press, New York (2005)
14. Dedecker, J.: Ambient-Oriented Programming. PhD thesis, Vrije Universiteit Brussel (2006)
15. Dedecker, J., Van Belle, W.: Actors for Mobile Ad-hoc Networks. In: International Conference on Embedded and Ubiquitous Computing EUC2004 (2004)
16. Dedecker, J., Van Cutsem, T., Mostinckx, S., D'Hondt, T., De Meuter, W.: Ambient-Oriented Programming in Ambienttalk. In: Proceedings of the 20th European Conference on Object-Oriented Programming (ECOOP) Nantes, France (2006)
17. Ernst, M.D., Kaplan, C.S., Chambers, C.: Predicate dispatching: A unified theory of dispatch. In: ECOOP '98, the 12th European Conference on Object-Oriented Programming, pp. 186–211, Brussels, Belgium (July 20-24, 1998)
18. Forgy, C.: Rete: A fast algorithm for the many pattern/many object pattern match problem. Artificial Intelligence 19, 17–37 (1982)
19. Gabbay, D., Laenens, E., Vermeir, D.: Credulous vs. sceptical semantics for ordered logic programs. In: Kaufmann, M. (ed.) Second International Conference on Principles of Knowledge Representation and Reasoning, pp. 208–217 (1991)
20. I.A. Group. Ambient intelligence: from vision to reality (September 2003)
21. Lieberman, H.: Using prototypical objects to implement shared behavior in object-oriented systems. In: Conference proceedings on Object-oriented Programming Systems, Languages and Applications, pp. 214–223. ACM Press, New York (1986)
22. Preuveneers, D., Van den Bergh, J., Wagelaar, D., Georges, A., Rigole, P., Clerckx, T., Berbers, Y., Coninx, K., Jonckers, V., De Bosschere, K.: Towards an extensible context ontology for ambient intelligence. In: Ambient Intelligence, pp. 148–159 (2004)
23. Ren, S., Yu, Y., Chen, N., Marth, K., Poirot, P.-E., Shen, L.: Actors, roles and coordinators - a coordination model for open distributed and embedded systems. In: COORDINATION, pp. 247–265 (2006)
24. Salber, D., Dey, A.K., Abowd, G.D.: The context toolkit: aiding the development of context-enabled applications. In: A. Press (ed.) CHI 99: Proceedings of the SIGCHI conference on Humon factors in computing systems, pp. 434–441. New York, USA (1999)
25. Salber, D., Dey, A.K., Abowd, G.D.: The context toolkit: aiding the development of context-enabled applications. In: CHI '99. Proceedings of the SIGCHI conference on Human factors in computing systems, pp. 434–441. ACM Press, New York (1999)
26. Schärli, N., Ducasse, S., Nierstrasz, O., Black, A.: Traits: Composable units of behavior. In: ECOOP 2003 – Object-Oriented Programming, LNCS, vol. 2743, pp. 248–274, Springer, Heidelberg (2003)
27. Sørensen, C.-F., Wu, M., Sivaharan, T., Blair, G.S., Okanda, P., Friday, A., Duran-Limon, H.: A context-aware middleware for applications in mobile ad hoc environments. In: MPAC '04. Proceedings of the 2nd workshop on Middleware for pervasive and ad-hoc computing, pp. 107–110. ACM Press, New York (2004)
28. Varela, C.A., Agha, G.: A hierarchical model for coordination of concurrent activities. In: Ciancarini, P., Wolf, A.L. (eds.) COORDINATION 1999. LNCS, vol. 1594, pp. 166–182. Springer, Heidelberg (1999)
29. Vos, M.D., Vermeir, D.: Choice logic programs and nash equilibria in strategic games. In: Flum, J., Rodriguez-Artalejo, M. (eds.) Computer Science Logic, vol. 1683, pp. 266–276. Springer, Heidelberg (1999)

Integrating Facts and Beliefs to Model and Reason About Context

Waltenegus Dargie and Thomas Springer

TU Dresden, Institute for Systems Architecture, Computer Networks Group,
Helmholtzstrasse 10, 01062 Dresden, Germany
{waltenegus.dargie, thomas.springer}@tu-dresden.de

Abstract. This paper presents a twofold context modelling approach
that integrates beliefs (uncertain knowledge) and facts to reason about
various everyday situations. Awareness of everyday situations enables
mobile devices to adapt to the social and conceptual settings in which
they operate; it also enables resources which share a similar context to
cooperate in order to carry out a distributed task on behalf of their user.
Our context modelling process involves the identification of the context
of interest, the determination of those aspects of a context which can be
captured by employing sensors, the determination of contextual states
for each aspect, and finally, the determination of logical and probabilistic relationships between the contextual aspects and the context they
represent. We demonstrate our approach by modelling physical places.
Data from various heterogeneous sensors build our system's belief, while
containment relationships build its factual knowledge regarding places.
The system utilises its belief and factual knowledge to reason about the
whereabouts of a mobile user.

1 Introduction

Human beings are apt to adapt to their surrounding by perceiving what is taking
place around them and by relating the perceived change in their surrounding
with their expectations and experiences. As he laid out his vision for ubiquitous
computing, Weiser asserted that the idea first arose from "contemplating the
place of today's computer in actual activities of everyday life. In particular,
anthropological studies of work life teach us that people primarily work in a
world of shared situations and unexamined technological skills [14]."

For example, when people attend a meeting, their eyes communicate to convey
agreements or disagreements to what is said or unsaid; voices are whispered to
exchange impromptu opinions; facial expressions reveal to the other participants
fatigue, boredom, or disinterest. More importantly, speeches may not be gram-
matically correct or complete. Previous as well as unfolding incidents enable the
participants to capture what cannot be expressed verbally. Speakers shift from
one language to another and use words with multiple meanings, and still the
other participants can follow.

Flexibility and adaptation is possible because the social and conceptual setting (i.e., the context) encompassing the interaction is effortlessly recognised by

J. Indulska and K. Raymond (Eds.): DAIS 2007, LNCS 4531, pp. 17–31, 2007.

all participants. As a result, within the perceived context, many activities unfold, some of which are unpremeditated, yet consistent with the context, while other activities express the freedom associated with the recognition of the context - for example, using incomplete or incorrect statements, or using words with multiple meanings. Still other activities reflect the participants' adjustment of behaviour in compliance with the context of the setting - for example, participants whispering to exchange impromptu ideas.

Capturing a context of interest and representing it in a meaningful way has been and still is the main focus of context-aware computing. The research community has approached this task from different perspectives. For example, Schilit et al. [12], Dey et al. [5], and Pasco [9] offer conceptual frameworks in which the different components required for context acquisition are proposed and explained. The various subtasks the components carry out represent a context at different levels of abstraction. Additional subtasks include discovery services and context storage. While their work identify the essential aspects of context computing, it offers little insight as to how the actual task of context recognition is carried out.

Gellersen et al. [6] offers a layered, conceptual architecture for context recognition which includes a sensor layer, a cue layer and a context layer. The sensor layer is responsible for obtaining raw data from physical sensors; the cue layer is responsible for obtaining meaningful features; the context layer is responsible for obtaining a context of interest by interpreting the relationship between several cues. Schmidt et al. [11] demonstrate the usefulness of the conceptual architecture by capturing various everyday contexts such as the state of a smart cup and the activity of a smart mobile phone.

While the conceptual approach proposed by Gellersen et al. is the basis of our work, we aim at complementing a context recognition task with a context modelling task. Subsequently, we proposes a context modelling and reasoning guideline for presenting the real-world to computers wholly, conceptually, and meaningfully. Our approach permits the integration of facts and beliefs regarding entities (people, places, device, etc.) which are useful for computing a context as a representation of a dynamic real-world situation. We will demonstrate that it is possible to compute a context even though only a subpart of its aspects can be captured by employing sensors, and even if it may not be possible to foresee which of these aspects can be captured at a given time.

The rest of this paper is organized as follows: in section 2 we discuss challenges associated with a context computing task; in section 3 we discuss related work; in section 4 we introduce our approach, and illustrate its implementation. Finally, in section 5 we will close the paper with a discussion and concluding remarks.

2   Aspects of Context Computing

Capturing a context as a representation of a conceptual or a social setting is not a straightforward achievement. Firstly, because conceptual and social settings are difficult to directly capture by employing sensor alone, a context as an abstraction of these settings is not explicitly available. Data have to be gathered from heterogeneous sources in a seamless fashion, desirable features should be extracted from the data, and a reasoning operation has to be performed. A context data source may abstract any type of sensor, framework, database, user input, or application. As far as a context is concerned, these data can be classified as factual or approximated data [4].

While factual data remain unchanged regardless of repeated observations of a given phenomenon, approximated data are modelled as *beliefs*, since different or repeated observations of the same phenomenon under similar circumstances may result in disparity. An example for the former is the profile of a user or a device in a database. Another example is the status of a device or an application: on, off or idle; an example for the latter is the thermal or acoustic property of a room. Secondly, a concomitant effect associated with approximated data is uncertainty – most physical sensors have different technical specifications and may be affected by environmental conditions differently. Thirdly, in a pervasive computing environment, the availability of sensing devices is dynamic; sensors may come and go over time, i.e., one may not be able to foresee what sensors can be employed for a given sensing task. In the literature, this problem is addressed by separating the concern of context acquisition from the context consumption, since applications are interested in the context they employ rather than in its acquisition process [5]. This, however, does not warrant the constant availability of a mechanism for capturing a certain contextual aspect at all time. Therefore, a context computing process should involve learning about new contextual aspects which are not foreseen previously but could provide indirect evidence about a situation of interest.

Finally, data fusion and recognition operations for manipulating sensed data entail assumptions and incomplete knowledge (world models), producing additional uncertainty. To minimise the effect of this, a context computing process should entail dynamic belief revision and update of models.

3   Related Work

Early research in context-aware computing focused on implementing specific applications. Based on the experiences learned, more generic solutions were developed introducing different levels of abstraction for gathering, interpreting, deriving and aggregating a context (refer, for example, Schmidt et al. [11] and Salber et al. [10]. The approach described in Schmidt et al. outlines a four layered approach to capture and process a context in order to drive higher-level situational information. Hence, sensors data are first transformed into predefined cues, and cues are processed by logical rules to determine the current situation of an application.

More recent approaches focus on the creation of comprehensive and generic models of a context to facilitate interoperability and context reuse. Henricksen et al. [7] employ ORM (Object Role Modelling) to model a context as an association of fact types and roles. Fact types represent physical objects while roles represent dependencies between them. The model enables the representation of a context as a fact type the property of which can be static, sensed, profiled, derived, or alternative; an alternative property signifies the potential presence of several (possibly contradictory) reports about a particular attribute. An interesting aspect of the modelling concept is the recognition of a context as a dynamic construct.

The model of Crowley et al. [3] consists of three basic elements of a dynamic real world situation: entities, roles, and relations. An entity is an association of correlated observable variables corresponding to a physical object; a relation is a predicate function describing the properties of entities; and a role is a potential set of actions within a task; where a task is defined to be the association of a current state and a goal state. Coutaz et al. [2] propose a conceptual architecture which manipulates the model proposed by Crowley et al. in order to reason about the context of a mobile user. The architecture consists of a sensing layer, a perceptual layer, a situation and context identification layer, and an exploitation layer. The sensing layer generates numeric observables; the perception layer is responsible for providing symbolic observables at the appropriate level of abstraction; the situation and context identification layer identifies the current situation and context from observables. The exploitation layer serves as an adapter between application semantics and the infrastructure, enabling applications to put declarative requests for context services. The architecture does not prescribe to any particular algorithm or schemes; thus, it is difficult to scrutinies the modelling concept as well as the architecture.

Chen et al. [1] propose a common context vocabulary based on a concept hierarchy. The proposed COBRA-ONT ontology contains general concepts which can be reused in the domain of pervasive computing. It models, among others, physical locations, devices, temporal concepts and privacy policies. The reasoning over this information is based on the OWL ontology requiring no additional rule framework.

Wang et al. [13] propose a hierarchical ontology consisting of upper and domain-specific ontology. The upper ontology models basic contextual entities while the domain-specific ontology contains domain or application related concepts which are modelled on the basis of the generic concepts of the upper ontology. They employ OWL DL for ontology representation and two additional reasoning schemes for consistency check: DL-reasoners and logic-based rules.

The approaches above consider a context as a construct which can be captured in its entirety. Subsequently, their usefulness is limited to model a dynamic real-world situation with factual data only.

Korpipää et al. [8] propose a context recognition framework, describing a context as an uncertain and dynamic construct. Among its most important tasks, the framework manages uncertainty of sensed data through the use of probability based inference and fuzzy membership. They employ ontology to model context which will be used by a nave Bayesian classifier to reason about various real-world situations. The framework supports the computation of the model parameters from training data. Though the Bayesian classifier employed a variety of contextual aspects, each was extracted from a single audio input. An additional limitation of the framework is its employment of a nave Bayesian classifier, which assumes the absence of causal dependencies between the input context atoms. In most practical cases, however, this assumption may not hold true. Similarly, Mntyjrvi et al. [16] apply k-means clustering and minimum-variance segmentation algorithms to capture the activity of a mobile user. The sensors they employ include motion, temperature, skin conductance, and temperature sensors.

In general, the above approaches employ either factual or probabilistic inputs to model and reason about context. We build on the experiences learned previously, but combine both factual and probabilistic aspects to tackle the problem of uncertainty at various stages.

4   A Guideline for Modelling Everyday Situations

In section 2, we discussed the causes of uncertainty in a context computing process. In this section, we will introduce a context modelling process which integrates facts and beliefs with the goal of reducing uncertainty. While the model enables probabilistic reasoning schemes to deal with inaccurately captured dynamic aspects, the additional factual knowledge in the model makes possible containment tests to resolve between equally probable contextual states. To motivate our approach, we give a brief scenario.

4.1   Scenario

Active monitoring is one example of an application domain where context-awareness plays a role. In this scenario, the task is to detect the presence of interesting entities and to determine the relationship between these entities. If a given pattern of relationship seems to be likely to be broken or violated, the application should take a predictive measure. A typical example of active monitoring can be watching children and their behaviour towards each other in a kindergarten. The specific task of the application may be to determine which child is playing with whom, but it can also be to determine whether there are children (regardless of their identity) in certain places and whether the social atmosphere is healthy. If, for instance, the application picks up an aggressive tone while children are playing, it should sound an alarm to avoid further escalation of events. An additional example is suppose we want the application to monitor the whereabouts of a particular child. To recognise and avoid dangerous situations, the application should determine whether the child is inside a room, in a corridor, or outdoors. If the child happens to be in a corridor or outdoors by itself, i.e., if no supervisor is with it, the system should alert the responsible supervisor; if the responsible supervisor does not respond, or if she is currently busy with another child, the system should alert the head supervisor.

In the second scenario, the relative whereabouts of a child triggers an action, but it may also trigger a set of actions, depending on the activity of its supervisor. The whereabouts of the child in itself cannot be taken as a context of interest. The same is true to the activity of the supervisor. This very well reflects the relative and relational nature of a context. Subsequently, the contexts of interest are: the relative whereabouts of a child in reference to its supervisor and the activity of the supervisor in reference to the whereabouts of the child.

The different aspects of a context of interest (the context model) depend on the available sensing mechanisms. For example, there is a plethora of location sensing mechanisms which are based on either infrared or RF or ultrasound technologies or a combination of some of these technologies. Use of any of these technologies makes the modeling task less of an issue compared to the actual sensing task. If, on the other hand, there is no direct mechanism to locate a person, the context of interest should be derived from other aspects which describe a place - these could be, for example, light intensity, temperature, humidity, sound pressure, ambient noise, etc., which provide indirect evidence about a place.

At an abstract level, the various contextual features which make up the model are the different forms of places (room, corridor and outdoors), the relationship of the supervisor not only with the child of interest, but also with other children, i.e., her activity. In the next subsections, we will present our context modelling approach step by step.

4.2   Determination of the Context of Interest

The main purpose of a context model is to describe a context of interest as well as its various states as exhaustively and as completely as possible. Since an interest in a context comes from applications which respond to it, the first step in the modelling process is to identify the set of contextual states which are relevant for a particular application. In the following subsection, we take the whereabouts of the child as a context of interest.

4.3   Identification of Aspects of a Context

Once a context of interest is known, the next step is to identify all of its aspects which can directly be captured by employing sensors. This decision is made based on the requirements of the application developer or the user. For the whereabouts of the child, the application developer may decide to employ already available sensors which capture humidity, temperature, light intensity, etc.

At this stage, it is not necessary to determine how exactly these aspects describe the context of interest. It is sufficient to know that some kind of relationship exists. In the next subsection, we shall demonstrate how a system can be trained to determine (at least in part) the nature of the relationship. The existence of a relationship between a context of interest and its aspects is modelled as an extensible factual relationship.

Figure 1 shows the major concepts and properties defining facts about persons, places, sensors, and physical values which can be measured by sensors. We use the Web Ontology Language (OWL) terminology in the model, depicting relationships between the concepts by labeled arrows. For example, a sensor

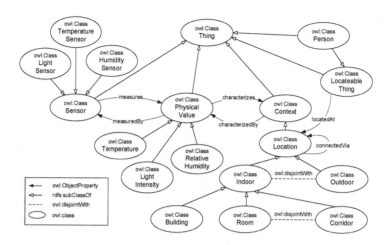

Fig. 1. A factual context model using the OWL terminology

measuring a certain physical property is modelled by the owl:ObjectProperty "measures" with its domain of owl:class "Sensor" and its range owl:class "PhysicalValue".

Relevant places are modelled as a hierarchy of location concepts. We distinguish between indoor and outdoor and model a building as a composition of rooms and corridors. The concepts indoor and outdoor as well as room and corridor are modelled as disjoint concepts using the owl:disjointWidth constructor, since they mutually exclude each other. Moreover, direct connections (such as a door, a passage, a stair case, an elevator, etc.) between places are described by the role "connectedVia" and by additional roles derived from the role "connectedVia"; for example, "connectedViaDoor". These factual relationships will be useful to validate a location context computed by a probabilistic reasoning scheme (to be discussed in section 4.5).

The relations between sensors and the corresponding context are modelled by the owl:ObjectProperty "characterizedBy" and "characterizes". The concept "Location" is described as a subclass of the "Context" concept. At the same time, location is characterized by the physical values temperature, light intensity, and relative humidity. To dynamically detect and bind to available sensors, an additional individual concept called "Sensor" is defined.

4.4   Determination of Factual and Probabilistic States

An aspect of a context can be modelled as either a discrete aspect or a continuous random variable. A discrete aspect has enumerable values, and it can be modelled as a factual concept, for example, the status of a device (on, off, or idle). Those aspects which are described by continuous numerical values are not straightforward to model. For example, the temperature of a place may be between -5C and 37C, depending on its spatial and temporal properties as well

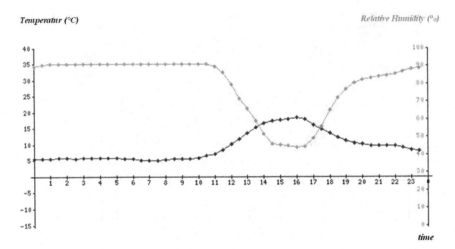

Temperatur (°C)   *Relative Humidity (%)*

Fig. 2. An average outdoor temperature (blue) and relative humidity (green) measurement

as other factors such as whether a heater is turned on. Moreover, such properties change frequently and thus two-valued assertions about them are not possible. Numerical properties can be modelled as beliefs by transforming the continuous values into discrete fuzzy values to imitate human reasoning. This process can be made semi-automatic. Consider a series of quantities, $x^{(1)}$, $x^{(2)}$, ..., $x^{(n)}$, representing some sensor measurements, each $x^{(i)}$ being independently subject to a random variation. It is possible to define a probabilistic model for the random process in which a set of unknown model parameters, Θ, determine the probability distributions of $x^{(i)}$. Such probabilities, or probability densities, will be written in the form of $P(x^{(i)}|\Theta)$. Learning about Θ is possible if the system has observed the values of some of the $x^{(i)}$. The impact of these observations can be captured by the likelihood function:

$$L(\Theta) = L(\Theta|x^{(1)}, x^{(2)}, ..., x^{(n)}) \tag{1}$$

Equation (1) yields the probability of the observed data as a function of the unknown parameters, which in turn is proportional to:

$$P(x^{(1)}, ..., x^{(n)}|\Theta) = \prod_{i=1}^{n} P(x^{(i)}|\Theta) \tag{2}$$

Figure 2 shows temperature and relative humidity readings of an outside place for October 2006 in Dresden, Germany. To make the sensor readings more meaningful to human consumers, we transformed them into meaningful fuzzy sets. To compute the model's parameters, i.e., the model's statistical parameters, we identify various fuzzy regions for each reading, and determine its temporal characteristics. The regions were classified into those which exhibit constant, decreasing, and increasing characteristics. The time context, ceteris paribus, forces the measurements to decrease or increase or to remain constant, and hence was classified as: *morning, afternoon,* and *noon.* These regions were in turn used to determine the fuzzy members of the temperature and humidity measurements. For temperature, these regions were labeled as: *very cold, cold, lukewarm, warm,* and *hot*; for relative humidity, they were labeled as: *dry, moderate,* and *moist.* The same process was applied for other aspects (light intensity: *dark, visible, bright,* and *very bright*; and sound pressure: *quite, normal, loud, noisy*).

Once the fuzzy regions of a given aspect for a given place were identified, the next task is to compute the model's parameters, $P(aspect = x | place = y, time = z)$; for example, for the above readings, the probability, $P(temperature = lukewarm | place = outdoor, time = noon)$, is equal to 0.45. The overall probability distribution of the temperature of an outdoor place at noon is given as: {{very cold, 0.15}, {cold, 0.35}, {lukewarm, 0.45}, {warm, 0.05}, {hot, 0.0}}. After the model's parameters were computed, the content of the ontology of figure 1 was updated to reflect the newly acquired knowledge.

4.5 Determination of Logical and Probabilistic Relationships

Establishing relationship – logical or probabilistic – between the context of interest and the various aspects by which it is represented is the necessary step to determine a reasoning scheme for a context computing task. Since the context model integrates both beliefs and facts, the reasoning scheme should be able to manage beliefs and facts. In general, probabilistic schemes are suitable for low-level context recognition, whereas logic- or rule-based reasoning schemes can be employed for higher-level context disambiguation. This will be illustrated shortly.

A reasoning scheme should also be able to deal with missing data as it may not be feasible to foresee which of the aspects of a context will be captured at a given time. This requires the reasoning schemes to deal with all possible combinations of available sensors. For example, in the previous section we identified *time, temperature, relative humidity, light intensity* and *sound pressure* – five aspects – as relevant aspects of the context of interest. Provided a time context will be available all the time – as the other aspects are influenced by it –, there are altogether 15 different combinations of sensors if we assume a random variation of sensors. In general, the random availability of sensors is described by equation (3) and (4), where p refers to the number of all possible combinations; n refers to the total number of aspects which can describe a place as accurately and unambiguously as possible; and r refers to the aspects which can be captured by the available sensors.

$$p = \sum_{r=1}^{n} \frac{n!}{(n-r)!r!} \tag{3}$$

For our scenario, this will be:

$$\sum_{r=1}^{4} \frac{4!}{(4-r)!r!} = 15 \tag{4}$$

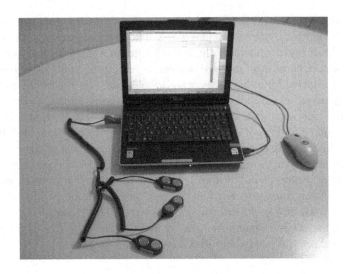

Fig. 3. The iButton Sensor network implementing the 1-wire protocol

5   Validation

In the previous section we illustrated by examples the four steps of a context modelling approach. To demonstrate the expediency of this approach, we implemented a system which reasons about the whereabouts of a mobile user.

We set up a 1-wire network (Figure 3) with various iButton sensor nodes on a laptop. The sensors we employed include: a DS1971-F3 and Java powered DS1957B data logger for storing secured profile information (the user's name and password to monitor which user has logged on to a device); temperature and humidity loggers with different sensing parameters (DS1921G, DS1921Z-F5, and DS2422, DS1923), and a light intensity data logger (PCE- 172). The sensors have different accuracy, sensing range, and resolution. We randomly vary the sensor nodes to simulate dynamic availability of sensors. A context provider will receive an event notification whenever a node arrives at or departs from a 1-wire network. When a node arrives, the provider binds to it and queries it periodically. The query interval and duration is defined by the user. The context provider translates each context type into a fuzzy set to enable human-like reasoning. The output of the context provider are supplied to a Bayesian probabilistic reasoning scheme, which computes a posterior probability distribution for all potential places – the whereabouts of a person – and determines the one which is most likely. However, there are situations in which some places appear equally probable – for example, a corridor and a room – in which case, the system applies containment test to avoid inconsistent reasoning and random decision.

Figure 4, Figure 5, and Figure 6 display three different configurations of a Bayesian network. In Figure 4, three aspects of a place are captured, namely

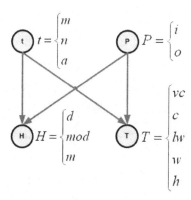

Fig. 4. A Bayesian Network with two parent nodes and two child nodes (relative humidity and temperature)

time, temperature, and relative humidity which were all measured by the sensors. The model's belief for the probabilistic relationship is that *place (P)* and *time (t)* are parent nodes and *temperature (T)* and *relative humidity (H)* are child nodes[1]. The various states each node can assume are as described in section 4.4.

When the data is obtained from the available sensors, they are mapped to corresponding linguistic variables each of which represents a particular aspect of a place, which is described by a fuzzy set. For example, 17C is mapped to the linguistic variable *lukewarm* of a temperature fuzzy set; 45% is mapped to the linguistic variable *dry* of a relative humidity fuzzy set; 1000 Lux is mapped to the linguistic variable *bright* of a light intensity fuzzy set, etc.

Once the linguistic variables of each node are determined, the Bayesian Network computes posterior probability for each potential place (corridor, room, or outdoors) using equation (5), which computes the posterior probability of a place given measurements of temperature, humidity, and time. The place with the highest posterior probability becomes the most likely place to which the sensed data refer.

For the case of Figure 4, the following input is an example: {time = September 15, 2005, 1:35 PM}, {temperature = 17C}, {relative humidity = 45%}. As can be seen in equation (6), the sensed data are mapped to *lukewarm* (for temperature), *moderate* (for relative humidity) and *noon* (for time).

$$P(P|T,H,t) = \frac{P(T|P,t)P(H|P,t).P(P)}{\sum_P P(H|P,t)P(T|P,t).(P))} \qquad (5)$$

---

[1] Except the time context, which influences other primitive contexts and hence should be modelled as a parent context, all primitive contexts are modelled as child nodes. On the other hand, the higher-level context which should be inferred is modelled as a parent node.

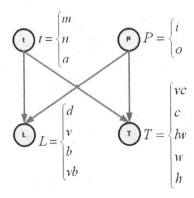

Fig. 5. A Bayesian Network with two parent nodes and two child nodes (light intensity and temperature)

$$P(P|T = lw, H = mod, t = n) = \frac{\begin{array}{l} P(T = lw|P, t = n)P(H = mod|P, t = n)P(P) \end{array}}{\begin{array}{l} P(T = lw|P = c, t = n)P(H = mod|P = c, t = n)P(P = c)+ \\ P(T = lw|P = r, t = n)P(H = mod|P = r, t = n)P(P = r)+ \\ P(T = lw|P = o, t = n)P(H = mod|P = o, t = n)P(P = o) \end{array}}$$

(6)

Applying Bernoulli's Principle of Insufficient Reason – a person can be anywhere with equal probabilities – to determine the probability distribution of a place, the posterior probabilities yield: {*corridor, 0.457*}, {*room, 0.44*}, and {*outdoors, 0.1*}. The difference in posterior probabilities between a CORRIDOR and a ROOM is not sufficiently large to discriminate between the two places. However, from the model description, we know that the two places are disjoint places, but both are subsumed by a building, which is an indoor place. Hence, the difference in posterior probabilities between both indoor places and outdoors is large enough to discriminate between INDOORS and OUTDOORS[2]. Here knowledge of containment relations between places has contributed to minimize uncertainty.

Figure 5 shows a different configuration for a similar topology, but for different availability of sensors - temperature and light intensity sensors. The posterior probabilities for this configuration are computed using equation (7), i.e., the conditional probability that a place is P given temperature, light intensity, and time measurements. This time the Bayesian Network was provided with the following sensor measurement: {time = September 15, 2005, 1:35 PM}; {temperature = 17C}; and {light intensity = 1000 Lux}.

$$P(P|T, L, t) = \frac{P(T|P, t)P(L|P, t).P(P)}{\sum_P P(T|P, t)P(L|P, t)(P))}$$

(7)

---

[2] To minimize error in decision making, we applied a heuristic-based decision threshold by setting the difference in posterior probability between two places to be more than 15%.

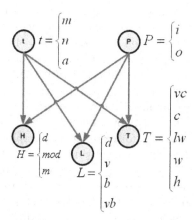

Fig. 6. A Bayesian Network with two parent nodes and three child nodes (relative humidity, temperature, and light intensity)

The light intensity of 1000 Lux was mapped to the linguistic variable: visible. This time the posterior probabilities yield: {*corridor, 0.39*}, {*room, 0.5*}, and {*outdoors, 0.1*}. Still the difference between the posterior probabilities of a room and a corridor is not significant enough to discriminate between the two places; but the difference between the posterior probabilities of the two indoor places and outdoors is significant enough to discriminate between indoors and outdoors.

Figure 6 displays a Bayesian Network with three child nodes: temperature, light intensity, and relative humidity. The posterior probabilities for this configuration are computed using equation (8), according to which the probability of a place having a state P is computed given humidity, light intensity, temperature and time measurements. The sensor measurements provided to the network were: {Time = September 15, 2005, 1:35 PM}; {temperature = 17C}; {light intensity = 1000 Lux}; and {relative humidity = 45%}.

$$P(P|T,H,L,t) = \frac{P(T|P,t)P(H|P,t)P(L|P,t)P(P)}{\sum_P P(H|P,t)P(T|P,t)P(L|P,t)(P))} \qquad (8)$$

Computing the posterior probabilities for the three different places yields: {*corridor, 0.38*}, {*room, 0.55*}, and {*outdoors, 0.06*}. Now the discrimination gap between a room and a corridor has increased. Therefore, with this configuration, the Bayesian Network could discriminate between a room and a corridor, and outdoors with minimised uncertainties.

6   Discussion and Conclusion

We motivated the integration of factual knowledge and beliefs about entities to model and reason about a context of interest. The motivation was followed by a twofold model comprising a probabilistic (beliefs) and a deterministic model (facts) for a comprehensive description of those aspects of a context we want to reason about. This model was produced in four steps: (1) identification of a context of interest; (2) identification of those aspects of the context which can be captured by employing sensors; (3) determination of meaningful contextual states for each aspect; and (4) determination of logical and probabilistic relationships between a context of interest and the various aspects it abstracts. We demonstrated our approach by modelling various physical places.

Our guideline can be employed for modelling several complex contexts. A health care application developer, for example, can employ our approach to determine the stress level (the higher-level context) of a person. Depending on available primitive context sources (e.g. oxygen sensors, blood pressure sensor, respiratory sensors, etc.) it is possible to determine with various degrees of uncertainty, whether a person is relaxed, mildly stressed, stressed, or significantly stressed. Other activities such as driving or maintaining a machine can also be modelled and reasoned about using our guideline.

Some final remarks regarding the modelling process: Determination of the contextual states of a primitive context may not be a straightforward process. Even though we encouraged the use of fuzzy sets, defining linguistic variables as well as their corresponding membership in a fuzzy set requires an adequate knowledge of the application domain as well as the characteristic and the range of measurements taken from the available sensors. for many real-world example, membership functions are complex. This can be an indication to the complexity of context modelling and reasoning in general. The other challenge is the way the states of the primitive contexts are related to the higher-level context of interest. In our demonstration, we used Bayesian Networks to model conditional independence, and the conditional probabilities were derived from the membership functions of the fuzzy sets. However, direct transition of membership functions into conditional probability does not apply all the time.

A typical challenge we faced during our experiment was the response time of the sensors employed. Most of our sensors were Dallas semiconductor sensors, which were enclosed in a 16 mm thick stainless still can. There was a delay of about 12 second before the sensors perceived an actual change in the environment. Though this might be acceptable for many human activities, for time critical applications this is not acceptable. Additional challenges included dealing with light intensity sensors: we had to make certain that light was received within the sensors specified incident angle; otherwise the amount received would fall significantly. A similar problem associated with light intensity was the sensors sensitivity to surrounding objects which absorb or reflect light. In the presence of such objects, we frequently observed counterintuitive results.

References

1. Chen, H., Finin, T., Joshi, A., Perich, F., Chakraborty, D., Kagal, L.: Intelligent agents meet the semantic web in smart spaces. IEEE Internet Computing, 8
2. Coutaz, J., Crowley, J., Dobson, S., Garlan, D.: Context is key. Communications of the ACM, pp. 49–53 (2005)

3. Crowley, J., Coutaz, J., Bérard, F.: Perceptual user interfaces: things that see. Communications of the ACM, vol. 43(3)
4. Dargie, W.: Dynamic generation of context rules. In: Lecture Notes in Computer Science, pp. 102–115 (2006)
5. Dey, A., Abowd, G.: Cybreminder: A context-aware system for supporting reminders
6. Gellersen, H., Schmidt, A., Beigl, M.: Multi-sensor context-awareness in mobile devices and smart artifacts. Mob. Netw. Appl. 7(5), 341–351 (2002)
7. Henricksen, K., Indulska, J.: A software engineering framework for context-aware pervasive computing. In: Proceedings of the Second IEEE international Conference on Pervasive Computing and Communications (Percom'04) (2004)
8. Korpipää, P., Mäntyjärvi, J., Kela, J., Kernen, H., Malm, E.-J.: Managing context information in mobile devices. IEEE Pervasive Computing (2003)
9. Pascoe, J., Ryan, N., Morse, D.: Using while moving: Hci issues in fieldwork environments. ACM Trans. Comput.-Hum. Interact. 7(3), 417–437 (2000)
10. Salber, D., Dey, A., Abowd, G.: The context toolkit: Aiding the development of context-enabled applications. CHI, pp. 434–441 (1999)
11. Schmidt, A., Beigl, M., Gellersen, H.: There is more to context than location. Computers and Graphics, vol. 23(6) (1999)
12. Shilit, B., Theimer, M.: Disseminating active map information to mobile hosts. IEEE Network, pp. 22–32 (1994)
13. Wang, X., Dong, J.S., Chin, C., Hettiarachchi, S., Zhang, D.: Semantic space: An infrastructure for smart spaces. IEEE Pervasive Computing 3(3), 32–39 (2004)
14. Weiser, M.: The computer for the 21st century. SIGMOBILE Mob. Comput. Commun. 3(3), 3–11 (1999)

Situation Specification and Realization in Rule-Based Context-Aware Applications

Patrícia Dockhorn Costa[1], João Paulo A. Almeida[1,2],
Luís Ferreira Pires[1], and Marten van Sinderen[1]

[1] Centre for Telematics and Information Technology, University of Twente,
PO Box 217, 7500 AE Enschede, the Netherlands
[2] Computer Science Department, Federal University of Espírito Santo (UFES),
Av. Fernando Ferrari, s/n, Vitória, ES, Brazil
{dockhorn, almeida, pires, sinderen}@cs.utwente.nl

Abstract. Context-aware applications use and manipulate context information to detect high-level *situations*, which are used to adapt application behavior. This paper discusses the specification of situations in context-aware applications and introduces a rule-based approach to detect situations. Situations are specified using a combination of UML class diagrams and OCL constraints. We support a wide range of situations, which can be composed of more elementary kinds of context. We discuss how to cope with distribution and to exploit it beneficially for context manipulation and situation detection. We employ a generic rule-based platform (DJess [2]) to support the derivation of situations in a distributed fashion.

1 Introduction

Context-aware applications use and manipulate context information to detect the situations of users and adapt their behaviour accordingly. Context-awareness has become an important and desirable feature for ubiquitous computing, in which applications not only use context information to react on a user's request, but also take initiative as a result of (continuously-running) context reasoning activities. In this sense, ubiquitous context-aware applications can be characterized as *attentive* in addition to *reactive*. An example is an application that adapts the quality of audio and video streams automatically according to battery power consumption and the kind of network connectivity available, without user intervention.

The design of context-aware applications is a challenging task, which justifies the development of novel methods, abstractions and infrastructures (e.g., [1, 3, 4, 6, 14]). This paper proposes an approach to the specification and realization of situation detection for attentive context-aware applications. Our aim is to facilitate application design by providing abstractions for the specification of context-aware applications, in particular those related to the detection of situations based on context information. In order to detect situations attentively, a rule-based approach to situation detection is proposed. This solution is based on the use of a general-purpose rule-based platform, which guarantees the efficiency of situation detection (triggers upon situation detection as opposed to query-based solutions).

J. Indulska and K. Raymond (Eds.): DAIS 2007, LNCS 4531, pp. 32–47, 2007.

Situations are specified using standard UML 2.0 [18] class diagrams which are enriched with OCL 2.0 [17] constraints to define the conditions under which situations of a certain type exist. We support a wide range of situations, which can be composed of more elementary kinds of context. To transform the specification into a set of rules to be executed directly on the rule-based platform, we identify a number of patterns for rule detection realization. The rule set which is derived systematically from the specification can be deployed directly in the Jess rule engine. We employ the DJess distributed rule-based platform [2] to support the derivation of situations in a distributed fashion. This paper extends the work presented in [7], by discussing situation realization, detection and distribution.

The paper is further organised as follows. Section 2 discusses how context is modelled in our approach drawing on our previous work [7, 8]. Section 3 discusses the specification of situation types. Section 4 elaborates on the realization of situation detection with the help of rule engines. Section 5 discusses how situation detection can be done in a distributed fashion according to different scenarios. This is done to exploit distribution beneficially for context manipulation and situation detection, not only for scalability purposes but also to address information privacy concerns. Section 6 discusses related work, and, finally, Section 7 summarises our results and indicates future research.

2   Context Models

A *context-aware application* is a distributed application that adapts its behaviour according to its users' context. Figure 1 depicts a user interacting with a context-aware application. The application obtains context information from the user's environment (e.g., by means of sensor technology) in order to reason about context and detect situations of interest.

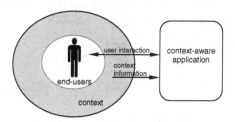

Fig. 1. Users, their context and a context-aware application

Context can be defined as "the interrelated conditions in which something exists" [15]. This definition reveals that context is only meaningful with respect to a thing (that "exists"), which we call here an entity. The concept of entity is fundamentally different from the concept of context: context is what can be said about an entity, i.e., context does not exist by itself. Examples of entities are persons, computing devices and buildings. The context of an entity can have many constituents ("interrelated conditions"). Examples of some constituents of the context of a person are the person's location, mental state, and activity. In the remainder of this paper, we use the term context to refer to constituents of the context of an entity. Together, these constituents form the entity's context.

The process of identifying relevant context consists of determining the "conditions" of entities in the application's universe of discourse (e.g., a user or its environment) that are relevant for a context-aware application or a family of such applications. The representation of these relevant conditions or circumstances is called here a *context model*. We define a context model as a conceptual model (in the sense of [16]) of context. In previous work [7, 8], we have defined conceptual foundations that can be used beneficially in context modeling. These conceptual foundations include the separation of entity and context types, which are represented here as UML classes. We briefly discuss these foundations in the sequel. The work presented in [7, 8] provides a more detailed discussion.

Intrinsic Context
We characterize context as either *Intrinsic* or *Relational*. Intrinsic context defines a type of context that belongs to the essential nature of a single entity, i.e., it does not exist separate from this entity. In addition, intrinsic context does not depend on the relationship with other entities. Figure 2 depicts examples of intrinsic context types which could be used in many health-related applications. Geographic location (GeoLocation) is context that inheres in all spatial entities. Similarly, battery power (BatteryPower) inheres in a computing device (Device). Analogous reasoning can be applied to other context types depicted here.

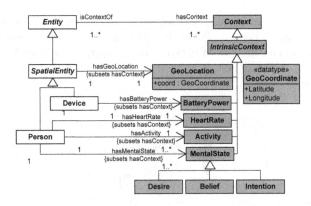

Fig. 2. Intrinsic context types

Intrinsic context types are associated with a data type such that an instance of an intrinsic context type is assigned to a value of this data type. The geographical location of an entity is an example of intrinsic context type, whose data type consists of all possible values in a geographical coordinate system, represented by the GeoCoordinate datatype.

Relational Context
While intrinsic context inheres in a single entity, relational context inheres in a plurality of entities. Relational context may be used to relate an entity to the collection

of entities that play a role in the entity's context. Figure 3 shows examples of relational context types. The NetworkAvailability relational context type relates a device to a collection of networks that are available through that device, and ChannelAvailability relates a device to a collection of communication channels supported by that device (e.g., e-mail, voice and SMS).

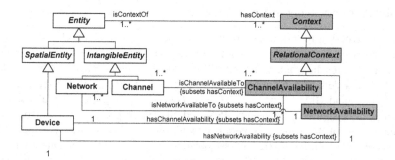

Fig. 3. Relational context types

Some other examples of relational context are DeviceAvailability and SocialNetwork. The DeviceAvailability relational context relates a person to a collection of devices that are available to that person. SocialNetwork relates a person to the collection of persons interacting with that person by any communication channels.

3 Situation Models

The context models we have discussed so far, allow application designers to represent a context-aware application's universe of discourse. This section introduces *situation models*, which explicitly represent particular situations of interest, given a certain context model.

Situations define particular states of affairs which are of interest to applications. They are composite concepts whose constituents are the elements of our context models, i.e., entities, and intrinsic and relational contexts. In this sense, situation models should extend and comply with the context models. For example, a situation model can represent the situation in which "John is near Alice and their mobile phones are available" or "John has a fever and influenza". The underlying context model for this example should define that a person may be near another person and that a person may own a mobile phone.

In our approach we define *situation types*, which aim at characterizing situations with similar properties. For example, the situation type "John is within 50 meters from Alice" consists of all situation instances in which the distance between John's and Alice's location values is less than 50 meters. Similarly, the situation type "Person is within 50 meters from another person" consists of all situation instances in which the distance between any two persons' location values is less than 50 meters. Although unanticipated situation instances are supported at application runtime, situation types are defined at application design-time.

The examples used throughout the paper illustrate a range of situation patterns that are relevant for context-aware applications. These patterns involve the different kinds of context (intrinsic and relational) and entities, which are the building blocks used to compose situations. We use a combination of UML class diagrams and OCL constraints to specify situations.

3.1 Situations Involving Intrinsic Context

Situations involving intrinsic context are composed by a unique entity and part of its intrinsic context. The following example represents a situation type (`SituationAvailable`) that captures the availability and willingness to communicate of MSN and Skype users. Figure 4 depicts a fragment of the structural context model that represents the `MsnStatus` and `SkypeStatus` intrinsic context types, which model the user's communication status while using MSN and Skype, respectively. A person, while playing the role of `MsnUser`, is associated with `MsnStatus` context type, and while playing the role of `SkypeUser`, is associated with `SkypeStatus` context type. The enumeration data types `SkypeStatusEnum` and `MsnStatusEnum` define all possible values for `SkypeStatus` and `MsnStatus`, respectively.

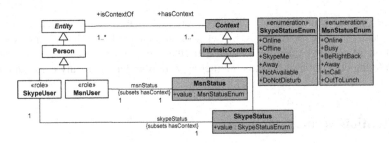

Fig. 4. Fragment of context model

Figure 5 depicts a situation model which builds on the context model presented in Figure 4, defining the situation type `SituationAvailable`.

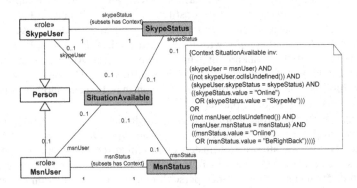

Fig. 5. SituationAvailable specification

The OCL invariant in this diagram is a predicate that must hold for all instances of `SituationAvailable`. It defines that instances of `SituationAvailable` must be either associated with a user available in Skype (with `SkypeStatus` set to `Online` or `SkypeMe`) or a user available in MSN (with `MsnStatus` set to `Online` or `BeRightBack`). The OCL operation `oclIsUndefined()` is part of the OCL standard library and tests whether the value of an expression is undefined.

Figure 6 shows an example of situation involving two entities and their intrinsic context. Their locations are compared such that instances of `SituationWithinRange` hold if two persons are located within a certain range (defined as an attribute of the `SituationWithinRange` class). This model builds on the context model defined in Figure 2.

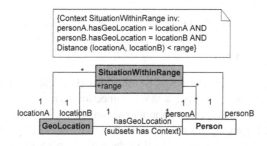

Fig. 6. SituationWithinRange specification

3.2 Situations Involving Relational Context

Situations involving relational context consist of at least two entities and part of their relational contexts. The following example discusses a situation in which a device has established a connection (relational context type) to each of the two network types, `WLAN`, and `Bluetooth` (entities). By explicitly modeling the connections as relational context, we are able to assign properties to these connections, such as access rights and negotiated QoS.

Figure 7 depicts the structural context models representing the types and relationships that are relevant for this example. According to this diagram, a `Device` may be connected to a `Network` through the relational context `Connection`.

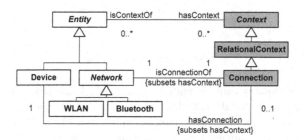

Fig. 7. Fragment of context model

Figure 8 depicts the situation type SituationConnected. The OCL invariant defines that instances of this situation must be associated with at least one connection object.

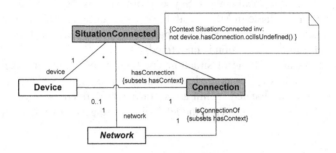

Fig. 8. SituationConnected specification

3.3 Situation of Situations

Situation themselves may be composed of other situations. Suppose we would like to know when a device switches from a WLAN connection to a Bluetooth connection in order to set new quality of service parameters. Since SituationConnected has been already defined in Figure 8, in order to detect SituationSwitch, we would have to verify whether SituationConnected held in the past for network WLAN, and currently holds for network Bluetooth. We may add the additional constraint that the handover time should not be longer than one second. This example is depicted in Figure 9, showing that SituationSwitch can be modeled by composing multiple occurrences of SituationConnection, one called wlan, and the other called bluetooth.

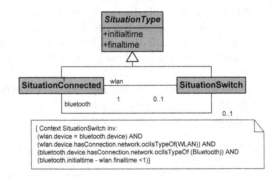

Fig. 9. SituationSwitch specification

This situation requires using temporal aspects, which are represented in our approach by means of initial and final times. Each situation type extends the SituationType class inheriting these temporal attributes. The initialtime attribute captures the moment a situation begins to hold, and the finaltime attribute, the moment a situations seizes to hold. Since we capture the finaltime, our model represents past occurrences of situations[1]. We also include temporal operations for relating situations in their occurrence intervals, such as precedence, overlapping, and post-occurrence. These operations are defined in OCL in terms of initial and final times, and can be used in the definition of situations.

4 Rule-Based Implementation

In a rule-based implementation, the designer defines rules which are applied to facts in a working memory. The mechanism used for rule application (and in our case situation detection) is based on the Rete algorithm [11], which efficiently matches the patterns for situations by remembering past pattern matching tests. Only new or modified facts are tested against the rules.

Figure 10 depicts the elements of our approach with the correspondence between the UML specification, the Java code and the Jess code at the template level (design-time). At the instance level (runtime), Figure 10 depicts the relations between the user's context and the rule-based implementation. Context sources provide context information, which is input as facts in the engine's working memory.

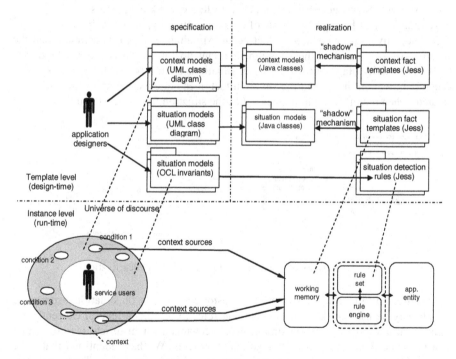

Fig. 10. Correspondences between UML specifications, and Java and Jess code

---

[1] The invariants as presented in the figures are violated for past occurrences of situations. In order to avoid that, we should include, for each invariant, a disjunction with a predicate that verifies whether this situation is a past occurrence (not finaltime.oclIsUndefined()). We omit this predicate in this paper for the sake of readability.

We have used *shadow facts* to implement our structural context models. This is a mechanism offered by Jess to serve as a connection between the working memory and a Java application. Objects created in Java are reflected in the working memory. Therefore, any alteration of the Java objects is automatically perceived by the Jess working memory. The Java classes in our implementation directly reflect the UML models defined at the context model, such that their generation can be automated. We have used Octopus (http://www.klasse.nl/octopus) for generating Java code from UML2.0 class diagrams.

Once we have defined the structural context models, we can carry out the situation detection realization. Similarly to the structural context model, each situation type, as specified in the UML class diagram, corresponds to a Java class, as well as a shadow fact template. Situation instances are represented as shadow facts that are created and deactivated by rules for situation detection. Each situation type leads to the definition of two rules, namely a rule for situation fact creation, and a rule for situation fact deactivation. Conditions for enabling these rules are derived from the invariants of situation classes. The rule for situation creation detects when an invariant becomes true, and the rule for situation deactivation detects when the invariant becomes false. We have identified patterns of situation types that are systematically mapped to Jess code. Automatic code generation from OCL to Jess is work in progress.

A situation fact life cycle consists of creation, activation, deactivation and destruction. The activation of a situation fact occurs simultaneously to its creation, and the deactivation occurs when the situation invariant no longer holds. Figure 11 uses a UML 2.0 activity diagram to show when situations should be created or deactivated. When the invariant holds and the situation fact does not exist yet, the situation fact is created; when the invariant no longer holds, the situation fact is deactivated.

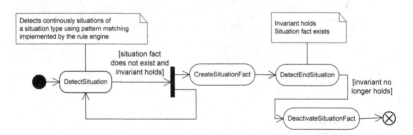

Fig. 11. Activity diagram for situation creation and deactivation

Deactivated situation facts consist of historical records of situation occurrence, which may be used to detect situations that refer to past occurrences. Currently, we implement a simple rule-based time-to-live mechanism for historical records, which considers the final time of deactivated situation facts. We have identified that situation realization in Jess follows certain patterns of implementation. Table 1 depicts how creation and deactivation rules should be formulated.

These rules are written in the Jess language. Conditions and actions are separated by the symbol "=>". The condition part (or left hand side) consists of patterns that match facts in the working memory. A pattern is represented in between parentheses,

Table 1. Creation and deactivation rules

Creation Rule	Deactivation Rule
`(situation type invariant)`	`(not (situation type invariant))`
`(not (situation exists))`	`(situation exists)`
`=>`	`=>`
`create (situation)`	`deactivate (situation)`
`[RaiseEvent()]`	`[RaiseEvent()]`

such as `(situation type invariant)`. The action part of a rule (or right hand side) contains function calls, such as the functions to create and to deactivate situations.

The condition part of a creation rule checks whether the OCL invariant holds, and whether there is already an instance of that particular situation currently active (final time not nil). If these conditions are met, a situation fact is created, and optionally, an event can be raised. Analogously, the condition part of a deactivation rule checks whether the OCL invariant no longer holds, and there is a current situation fact active. When these conditions are met, this situation instance is deactivated, and optionally, an event can be raised. Figure 12 depicts how `SituationConnected` and `SituationSwitch` (see section 3) are implemented in Jess.

```
;Creation rule (SituationConnected)
(defrule create_situation_connected
    (Device (OBJECT ?dv) (hasContext ?contexts) (sizeContexts ?s))
    (test (?dv hasContextType "context_control.Connection"))
    (not (SituationConnected (OBJECT ?st) (device ?dv) (finaltime nil)))
    =>
    (bind ?SituationConnected (new situation_control.SituationConnected ?dv))
    (definstance SituationConnected ?SituationConnected))

;Deactivation rule (SituationConnected)
(defrule deactivate_situation_connected
    (Device (OBJECT ?dv) (identity ?id) (hasContext ?ctxs) (sizeContexts ?size))
    (test (not (?dv hasContextType "context_control.Connection")))
    (SituationConnected (OBJECT ?st) (device ?dv) (finaltime nil))
    =>
    (call ?st deactivate))

;Creation rule (SituationSwitch)
(defrule create_situation_switch
    (Device (OBJECT ?dv) (identity ?dvid))
    (SituationConnected (OBJECT ?SWlan)
                        (device ?device&:(eq (call ?device getIdentity) ?dvid))
                        (network ?net&:(instanceof ?net context_control.WLAN))
                        (finaltime ?finaltime&:(neq ?finaltime nil)))
    (SituationConnected (OBJECT ?SBlue) (device ?dv)
                        (network ?net2&:(instanceof ?net2 context_control.Bluetooth))
                        (starttime ?start) (finaltime nil))
    (test (<= (- (call ?start getTime)(call ?finaltime getTime)) 60000))
    (not (SituationSwitch (OBJECT ?st) (wlan ?SWLAN) (bluetooth ?SBlue)
                        (finaltime nil)))
    =>
    (bind ?SituationSwitch (new situation_control.SituationSwitch ?SWlan ?SBlue))
    (definstance SituationSwitch ?SituationSwitch))
```

Fig. 12. Situation realization in Jess

The condition part of the `create_situation_connected` rule checks whether there is a `Connection` relational context in the list of contexts of that device. This part of the condition corresponds to the OCL invariant defined in Figure 8. In addition, it checks whether a `SituationConnected` instance does not already exist for that device. When these conditions are met, the action part is triggered, i.e., an instance of `SituationConnected` is created for that device.

The condition part of the `deactivate_situation_connected` rule, on the contrary, checks whether the device is no longer connected to a network, and if there is an existing `SituationConnected` for that device. If these conditions are met, that particular instance of `SituationConnected` is deactivated, and can be used in the future as a historical record.

The condition part of the `create_situation_switch` rule checks whether there was an instance of `SituationConnected` with network `WLAN` in the past (`finaltime` not nil), and currently there is an instance of `SituationConnected` with network `Bluetooth`. In addition, the handover time should not be longer than 60 seconds. These parts of the condition correspond to the OCL invariant depicted in Figure 9. As in all creation rules, the condition also checks whether there is no instance of `SituationSwitch` for that particular handover currently active. When these conditions are met, an instance of `SituationSwitch` is created. We did not include here the `deactivate_situation_switch` rule due to the lack of space.

To allow maintenance of past situations, we use a mechanism based on object serialization to preserve the situation state at the time the situation was deactivated. When a situation is deactivated, a serialized copy of the situation is created and stored for future use. Serialized objects are given unique identifiers, so that they can be retrieved unambiguously. For this reason, when checking the existence of a past instance of `SituationConnected`, we have used an unique identifier of the device (`call ?device getIdentity`), instead of the object identifier (`device ?dv`) as in the currently active instance.

5 Distribution Issues

So far, we have focussed on the various rule patterns for the detection of the various kinds of situation. We have presented the realization solutions without regard for distribution, as if situation detection were based on a single rule engine, working with a single set of rules and a single working memory. In this section, we consider alternative distribution scenarios, and discuss their trade-offs.

Firstly, we consider the fully centralized scenario, in which no distribution is employed. In this scenario, context sources feed context information into the central rule engine's working memory, as depicted in Figure 13. This is the simplest scenario, and has limited scalability with respect to the number of situations detected, even when situations are entirely independent of each other, i.e., when situations are detected using context conditions that are sensed independently, and are not composed of other situations. The centralized approach introduces a single point of access to context information, which can be considered a potential (privacy) hazard, due to the sensitive nature of particular kinds of context information.

Secondly, we consider a scenario with multiple hub-and-spokes for situation detection. In this scenario, multiple engines detect independent situations. The level of distribution is constrained by the nature of the situation model, each hub-and-spoke

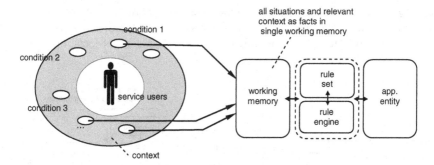

Fig. 13. Centralized scenario

pattern consisting of a centralized solution. In this approach, each rule engine may be associated to a different administrative domain, which enables more fine-grained control of the (privacy) policies which apply to the context information for that domain. The solution is highly constrained by the nature of the situation model, since all related situations must be detected in the scope of the same rule engine. Figure 14 depicts this solution with two rule engines detecting independent situations 1 and 2.

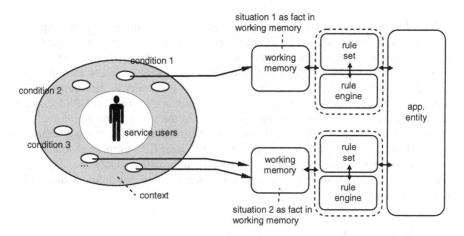

Fig. 14. Multiple hub-and-spokes scenario

Finally, we consider a distribution scenario with a higher level of distribution that not only exploits possible independent situations, but that is able to decompose situation detection further, and distribute parts of the rule detection functionality to different rule engines. Different distribution strategies and rule engine configurations can be accommodated using this approach. Figure 15 depicts a possible configuration with two independent situations 1 and 2 detected independently in rule engines A and B (as in the hub-and-spokes scenario). The facts corresponding to those situations are shared with a rule engine C, which detects a situation 3 which is derived from situations 1 and 2. We propose a shared working memory mechanism that is part of the DJess infrastructure [2] to realize this approach. With this mechanism, rule engines running in different nodes can apply rules on shared sets of facts. A rule engine may participate in multiple shared memory partnerships (which are called Web of Inference Systems in DJess), each of which defining a shared set of facts, thus allowing arbitrary configurations.

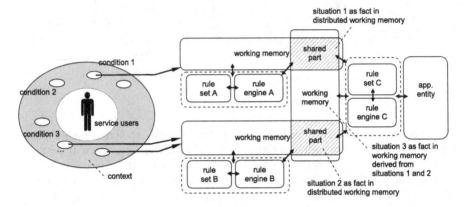

Fig. 15. Distributed scenario

The distributed scenario enables fine-grained control of the policies that apply to context information, since different rule engines and parts of situation detection can be associated with different administrative domains. The policies for context information may justify in this scenario different distribution strategies. For example, consider an application that uses the distance between two users to determine whether users can view each other's contact information. Suppose further that GPS location is used to compute the distance between users. Due to the sensitive nature of the "raw" GPS location, different policies apply to this information, and to the aggregate and usually less sensitive distance information. In this case, GPS location should be only available to the engines that derive proximity information. Only the aggregated proximity information should be shared with other engines that define contact information visibility.

6   Related Work

Several approaches presented in the literature [12, 13, 19] support the concept of situation as a means of defining particular application's states of affairs. These approaches usually apply centralized mechanisms, and instead of detecting situations attentively, they offer reactive query interfaces, which do not take the initiative of generating events upon situation detection.

The work presented in [13] discusses a situation-based theory for context-awareness that allows situations to be defined in terms of basic fact types. Fact types are defined in an ORM (Object-Role Modeling) context model, and situation types are defined using a variant of predicate logic. The realization supported by means of a mapping to relational databases, and a set of programming models based on the Java language. Although CML is based on a graphical notation, to the best of our knowledge, there is no modeling tool available for graphical situation specification. In addition, the implementation, as reported in [13], does not consider situation detection distribution.

None of the approaches we have studied use UML 2.0 in combination with OCL invariants for defining situation types. UML is unfairly underestimated in the context-awareness community. As we have seen in this paper, UML can be an appropriate and effective tool for modeling context and situations types. Furthermore, UML is currently widely adopted as a general modeling language, with extensive documentation and tool support.

7 Conclusions

We have proposed a novel approach for the specification and realization of situation detection for attentive context-aware applications. The specification approach is based on our earlier work on conceptual modeling for context information, and uses standard UML class diagrams for graphical representation of context models and situation models. Situations can be composed of more elementary kinds of context, and in addition can be composed of existing situations themselves. We have addressed the temporal aspects of applications, and included primitives to relate situations based on their temporal aspects.

The realization is rule-based, and executes on mature and efficient rule engine technology available off-the-shelf. The rule set is derived systematically from the specification and has been deployed directly in the Jess rule engine. We have argued that a distributed solution to situation detection has benefits, which apply to context-aware applications in particular. We have realized communication between rule engines by using the DJess shared memory mechanism, which allows different engines to execute their rule base in a shared set of facts.

This work is part of a larger effort towards a generic infrastructure to support context-aware applications. The use of a rule-based approach enables us to perform situation detection efficiently, and to generate events for situation detection with little effort. In addition, we also apply rule-based approaches to implement Event-Condition-Action (ECA) rules in our infrastructure [9].

As part of future work, we intend to study more complex mechanisms for discarding historical situation records that will no longer be used. Our current solution uses time-to-live for discarding historical records. An alternative solution is to eliminate all historical data that is not referred by any active situation. This requires complex inspection on situation type dependencies.

Acknowledgements

This work is part of the Freeband AWARENESS and A-MUSE projects (http:// awareness.freeband.nl and http://amuse.freedband.nl). Freeband is sponsored by the Dutch government under contract BSIK 03025.

References

1. Almeida, J.P.A., Iacob, M.E., Jonkers, H., Quartel, D.: Model-Driven Development of Context-Aware Services. In: Eliassen, F., Montresor, A. (eds.) DAIS 2006. LNCS, vol. 4025, pp. 213–227. Springer, Heidelberg (2006)
2. Cabitza, F., Sarini, M., Dal Seno, B.: DJess - a context-sharing middleware to deploy distributed inference systems in pervasive computing domains. In: Proceeding of International Conference on Pervasive Services (ICPS '05), pp. 229–238. IEEE CS Press, Washington, DC (2005)
3. Dey, A.K., Salber, D., Abowd, G.D.: A Conceptual Framework and a Toolkit for Supporting the Rapid Prototyping of Context-Aware Applications. Human-Computer Interaction 16(2-4), 97–166 (2001)
4. Chen, H., Finin, T., Joshi, A.: An ontology for context-aware pervasive computing environments, Knowledge Engineering Review. In: Special Issue on Ontologies for Distributed Systems, vol. 18(3), pp. 197–207. Cambridge University Press, Cambridge (2003)
5. Dockhorn Costa, P., Ferreira Pires, L., van Sinderen, M.: Architectural Support for Mobile Context-Aware Applications. In: Handbook of Research on Mobile Multimedia, Idea Group Inc. (2005)
6. Dockhorn Costa, P., Ferreira Pires, L., van Sinderen, M.: Designing a Configurable Services Platform for Mobile Context-Aware Applications, International Journal of Pervasive Computing and Communications (JPCC), vol. 1(1). Troubador Publishing (2005)
7. Dockhorn Costa, P., Guizzardi, G., Almeida, J.P.A., Ferreira Pires, L., van Sinderen, M.: Situations in Conceptual Modeling of Context. In: Workshop on Vocabularies, Ontologies, and Rules for the Enterprise (VORTE 2006) at IEEE EDOC 2006, IEEE CS Press, Washington, DC (2006)
8. Dockhorn Costa, P., Almeida, J.P.A., Ferreira Pires, L., Guizzardi, G., van Sinderen, M.: Towards Conceptual Foundations for Context-Aware Applications. In: Proc. of the Third Int'l Workshop on Modeling and Retrieval of Context (MRC'06), Boston, USA (2006)
9. Etter, R., Dockhorn Costa, P., Broens, T.: A Rule-Based Approach Towards Context-Aware User Notification Services. In: Proc. of the IEEE International Conference on Pervasive Services 2006, Lyon, France (2006)
10. Freeband A-MUSE Project, http://www.freeband.nl/project.cfm?id=489
11. Friedman-Hill, E.: JESS in Action: Rule-Based Systems in Java. Manning Publications Co., (2003)
12. Hang Wang, X., Qing Zhang, D., Gu, T., Keng Pung, H.: Ontology-Based Context Modeling and Reasoning Using OWL. In: Proc. of the 2nd IEEE Annual Conf. on Pervasive Computing and Communications Workshops (PERCOMW04), USA, pp. 18–22 (2004)
13. Henricksen, K., Indulska, J.: Developing context-aware pervasive computing applications: Models and approach. Journal of Pervasive and Mobile Computing, vol. 2(1), pp. 37–64. Elsevier (2006)
14. McFadden, T., Henricksen, K., Indulska, J., Mascaro, P.: Applying a Disciplined Approach to the Development of a Context-Aware Communication Application. In: 3rd IEEE Conf. on Pervasive Computing and Communications (Percom 2005), IEEE CS Press, Washington, DC (2005)
15. Merriam-Webster, Inc.: Merriam-Webster Online: http://m-w.com
16. Mylopoulos, J.: Conceptual modeling and Telos. In: Loucopoulos, P., Zicari, R. (eds.) Conceptual modeling, databases, and CASE, John Wiley and Sons Inc., New York (1992)

17. Object Management Group: Unified Modelling Language: Object Constraint Language version 2.0, ptc/03-10-04 (2003)
18. Object Management Group: UML 2.0 Superstructure, ptc/03-08-02 (2003)
19. Strang, T., Linnhoff-Popien, C., Frank, K.: CoOL: A Context Ontology Language to enable Contextual Interoperability. In: Proc. of the 4th IFIP International Conference on Distributed Applications and Interoperable Systems (DAIS2003), pp. 236–247 Paris (2003)

Observability and Controllability of Wireless Software Components

Fabien Romeo, Franck Barbier, and Jean-Michel Bruel

LIUPPA, Université de Pau et des Pays de l'Adour
Av. de l'Université, B.P. 1155, F-64013 PAU - France
fabien.romeo@univ-pau.fr, franck.barbier@franckbarbier.com,
jean-michel.bruel@univ-pau.fr

Abstract. Software components embedded in wireless devices are subject to behavior which cannot be fully and realistically predicted. This calls for a runtime management infrastructure that is able to observe and control the components' states and to make their behaviors explicit, tangible and understandable, in any case and at any time. In this paper, we propose a framework for remotely administrating the functional behavior of software components deployed on wireless nodes. This framework is based on components which are locally managed by internal managers on the wireless side. The controllable nature of components relies on executable UML models that persist at runtime. On the administration side, models are replicated and synchronized with the models that constitute the inner workings of the wireless components.

1 Introduction

Component-based development is a challenging topic in the area of ubiquitous systems. More particularly, this is illustrated by research on specialized component models (*e.g.*, pect [1], koala [2], pecos [3], beanome [4] or frogi [5]) which themselves may support composition techniques that are specific to ubiquitous systems.

Many studies have shown that embedded system developers expect better analysis supports of software behavior. Better testability and debuggability are among these major requirements [6, 7]. Component-based development may be seen as a breakthrough with respect to this topic. Indeed, building software by means of components enables the identification and the setup of deployment properties. As for the compositions of components, they may express links which may reflect wireless infrastructures in a structured and logical way. If one has at one's disposal an appropriate formalism to design the inside of components (implementation) and the outside (interfaces and their dependencies embodying compositions), runtime management may benefit from this formalism. More specifically, this concerns the executable component/composition behavior models that result from using this formalism. Therefore, models act as tracking and monitoring supports.

In the area of ubiquitous systems, mastering deployment conditions includes overcoming some stumbling blocks. Instable communication connections that may be broken, damaged modes are frequent, runtime environments/infrastructures are mobile

J. Indulska and K. Raymond (Eds.): DAIS 2007, LNCS 4531, pp. 48–61, 2007.

and may quickly evolve, etc. Thus, emphasizing the management-centric or model-driven design of software components is not enough. A management system on the top of a distributed application composed of several varied wireless components also requires specific attributes: self-management as defined by autonomic computing [8], special manager roles and distribution of the management layer itself.

In this paper, we describe WMX (Wireless Management eXtensions) [9], an adaptation of JMX, which is the standardized management API and framework in the Java world [10]. Although WMX is the adaptation of JMX for ubiquitous systems, we add in WMX an enhanced support to have "true" manageable software components and compositions. While JMX stresses the management infrastructure (inspired by norms like GDMO - Guidelines for the Definition of Managed Objects), it does not provide a component design method. This means that the inside of these components, at any time, may not really be interpretable and intelligible by management systems; these being human or autonomic. Like JMX, we offer a coercive framework in which components comply with design rules so that they may be deployed in WMX-compliant environments. This point mainly relies on the idea of embedded internal managers which interact with the management side. Components are in particular endowed with dedicated management interfaces in order to sort out what is and has to be managed.

Contrary to JMX, we organize and implement the inside and thus the behavior of components based on executable UML 2 State Machine Diagrams, a variant of Harel's statecharts [11]. To enable the persistence of these models at runtime, we have a J2ME (Java 2 Micro Edition)-compliant library which includes and organizes observation and control activities around the components' abstract states. This includes the dependencies between these states (exclusiveness, orthogonality and nesting) and the logical communications of components (event sending) which embody compositions. Concretely, complex state machines may graphically appear in consoles or GUIs and act as the key entry point for management: forcing states for instance.

To present and explain WMX, this paper first discusses the idea of locally managed components, which are the basis of the proposed infrastructure. Next, the relationships between internal managers and the global management system are described. Finally, a case of composition management is illustrated by means of an example. Before we conclude, synthetic performance measures are listed.

2   Internal Management of Components

We first present the design of a locally managed component, made up of business functionalities embodied in a business subcomponent and a modeled behavior controlled by its internal manager. The correlation between these two subcomponents and the behavior model are detailed in the section 2.2.

2.1   Internal Managers and Business Components

In classical management solutions [8, 13] the application and the management system interact through sensors and actuators – or effectors in the autonomic metaphor. Sensors are used by managers to probe the application and actuators are used to execute application actions.

In CBSE, [14] has defined a specific interface, *the Diagnostic and Management interface*, which provides selective access to the internals of the components for management purposes. Since components communicate through their interfaces, it is natural to specify sensors and actuators as interfaces. Figure 1 depicts, through UML 2 Component Diagrams the resulting architecture of our notion of locally managed component. We have gathered in management ports three types of interfaces acting as sensors and actuators to relay information between the business component and the internal manager inside the locally managed component.

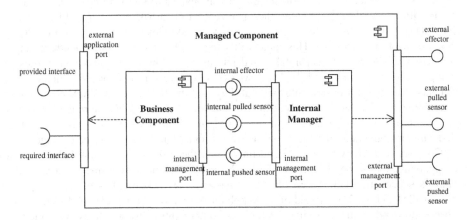

Fig. 1. Managed Component Architecture

From a design perspective, we have on one side the business component, which implements the concrete business functionalities, *i.e.* the computation, and on the other side the internal manager, which controls the component according to its defined behavior model. In this way, the internal manager totally encapsulates the control logic, which is then externalized from the business component (as recommended by [15]) to maximize loose coupling between the components. We have thus been able to compose components according to their behavior models [16], but the definition of such a composition mechanism is out of the scope of this paper.

The managed component can also communicate with other external components through classical provided and required interfaces. These interfaces are part of an external application port that is connected to the business component that is responsible for business functionalities. The internal management is connected with an external management port, which is comprised of sensors and actuators, through which the management system can query the manager about its component's states and act on its behavior (see section 3).

2.2 Behavior Model Facilitating the Management of Components

The principle of the management framework is to include a statechart [11] within each managed component's internal manager. This statechart specifies the component's behavior by a set of states and transitions. Figure 2 represents a detailed UML 2 diagram relating to an example of a managed component. Its behavior is defined by the statechart in Figure 3. The detailed component diagram explicits the

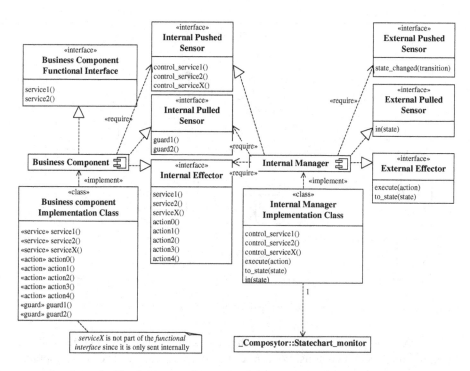

Fig. 2. Managed Component's Detailed Architecture

interfaces defined in Figure 1 and the implementation classes of this managed component. The behavior of this component is executed by a statechart engine, the *Statechart_monitor* associated with the internal manager.

During its execution, this managed component can only be in one of its two mutually exclusive states *SA* or *SB*. According to statechart formalism, *SA* is the initial state. In this state, a request on *service1* exposed in the component's functional interface would generate an event in the internal manager that would trigger a transition from *SA* to *SB*, whereas requests on any other service would have no effect. Conversely, in state *SB* this same event would trigger a transition to *SA*, no matter what substates the component may have. *SB* is a composite state divided into orthogonal regions. At *SB* entry, the component is simultaneously in substates *S10*, *S2* and *S3*, which causes the internal manager to execute in parallel through the internal effector *action0* and *action3* on the business component which implements them. In *S10* substate, a call to *service2* could trigger a transition to *S11* or a transition to *S12* depending on whether *guard1* or *guard2* hold. Note that only one of these two guards can hold simultaneously as specified, if they could hold two at the same time there would have been a consistency error in the statechart due to indeterminism. So if *guard1* holds, *action1* is executed and the component enters into substate *S12*. Notice that it also re-enters into *S2*, as a self-transition is defined for this state upon detection of event *service2*, regardless if *guard1* or *guard2* hold. If *guard2* holds, then a signal is sent to component *self*, *i.e.* to itself, as specified by the following notation ^*self.serviceX*.

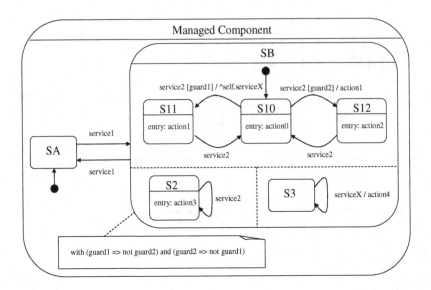

Fig. 3. Managed Component Behavior

This example illustrates the relationship between the internal manager and the business component it controls. We can see that two kinds of data need to be captured by the manager: service requests and low-level states. Low-level states are values of objects' attributes that are traditionally monitored in management and are collected here in an abstract way by the evaluation of predefined guards. In management, two different models are used to monitor data: push and pull models [17]. The pull model is based on the request/response paradigm. In this model, the manager sends a data request to the managed host according to its needs, then the managed host replies. Such a sensor, which we call *pulled_sensor*, is used to evaluate the statechart's guards whenever required by adding a provided interface to the business component. Conversely, the push model is based on the publish/subscribe/distribute paradigm. In this model, the manager specifies the data it is interested in, then the managed host is responsible for pushing this data to the manager whenever they change. Thus a *pushed_sensor* is perfectly adapted to collect the business component's incoming events upon reception. We have added a required interface to the business component to equip it with such a sensor.

3   External Management of Components

Management involves two dual activities, monitoring and control. The first part of this section focuses on the way monitoring is considered between a managed component and our management system and the second presents the different control functionalities that are provided.

3.1 Monitoring

Monitoring is the activity of making continuous observations of the evolution of state variables that reflect system dynamics. In the last section, we have seen that the internal manager is responsible for the direct monitoring of the managed component's business activity. But since it is not fully self-manageable, management information needs to be acquired by a higher level management system. In our context of deploy-ing components in embedded systems, the management system has to perform wirelessly, away from managed components. The reason for not integrating this management system into the application system itself is two-fold. First, as we are in a wireless context, we aim at avoiding the overload of wireless devices with heavy management computation. Second, the user interfaces of such systems, often mechanical, are minimal when they exist and thus are not appropriate for management activity.

Hence, we choose to replicate the behavior, *i.e.* the statechart, of managed compo-nents on the management side. In managed component internals, the data we managed are events and low-level states (as shown in section 2). A first approach is to reproduce the same scheme. In [18] we forwarded only the events and not the low-level states, which would have been too heavy and inefficient since we do not need to know every change in this data. But this caused synchronization problems since the value of this data is used in guards for firing transitions. As a result, we could not deduce all the transitions that were actually fired.

In order to avoid this problem, we now forward fired transitions instead of events. Hence, we ensure that the replicated statechart evolves in the same way as the original does. In addition, there is no need for the management system to know about low-level states, since the transition choice is already carried out by the internal manager. Data is abstracted to a higher level and the management system only requires the statechart's states in order to work. To allow this communication between the managed component and the management system, we have once again the same two possible models we used in section 2, namely push and pull models. Therefore, we have added an *external_pushed_sensor* as a required interface to the managed component, so that it can notify the management system of any state change. We have also added an *external_pulled_sensor* for re-synchronization purposes in case of communication breakdown. What we have described above is only the information transferred from a running management session. A protocol for starting the process of replication can be worked out, but it is out of the scope of this paper.

3.2 Control

The boundaries of control activity are hard to define because it is involved both in business activity and management activity. Every application has its own control logic and behavior, which coordinates its different functionalities. Control in manage-ment interferes with this control logic to activate such or such functionality. In the managed component, we have delegated the whole control responsibility to the intern-al manager. Contrary to classical applications, in which the control logic is combined with business functionalities, the behavior of our managed component is explicitly defined in a statechart that is directly executed by the *Statechart_monitor* of its internal manager. The latter in turn triggers the corresponding actions on its business component. This allows the internal manager to propose a specific interface to the management system, the *external_effector*, in order to inflect the component's behavior.

Our management system supports three types of control:

- control by event: an event corresponding to a request of service from the component's functional interface is sent to the managed component. This is equivalent to what could be done by a component's client.
- control by state: the managed component is forced into a specified state defined in its statecharts. The control induced by the statechart's transitions is bypassed to put the component directly into the desired current state.
- control by action: it provokes the direct execution of an action in the business component of the managed component without making any change in its current behavior state.

4   Management of Compositions

In the previous two sections, we have seen how management is provided with abstract knowledge of managed components' behavior through their internal managers. This enables high-level management policies for an assembly of managed components, which otherwise could not be taken into account by the internal managers themselves. We first describe a special type of behavior composition used in component based modeling. We then show a management policy for this type of composition that maintains the consistency of the application's overall behavior at runtime.

4.1   Behavior Composition

In CBSE, a software system is considered as an assembly of components. The focus is on practical reuse through the building of new solutions by combining external and home made components. However, building systems from existing parts is known to be a difficult task, especially due to architectural mismatching [19]. In order to represent compound behaviors, Pazzi proposes the adoption of Part-Whole Statecharts (PWS) [20]. In his proposal, compounds' (or parts') behaviors, which are specified by statecharts, are composed through the parallel AND mechanism, which yields a global automaton containing all the compounds' statecharts in different orthogonal regions. An additional region representing the composite's (or the whole's) behavior is added to this automaton. The composite controls its compounds by event sending, but is not notified of its compounds' state change. This could lead to the desynchronization of the composite's statecharts with regards to its compounds' statecharts. Pazzi deals with the problem by obliging the encapsulation of the compoundss. But in [21]'s definition of several forms of composition, the encapsulation property is not a systematic characteristic of this relationship and thus the behavior of the compounds and the composite can diverge. In the following part, we show an example of how a management policy can detect this particular scenario and automatically handle it.

4.2 A Management Policy to Ensure Rigorous Behavior Composition

Let's consider a traffic light component made up of three light components, a red, a yellow and a green one. These components are involved in a relationship where the traffic light is the composite and the lights are the compounds. All the lights have the same behavior, which has two states, *On* and *Off*, as represented by the state-chart of Figure 4.

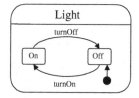

Fig. 4. The Light's Behavior

The behavior of the traffic light is depicted by the statechart of Figure 5. It is composed of three main states *Red*, *Yellow*, and *Green*, and is set to *Red* by means of the *Start* state. When a transition is triggered, it sends signals (notation: ^*component.signal*) to switch on or off appropriate lights in order to light only the correct light named by the state that has been reached by the transition.

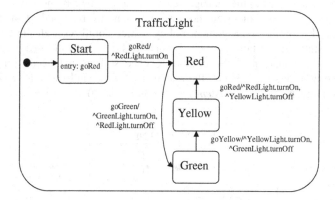

Fig. 5. Traffic Light Behavior

Specified like this, the system works well as long as the control of the compounds only comes from the traffic light component, the composite. Indeed, if for any reason, such as an unforeseen event, a hack attack, or a management operation, a light changes its state without the traffic light that initiated it, the behaviors of the composite and its compounds would be desynchronized. This is an illustration of the previously described problem.

To handle this situation, we build, thanks to our framework, these four components as managed components executing the statecharts of Figures 4 and 5. Then we build their corresponding external managers, which replicate the statecharts of the components and allow to control them through the management system. This is depicted with the orthogonal states *Monitor* and *Control* in the managers' behavior specification of Figures 6 and 7.

This allows us to define a management policy in the management system based on the informations provided by these managers. The idea is to specify composite's states as abstract states that belong to a subset of the Cartesian product of the compounds' states. In our example, the traffic light is composed of three lights and the behavior of each light is composed of two states. The Cartesian product yields 2^3 states and only three are defined for the traffic light, namely *red light on only*, *yellow light on only* and *green light on only*. Other states, in which more than one light are on, are undefined for the traffic light. The next table summarizes this situation.

Table 1. States mapping between composite and components

Components	Valid States		
RedLight	On	Off	Off
YellowLight	Off	On	Off
GreenLight	Off	Off	On
TrafficLight	Red	Yellow	Green

Hence, the composition between the traffic light and its lights can be qualified by two states, *Defined* or *Undefined*, depending on whether the states of the lights reflect a valid state for the traffic light or not (see *valid_state_guard* in Figure 6). The *Undefined* state indicates to the management system that the assembly of components is in a state that has not been designed. It has to be handled manually or autonomically by another management policy, which could reset all the components in a proper state for instance. If the compounds are in a defined state for the composition, the manager of the composite checks if its managed component is synchronized with this state. If not, the manager autonomically sets the composite to the corresponding state (see *consistency_guard* in Figure 6).

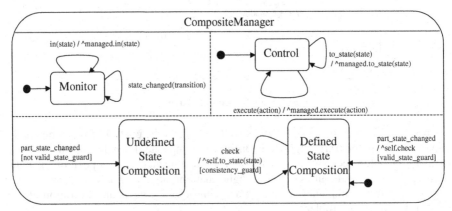

valid_state_guard: (RedLight.in(On) ∧ YellowLight.in(Off) ∧ GreenLight.in(Off))
           ∨ (RedLight.in(Off) ∧ YellowLight.in(On) ∧ GreenLight.in(Off))
           ∨ (RedLight.in(Off) ∧ YellowLight.in(Off) ∧ GreenLight.in(On))

consistency_guard:
(state = Red) ⇒ (managed.in(Red) ⇒ (RedLight.in(On) ∧ YellowLight.in(Off) ∧ GreenLight.in(Off))
∨
(state = Yellow) ⇒ (managed.in(Yellow) ⇒ (RedLight.in(Off) ∧ YellowLight.in(On)
∧ GreenLight.in(Off))
∨
(state = Green) ⇒ (managed.in(Green) ⇒ (RedLight.in(Off) ∧ YellowLight.in(Off) ∧ GreenLight.in(On))

Fig. 6. Composite Manager's Behavior

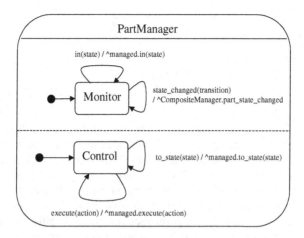

Fig. 7. Compound Manager's Behavior

5 Implementation

The implementation of the presented infrastructure is named WMX, which stands for Wireless Management Extensions. It has to be seen in as an overall effort to rigorously develop component-based complex systems. WMX is part of a framework dedicated to the development of autonomic component-based applications. It is based on a Java library that enables the execution of Harel's Statecharts: the PauWare library [16]. In WMX, both internal and external managers are built on top of this library: internal managers use the J2ME version, called Velcro, and external managers use the J2SE standard version. Communications between these components have been generalized and they are delegated to specific adapters, which support the chosen wireless technologies (Wifi, Bluetooth, WMA, ...). The overall management system relies on the management standard JMX and thus can be incorporated into existing JMX-compliant management solutions.

5.1 Wireless Software Components

WMX provides the necessary facilities to directly implement managed components as specified in Figure 1. From a design viewpoint, this simply leads to extending the *WMX_component* class provided by WMX and to incorporating the statecharts controling its behavior by using the Velcro library. Here is the code of the Light component in Figure 4 (the code is incomplete):

```
public class Light extends WMX_component {
    protected AbstractStatechart _On;
    protected AbstractStatechart _Off;
    protected AbstractStatechart_monitor _Light;
    public Light() throws Statechart_exception {
        // init states
        _On = new VelcroStatechart("On");
        _Off = new VelcroStatechart("Off");
        _Off.inputState();
```

```
    _Light = new VelcroStatechart_monitor(
                        _On.xor(_Off),"Light");
    registerStatechart_monitor(_Light);
    // init transitions
    _Light.fires("turnOn",_Off,_On,[...]);
    _Light.fires("turnOff",_On,_Off,[...]);
    }
    [...]
}
```

In the above code, *Light* is composed of *On* and *Off* states using the XOR operator and it is declared as a statechart monitor, which is the access point to the overall statechart of the Light component. The *registerStatechart_monitor* method (in bold print), which is a member of *WMX_component* class, effectively registers the statechart monitor to be used for management purposes. Then all the management communication matters are automatically handled by the *WMX_component*.

Events in the statecharts are implemented as method calls which notify the statechart monitor to start a run-to-completion process to execute eligible transitions:

```
public void turnOn() throws Statechart_exception {
    _Light.run_to_completion("turnOn");
}
public void turnOff() throws Statechart_exception {
    _Light.run_to_completion("turnOff");
}
```

When declaring a transition between states with the *fires* method, it is possible to specify a guard that will have to be satisfied in order to trigger the transition and an action to be performed when the transition is actually triggered. Here is the signature of the *fires* method:

```
public void fires(java.lang.String event,
                  AbstractStatechart from,
                  AbstractStatechart to,
                  boolean guard,
                  java.lang.Object object,
                  java.lang.String action,
                  java.lang.Object[] args)
         throws Statechart_transition_based_exception
```

In the above signature, it is important to notice that the object in charge of the execution of the action can be specified. In this way, components deployed in the same JVM and can communicate asynchronously through their statechart monitors.

5.2 Wireless Management Communication and Remote Management System

In our proposition, the statechart of a managed component deployed on a wireless device is replicated and kept up to date in its remote management system. The replicated statechart is also implemented by using the PauWare library, but only the states of the original statechart are duplicated; not the transitions. The triggered transitions are directly forwarded by the managed component and there is no event processing to execute the eligible transitions.

In WMX, management communication is done through *Wireless Communicators* which target specific wireless networks such as WiFi, Bluetooth, or WMA (SMS) for instance. Like this, depending on the available network, one can choose to connect such or such communicator to one's managed component and corresponding manager. Of course our framework depends on the reliability of the wireless network that is used. However in our current implementation, even if communications are temporarily broken, the management system will eventually be updated since our statecharts support asynchronous communications. Moreover, we have deployed the TrafficLight case study on a PDA, which is an HP iPAQ hx4700 embedding J9 Java virtual machine from IBM, using Wifi and the application goes perfectly well, as long as the device remains within the network range. And if it loses connection for a moment the management system restarts in the current state of the managed component.

Lastly, managers in WMX are implemented as MBean in order to be accessible through JMX, which is the standard for management in the Java Platform. Thus, WMX components are manageable through common management systems such as the JMX console or even through a simple web page by using the JDMK HTML adaptor.

6 Performance Issues

In order to evaluate our framework, we employ a benchmark to quantify the execution time overhead per state change. For our purpose, iterations of 100000 state changes are performed on different test components. Table 2 reports the results from this experiment on our test system: a Pentium M 1,6GHz processor with 512 Mo of RAM running Java 1.5 on Windows XP. We chose this system over a handheld device in order to compare WMX with JMX, which can not be run on Java ME. Moreover, this choice also allows us to quantify the cost of the adaptation of PauWare for wireless systems in Velcro.

At first glance the results show that PauWare is twice heavier than JMX, but this is acceptable when considering that the State Machine engine performs a lot more controls than JMX. Moreover, the performances of Pauware are improved by the use of cached transitions: the transitions that are not dynamically resolved at runtime can

Table 2. Benchmarks

Implementation	Benchmark	Overhead per state change
Pure Java	2 ms	0 µs
Java + reflect API	14 ms	0,12 µs
JMX (internal access)	721ms	7,19 µs
PauWare (w/o cache)	1491 ms	14,89 µs
PauWare (w cache)	1027 ms	10,25 µs
Velcro (w/o cache)	1529 ms	15,27 µs
Velcro (w cache)	1038 ms	10,36 µs
Following implementations include I/O or networking		
Pure Java + System.out.print()	2584 ms	25,82 µs
WMX (velcro + sockets)	3893 ms	38,91 µs
JMX + RMI connector	22077ms	220,75 µs

be statically defined once and for all. Another interesting result is that the adaptations made in Velcro to render the State Machine engine compliant with Java ME do not much affect the performance.

At last in more realistic situations, *i.e.* when the management involves logging or networking, WMX is only 50 percent slower than a simple log console (Pure Java + System.out.print()) and it clearly outperforms JMX used with an RMI connector.

7 Conclusion

In this paper, we have presented a management system for software components deployed in wireless embedded systems. The solution focuses on the management of model-driven behaviors. To that end, we have introduced internal managers which are responsible for observing and controlling managed component behaviors. Thanks to these wireless-side managers, we have shown how the global management system is organized. More precisely, we have illustrated the exchanges flows induced by management activities. Then, we have described an example of management policy based on a particular type of composition. Finally, performances issues were briefly evoked.

At this time, we have experimented and validated our approach by a prototype running on real devices (PDAs especially). The wireless management side is obviously based on J2ME and PauWare (the support for executable UML 2 State Machine Diagrams). As for the global implementation of the prototype, we have kept JMX on the non-wireless side in order to take advantage of all of the features of this standard. Our existing implementation is not bound to any specific running environment or component model. We on purpose are currently investigating the OSGi platform which has become highly used in wireless systems.

We are also currently working on "autonomous" management policies that might rely on our system to make management activities more and more autonomic. Clearly, self-healing for instance, a kind of fault recovery mechanism, might take advantage of rolling back state machines to stable consistent configurations when abnormal situations exist or persist. Self-configuration may also be more easily and more straightforwardly instrumented by forcing states of components.

References

1. Wallnau, K.C.: Volume III: A Technology for Predictable Assembly from Certifiable Components. Technical report, Software Engineering Institute, Carnegie Mellon University, Pittsburgh, USA (2003)
2. van Ommering, R., van der Linden, F., Kramer, J., Magee, J.: The Koala Component Model for Consumer Electronics Software. Computer 33(3), 78–85 (2000)
3. Winter, M., Genssler, T., Christoph, A., Nierstrasz, O., Ducasse, S., Wuyts, R., Arvalo, G., Mller, P., Stich, C., Schnhage, B.: Components for Embedded Software – The PECOS Approach. In: Second International Workshop on Composition Languages. In conjunction with 16th European Conference on Object-Oriented Programming (ECOOP), Malaga, Spain (2002)

4. Cervantes, H., Hall, R.S.: Beanome: A Component Model for the OSGi Framework. In: Proceedings of the Workshop on Software Infrastructures for Component-Based Applications on Consumer Devices, Lausanne, Switzerland (2000)
5. Desertot, M., Cervantes, H., Donsez, D.: FROGi: Fractal components deployment over OSGi. In: 5th International Symposium on Software Composition SC'06, Vienna, Austria (2006)
6. Crnkovic, I.: Component-based Software Engineering for Embedded Systems. In: International Conference on Software engineering, St. Luis, USA, ACM, New York (2005)
7. Möller, A., Fröberg, J., Nolin, M.: Industrial Requirements on Component Technologies for Embedded Systems. In: International Symposium on Component-Based Software Engineering, Edinburgh, Scotland, Springer Verlag, Heidelberg (2004)
8. Kephart, J., Chess, D.: The Vision of Autonomic Computing. In: Computer Magazine, vol. 36, pp. 41–50. IEEE Computer Society, Washington, DC (2003)
9. Romeo, F.: WMX, http://www.univ-pau.fr/ fromeo/wmx
10. Kreger, H., Harold, W., Williamson, L.: Java and JMX. Addison Wesley, London (2003)
11. Harel, D.: Statecharts: A Visual Formalism for Complex Systems. Science of Computer Programming 8(3), 231–274 (1987)
12. Grieskamp, W., Heisel, M., Dörr, H.: Specifying Embedded Systems with Statecharts and Z: An Agenda for Cyclic Software Components. In: Astesiano, E. (ed.) ETAPS 1998 and FASE 1998. LNCS, vol. 1382, pp. 88–115. Springer, Heidelberg (1998)
13. Buzato, L.E.: Management of Object-Oriented Action-Based Distributed Programs. PhD thesis, University of Newcastle upon Tyne (1994)
14. Kopetz, H., Suri, N.: Compositional design of RT systems: A conceptual basis for specification of linking interfaces. In: 6th IEEE International Symposium on Object-oriented Real-Time Distributed Computing, Hokkaido, Japan (2003)
15. Lau, K.K., Elizondo, P.V., Wang, Z.: Exogenous Connectors for Software Components. In: Eighth International SIGSOFT Symposium on Component-based Software Engineering, Springer, Heidelberg (2005)
16. Romeo, F., Ballagny, C., Barbier, F.: PauWare : un modèle de composant basé état. In: Journées Composants, Canet en Roussillon, France, pp. 1–10 (2006)
17. Martin-Flatin, J.P.: Push vs. Pull in Web-Based Network Management. In: Proc. 6th IFIP/IEEE Intl. Symposium on Integrated Network Management (IM'99), Boston, MA, pp. 3–18 (1999)
18. Romeo, F., Barbier, F.: Management of Wireless Software Components. In: The 10th International Workshop on Component-Oriented Programming in the 19th European Conference on Object-Oriented Programming, Glasgow, Scotland (2005)
19. Garlan, D., Allen, R., Ockerbloom, J.: Architectural Mismatch or Why it's hard to build systems out of existing parts. In: 17th International Conference on Software Enginneering, Seattle, Washington, ACM SIGSOFT, pp. 179–185 (1995)
20. Pazzi, L.: Part-Whole Statecharts for the Explicit Representation of Compound Behaviors. In: UML, pp. 541–555 (2000)
21. Barbier, F., Henderson-Sellers, B., Parc, A.L., Bruel, J.M.: Formalization of the Whole-Part Relationship in the Unied Modeling Language. IEEE Trans. Software Eng. 29(5), 459–470 (2003)

Service Level Agreement Management
in Federated Virtual Organizations

Tuomas Nurmela[1] and Lea Kutvonen[2]

[1] Tietoenator Processing & Network Oy, Espoo, Finland
`Tuomas.Nurmela@tietoenator.com`
[2] Department of Computer Science, University of Helsinki, Finland
`Lea.Kutvonen@cs.helsinki.fi`

Abstract. The present emergence of loosely-coupled, inter-enterprise collaboration, i.e., virtual organizations calls for new kind of middleware: generic, common facilities for managing contract-governed collaborations and the autonomous business services between which those collaborations are formed. While further work is still needed on the functional governance of the collaborations and services, even more work is awaiting on the management of non-functional aspects of the virtual enterprises and their members. In this paper, languages and architectures for service level agreement between Web Services are discussed and the maturity of the service level management solutions is reflected against the needs of federated virtual organizations.

Keywords: virtual organizations, Web Services, service level agreements.

1 Introduction

The present emergence of loosely-coupled, inter-enterprise collaboration, i.e., virtual organizations calls for new kind of middleware: generic, common facilities for managing contract-governed collaborations and the autonomous business services between which those collaborations are formed. These facilities are required to manage the collaboration lifecycle and interoperability at technical, semantic and pragmatic levels. We call these facilities B2B middleware [1, 2].

While further work is still needed on the functional governance of the collaborations and services, even more work is awaiting on the management of non-functional aspects of the virtual enterprises and their members. In the category of non-functional aspects three types of phenomenon can be seen: 1) policies and business rules that determine pragmatic decision between alternative business processes or collaborations, 2) private decision-making rules, for example determining trust relationships or quality of service level satisfaction, that have effect on the collaboration memberships (or in breach recovery actions at the collaboration level), and 3) non-functional aspects related to communication between business services, including security, QoS, or other selectable transparencies of the abstract communication channel.

J. Indulska and K. Raymond (Eds.): DAIS 2007, LNCS 4531, pp. 62–75, 2007.

As part of the work on refining the non-functional aspect management in federated virtual organizations and in the Pilarcos architecture [2], we have separately studied sub-architectures for multiparty eContracting [2], binding between peers by federated, open channels, and trust management [1]. To complement this theme, the present paper studies the management of service level agreements, associated either to the communication architecture, or more interestingly to the quality of peer services in the collaboration. The study addresses adaptation to changes either at the organizational, local level, or in the operational environment of the services by different type of runtime agreements on the service level. The present trend on service level management enables the service markets to move from basic cost-competition towards differentiation through variation of service capabilities.

Service level management (SLM) [6] is the business process that contains all the activities relating to *service level agreements* (SLAs, formally negotiated contracts) and their management. In business environments, SLM as a process roughly contains the activities of defining SLAs, negotiating SLAs (or buyer selection based on classes of service), monitoring and evaluation of SLAs and managing breaches of SLAs. SLM also contains the notion of reporting the results to the customer. This business-centric approach can be seen as the central difference between thinking about management of QoS contracts and management of SLAs.

As can be seen, the SLM process activities are nearly the same as for eContracting process [2, 8]. However, the difference lies in the scope: in open, dynamic environments, eContracting is required to negotiate and agree the common process between collaborators (e.g. when forming a virtual breeding environment) and between a virtual organization instance and customers when forming an external contract and ensuring that what is agreed will be honored by all parties. Likewise, issues such as capability to utilize support infrastructure in a federation is required. However, in SLM, the focus is only on managing the SLA commitments.

The practical service level management approach complements the present work on extended service-oriented architectures (SOA) [3, 4], also taking into account adaptation to heterogeneity and autonomy of partners [5]. On implementation level, different research initiatives on Web Services QoS have approached the issue from both performance-perspective and from non-functional aspects (NFA) perspective in general. The approaches focus either on model-driven development (MDD) or policy-expressions or runtime service management.

In this paper, languages and architectures for service level agreement between Web Services are discussed and the maturity of the service level management solutions is reflected against the needs of federated virtual organizations. After presenting a frame of reference in Section 2, the paper surveys Web Service languages that focus on the performance-perspective and in particular include service level agreements (SLAs) and reflect the various architectures behind their development and the SLM phase for which they support in Section 3. The maturity and sufficiency of these approaches, reflected against the Pilarcos architecture design principles, conclude the paper.

2 Service Level Management

The discussion of service level management is dependent on the type and scope of agreements as well as the agreement management lifecycle. In terms of different *types of SLAs* [6], service providers typically create both internal SLAs and external SLAs. *Internal SLAs* define the requirements between service producers. *Operational Level Agreements (OLAs)* codify what is expected of different units within the service provider company that offers the service to customers. If the service provider utilizes a third party as sub-contractor to provide the service, an *underpinning contract (UC)* is created between the third party and the provider. *External SLAs* codify what is being offered to the external customer. A central tenant is that internal SLAs relating to the service (whether OLAs and UCs) are more stringent than external SLAs. SLAs contain among other things *SLA parameters* (e.g. availability), with each having a service level objective (SLO), i.e. target value for the given SLA parameter.

The different types of SLAs relate especially to organizational form, i.e. whether the virtual organization is a temporary organizational structure like a consortium or a more permanent structure such as a partnership [7]. The virtual organization in practice requires means of either aggregating the SLAs to determine the composite SLA for the whole service (offers-based approach) or using the external SLA in the contractual agreement with the customer to make negotiation demands on the potential members in the virtual organization (reverse-auctioning approach). The latter assumes the service provider either takes the risk that fulfillment of service is not really possible or uses an already existing virtual breeding environment as the basis for negotiation, without having negotiated the details with participating members.

Alternatively service providers could approach the issue as a risk management scenario and include SLA breach-related monetary compensation to service pricing without regard to actual requirements. However, intuitively this does not lead to long customer relationships given that customer probably cannot negotiate the actual financial loss as part of the breach management payoff.

SLA contract scope needs to be considered in addition to considering the different roles that may be related to producing the service. The SLAs can either deal with technical metrics or it can deal with business metrics as part of the eContract. Ideally the technical metrics can be aggregated to business metrics. Yet the business metrics are domain dependent. Therefore, the mapping is problematic.

Figure 1 describes a suggestion for minimal content in regard to different types of SLA and eContracting. Possibility for separation of SLA management from the eContracts provides benefits in terms of reuse and breadth of situations to which the language can be applied. The separation of technical metrics from business metrics supports system modularity. It also supports specification of third party roles in order to manage a specific area of responsibility (e.g. monitoring and evaluation of purely technical SLA parameters). This approach would benefit from indicating dependencies between different metric types.

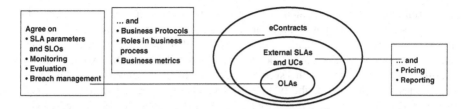

Fig. 1. Minimal scope of contract content from SLM perspective

In addition to the contents of the agreements and the scope of content amongst the involved parties, the service level management lifecycle has to be determined. In the following, the steps of template design, SLA-enhanced process design, negotiation and selection, monitoring, evaluation, breach and bonus management and reporting are identified. The lifecycle is captured in Figure 2. This is loosely based on the ITIL SLM process description [6] and the eContracting process [8].

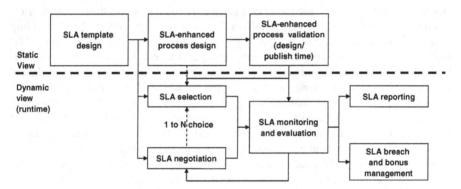

Fig. 2. Frame of reference for SLM

The SLA template design consists of defining the SLA elements, for example in XML. If the SLA is to be negotiated, SLOs are dynamically established. Only SLA parameters and parameter boundaries need to be defined. Alternatively, if a class of service–approach is used, classes need to be defined. This means defining the SLA parameters and the SLOs prior to offer of the service. The class of service approach is beneficial in the sense that possible conflicting technical demands (e.g. minimal latency but assured delivery) can be screened and will not need runtime resolution. However, because customer specific requirements cannot be matched, it fits better to environments focusing only on technical metrics. The template design is particularly impacted by the SLA language design choices.

The SLA-enhanced process design relates to utilization of composite services: SLAs may be involved at design time of the process (composite service), especially if the process is private and therefore only internal SLAs are involved. SLA-enhanced process design requires that process design tool supports SLAs.

After creation of the process, the SLA-enhanced process design may be *validated* at design time or the time of publishing a Web Service. This requires extending the type repository to include SLA validation support.

At runtime, after deployment of service, the consumer either *negotiates* the required SLOs or *selects* an appropriate class of service. In the case where services are provided in an open market, it is possible that the Web Service consumer participates in an auction for the best possible Web Service. This would require a negotiation mechanism with support for multiparty negotiation. Alternative approaches include the capability to select an identical service from each service provider and only provide payment for the fastest [9]. In addition, the offered services can be provider resource-constrained. In this case the negotiation may be may revolve around multiple consumers competing in an auction for single provider resources.

As can be seen, the SLA determination can be modeled as a full-blown auction or bargaining scenario. However, this is typically not required in practice, because of SLA having limited scope. Likewise, the negotiation can be separated under a separate negotiation protocol.

The monitoring of SLA parameters contains at least two issues. First, the monitoring can be done either in-band or out-of-band. Second, the link between monitoring and evaluation can be passive, reactive or proactive [8]. *Out-of-band monitoring*, following a typical probe-approach, is suitable for performance metrics. *In-band monitoring* on the other hand can be located on the service host providing host or on a separate tier consisting of e.g. access control, message routing and XML firewall protecting the service. Especially non-performance based metrics utilize in-band monitoring. *Passive monitoring link* merely refers to logging monitoring data at run time. Evaluation is done later as a separate action. *Reactive monitoring link* provides the means for evaluation of SLO breaches for corrective actions. *Proactive monitoring link* would support the use of internal thresholds prior to SLO breach and actions that would try to ensure breach of SLO would not happen. Evaluation therefore includes threshold evaluation in addition to SLO breach evaluation.

The evaluation of SLOs can be based on different *modes*, being *event-based* (with e.g. schedules) or *request-based*. Likewise, it can support *complete evaluation* (i.e. utilize all available monitoring data) or *statistical evaluation* (i.e. evaluate only a sample of monitoring data). *Evaluation accuracy* is dependent on the monitoring data sources: for an example, if availability data source consists of trouble tickets, a human element is involved. On the other hand, in case of an end-to-end polling, frequency of polling denotes the accuracy.

The SLA breach management governs SLO or proactive threshold breaches, i.e. it is closely tied to the monitoring link. For example, with passive monitoring link, breach management is typically done a posteriori by people. While little research on automated breach management is available, intuitively this is done by consumer and/or provider. Not all possible mechanisms fit the different monitoring link types (reactive or proactive). Intuitively, a number of mechanisms are possible, including the following:

- Using long-running transactions and their compensation mechanisms as part of the breach management scenarios (provider, reactive monitoring link).
- Reselecting the class of service or renegotiating the SLA (consumer and or provider, reactive monitoring link).
- Automatically or semi-automatically redesigning the process tasks (provider, reactive monitoring link).

- Forcing the virtual organization to undergo an evolution to replace the misbehaving member with another one (provider, reactive monitoring link).
- Making monetary compensation based on the sanctioning clauses of the SLA and continuing business as usual (provider, reactive monitoring link).
- Reducing the reputation of the misbehaving member and continuing business as usual (consumer and/or provider, reactive monitoring link).

Some additional mechanisms may be possible for systems considering only technical metrics such as adapting platform configuration through workload managers or deploying new servers or deploying new servers.

Few issues are worth noting. First, participation of other third party roles depends on the mechanism. Secondly, the mechanisms above assume the relationship between consumer and provider still remains valid. Alternatively the consumer may decide to switch provider. Third, in case of failure due active coordinator node failure (i.e. service aggregator, virtual organization coordinator), many of the approaches are void. In this case possibly reliable messaging and local node self-healing and self-management mechanisms could be utilized for avoidance of unnecessary breach management.

SLA bonus management could provide additional monetary or reputation bonuses based on over-performance of a member. If no bonus management is utilized, degradation of service is a provider option, though this is suitable only in completely automated services.

SLA reporting in all likelihood needs to provide both operational reporting and management reporting. This is especially important for the next evolutions of workflow systems, which suffered in comparison to ERPs due to lack of reporting facilities [10].

3 SLA Languages and SLM Architectures

In the following, examples of different types of SLA languages and SLA architectures behind them are discussed. The goal of the survey was to find existing candidates for the SLA templates, negotiation and monitoring, as well as SLA post-processing in federated virtual organizations. As the technical environment, the Pilarcos architecture [1, 2] was used with the following points of interest.

The Pilarcos architecture provides for both the static and dynamic views of SLM (see Figure 2). For the static view, service type definitions include attributes that form part of the SLA template; other parts can be derived from the business network model defining the topology of the collaboration providing the composite service in question. For the dynamic view, each service provider registers its service offer that contains the service interface description (including a process description) and its service level offers and requirements that can be used in the selection and negotiation phases. The negotiation is performed partially by a populator agent, that takes a suggested business network model (defined in terms of service roles, interactions between them, and nonfunctional requirements to be jointly filled by the collaboration) and imports matching service offers to it. Further, the negotiation continues by allowing each potential partner to review the proposed collaboration structure and conditions gathered to the eContract. In this phase, privately held motivations for decision-making and preferences take effect, for example, trust-based decisions can determine what kind of policy values become accepted, or whether a collaboration is entered at all. For monitoring purposes there are two sources of NFA-related rules. First, from the business network model itself, monitoring rules for business-related aspects can be gathered – these can be expressed either in terms of business concepts, associated to processes and thus multiple services at the same time, or in terms of technical concepts in cases where no translation between business concepts and technical concepts exist. Second, as a result of the negotiations, for each role there is an associated service and functional and non-functional requirements placed on that service alone.

Beyond the languages surveyed in this paper a number of others exist, including those in the semantic Web Service arena (e.g. WSML/WSMO QoS extension [18]) and eContracting languages and systems extensions, such as Laura [19] extending ebXML.

3.1 SLAng

SLAng [11, 12] was developed in University College London by deriving SLA requirements from real world SLAs. SLAng approaches SLAs from service management perspective, focusing on performance metrics and automation of system management, a subset of service management. It focuses on utilization of SLAs in support of model-driven development. No implementations using SLAng were found during research for the paper.

SLAng main concepts are SLA metrics, SLA categories and responsibilities. *SLA metrics* are part of the SLAng definition. The exact metrics depend on the domain of SLA. For application service provider (ASP) domain, metrics are categorized to four *QoS characteristic groups*: service backup, service monitoring, client performance and operational QoS characteristics. SLA metrics are valid during a schedule, which defines the contract period.

SLAs categories divide to vertical and horizontal SLAs. *Vertical SLAs* identify different parts of a Web Service platform in order to establish internal SLAs between them. This is intended to enforce behavior with network elements, databases, middleware and application servers. Vertical SLAs include communications SLA (between network element and host OS), hosting SLAs (between host OS and application server), persistence SLAs (between host OS and database) and application SLAs (between Web Services and applications servers).

Horizontal SLAs are used to establish SLAs between "same layer" elements (i.e. to describe horizontal dependencies). Horizontal SLAs include networking SLAs (between network elements), container SLAs (between application servers) and service SLAs (between Web Services).

Responsibilities enable description of individual and mutual commitments. *Client* and *server responsibilities* describe individual commitments. The approach supports different WSDL message exchange patterns on service SLA level and enables inter-composition of SLAs to take into account requirements on both members. *Mutual responsibilities* are responsibilities that both members have agreed to. These can be established with a separate negotiation mechanism. Mutual responsibilities can be used to describe the compensation for a given SLO breach. Different types of compensation descriptions are not yet part of SLAng.

SLAng focuses on complementing an abstract description of the behavioural model of the service. Therefore, QoS is modeled as part of the application in Web Services consumer and producer behaviour. The approach is supported by UML Profiles for QoS have been defined by OMG [13]. Use of this for QoS modeling has been discussed also by Pataricza, Balogh and Gönczy for both QoS performance and fault tolerance modeling, validation and evaluation [14].

However, SLAng designers correctly note that in order to support validation from type systems perspective, a number of extensions are required beyond application QoS modeling. They advocate using UML and UML Profiles to model SLAng SLA metrics, participants and participant behavior and defining SLAng constraints that define the service level objectives through Object Constraint Language (OCL). Currently available actual formal definitions limits to defining ASP reference model.

Researchers behind SLAng are proponents for MDD-based approach. SLAng approach is for both design time validation support especially intra-service SLA and monitoring and evaluation of runtime behavior between negotiated SLAs. Inter-service SLA composition is also noted. However, much of this seems to be still in the works as future work noted includes service composition and analysis toolkit and incorporating the constraints to applications through code generation for runtime evaluation. Likewise, the lack of negotiation mechanism description would indicate that the issue is not currently addressed. Additional work noted includes transformations from formal descriptions to a human-friendly business contract and SLA document.

SLA metrics, categories and an MDD-approach provides a view to the design principles behind SLAng usage in ASP domain: first the system management environment is spliced to elements. After this, each of their QoS characteristic groups and SLA metrics defined. This is followed by relationship definition. The assumption is that after this, one can (i) validate that there are no mismatches and (ii) incorporate the behavioral constraints to applications.

SLAng contains no support for breach and bonus management or service pricing. These, with addition of reuse through SLA templates are also considered part of future work for SLAng. Lack of dependency expression between different types of SLA metrics is not addressed.

In terms of eContracting, SLAng is seen as the main mechanism to complement BPEL with behavioral model all the way to eContracting requirements. However, given that the language has to be extended to other domains beyond ASP and lacks breach and bonus management support, the current approach seems insufficient for virtual organization requirements.

3.2 Web Services Level Agreement

Web Services Level Agreement (WSLA) [15, 16] has been developed and prototyped by IBM during 2000-2003. WSLA perceives SLAs for Web Services from a service management perspective with narrow scope, implicitly focusing on providing a customized SLA containing such as response time, availability and throughput. WSLA is currently utilized in TrustCoM. TrustCoM [20] focuses on enabling dynamic virtual organizations through inclusion of security, trust relationships and contracts. The SLA management subsystem is partitioned among participants. It includes *local SLA management services*, which contain SLA monitoring and management and a *separate third party SLA evaluator service* for actual SLA evaluation. This uses the notification infrastructure to inform of violations, without regard to the actual breach management mechanism. A separate negotiation mechanism is used to establish the SLAs.

Main concepts of WSLA SLAs are parties, service definition and obligations. These are utilized in WSLA templates and contracts, although neither of the terms is part of the WSLA definition. *Parties* define the signing parties (Web Service consumer and provider) and supporting parties (third parties). Third parties include measurement (i.e. monitoring) providers, condition evaluators and management providers (i.e. breach management handlers). The different participating parties enable different contract types, related to composition of services. Likewise, although the contract is for two parties, composition of contracts enables multi-party fulfillment of SLA. This also means a contract can be split into multiple sub-contracts.

Service definition defines the service (or group of services) and the SLA parameters that relate to it. The SLA parameters support hierarchies. The foundation is based on *resource metrics* (e.g. SNMP MIB counters), which is collected based on a *measurement directive*. Multiple resource metrics can be aggregated to a *composite metrics* according to some function, which is computed based on an interval defined by a schedule. Composite metrics can be either directly mapped or aggregated to *SLA parameters* which are defined by the Web Services consumer. SLA itself is established through a separate negotiation mechanism outside the scope of WSLA. The optimal end result would be that a single or group of SLA parameters would reflect a business metric for the Web Service consumer. WSLA itself does not define any QoS metrics but provides the XML elements to make the resource-based definitions. It should be noted that while dependencies through aggregation of metrics can be expressed, dependencies between SLA parameters cannot be expressed.

Obligations provide means to express *service level objectives*, which define the party responsible, validity period and target values of SLA parameters. Obligations also define *action guarantees*, which define service management actions (i.e. breach management mechanism) to be done in case SLO is not achieved. Definitions for workload manager resource management and service deployment are examples of management actions, although these are not defined in WSLA. An evaluation event or evaluation schedule provides information on evaluation condition.

WSLA template consists of two parts: first part provides a partially filled contract that defines basic characteristics (e.g. who the parties are). Second part extends the first with an "offer document", which defines constraints for the template SLA parameters. For an example, constraints can be used to define a range or list of acceptable values for an SLA parameter to limit negotiation. While WSLA templates are used to describe service offer through the negotiation process, they can be reusable in a sense that a base template is used, which is only refined in the negotiation process.

WSLA contracts emulate the technical part of business contracts. In order to make them legal, a contracting framework utilizing WSLA must provide a separate eContracting mechanism. WSLA contracts contain the SLA parameters and SLOs formed based on the WSLA template offered to the consumer. Contract types depend on parties involved and the contracting framework. This also defines service composition support, which is not limited by the language itself, but can be difficult to implement.

As an example, the following contract types are used in one implementation of WSLA [16]: *offers* are WSLA templates that provider provides to consumer (i.e. they are external SLAs). *Usage contracts* are realized contracts for a particular service by a particular consumer. *Provider contracts* are aggregated SLAs by multiple providers to enable one provider to represent others in a composite service or group of independent services. *Basic contracts* provide the business contract part outside the scope of WSLA.

WSLA contracts attach to Web Services by pointing to the WSDL description that defines the services for WSLA contract is created for. No discussion is provided on utilizing WSLA with UDDI directories, or consumer inquiry of WSLA composite metrics without requesting actual service (i.e. metadata exchange). Presumably latter is to be done with a separate management protocol.

WSLA is not tied to a particular eContracting language or mechanism and can be used to supplement basic contract definitions. However, the underlying assumption is that the business metrics can be defined by the Web Service consumer based on SLA parameters.

WSLA provides means for expressing what is measured, by whom and how. It also defines means to express actions based on breaches. Yet it does not provide information on meaning of any of the third party functions regarding monitoring, evaluation and breach management. These have to be separately defined. These definitions impact the formality of the language: validation of WSLA-enhanced process designs seems problematic even based on the basic language specification. Likewise, clearly a comprehensive support infrastructure is required to provide a suitable support for applications that wish to utilize WSLA.

3.3 Web Services Offerings Language

Web Services Offerings Language (WSOL) [17] has been developed and prototyped in Ottawa-Carlton Institute of Electrical and Computer Engineering during 2001-2005. WSOL perceives QoS for Web Services from a networking perspective, extending this with "design by contract" –concepts. However, implicitly the focus is on describing performance metrics. WSOL is utilized in Web Services Offerings Infrastructure (WSOI). WSOI is basically an XML parser for checking WSOL definition syntax correctness and a SOAP engine extension, which provides an in-band monitoring and evaluation by using WSOI handlers for interception. Future work includes WSOL code generator to create WSOI handlers from WSOL definitions.

Main concepts of WSOL include the service offerings, constraints and management statements. These are supported by reusability elements and service offering dynamic relationships. *Service offerings* utilize a class of service –approach, i.e. offerings (SLAs) describe different levels of service for the Web Services consumer to select from. No negotiation mechanism is possible for either customization of SLAs or bidding in case multiple parties provide the same service offer on an open market. The service offerings reusability is done through service offering items, i.e. constraints, management statements and reusability elements.

Constraints express evaluated conditions, which can be behavioral, QoS and access related. Behavioral constraints enable pre- and post-condition and invariant expressions. Also "future-conditions" are expressible, i.e. conditions that surface after some specific amount of time has passed from the service request. QoS constraints describe QoS metrics and the monitoring entity. QoS metrics themselves are defined by an external ontology. QoS metrics are evaluated with each service request. Alternatively, "periodic QoS" can be expressed, whereby evaluation is done to random requests. Only the average of evaluation is expressed. Access rights can be related to service hours and number of invocations.

While overall the QoS approach seems to fit request-response WSDL message exchange pattern (MEP), use with other WSDL MEPs are not discussed.

Management statements contain management information for different classes of service. This includes price statements, monetary penalty statements and management responsibility statements. Price statements divide to pay-per-use and subscription payments. The pay-per-use payment supports default price and grouping of operations to limit definition length. Subscription payments are intended to support time- based billing. The payment statements are separate XML-schemas, alternative models, such as volume pricing could be defined as an alternative XML schema. Monetary penalty statements are the only supported breach management mechanism currently in WSOL. WSOL implicitly assumes management parties will send notifications [17, pp. 91]. Monetary units are defined in an external ontology. Management responsibility statements specify role responsibilities for particular constraints, supporting third trusted parties. No link to reputation services is provided to evaluate the third parties.

Reusability elements are a central enabler in reusing the service offering items. Basically it provides means to reuse service offering items by defining templates and specializing these with parameter definitions. The approach supports specifying different levels (e.g. groups of expressions, individual expressions) of reuse. Likewise "applicability domains" enable scoping these in terms of WSDL. Constraints, management statements and reusability elements are formally specified in UML. Extension with ontologies to enable semantic validation is within scope of the ongoing research work.

WSOL descriptions point to the WSDL file describing the operations. WSDL extensions were considered but discarded. No discussion is provided on utilizing WSOL with UDDI directories. WSOL information (i.e. metadata) can be requested with a management protocol.

WSOL provides excellent means for dependency expressions by supporting both static and dynamic relationships. Static relationships are expressed in service offerings themselves. Service offerings can be created, updated or deleted after deployment of service. However, given the performance focus of the design, these are insufficient to accommodate runtime changes to a service that is utilized by a consumer. WSOL uses *service offering dynamic relations* (SODRs) as means of runtime adaptation by describing replacement of a particular service offering with another particular service offering in case of a particular constraint violation.

Table 1. Comparison of Web-Services –related SLA-language initiatives

Attribute	SLAng	WSLA	WSOL
Background and approach	Service management, Model-driven development	Service management, Runtime support infrastructure	Network QoS, Runtime support infrastructure
SLM infrastructure or toolset for language	Unknown	TrustCoM	Web Services Offerings Infrastructure (WSOI)
Main concepts	(Domain-specific) SLA metrics, SLA categories, responsibilities	Parties, service definition, obligations	Service offerings (SOs), constraints, management statements
SLA verification	Design-time validation and run-time evaluation	Run-time evaluation	Run-time evaluation
Association mechanism to service descriptions and service offers	Behavioural model	SLA points to WSDL	Service offering points to WSDL
Reusability	None currently	WSLA templates	Reusability elements
Denotations and formal background	UML, UML profiles and OCL	UML	UML
Composition support for aggregated services	Intra-composition and inter-composition based on conformance	Not constrained by language, depends on contracting	Not constrained by language, seen as problematic
Selection or negotiation mechanisms and multiparty aggregations	None currently, separate negotiation protocol intended	Separate negotiation protocol, custom SLAs	Selection, predefined classes of service
Pricing support	None currently	None currently	Yes, in management statements
Breach management support	None currently	Yes, in action guarantees	Yes, in management statements
Dependency expressions between SLAs and SLOs	None	None	SO dynamic relationships
Relationship to eContracting	Used with BPEL	Aggregation of technical metrics to business metrics	Independent of eContracting

Composition of WSOL service offerings is not currently addressed. This is a problematic area given that the QoS metrics are defined by an external ontology. Some preliminary work has been done in this area, but it has been noted that "implementation of these mechanism to the management infrastructure would not be trivial" [17, pp. 63].

Overall the language design leaves relationship to eContracting open: means for legal binding of SLAs and using WSOL with business protocols remains an open topic, possibly due to the background and scope of investigation.

3.4 Summary

In the survey, special attention was given on properties related to potential for composing service and their SLA notions, whether the language was designed for the static or dynamic environments, and their relationship to eContract structures. The SLA languages are summarized in Table 1.

We note that at its current state SLAng is designed for development time descriptions and, on service SLA level, is used to complement BPEL by expressing behavioral constraints. On the other hand, WSLA and WSOL focus on runtime support in terms of negotiation or selection and evaluation of offers. However their relationship to eContracting is different. WSLA assumes that Web Services consumer can establish relationship to business metrics based on providers technical metrics, whereas WSOL simply focuses on technical metrics without regard to eContracting.

4 Conclusions

Taking the reviews and the frame of reference into account the presented languages all provide good approaches in specific areas. In particular, the SLAng level of formality and client requirements provide support for design validation and service inter-composition. This is in-line with populator requirements. Second, WSLA provides a comprehensive conceptual frame and does not limit to particular metrics even though it lacks means to express support of runtime dynamism. Third, the use of WSLA in TrustCoM shows that modularity is achievable, potentially supporting separation of evaluation and breach management mechanisms from local monitoring. Finally, the WSOL service offering dynamic relationships provide means of pre-defining runtime support for autonomous service adaptation.

In general, further development is needed on languages that provide better support for NFA-related QoS beyond communications and technical QoS, support composition of service offers, and allow expressions of monitoring rules to complement the associated service level requirements.

As a conclusion, there is need for further developing a family of aspect languages for NFAs with a number of requirements: Each language should have a sufficient set of joint basic concepts so that aggregations can be negotiated over them in a sensible way. Consequently, each broad category of business services has a separate set of concepts and related metrics, so that these are understandable to the business process designers in business terms. At the more technical level, it is required that each concept and metrics has a supported transformation to technical terms in a transparent way. Also, it is necessary that the technical level concepts and metrics are provided for communication service business.

References

1. Kutvonen, L., Ruokolainen, T., Metso, J.: Interoperability middleware for federated business services in web-Pilarcos. International Journal of Enterprise Information Systems 3(1), 1–21 (2007)
2. Kutvonen, L., Metso, J., Ruohomaa, S.: From trading to eCommunity population: Responding to social and contractual challenges. In: Proceedings of the 10th IEEE International EDOC Conference (EDOC 2006), Hong Kong (October 2006)
3. Papazoglou, M.P.: Service oriented computing: concepts, characteristics and directions. In: 4th International Conference on Web Information Systems Engineering (WISE'03) (2003)
4. Papazoglou, M.P., Georgakopoulos, D.: Service oriented computing. Communications of the ACM 46(10), 25–27 (2003)
5. Singh, M.P., Huhns, M.N.: Service-Oriented Computing: Sematincs, Processes, Agents. John Wiley & Sons, New York, NY (2005)

6. OCG, ITIL Service Delivery, The Stationary Office (2001)
7. Camarinha-Matos, L.M., Afsarmanesh, H.: Virtual Enterprise Modeling and Support Infrastructures: Applying Multi-agent System Approaches. In: Luck, M., et al. (eds.) Multi-Agent Systems and Applications, ACAI 2001, LNAI 2086, pp. 335–364 (2001)
8. Milosevic, Z., Berry, A., Bond, A., Raymond, K.: Supporting business contracts in open distributed systems. In: 2nd International Workshop on Services in Distributed and Networked Environments (1995)
9. Ludwig, H.: Web Services QoS: External SLAs and Internal Policies, Or: How do we deliver what we promise? IBM research center report (2003)
10. Cardosa, J., Bostrom, R.M., Sheth, A.: Workflow Management Systems and ERP Systems: Differences, Commonalities, and Applications. In: Information Technology and Management 5, pp. 319–338. Kluwer, Dordrecht (2004)
11. Skene, J., Lamanna, D.D., Emmerich, W.: Precise Service Level Agreements. In: 26th International Conference on Software Engineering (ICSE'04) (2004)
12. Lamanna, D., Skene, J., Emmerich, W.: SLAng: A Language for Defining Service Level Agreements. In: Proc. of the 9th IEEE Workshop on Future Trends in Distributed Computing Systems, FTDCS 2003 (Puerto Rico, May 2003) (2003)
13. Object Management Group (OMG), UML profile for quality of service and fault tolerance characteristics and metrics (2004)
14. Patarizca, A., Balogh, A., Göczy, L.: Verification and validation of Nonfunctional aspects in Enterprise modeling. In: Rittgen, P. (ed.) Enterprise Modeling and Computing with UML, Idea Group, pp. 261–303 (November 2006)
15. Ludwig, H., et al.: Web Service Level Agreement (WSLA) Language Specification, Version 1.0, revision wsla-2003/01/28. available from: www.research.ibm.com/wsla/WSLASpecV1-20030128.pdf
16. Dan, A., et al.: Web Services on demand: WSLA-driven automated management. IBM systems journal 43(1), 136–158 (2004)
17. Tosic, V.: Service Offerings for XML Web Services and Their Management Applications, PhD Thesis, Carleton University, Department of Systems and Computer Engineering (August 2004)
18. Toma, I., Foxvog, D., Jaeger, M.C.: Modelling QoS characteristics in WSMO. In: Proceedings of the 1st workshop on Middleware for Service Oriented Computing (MW4SOC 2006), Australia (November 27–December 01, 2006)
19. Svirskas, A., Roberts, B.: Towards business QoS in Virtual Organizations through SLA and ebXML. In: 10th ISPE International Conference on concurrent engineering: Research and Applications (2003)
20. TrustCoM, TrustCoM Reference Architecture, Version 1, Deliverable D09, Work package 27 (14.8.2005)

Construction and Execution of Adaptable Applications Using an Aspect-Oriented and Model Driven Approach

Sten A. Lundesgaard[1], Arnor Solberg[2,*], Jon Oldevik[2], Robert France[3],
Jan Øyvind Aagedal[2], and Frank Eliassen[1]

[1] Simula Research Laboratory, Network and Distributed Systems,
P.O. Box 134, N-1325 Lysaker, Norway
{stena, frank}@simula.no
[2] SINTEF, ICT,
P.O. Box 124, N-0314 Oslo, Norway
{arnor.solberg, jon.oldevik, jan.aagedal}@sintef.no
[3] Colorado State University,
Fort Collins, CO-80532, USA
france@cs.colostate.edu

Abstract. Constructing and executing distributed applications that can adapt to their current operating context, in order to maintain or enhance Quality of Service (QoS) attribute levels, are complex tasks. Managing multiple, interacting QoS features is particularly difficult since these features tend to be distributed across the system and tangled with other features. The crosscutting nature of QoS features can make them difficult to evolve, and it can make it complicated to dynamically optimize with respect to provided QoS during execution. Furthermore, it complicates efficient construction of application variants that differ in their QoS characteristics to suit various execution contexts. This paper presents an aspect-oriented and model driven approach for constructing and a QoS-aware middleware for execution of QoS-sensitive applications. Aspect-oriented modeling techniques are used to separate QoS features from primary application logic, and for efficient specification of alternative application variants. Model driven engineering techniques are used to derive run-time representations of application variants from platform independent models. The developed middleware chooses the best variant according to the current operating context and the available resources.

1 Introduction

Distributed systems often execute in heterogeneous environments, in which the availability of resources such as bandwidth, memory, and computing power change over time. The increasing mobility and pervasiveness of computing systems require the consideration of the dynamic environment, when building suitable QoS features for maintaining desired QoS. Adaptive middleware addresses these challenges. It performs run-time configuration and adaptation by choosing between alternative application variants with similar functional properties but different QoS characteristics and

---

* Two first authors are in alphabetical order.

J. Indulska and K. Raymond (Eds.): DAIS 2007, LNCS 4531, pp. 76–89, 2007.

resource demands. Criteria for choosing an application variant are generally based on the context [1] or QoS characteristics [2][3].

Many concerns need to be considered when constructing alternative application variants, e.g., QoS preferences, context dependencies, and resource allocation. To manage this complexity, separation of concerns and support for defining and using suitable abstractions are needed. In Model Driven Engineering (MDE), abstractions and transformations between levels are used to manage complexity. For example, the Model Driven Architecture (MDA) [4] specifies three abstraction levels; a Computation Independent Model (CIM) describes the environment and specifies requirements; a Platform Independent Model (PIM) describes the parts that do not change from one platform to another; and a Platform Specific Model (PSM) includes descriptions of platform dependent parts. To further control the complexity of developing application variants that have similar functionality but differ in their QoS characteristics, mechanisms for separating crosscutting QoS features from the primary application logic are needed. Examples of QoS characteristics are security, integrity, robustness, and performance. Examples of corresponding QoS features are authentication, transaction control, error handling, and compression. Aspect-Oriented Software Development (AOSD) approaches [5]-[8] provide mechanisms for encapsulating crosscutting features. In the Aspect Oriented Modeling (AOM) approach presented in [8], crosscutting features are modeled as aspects and composed with the primary design model, to form integrated models.

This paper presents an approach for Construction and Execution of Adaptable applications (CEA-Frame). CEA-Frame integrates MDE and AOM techniques to model application variants in platform-independent terms and to automatically transform PIMs to PSMs. QoS features are separated from the primary functionality as aspect models and designed to fit particular operating contexts. For the execution we have developed a context- and QoS-aware dynamic middleware named QuAMobile, which identifies and chooses the application variant that is considered best for the current context and available resources. The alternative application variants are deployed using platform independent specifications, called *service plans* [11].

The separation of concern mechanisms in CEA-Frame improve the reusability of both design- and run-time artifacts through application-independent models of crosscutting QoS-features, and service plan specifications that separate meta-data from implementation code. Furthermore, modeling the QoS features separately in aspect models enables efficient representation of QoS variability from which a large number of application variants can be derived. The MDE based transformations make the transition from PIMs to PSMs faster, smoother and less error prone.

Sect. 2 presents the integrated construction and execution concepts, mechanisms and activities of CEA-Frame. In Sect. 3 the CEA-Frame is illustrated and validated using a live media streaming application example. Sect. 4 discusses related work. Sect. 5 draws some conclusions and outlines future work.

2 Construction and Execution of Adaptable Applications

CEA-Frame (Fig. 1) provides: i) methods for specification of application variants combining model driven and aspect-oriented modeling techniques, ii) mappings

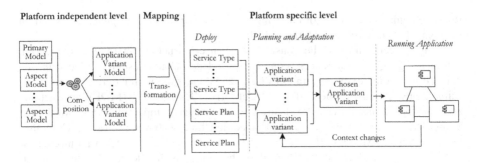

Fig. 1. Overview CEA-Frame

generating platform level constructs from platform independent specifications, and iii) a QoS-aware planning and adaptation supplied by the QuAMobile middleware.

At the platform independent level, a primary model and a set of aspect models are developed. Alternative application variants are obtained based on the following two mechanisms: i) compositions are used to derive application variants by composing the primary model with different subsets of the aspect models, and ii) variants of aspect models and primary models are described by means of model-based variability mechanisms such as specialization and parameterization. From the PIMs, service types in the form of Web-Service Description Language (WSDL) files and XML-based service plans are generated by our transformation engine. These mappings are implemented using the MOFScript Eclipse plug-in [10]. At the platform specific level, the QoS-aware planning process (in QuAMobile) uses the deployed service types and service plans to select the application variant that is considered best for the current context in order to meet the user's QoS preferences. This also includes checking context dependencies (e.g., run-time environment, communication technology, and storage facility dependencies), and predicting the end-to-end QoS according to the available resources (e.g., processing load, data rate and memory usage).

2.1 The Conceptual Service Model

The CEA-Frame defines *service, service type,* and *service plan* as central architectural concepts (see Fig. 2). A service type can be composed from a set of service types. An *application type* is a *service type.* Services realize service types and their meta-information is specified in *service plans.* Consequently, there may be different service plans for a service type. Services can be atomic or composite. Accordingly, there are atomic and composite plans. An atomic plan describes an atomic service, while a composite plan recursively describes a composite service by specifying the involved service types and the connections between them. In addition, both types of service plans contains: i) information about dependencies to context elements, ii) specification of the parameter configurations and iii) specification of the QoS characteristics. These are vital information for the QoS-aware planning and adaptation. It is tedious to

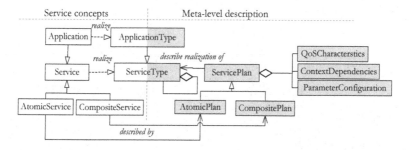

Fig. 2. The service and service plan concepts of CEA-Frame

develop the service plans manually, because many alternative application variants are required to support the different operating contexts of the application. In CEA-Frame the service plans are automatically generated from the more abstract PIMs. Service plans are further elaborated in [11].

2.2 Constructing Application Variants

The basis for the modeling in CEA-Frame is our Aspect-Oriented Model Driven Framework (AOMDF) [12], which combines aspect-oriented and model driven techniques to separate both vertical concerns such as technical platform, and user defined crosscutting concerns such as QoS. CEA-Frame extends AOMDF to support construction and execution of QoS-aware adaptable applications.

A design is expressed in terms of the following artifacts [7]: i) the *primary model (PM)* describes the application logic; ii) the *aspect models (AM)* describe crosscutting QoS features; iii) the *bindings* define where in the primary model the aspect models should be composed; and iv) the *composition directives* govern how aspect models are composed with primary models.

Before an aspect model can be composed with a primary model in an application domain, the aspect model must be instantiated in the context of the same application domain. An instantiation is obtained by binding elements in the aspect model to elements in the application domain. The result is called a context-specific aspect model. Context-specific aspect models and the primary model are composed to obtain an integrated design view [8]. Fig. 3 shows the modeling and mapping activities when constructing alternative application variants using CEA-Frame.

Starting at the *platform independent level*, the primary model is specified. Variability is specified using variability mechanisms provided in UML such as specialization, templates and multiplicity (e.g., "0..1" for optional elements). Then, QoS features are specified in aspect models. In our approach aspect models are reusable patterns that describe application specific QoS features when instantiated. In the composition, the aspects models are instantiated and composed with the primary model. An aspect model is instantiated by binding template parameters to actual values.

Platform independent level

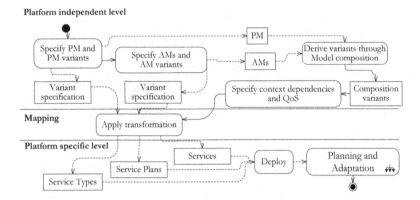

Fig. 3. CEA-Frame modeling and mapping activities

2.3 Execution of Adaptable Applications

In our implementation of CEA-Frame the distributed dynamic middleware QuAMobile and the Java virtual machine constitute the execution environment. QuAMobile implements a plug-in architecture for inserting domain specific managers: *service planner, context manager, resource manager, configuration manager*, and *adaptation manager* as depicted in Fig. 4. Service types and plans are interpreted during deployment using the Java Document Object Model (JDOM) open source parser. Service implementations reside in the *repository*, while service types and plans are published to the *broker*. During executing, service types and plans represent the meta-level model of the running application. This model is causally connected to the application, that is, any changes made to the meta-level causes corresponding changes in the application.

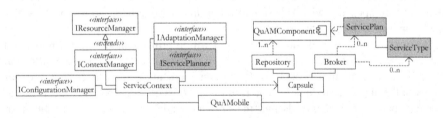

Fig. 4. QuAMobile core architecture

In dynamic heterogonous environments QoS guarantees can not be made. Instead QuAMobile re-plans and adapts the applications to meet the changes in context and resource availability. In the middleware the two plug-ins service planner and adaptation manager performs QoS-aware planning and adaptation. Service planning is a process that identifies suitable application variants for the context in which the application shall execute and choose the one that is considered most optimal with respect to the user's QoS preferences. The planning commences when the user (i.e., client software) submits a service request with user QoS preferences in the form of utility functions to the platform. In CEA-Frame, utility is a measure of usefulness and is expressed by a real number in the range [0, 1], where 0 represents *useless* and 1 represents *as good as perfect*. Service planning is a four step process starting with i) identifying all the alternative application variants, ii) context dependency filtering, iii) QoS prediction, and iv) choosing the best suited variant according to the specified utility functions.

The adaptation mechanisms operate on a meta-level, where the service types and service plans are used for reasoning and altering the running application. When changes in the context are detected, i.e., there is updated context and resource information available, the service planner performs a re-planning of the running application. If another application variant matches the user's QoS preferences better, the middleware adapts the application. First, existing plans that constitute the meta-model of the running application are made available (reification). Then components involved in the adaptation are pushed to a safe-state (if this state is reachable), and changes are made to the meta-model. Lastly, the changes are absorbed by the application. Fig. 5 shows the activities involved in the execution of an adaptable application, and is a detailing of the planning and adaptation activity of Fig. 3.

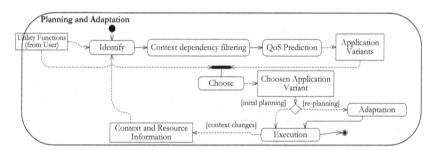

Fig. 5. Planning and adaptation activities

3   Illustrative Example

This section illustrates the CEA-Frame by describing the construction and execution of a live media streaming system. The system captures events (e.g., news and sports), encode onsite, and forward the media stream to streaming servers that the users access over the Internet (see Fig. 6). Users are mobile, and switch from Local Area Network (LAN) to a Wireless LAN (WLAN), and between WLAN subnets.

3.1   Modeling and Mapping

The illustrative example of the modeling and mapping process is structured according to the CEA-Frame activities depicted in Fig. 3.

Specify Primary Model and Primary Model Variants. The application level composite structure of the media streaming primary model is shown in Fig. 6.

SgnlCommunication initiates and controls the media stream on request from the *MediaPlayer*. *LiveMediaSrc* provides the video images, and *MediaStrmService* sends the stream to *MediaPlayer* through the *StrmCommunication* service. These services

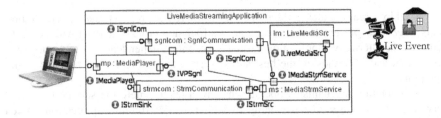

Fig. 6. Live media streaming system, application level composite structure

are all composite. In this example we will look into details of the *StrmCommunication* service and its variants (Fig. 7). This service has both alternative compositions and parameter configurations from which variants are derived, high-lightening variability mechanisms and variant derivation provided in CEA-Frame.

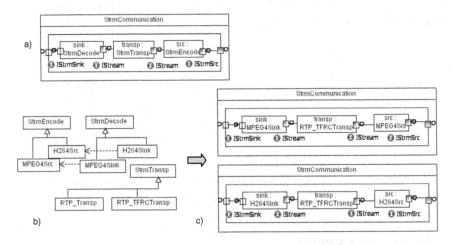

Fig. 7. a) primary model of *StrmCommunication* and b) variations of types

The types of the parts contained in the general *StrmCommunication* (Fig. 7a) are abstract and represent variation points. Possible variations of these types can be represented as a specialization hierarchy as shown in Fig. 7b. Here the allowed specializations for the encoder and decoder are MPEG-4 and H.262, and the allowed transport protocols are RTP and RTP_TFRC. Fig. 7c shows two of the four possible variants for this case. The dependency relationships in the specialization hierarchy ensure compliance for the source and sink of a particular variant.

Specify Aspect Models and Aspect Model variants. QoS features are specified in aspect models. For wireless communication bit errors represent an inherent problem. To ensure a satisfactory video quality, Forward Error Correction (FEC) algorithms can be used to minimize the effect of bit errors. Also, due to the handover and roaming between WLAN sub-nets, pre-fetching (using a buffer) can be used to reduce jitter. To improve smoothness and timeliness of the video when streaming over WLAN, the two aspect models depicted in Fig. 8a and Fig. 8b are specified.

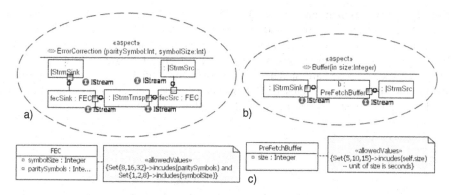

Fig. 8. Aspect Models a) error correction, b) pre-fetching, and c) allowed values

The aspect models are parameterized. The *allowedValues* stereotype is used to specify the values of these parameters for the particular application (Fig. 8c). For the *ErrorCorrection* and *Buffer* aspects, parameters that must be specified are buffer sizes, symbol sizes, and parity symbols. The set of combinations of these parameter configurations signify a corresponding set of aspect model variants (i.e., nine *Error-Correction* variants and three *Buffer* variants) with different QoS characteristics and resource demands. For example, increasing the values for the parity symbols and the symbol size increase the protection level of the error correction, but at the cost of CPU usage and start-up time.

Derive Variants Through Model Composition. The aspect models consist of template forms of composite structure diagrams, expressed using a template variant of the Role Based Meta-Modeling Language (RBML) [18]. RBML is a pattern description language which characterizes a family of UML models. The aspect templates are instantiated by binding template parameters to values. The parameters are marked using the symbol "|" (see the aspects models in Fig. 8). When the role binding is specified the primary model is composed with the aspect models according to specified composition rules.

We obtain four alternative compositions of the *StrmCommunication* service, two of which are shown in Fig. 9 (pre-fetching without FEC and usage of the primary model without including any aspects is not shown).

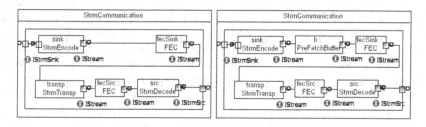

Fig. 9. Composition variants of *StrmCommunication*

Specify Context Dependencies and QoS. Applying CEA-Frame, application specific QoS characteristics, resources, and context elements need to be defined. The QoS characteristics and resources definitions in our example are based on the ISO/IEC 9126 QoS characteristics catalogue [14] and the General Resource Model (GRM) [15]. The specifications are modeled according to the guidelines of the UML profile for QoS standard [13]. A subset of QoS characteristics resource and context types used for the live media streaming application is shown in Fig. 10a.

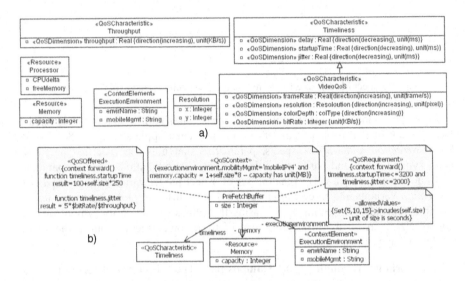

Fig. 10. a) QoS characteristics, resource, and context types, and b) context dependencies and QoS specification

The specified services are associated with context dependencies, QoS require-ments, and QoS prediction functions. For context dependency specifications we use the stereotype *QoSContext*. The *QoSOffered* stereotype us used to specify predicted QoS. Both stereotypes are provided by the UML profile for QoS standard [13]. In addition we have defined the *QoSRequirement* stereotype, which is used to specify the QoS levels a service needs to fulfill, e.g., min and max values. A *QoSRequirement* specification is identified based on expected usage of the service.

QoSOffered specifies QoS prediction functions that the middleware uses to calcu-late the QoS for a given set of context and resource QoS values. For example, *StrmCommunication* is associated with functions that predicts a long start-up time when the *PreFetchBuffer* is part of the composition. However, when connected to WLAN these functions predict increase in the frame drop rate and jitter. When streaming live media (e.g., news and sport events), the user defined trade-off may be to have low start-up time as long as the frame drop rate is below a certain limit. Fig. 10b shows examples of application specific context and QoS specifications using the *QoSContext, QoSOffered,* and *QoSRequirements* stereotypes (the Object Constraint Language (OCL) is used for specification).

For composite services, *QoSOffered* is dependent on the QoS offered by its parts. Thus, QoS prediction in these cases need to take into account that the composite do not know what parts it consist of, since new parts can be added when composing aspect models. For example the offered *startupTime* for the *StrmCommunication* is a summation of the *startupTime* of its parts; consequently, the different composition variants will have different start-up times as expressed with the following OCL-based predictor function:

(self.timeliness.startupTime = self.parts.collect(part:Property | part.type.feature->select (f:Feature | f.name = 'timeliness'))->collect (f:Feature | f.type.attribute->select (a:Property | a.name = 'startUpTime')) -> sum ()).

Apply Transformation. To bridge the model and platform levels of the adaptable application, automated transformations are used for mapping UML models to application variants and service type specifications. The PIM transformation source consists of the four composed models derived from the compositions of aspect and primary models, two of these are shown in Fig. 9. We refer to these as the base compositions. Additional input to the transformation, for our example, is the specialization hierarchy specifying primary model variants, the allowed values associated with aspect models parameters determining aspect model variants, and context and QoS specifications. From these a total number of 432 alternative variants of the *StrmCommunication* service can be derived (4 base compositions*4 primary model variants*9 ErrorCorrection aspect model variants*3 Buffer aspect model variants). Thus, this specific case illustrates the general challenge that the set of variants can be very large. To avoid a large number of variants, one can identify combinations of the parameter values that imply significant variation in the end-to-end QoS characteristics. Only these are deployed as possible run-time variants. In the example this led to a reduction of combinations of the three different sets of parity symbol lengths and symbol sizes for the FEC service from nine combination to the following three value pairs: {8, 1}, {16, 2}, or {32, 8}). The number of derived PSM variants then becomes 144.

The transformations have been implemented using the MOFScript Eclipse plug-in [10]. MOFScript was one of the proposed languages in the standardization process of MOF Model to Text Transformations, which has been adopted and is now in its finalizing stage [9]. In general, the implemented transformations map CEA-Frame PIM concepts such as *QoScharacteristics*, *QoScontext*, and service specifications in primary and aspect models, to CEA-Frame PSM concepts such as service types, service plans, and service realizations.

3.2 QoS-Aware Planning and Adaptation

In our example QuAMobile is installed on a laptop and a streaming server. The installation creates a common service context that provides protocols for service discovery and context information sharing between the domain specific management plug-ins. The service planner residing on the streaming server is configured as master, i.e., centralized planning and local adaptation. To illustrate the QoS-aware planning and adaptation (tasks shown in Fig. 5) it is assumed that the user has the laptop connected to the LAN. After some time the user disconnects and moves over to WLAN.

Deploy. Generated service types (WSDL), service plans, and components are deployed and published on the machine on which the service is to execute.

Identify. When the user requests access to the live streaming service, alternative application variants are synthesized from the published services and discovered service plans. QuAMobile identifies all of the 720 application variants (144 variants of the *StrmCommunication* and additional 5 variants of the *LiveMediaSrc* services, resulting in 720 variants of the *LiveMediaStreaming* application (see Fig. 6).

Context Dependency Filtering. Application variants that can not execute in the current operating context are filtered, by comparing gathered context information against the specified context dependencies (*QoSContext* in the composite models). In QuAMobile, it is the context manager that gathers and processes data about the context and makes information available to the service planner plug-in. For the identified application variants, it is the specified dependencies to the screen resolution that are caught by the context dependency filter, since three of the *LiveMediaSrcs* services require a screen with a higher resolution than what the laptop has. After context dependency filtering 288 variants remains.

QoS Prediction. End-to-end QoS characteristics are predicted using the specified functions (*QoSOffered* stereotype) in a bottom-up style, i.e., start by calculating the QoS of each atomic service and finishing of with the composite service. The QoS prediction functions are specified and deployed as text strings; hence, the expressions are calculated for each planning and adaptation process. Predicted QoS are checked against QoS requirements specified by the application developer (*QoSRequirement* stereotype).

Choose. Utility functions are used to specify the user's QoS preferences and tradeoff between user QoS dimensions, e.g., $start\text{-}up\ time \geq 0.6$, $detail\text{-}level \geq 0.6$, and $smoothness \geq 0.6$. By using the provided utility functions (see Fig. 11Fig. 11) and the predicted QoS QuAMobile calculates the utility of the application variants and chooses the one, which i) meets the specified minimum utility values and ii) has the highest utility-to-user QoS ratio. When the laptop is connected to the LAN it is the application variant with the *StrmCommunication* composition without the *FEC* and *PreFetchBuffer* services that is chosen, i.e., the primary model as depicted in Fig. 7. This variant is selected since the increase in utility for the *detail level* and *smoothness* dimensions are small compared to the increase in *start-up time*.

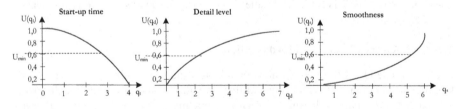

Fig. 11. Utility Functions

Execution. The application variant chosen is forwarded to the configuration managers on the laptop and streaming server. They create the components, configure, and bind them together. Execution of the initial application variant is like any other non- adaptable applications.

Adaptation. In our example the user disconnects the laptop from the LAN during the streaming of a particular news event, i.e., the streaming connection is moved over to WLAN by the *RTP_TFRCTransport* service. The context change makes the current application variant unsuitable, as the bit error rate associated with WLAN causes video frame to be dropped, i.e., too low utility for the *smoothness* dimension. QuAMobile therefore initiates re-planning and chooses the application variant which includes both the *FEC* and *PreFetchBuffer* services. This variant has a better balance between the *start-up time* and *smoothness* QoS dimensions. During adaptation service plans are used as a meta-model of the running application, enabling QuAMobile to make changes to the running application.

4 Related Work

Atkinson et al. [19] combine model driven and aspect-oriented development. Aspect-oriented techniques are used for refining specific aspects of the model (vertical separation of concern) by architecture stratification. This approach differs from the aspect approach employed in CEA-Frame, in that the aspects are not composed but represent refinements of a particular part of the model at higher level stratums. Thus, each stratum represents the whole system. Furthermore, Atkinson et al. define possible refinements as pattern-based aspects applied through framework instantiations. In our approach we use standard AOM and MDE mechanisms such as compositions and transformations.

MDE is used by Kulkarni et al. [16] for providing separation of concern between system concerns at both model and code level using templates and code weaving. This is similar to the AOM approach we employ, except that we use parameterized UML to specify aspects and perform model level composition avoiding the need for code level weaving. Clarke et al. [17] and Ray et al. [7] also apply aspects for separation of concern. The aspects models are weaved with application models, by adding and replacing both classes and operations. Kiczales et al. [5] employ aspect models for multiple concerns; functional behavior and crosscutting concerns. Hyper/J multiple models are integrated, making it possible to model alternative static application variants. CEA-Frame integrates aspect models with the application logic in a similar manner, but has additional support for parameter configuration, context, and QoS requirements. In addition, MDE principles are used to generate platform specific artifacts.

There are examples of adaptive middleware platforms that are combined with software engineering tools; $2K^{Q+}$ [2], QuO [3], and CoSMIC [20]. $2K^{Q+}$ provides an environment for specifying alternative service compositions, their QoS characteristics, and adaptation steps. A platform dependent compiler produces executable code for adapting the application. QuO introduces description languages for specifying QoS, which is compiled to executable code for monitoring QoS and controlling the interaction between distributed objects. CoSMIC is a MDE toolkit, which model compositions and QoS requirements at the platform level (a component based QoS-aware CORBA middleware). CEA-Frame addresses the same problems as $2K^{Q+}$, QuO, and CoSMIC, but at a platform independent level. This avoids specification of all possible context and resource allocations, and enable integration of the framework with any development environment and middleware platform. Furthermore, CEA-frame pushes the task of identifying and choosing a variant to run-time, giving a larger solution space and higher probability of finding the best application configuration.

5 Conclusion and Future Work

The task of developing and operating distributed applications for heterogeneous dynamic environments is particularly difficult in the presence of multiple crosscutting QoS features. Our approach to tackle this problem is to separate the QoS features from the application logic, and place the responsibility of choosing and configuring the application at the middleware level.

CEA-Frame combines AOM and MDE techniques for efficient construction of a potentially large number of alternatives application variants needed due to the dynamics and heterogeneity of the execution environment. A context and QoS-aware middleware is developed to handle adaptation. The framework provides: i) methods and activity descriptions for constructing adaptable applications, ii) variability mechanisms using aspects and model composition as well as parameterized primary and aspect models, iii) separation of crosscutting QoS features iv) automatic model transformation and code generation, and v) a QoS-aware planning and adaptation process that configures and adapts the application to suit the operating context and resources available. The implementation of the framework has been validated by using it to construct and execute a live video streaming application.

The construction of application variants is accomplished by separating QoS variability specifications from variability of the primary model and the composition of the primary model with different subsets of the aspect models. The automatic transformations support efficient derivation of a large number of alternative application variants and eliminate tedious error-prone manual implementations. At the platform specific level separating specifications of the alternative application variants and their QoS characteristics (using the service plan concept) improves reusability of the services. All information needed for the middleware to filter, order, and choose a suitable application variant, is generated from platform independent models. CEA-Frame is based on standards such as the UML profile for QoS [13], GRM [15], ISO/IEC 9126 [14], and MOF Model to Text [9].

To develop the CEA-Frame, we will work further on the model composition techniques and related tool support. We are also working on OCL-based templates that are easier to work with and more readable.

References

1. Capra, L., Emmerich, W., Mascolo, C.: CARISMA: Context-Aware Reflective mIddleware System for Mobile Applications. IEEE Trans. on Software Engineering 29(10), 929–945 (2003)
2. Nahrstedt, K., Xu, D., Wichadakul, D., Baochun, L.: QoS-Aware Middleware for Ubiquitous and Heterogeneous Environments. IEEE Communications Magazine 39(11), 140–148 (2001)

3. Loyall, J., Bakken, D., Schantz, R., Zinky, J., Karr, D., Vanegas, R., Anderson, K.: QoS Aspect Languages and Their Runtime Integration. In: O'Hallaron, D.R. (ed.) LCR 1998. LNCS, vol. 1511, pp. 303–318. Springer, Heidelberg (1998)
4. OMG, MDA TM Guide v1.0.1, http://www.omg.org/docs/omg/03-06-01pdf
5. Kiczales, G., Lamping, J., Mendhekar, A., Maeda, C., Lopes, C., Loingier, J., Irwin, J.: Aspect-Oriented Programming. In: Aksit, M., Matsuoka, S. (eds.) ECOOP 1997. LNCS, vol. 1241, pp. 220–241. Springer, Heidelberg (1997)
6. Ossher, H., Tarr, P.: Using Multidimensional Separation of Concerns to (Re)shape evolving Software. Communications of the ACM 44(10), 43–50 (2001)
7. Ray, I., France, R., Li, N., Georg, G.: An Aspect-Based Approach to Modeling Access Control Concerns. Journal of Info. and Software Tech. 46(9), 575–587 (2004)
8. France, R., Ray, I., Georg, G., Ghosh, S.: An aspect-oriented approach to design modeling. IEE Proc. Software, vol. 151(4) (2004)
9. OMG: MOF Models to Text Transformation Language Final Adopted Specification. Technical report, OMG document ptc/06-11-01 (2006)
10. MOFScript Eclipse plug-in, http://www.modelbased.net/mofscript
11. Lundesgaard, S., Lund, K., Eliassen, F.: Utilising Alternative Application Configurations in Context- and QoS-aware Mobile Middleware. In: Donatelli, S., Thiagarajan, P.S. (eds.) ICATPN 2006. LNCS, vol. 4024, pp. 228–241. Springer, Heidelberg (2006)
12. Simmonds, D., Solberg, A., Reddy, R., France, R., Ghosh, S.: An Aspect Oriented Model Driven Framework. In: Proc. the Enterprise Distributed Object Computing Conference, pp. 119–130 (2005)
13. UML profile for modeling QoS and Fault Tolerance characteristics and Mechanisms. Adopted standard, OMG May 2005, Document ptc/05-05-02 (2005)
14. ISO/IEC JTC1/SC7, 1999a, Information Technology -Software product quality -Part 1: Quality model, ISO/IEC, Report: 9126-1
15. Object Management Group, UML Profile for Schedulability, Performance, and Time Specification, ad/2000-08-04 (2002)
16. Kulkarni, V., Reddy, S.: Separation of Concerns in Model-driven Development. IEEE Software 20(5), 64–69 (2003)
17. Clarke, S., Harrison, W., Ossher, H., Tarr, P.: Subject-Oriented Design: Towards Improved Alignment of Requirements, Design and Code. In: Proc. of 14th ACM SIGPLAN Conference on Object-oriented Programming, Systems, Languages, and Application, pp. 325–339 (1999)
18. France, R.B., Kim, D., Ghosh, S., Song, E.: A UML-Based Pattern Specification Technique. IEEE Trans. on Software Eng. 30(3), 193–206 (2004)
19. Atkinson, C., Kühne, T.: Aspect-Oriented Development with Stratified Frameworks. IEEE Software 20(1), 81–89 (2003)
20. Gokhale, A., Balasubramanian, K., Krishna, A., Balasubramanian, J., Edwards, G., Deng, G., Turkay, E., Parsons, J., Schimdt, D.: Model Driven Middleware: A New Paradigm for Developing Distributed Real-time Embedded Systems. Science of Computer programming (2005)

Component Adaptation in Contemporary Execution Environments

Susan Eisenbach[1], Chris Sadler[2], and Dominic Wong[3]

[1] Department of Computing, Imperial College London
[2] School of Computing Science, Middlesex University
[3] Morgan Stanley, London
S.Eisenbach@imperial.ac.uk

Abstract. Because they are required to support component deployment and composition, modern execution environments embody a number of common features such as dynamic linking and support for multiple component versions. These features help to overcome some classical maintenance problems focused largely on component evolution, where successive generations of collaborating components need to be kept collaborating. What has been less studied has been component adaptation, whereby a component developed in an environment consisting of one set of service components is required to operate in one or several other environments containing qualitatively different components. In this paper we examine the needs developers and deployers have arising out of component adaptation and explore the concept of Flexible Dynamic Linking as a means of satisfying them. We describe a suite of tools developed to demonstrate this approach to component adaptation support within the .NET Common Language Runtime.

Keywords: component adaptation, component evolution, dynamic linking, execution environments, .NET, runtime systems.

1 Introduction

Applications based on software components offer computer users a variety of benefits including widespread utilization of robust 'industrial-strength' subcomponents; optimal exploitation of system resources through resource sharing and conditional loading; and potentially frequent and transparent updating. There are also benefits for the developers of the components who can continue improving and updating their products, even after their clients have taken delivery of and started to use their software.

Modern execution environments that have been built to run such applications need to embody a number of characteristic features in order to deliver these benefits. In the first place they need to be able to manage all the components. This has proved more difficult than might at first be thought and the history of recent operating systems development is sprinkled with cases where this rather obvious requirement has been inadequately accomplished. In an environment where any given component may be required by more than one application, it is essential that the component management system can deal with multiple versions of the component, since an upgrade which is

J. Indulska and K. Raymond (Eds.): DAIS 2007, LNCS 4531, pp. 90–103, 2007.

beneficial to one application can easily prove disastrous to another. This phenomenon is known as DLL Hell in Microsoft[32] and is not unknown in other runtime environments[13].

The second feature that is needed for component-based support is dynamic linking, by means of which the components that an application depends on are located and loaded only at runtime and only on demand. This is how the use of system resources can be optimized. When code is compiled, information about the nature and location of external references needs to be recorded and retained with the object. In statically linked systems, the location tends to be recorded as a memory offset and all the code must be loaded together. In a dynamic linking system, the information will more likely be a symbolic reference (for example, a pathname) that can be passed to the operating system at runtime.

When these two features are combined in an execution environment, what emerges, in principle, is a powerful maintenance regime. *Component evolution* – implying that the improvements made to the next generation of one component will be automatically propagated to its existing clients – is generally well provided for in modern execution environments[15]. *Component adaptation* - porting an application from one environment to another - should not require significant intervention provided that compatible service components exist. So an application written to exploit, say, the ODBC of SQLServer should be able to execute with some generic ODBC without requiring an entire new build. In practice, applications are conventionally bound only to the actual components they were compiled against. The best the runtime system can do is use the symbolic references to re-locate those resources in the new (deployed) environment – so although linking is dynamic because it occurs at runtime, it is still essentially fixed. However, the redirections required to achieve both evolution and adaptation can be obtained by interfering with the symbolic reference data between compile-time and runtime. This intervention has been termed flexible dynamic linking[8] and different execution environments permit this to a greater or lesser extent.

In this paper we discuss the limitations of dynamic linking in section 2 and explore the interventions needed to achieve flexible dynamic linking in the .NET Common Language Runtime in section 3. Section 4 describes the various elements of the FLAME toolset that was developed to accomplish flexible dynamic linking to support specifically component adaptation. The paper concludes with related and future work.

2 Dynamic Linking

Dynamic Linking was first used in the MULTICS (Multiplexed Information and Computing Service) system[10]. It has found its way into many of today's programming environments including Java[17] and the .NET Framework[22] primarily as a means of satisfying the late binding requirements of modern object-oriented programming languages. The impact of dynamic linking on the efforts of software maintainers is therefore something of a side-effect. Nevertheless, component evolution has been rather well catered for by the approach taken which goes a long way to resolving DLL Hell[14]. Component adaptation has not received the same amount of attention partly because it has not been perceived of as such a big problem.

Since the dawn of Commercial Off-The Shelf (COTS) software, it has been the case that the computer system that a piece of software was developed on has not necessarily been the same as the sort of system that it eventually runs on. The developer needs to make some attempt to ensure that the software's clients' expectations of success will not be thwarted by missing or underspecified resources. The traditional method of tackling this problem consists of publishing a 'minimum specification' that the software will be guaranteed to run on.

In a component-based software environment, this approach can lead to situations where, at the majority of deployment sites, applications are bound to suboptimal resources. For example, an application might use software floating point processing on a system where floating point hardware exists. The developer's policy here is "The speed of the convoy is the speed of its slowest ship". This policy is not satisfactory for clients who have invested in higher-specification hardware or richer software resources. A generally more satisfactory approach is for developers to program to an Applications Programming Interface (API). Each client then has the obligation to provide an implementation of the API requirements as best as the system will allow. For existing component-based software environments, this involves creating or configuring components with the same signatures as those on the development system. The systematic approach to this process is termed *component adaption* (regrettably similar to component adaptation) where API mismatches between components are bridged by intermediate components, or *adaptors* [5].

However, this approach is still restrictive, as linking is constrained by compiler decisions. Compiling in a Microsoft environment will result in the expectation that `System.Console.Writeline` will come from `mscorlib`. Trying to execute the same code on a Linux system, where `System.Console.Writeline` comes from `monolib`, will result in a resolution error. Similar errors occur if the class names are not identical. The compiler has hardwired the symbolic reference with the classname and no further flexibility is possible.

In the context of this paper, another potentially confusing nomenclature is *compositional adaptation* [21] which describes a similar but essentially harder problem – the dynamic update, or hot-swapping of components *during runtime*. Considerations of these capabilities is largely focused on systems supporting ubiquitous computing [26] or autonomic computing [6].

3   Flexible Dynamic Linking

How often would the flexibility sought after in Section 2 make a difference to the applicability or portability of real-world components? This line of research was motivated by two cases where proprietary software that our components depended on could not be shipped to or otherwise accessed by some clients. In the first case a research package [20] utilized some routines derived from embargoed NASA algorithms. In order to make this tool available to a wider research community, it was necessary to embed some complex reflective code so as to effect the appropriate redirections.

In the second case an international merchant bank had developed a specialised DLL which was optimised for writing to their database. For confidentiality reasons they declined to distribute it to external software subcontractors. The subcontractors therefore had to develop using a generic database writer with no optimisation (see Table 1).

Table 1. Instead of the database library how can a database library be targeted?

Source code	Compile-time classes		Runtime classes	
New DBLib()	DBLib	OK	SQLSvrLib	??
New DBLib()	(None)	??	DBLib,	OK
			SQLSvrLib	OK

The idea behind Flexible Dynamic Linking is to allow the hardwiring performed by the compiler to be bypassed in some fashion. On the developer's side, this could allow for a range of alternative components to be suggested as binding partners at remote sites. On the deployer's side, it would permit the substitution of one component for another. This should make things more satisfactory in both of the real-life cases, without compromising type safety.

3.1 The Common Language Infrastructure

Like the Java Virtual Machine, the .NET Common Language Runtime (CLR) offers a managed environment for safe and secure program execution. Both systems take programs in the form of bytecode (called Microsoft Intermediate Language - MSIL - in the case of .NET). In .NET the MSIL is compiled into native code by the runtime just before it is executed whereas Java bytecode is normally interpreted. One of Java's strengths is its platform independence and at first glance it would seem the .NET Framework is missing this valuable attribute. However Microsoft has released its specification and it was standardised by the European Computer Manufacturers Association (ECMA). ECMA-335[16] defines the Common Language Infrastructure (CLI) where applications written in different languages can be run on differing systems without the need to take into account the characteristics of that environment.

The central store for shared libraries to be used by the CLR is called the General Assembly Cache (GAC). Microsoft's .NET Framework *assemblies* (Microsoft's term for components) are placed here for shared access. Only globally unique assemblies are allowed to be shared and installed into the GAC, all others are considered to be private, not trusted for sharing, and are usually kept within the application folder. Fusion is the assembly loader that handles the dynamic linking within the CLR and it is invoked whenever a reference to an external assembly is made.

Three important open source implementations of the ECMA-335 standard are Mono[31], DotGNU[11], and Rotor (Microsoft's own Shared Source Common Language Infrastructure (SSCLI)) [24,29].

3.2 Definition

Dynamic linking allows the linking at runtime to a class that was identified at compile-time. Flexible Dynamic Linking defers the decision of which class to link to *until* runtime when the linker will make the final decision. This serves to decouple the runtime environment from the compile time environment. Flexible Dynamic Linking, as set out in [8], achieves this by using *type variables* instead of class names in the bytecode generated during compilation. A type variable is a placeholder for a type. At runtime the decision on which type is used as a substitute is taken by the linker normally based on some predefined policy. For example, consider:

```
public class Class1
{
  static X list;
   public static void Main(string[] args)
   {
list = new X(); list.Add("foobar");
   }
}
```

The type variable X is a placeholder for a real type. This will be compiled into the bytecode and when it comes to executing the code the linker will recognise this as a type variable and make a decision as to which type it should substitute in its place. In theory, as long as the chosen substitute has an empty constructor and has the method Add(String s) then it will execute without error. This conception of linking can assist component adaptation since creating platform independent code is simply a matter of using type variables and ensuring that there is a type on the target platform which provides the same interface as that being used by the type variable. The same applies to utilising DLLs which are known to be on the target system.

However, when we come to apply this strategy to .NET there is a slight modification which is needed due to the way in which external types are referenced in MSIL bytecode. Consider the following "Hello World" program in .NET:

```
.method private hidebysig static void Main(string[] args)
cil managed
    {
      .entrypoint
      .maxstack   8
      IL_0000: nop
      IL_0001: ldstr "Hello World"
      IL_0006:call void[mscorlib]
        System.Console::WriteLine(string)
      IL_000b: nop
      IL_000c: ret
    } // end of method Program::Main
```

The reference to the type System.Console is tagged with the assembly in which it is found, mscorlib. As a consequence of this, every type variable which we generate for the bytecode must be represented in two parts; an assembly type variable and a class type variable.

4 FLAME

The tool described in this paper is named FLAME. It is based on CUPID[1] an implemention of Flexible Dynamic Linking that was designed so as to give developers the ability to indicate compatible substitutions at both the class and assembly levels. CUPID implements *logical* type variables – metadata inserted into the bytecode that tags specific classes and assemblies as potentially variable. CLIs that cannot interpret the metadata can execute the assembly as normal, linking to the original build references. The metadata is created via the use of *custom attributes*. These allow the developer to define the assemblies/classes to be replaced, what to replace them with, and some other linking options. A risky alternative would be to allow *any* assembly which provides the correct API (called a *binary compatible* assembly) to be a possible substitution candidate.

CUPID ensures type safety by analysing the bytecode of the application and automatically generating appropriate *member constraints* to be inserted. Member constraints specify all class/field accesses that the substitute member must satisfy during execution of the program. CUPID also allows the (manual) specification of *structural constraints* - ensuring that, if there is a supertype-subtype relationship between two classes, then whatever type replaces the supertype must be a supertype of the type that replaces the subtype.

The FLAME system was designed to automate the specification of the structural constraints for the developer and then to develop a deployer-centric solution. To achieve these two goals we have three distinct components; the FLAMEConstraint tool, the FLAME runtime and the FLAMEConfig tool. Fig. 1 shows how the three components are related.

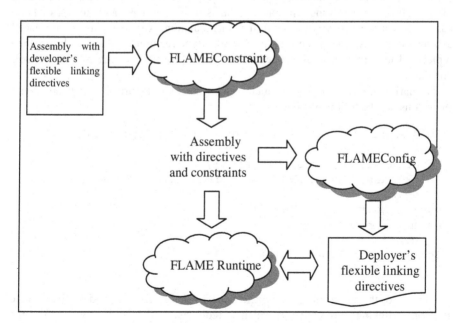

Fig. 1. Architectural overview of FLAME

In the CUPID system member constraints are generated by a Perl script (dubbed flxibl). In order to improve efficiency FlameConstraint utilises the Phoenix compiler framework [23] to provide the basis for a new post-compilation tool which will generate both member and subtype constraints. Two attributes, LinkAssembly and LinkClass, are used to create linking directives attached at the appropriate scope: assembly, module, class or method. The constraints for substitute assemblies and classes are derived from these directives and are then inserted into the bytecode, again at the appropriate scope level. The constraints are defined using two custom attributes, LinkMemberConstraint and LinkStructureConstraint.

LinkAssembly Attribute. A LinkAssembly attribute redirects all class references, within a given scope, from its original assembly to a new one by essentially replacing the original assembly name with a new one. The LinkAssembly attribute has parameters that fully describe the original and new assembly.

LinkClass Attribute. The LinkClass attribute does for classes what LinkAssembly does for assemblies. However, since a class reference includes both the assembly and class names a LinkClass attribute must have a corresponding LinkAssembly attribute that contains the same InterfaceName.

LinkMemberConstraint Attribute. When we substitute one class for another, the new class must provide all of the method calls and field references that the program makes on the old class. These required methods and fields are called member constraints and are expressed through the LinkMemberConstraint attribute.

LinkStructureConstraint Attribute. The types referenced in a program have a complex set of subtype and supertype relationships. Among other things, subtypes are often used in place of supertypes as arguments to method calls and subtypes can be cast to one of their supertypes for further manipulation. Any new classes introduced as substitutes must satisfy the subtype and supertype relationships as the classes they replace. These relationships are expressed as LinkStructureConstraint attributes.

To clarify the usage of the attributes and what FLAMEConstraint does with them consider the following code:

```
[LinkAssembly("System.Windows.Forms", "SpecialForms",
"1.1.*", null, null, true, "special",
InterfaceType.LOCAL_INTERFACE)]
[LinkClass("System.Windows.Forms.Form", "BlueForm",
"special")]
public static void Main {
Form f = new Form();
f.Show()
Form d = new MDIWindowDialog();
}
```

The use of the two attributes LinkAssembly and LinkClass describe a single flexible linking directive which redirects all references to the System.Windows.Forms.Form class (which has been defined in the

`System.Windows.Forms` assembly) to the `BlueForm` class (defined in the `SpecialForms` assembly). When this code is parsed by the `FLAMEConstraint` tool it generates member and subtype constraints based on the usage of all instances of the `System.Windows.Forms.Form` and results in the augmented code given below:

```
[LinkAssembly("System.Windows.Forms", "SpecialForms",
"1.1.*", null, null, true, "special",
InterfaceType.LOCAL_INTERFACE)]
[LinkClass("System.Windows.Forms.Form", "BlueForm",
"special")]
[LinkMember("System.Windows.Forms",
"System.Windows.Forms.Form", "Application1.exe",
"100663300", false)]
[LinkMember("System.Windows.Forms",
"System.Windows.Forms.Form", "Application1.exe",
"100663323", false)]
[LinkStructure("System.Windows.Forms",
"System.Windows.Forms.Form", "100782403",
"System.Windows.Forms",
"System.Windows.Forms.MDIWindowDialog", "1008392532",
"Application1.exe")]
public static void Main {
  Form f = new Form();
  f.Show()
  Form d = new MDIWindowDialog();
}
```

The `FLAMEConstraint` tool has generated `LinkMember` constraints which specify that the replacement must provide the constructor and `Show()` methods, although this is hard to see since they are referred to only by metadata token numbers (for example "100663300"). A subtype constraint, in the form of a `LinkStructure` attribute, says its replacement must be a supertype of the `MDIWindowDialog` type.

4.1 FLAME Runtime

The *application configuration file* is an XML file which resides in the application's directory and is named `<applicationName>.exe.config`. Under the normal .NET runtime when the application is run, execution will proceed as normal until an external type is referenced. Fusion will then find the referenced type's enclosing assembly and load it into the runtime. .NET *strong-name* assemblies are identified by name, a public key ID, a 'culture' and a four-part version number. The first time that Fusion is invoked it searches the application directory for a corresponding application configuration file. If one is found, it will parse the XML and cache the information for future reference. Whenever Fusion receives an assembly load request it will first consult its cached application configuration file to see whether the assembly is subject to a version redirect and if so it will attempt to load the specified version else it will load the originally requested version. A typical binding redirection looks like this:

```
<assemblyIdentity name="TestLibrary1"
                  publicKeyToken="9D9229CF9B3C922D"
                  culture="neutral"
  />
  <bindingRedirect oldVersion="1.0.0.0"
                   newVersion="2.0.0.0"
  />
```

To specify our flexible linking directives in FLAME we extended the existing <bindingRedirect> tag of the application configuration file so that we can describe a new assembly. This means accommodating the name, culture and public key token of the new assembly. Thus:

```
<bindingRedirect interfaceName="macosx"
                 interfaceType="ANY_INTERFACE"
                 oldVersion="1.0.0.0"
                 newVersion="2.0.0.0"
                 newAsmName="TestLibrary2"
                 newPublicKeyToken="9B9287CC6B3C809A"
                 newCulture="neutral"
  />
```

This redirects all references from TestLibrary1 to TestLibrary2. This means that TestLibrary2 must define all of the types which TestLibrary1 offers and which are referenced in the application otherwise we will find a type load exception at runtime. We also need the capacity to redirect individual types within an assembly. This is achieved through varClass and newClass attributes of the <bindingRedirect> tag.

To carry out the deployer defined flexible linking directives in FLAME we could create and insert metadata into the assembly's bytecode to describe the substitutions. This would involve invoking a tool before the code is executed to modify the original assembly with some new metadata. The underlying runtime would not have to be touched because in essence it is performing the same steps as the FLAMEConstraint tool with two major differences:

(i)   The metadata would be generated from a given list of substitutions, not from custom attributes.

(ii) The bytecode changes would occur just before runtime at the deployer side, instead of occurring just after compilation at the developer side.

Unfortunately, to modify the metadata requires the assembly to be disassembled and then reassembled, and if the original assembly was signed with a private key by the developer it would need to be resigned when it was reassembled. The deployer would not be in possession of this key so would be unable to re-sign the assembly thus restricting usage to unsigned applications.

Therefore it is necessary to modify the runtime directly so that it can parse the additional binding redirection XML and then act upon it. The enhanced FLAME runtime does not check constraints on any types that it flexibly links. This means that after loading a substitute assembly/class it is possible that the runtime will not be able to load the required type or invoke the required method.

One possible solution is to use the application configuration file for storing the constraints, but this has two main drawbacks. First of all, XML is a very verbose representation format and representing a single member or subtype constraint takes several lines of XML. A reasonably sized application with a large number of constraints would end up with an extremely bloated application configuration file. Secondly, the application configuration is usually edited by hand which makes it very easy for someone to accidentally remove or alter a constraint.

A further reason for not incorporating runtime constraint checking is the potential performance decrease when verifying a large number of constraints. Member constraints are quite fast to check since it is only querying the existence of a method or field in the loaded class. However, subtype constraints can potentially take much longer. Consider a type T1, defined in assembly A1, with a subtype constraint which says that whatever replaces T1 must be a supertype of type T2. To check this constraint we must load type T2, which is defined in assembly A2, and then check the relationship between the two types. Unfortunately type T2 is also subject to flexible dynamic linking, it is to be replaced by type T3. So we must now also verify that T3 satisfies all of T2's constraints. Loading these types from the different assemblies, which may not be required during the run, causes delays in the execution and also increases the memory footprint of the running application.

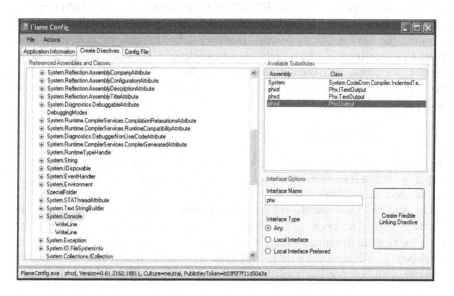

Fig. 2. Screenshot from the FLAMEConfig tool

4.2 FLAMEConfig

Without storing a great deal of semantic information, it is not feasible to perform constraint verification automatically at runtime, so it is essential to ensure that any substitute assembly identified in a flexible linking directive will be binary compatible with the application. FLAMEConfig is an interactive tool which is designed to achieve the required type-checking in an intermediate step taken at the deployment site. The operation of FLAMEConfig is as follows:

(i)   The application for which flexible linking directives are to be created is loaded into the tool.

(ii)   A list of all the assemblies and classes referenced within the loaded application is displayed to the user. (If the assembly is missing for some reason FLAMEConfig will inform the user.)

(iii)   The user picks the assembly/class they wish to flexibly link and the list of possible substitute assemblies/classes is displayed to the user.

(iv)   The user chooses the substitute from the list and defines what interface type and name they want for the directive. (see Fig. 2)

(v)   Finally, the tool creates the appropriate XML to express the flexible linking directive and adds it to the application configuration file.

The list of possible substitutes is generated by examining the GAC and local application folder for every assembly. An assembly/class is then added to the list of eligible substitutes if it can satisfy the member and subtype constraints inferred from the selected referenced assembly/class. Provided that the application configuration file is not manually edited subsequent to this step, the flexible linking directives are guaranteed to substitute binary compatible assemblies/classes (as long as the execution environment does not change).

The three components of the FLAME system combined with CUPID make a complete system for flexible dynamic linking, enabling both developers and deployers to control the flexible linking process. Deployer-defined directives are located in the application configuration file whilst developer-defined ones are embedded in the assembly metadata. Thus there is no danger that they will conflict syntactically, so to speak. In circumstances where they conflict semantically, it is the deployer-defined directive that takes precedence.

4.3 Case Study: xmlValid

The FLAME system was tested on a real-world application called xmlValid - a simple command line XML validation tool[30] which checks whether an XML file is well formed and validates it against a given XSD file.

The xmlValid assembly references two external assemblies; mscorlib and System.Xml. The class System.Xml.XmlTextReader was chosen as the target for flexible dynamic linking. A new class, MyXml.MyXmlTextReader was developed as a binary compatible replacement. We ran timing tests to gauge the performance difference, the results of which are presented in Table 2.

Table 2. Execution times of with and without flexible linking

Run	Normal Time (s)	Flex Linked Time (s)	Difference (s)
1	9.51	10.12	0.61
2	9.17	10.08	0.91
3	9.78	10.00	0.22
4	9.14	9.98	0.84
5	9.10	9.93	0.83
6	9.24	10.23	0.99
7	9.07	10.01	0.94
8	9.12	10.29	1.17
9	9.16	10.60	1.44
10	9.20	9.92	0.72
Average	9.25	10.12	0.87

Flexible dynamic linking added an average 0.87 seconds or around a 9.4% increase in execution time using a test input file. Since (typically) larger XML files would take longer to validate, this overhead could be expected to fall. So the performance cost for having flexible dynamic linking does not seem unacceptable.

5 Related and Future Work

The idea of keeping types unspecific at compile-time by means of type variables has been examined in several programming communities [28,18,3]. In the meantime, linking-time behaviour, both for .NET and for the Java Virtual Machine has received some formal attention [2,12,7].

The current work is built on a number of earlier projects, focused initially on component evolution [14], which anticipated the .NET 2.0 introduction of type forwarders [19]; and then on component adaptation [9,1]. Execution environments that support the runtime interpretation of metadata, in conjunction with pertinent configuration files, are bound to receive increasing attention [25,27,4].

A number of future extensions to the FLAME toolset itself are possible. Instead of asking the developer or deployer to choose replacement assemblies or classes, an enhanced runtime could make the decision based on some heuristics. The heuristics used to decide which substitution is most appropriate would have to be based on the properties of the assembly.

The Phoenix framework offers a rich toolset for dataflow analysis and generation of member and subtype constraints could be based on dataflow information. Those referenced methods and fields and subtype relationships which applied during a typical run of the program could be used to constrain the possible replacement assembly.

Application configuration files are not the only files that the Fusion checks for binding information. The machine configuration file redirects the loading of particular assemblies for every executable run on that machine. The schema for the machine configuration file is identical to that for the application configuration file so modifying FLAME to extend flexible linking to this file should not be particularly difficult. Finally developers could distribute application configuration files directly with their programs, then these could be fed into the FLAMEConfig tool at the deployer end to verify that they obey the member and subtype constraints.

The main goal of this project was to provide a method for the deployer to specify any assembly or class which should be subject to flexible dynamic linking and to ensure that it will be carried out in accordance with all the directives and binary compatibly. Additionally the tools to help the developer were improved. The Flame toolset lets the developer suggest and the deployer choose different assemblies and classes than were available in the compilation environment. We have developed our toolset on .NET because it had metadata which made the implementation reasonably straightforward. However, we believe that the ability to do component adaptation should be more widely applicable.

Acknowledgments. The software described in this paper was inspired by Alex Buckley's PhD thesis work on Flexible Dynamic Linking. We would like to thank him for all his help in the development of Flame.

References

1. Aaltonen, A., Buckley, A., Eisenbach, S.: Flexible Dynamic Linking for.NET. Journal of .NET Technologies, vol 4 (June 2006)
2. Abadi, M., Gonthier, G., Werner, B.: Choice in Dynamic Linking. In: Walukiewicz, I. (ed.) FOSSACS 2004. LNCS, vol. 2987, Springer, Heidelberg (2004)
3. Ancona, D., Damiani, F., Drossopoulou, S., Zucca, E.: Polymorphic Bytecode: Compositional Compilation for Java-like Languages. In: ACM SIGPLAN-SIGACT Symposium on Principles of Progamming Languages. Long Beach, California (2005)
4. Attardi G., Cisternino, A., Colombo, D.: CIL + Metadata > Executable Program. Journal of Object Technology, Special issue: .NET: The Programmers Perspective: ECOOP Workshop (2003)
5. Bracciali, A., Brogi, A., Canal, C.: A formal approach to component adaption. In: J. Syst. Softw. vol. 74(1) (2005)
6. Bialek, R., Jul, E., Schneider, J.-G., Jin, y.: Partitioning of Java Applications to Support Dynamic Updates. In: 11th Asia-Pacific Software Engineering Conference (APSEC'04)(2004)
7. Buckley, A.: A Model of Dynamic Binding in .NET in ECOOP Workshop on Formal Techniques for Java-like Programs. Oslo, Norway (2005)
8. Buckley, A., Drossopoulou, S.: Flexible Dynamic Linking. In: ECOOP Workshop on Formal Techniques for Java-like Programs. Oslo, Norway (2004)
9. Buckley, A., Murray, M., Eisenbachm, S., Drossopoulou, S.: Flexible Bytecode for Linking. In: .NET in ETAPS Workshop on Bytecode Semantics, Verification, Analysis and Transformation. Edinburgh, Scotland (2005)
10. Corbato, F.J., Vysssotsky, V.A.: Introduction and Overview of the MULTICS System. AFIPS Fall Joint Computer Conference (1965)
11. DotGNU Project: Available from: http://dotgnu.org/
12. Drossopoulou, S., Lagorio, G., Eisenbach, S.: Flexible Models for Dynamic Linking. In: European Symposium on Programming. Warsaw, Poland (2003)

13. Eisenbach, S., Jurisic, V., Sadler, C.: Feeling the Way Through DLL Hell. In: First Workshop on Unanticipated Software Evolution. Malaga, Spain (2002)
14. Eisenbach, S., Kayhan, D., Sadler, C.: Keeping Control of Reusable Components. In: International Working Conference on Component Deployment. Edinburgh, Scotland (2004)
15. Eisenbach, S., Sadler C.: Reuse and Abuse. Journal of Object Technology, (January 1, 2007) vol 6. ETH Swiss Federal Institute of Technology (2007)
16. ECMA International: Standard ECMA-335 Common Language Infrastructure (CLI) (2005) Available from: http://www.ecma-international.org/publications/standards/Ecma-335.htm
17. Gosling, J., Joy, B., Steele, G., Bracha, G.: Java(TM) Language Specification, 2nd edn. Addison Wesley, London (2000)
18. Kennedy, A., Syme, D.: Design and Implementation of Generics for the .NET Common Language Runtime. In: ACM SIGPLAN Conference on Programming Language Design and Implementation. Snowbird, Utah, USA (2001)
19. Lander, R.: The Wonders of Whidbey Factoring Features. Part 1: Type Forwarders (September 14, 2005) Available from http://hoser.lander.ca/
20. Magee, J., Kramer, J.: Concurrency : state models & Java programs Chichester, England, Wiley (2006)
21. McKinley, P., Sadjadi, S.M., Kasten, E.P., Cheng, B.H.C.: A Taxonomy of Compositional Adaptation in Software Engnieering and Network Systems Laboratory Technical Report MSU-CSE-04-17 (2004)
22. Microsoft Corporation: Microsoft Developer Network. Available from: http://msdn.microsoft.com
23. Microsoft Corporation. Phoenix Documentation (2005) Available from: http://research.microsoft.com/phoenix/
24. Microsoft Corporation. SSCLI Documentation (2002) Available from: http://research.microsoft.com/sscli/
25. Mikunov, A.: Rewrite MSIL Code on the Fly with the .NET Framework Profiling API. MSDN Magazine (September 2003)
26. Paspallis, N., Ppapadopoulos, G.A.: An approach for Developing Adaptive, Mobile Applications with Separation of Concerns. In: Proc. COMPSAC'06 (2006)
27. Piessens, F., Jacobs, B., Truyen, E., Joosen, W.: Support for Metadata-driven Selection of Run-time Services In: .NET is Promising but Immature. Journal of Object Technology, Special issue: .NET: The Programmers Perspective: ECOOP Workshop (2003)
28. Shao, Z., Appel, A.W.: Smartest Recompilation. In: Proceedings of the 20th ACM SIGPLAN-SIGACT Symposium on Principles of Programming Languages (POPL'93), Charleston, South Carolina, USA (1993)
29. Stutz, D., Neward, T., Shilling, G.: Shared Source CLI Essentials. O'Reilly (2003)
30. Sells, C.: .NET and Win 32 tools. available from :http://www.sellsbrothers.com/tools
31. What is Mono? Available from: http://www.mono-project.com/Main_Page
32. Wong, F.: DLL Hell, The Inside Story (1998) available from: http://www.desaware.com/tech/dllhell.aspx

Managing Distributed Adaptation of Mobile Applications

Mourad Alia[1], Svein Hallsteinsen[2], Nearchos Paspallis[3], and Frank Eliassen[4]

[1] Simula Research Lab, Martin Linges v 17, Fornebu, P.O.Box 134, 1325 Lysaker, Norway
mouradal@simula.no
[2] SINTEF ICT, S.P. Andersens vei 15 b, Trondheim, Norway
svein.hallsteinsen@sintef.no
[3] Department of Computer Science, University of Cyprus, P.O. Box 20537, Nicosia, Cyprus
nearchos@cs.ucy.ac.cy
[4] Department of Informatics, University of Oslo, P.O.Box 1080 Blindern, Oslo, Norway
frank@ifi.uio.no

Abstract. Mobile computing is characterised by variations in user needs and in the computing and communication resources. We have developed a middleware centric approach for the development of software capable of dynamically adapting to such variations. The middleware leverages models of needs and resources and the adaptation capabilities of the software and performs context monitoring, adaptation planning and dynamic reconfiguration at runtime. In this paper we focus on the modelling of resources of a distributed mobile computing infrastructure and how the resource model is used in adaptation planning. We present a distributed resource management framework and mechanisms necessary to maintain an up to date resource model at runtime. The challenge is to balance the level of abstraction so as to hide some of the heterogeneity of the actual infrastructure while retaining sufficient detail to serve the needs of distributed and centralized adaptation planning. The proposed framework is illustrated through a running example.

1 Introduction

With the increasing mobility and pervasiveness of computing and communication technology, software systems are commonly accessed through handheld, networked devices, carried by people moving around. This introduces dynamic variation both in the user needs and in the operating environment of the provided services. For example, communication bandwidth changes dynamically in wireless communication networks and power is a scarce resource on battery-powered devices when outlet power is not available. Under such circumstances, applications need to adapt dynamically in order to retain usability, usefulness, and reliability. To design such applications many recent works have proposed general solutions based on an adaptation loop control monitoring user needs and available resources and adapting the application accordingly. However, most of these solutions concentrate on the dynamic reconfiguration of the mobile application on the client device, without properly exploiting the computing resources available throughout the wireless networks it is mostly connected to [1,2].

J. Indulska and K. Raymond (Eds.): DAIS 2007, LNCS 4531, pp. 104–118, 2007.

In the MADAM[1] approach, adaptations are carried out by generic middleware where earlier implementation of the running application are reconsidered in response to context changes [4]. This is also referred to as planning. The (re)planning is based on runtime architecture models of applications with their adaptation capabilities explicitly modelled. During re-planning, alternative architecture models of the running applications are dynamically generated by considering alternative implementation choices for the component types of the applications. The adaptation reasoning relies on the use of utility functions allowing the computation of the utility for the user of an application variant given the current user needs and available computing and communication resources. The utility functions are designed and implemented with the aim of dynamically measuring the benefit of a given variant.

In this paper, the current MADAM approach is extended to enable the adaptation planning process to leverage the deployment (and possible re-deployment) of the application components in a distributed mobile computing infrastructure. Such an infrastructure will usually consist of several nodes connected via one or more communication networks. Distributed adaptation planning can then be used to increase the performance of the user application and to minimize the latency and the communication overhead – as in classical grid-like infrastructures – or yet to increase the availability of the end user service.

The main contribution of this paper is the combination of a resource management framework and utility-based adaptation reasoning used to manage distributed mobile adaptation. The aims of the resource management framework are (i) the modelling of the resources of the distributed infrastructure so as to hide the heterogeneity of the infrastructure and to provide a uniform and generic method to access the resources and (ii) resource control and management, both locally in one node and globally by maintaining a global view of the distributed computing infrastructure composed of a set of discoverable resources. The adaptation reasoning uses the resource management framework to discover the available and surrounding resources (the different networks, servers, etc.), select the best placement using the utility functions and finally allocate the selected resources with the associated amounts.

We start the presentation of this paper by a motivating example in section 2. Then section 3 presents the overall MADAM middleware-centric approach for the management of distributed adaptation. The resource management framework , as part of the proposed middleware, is presented by the section 4. Section 5 explains how the adaptation manager interacts with the resource manager component to perform distributed adaptation reasoning. An implementation status is given in section 6. Finally, section 7 discusses some relevant related works before concluding in section 8.

2   Motivating Example: On-Site Worker Application

The following scenario shows how self-adaptation is crucial to retain the usefulness of the application across typical context changes. The scenario describes an application, which is used to assist a maintenance worker with on-site work. Because of the nature of her work, the worker may not always be able to visually interact with the mobile

---

[1] MADAM is a European IST Project [3].

device (e.g. a PDA running the application). Consequently, the application is designed to offer two modes of user interaction: visual and audio interfaces. The visual interaction communicates with the user with visual messages (e.g. text in popup windows) while the audio interaction uses the PDA's speakers and microphone to communicate information to and from the user.

Consider the case where the worker is in her office, interacting with the PDA in order to prepare the application for the on-site visit. In this case, the application has the full attention of the user, and consequently the visual interaction is selected as it is more responsive (e.g. faster interaction) and more resource efficient (i.e. requires less memory and CPU, and no networking). But when the worker starts working on the gear to be maintained, the application switches to audio interaction, thus releasing the worker from the burden of having to visually interact with the application. Finally, when the network is sufficiently fast and cheap, and the resources are low (e.g. because the PDA starts other applications as well), the application switches to the audio mode where the speech-to-text component is hosted by another computer, for example a pc at the site. As illustrated by this scenario, the main effort of the self-adaptation mechanism is to monitor the context (i.e. the status of the hosting device and the user), and dynamically respond to changes by selecting the most appropriate application variant. To keep things simple, this scenario considers three modes only: the visual, the audio, and the audio with remote text-to-speech processing modes.

This scenario demonstrates that certain applications can improve their provided utility by switching between alternative application behaviours and deployment. It therefore stresses the need for a distributed resource management framework for the management of the distributed adaptation.

3   Distribution Adaptation Management

We focus on the resources directly surrounding one mobile user such as the handheld device, the home PC, or the laptop in the suitcase. This collection of computers together with the communication networks they are connected to, is referred to as an adaptation domain Within an adaptation domain all computers run an instance of the MADAM middleware and there is one client (the handheld device) and zero or more servers. The domain is formed dynamically by the means of a discovery protocol, whereby servers regularly advertise their presence, and the client keeps track of available servers. Servers may be shared, meaning that they are members of more than one domain. All the servers in a domain have a network connection to the client and servers may be connected to other servers.

The client runs the adaptation control loop and manages the adaptation of the set of active applications, including (re)deployment of their components on the resources in its domain, seeking to maximise the utility to the user.

The applications running inside a domain may depend on services provided outside the domain. This may include both web services and shared peripherals. Discovering, selecting and binding to suitable service instances is also part of the responsibility of adaptation management, as well as replacing or removing the need for services that disappear or otherwise break the service level agreement. However, this is outside the

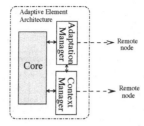

Fig. 1. MADAM Adaptive Element Architecture

scope of this paper. Here we focus on adapting the deployment of the components of the active applications on the resources available inside an adaptation domain.

3.1 MADAM Adaptive Element Architecture

Figure 3.1 shows the architecture of an instance of the MADAM middleware, which represents an adaptation control loop in one node. Its main components are the core, the adaptation manager and the context manager. The core provides platform-independent services for the management of component instances including application components, context components, and resources that are also reified through components. The management of such components involves the supporting of lyfecycle operations such as loading, unloading, binding, unbinding and setting parameters of components. This is implemented using reflective mechanisms similar to those in Fractal [5] and Open-Com [6].

The Adaptation Manager is responsible for reasoning on the impact of context changes on the application, determining when there is a need to trigger adaptation of the application, and for selecting an application variant that best fits the current context. The Context manager is responsible for managing and monitoring contexts relevant for the adaptation. It manages the contextual information available to the node, including the execution platform, with its networks and computing resources, and the physical environment information such as light and noise and user needs [7]. Furthermore, as the context manager enables distributed context information sensing and aggregation operations, additional services such as network and node discovery and context sharing are enabled.

3.2 Adaptation Approach: Property-Driven Variability

The working of the MADAM middleware is based on architectural reflection, meaning that the middleware maintains models of the running applications, with adaptation capabilities modelled explicitly in the form of variation points. It also maintains models of the user needs and the computing and communication resources available within the adaptation domain. These models are represented according to the conceptual model depicted in figure 2.

We view a software system and its context as a system of interacting entities. Entities may represent applications, instances of software components making up applications,

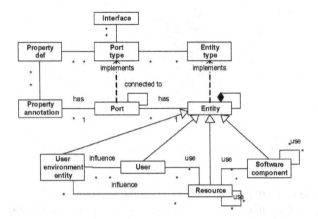

Fig. 2. Conceptual adaptation model

computing or communication resources, the user, and elements in the environment which influence the user needs. Entities interact with other entities by providing and making use of services through ports. A port represents a service offered by an entity or a service needed by an entity. Entities may be composed of smaller entities, allowing for a hierarchic structure. Distribution is modelled by dependencies of software components on resource entities representing computing devices.

To model variation points, both in the application and in the computing infrastructure, we introduce the concept of entity types. An entity type defines a class of entities with equivalent ports which may replace each other in a system.

With these concepts, we are able to model the architecture of an adaptive application as a possibly hierarchical composition of entity types, which define a class of application variants as well as a class of contexts in which these applications may operate. The latter include the computing infrastructures, on which the applications may execute. In addition to this , we need a way to enable the derivation of the software variant and its deployment on the available computing infrastructure that best fits the current user needs. Our approach is based on property annotations associated with the ports. The property annotations characterises the service provided or required by the port. For example, a property annotation might denote the response time of a service provided by an application, the latency of a communication link, the maximum latency tolerated by an application, or the noise level at the current location of the user.

Property annotations allow us to reason about how well an application variant matches its context, by comparing the properties of the services provided by the application with the properties required by the user, and the properties expressing the resource needs of the application with the property annotation describing the resources provided by the current computing infrastructure. The match to user needs is expressed in a utility function associated with each application. By default the utility function is a weighted mean of the differences between properties representing user needs and properties describing the service provided by the application, where the weights represent

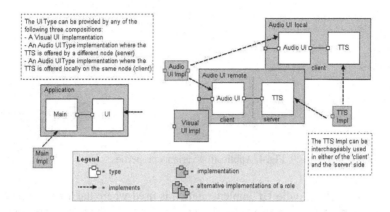

Fig. 3. Application Compositions

priorities of the user [8]. However, the developer may also provide a tailored utility function for an application. The following section shows how this model is applied to our motivating example.

3.3   Example Revisited

The architecture of our application example consists of four components namely the main logic, the visual UI impl, the audio UI impl, and the TTS components (see figure 3). The main logic component encodes the basic control loops of the application, and is responsible for the functional implementation. This component has one dependency only: the UI type. This type can be interchangeably provided by any of the three implementations: Visual component impl, the Audio UI local, and the Audio UI remote.

By using these basic components as building blocks, the application can be configured in three different compositions (i.e. variants). The three possible compositions are as follows: (i) the main logic component is connected to the visual UI component, (ii) the main logic component is connected to the audio UI component which is itself connected to a local instance of the TTS component, and (iii), the main logic component is connected to the audio UI component which is itself connected to a remote instance of the TTS component (i.e. on a server node).

Regarding properties annotations, as it is illustrated in figure 4, our application example is modeled around two main properties: the *response* and *handsfree*. At runtime, the adaptation process tries to match the required properties to the offered ones, something which is depicted by the depicted utility function. This function is expressed as a weighted average of the user's need for handsfree functionality and quick response time. The preference among the two is controlled with the c_1 and c_2 parameters (where higher c_1 indicates greater dependency on the handsfree functionality, and greater c_2 indicates higher dependency on the response time).

Concerning the UI type, again the offered and needed properties are the same as for the application, as it is shown in the figure. In the case of using the "Visual UI" implementation, the response and the handsfree properties offered take a fixed value.

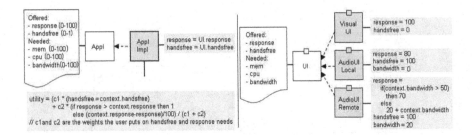

Fig. 4. Application variants properties

Similarly, when the "Audio UI"implementation is used where the TTS component is local, the two properties are also of fixed value. Furthermore, the required bandwidth is 0 (as no networking is involved). In the case of the "Audio UI" implementation where the TTS is remotely deployed though, the response is expressed by a function which expresses that the value depends on the bandwidth, which is reasonable as the networking affects the way the two nodes interact. In this case, the bandwidth is also set to a fixed value (i.e. 20) which is the minimum required.

4   Resource Management Framework

We understand a resource simply as a reusable entity in the system, that is employed to fulfill the resource request by a resource consumer. In our adaptation approach presented in the previous section, dependencies of a given application on resources are expressed through properties. Therefore, the resource management component is an indispensable component to the adaptation manager in order to enable deciding for the appropriate application variant and (re)deployment within an adaptation domain with respect to the user needs. To achieve that, the resource management framework should provide facilities for *discovering*, *monitoring*, *allocating and releasing*, and *configuring* resources.

4.1   Distributed Infrastructure Resource Model

A prerequisite for allowing the observation of resources is to model them so that their runtime behaviour is reified. Resources are modeled uniformly as special entities according to our conceptual model (see figure 2). In one hand this allows hiding the heterogeneity of the different resources and in the other hand, it facilitates their runtime management as every component instance.

As shown in figure 5, a resource may be atomic - e.g. network and computational node resources -, or composite - e.g. clusters of nodes -. A resource has a type and all resources of the same type provide the same set of services types which are qualified with a set of properties. These properties includes particularly QoS characteristics that represents the usage and the capacity of consumable resources. More precisely, we distinguish between three types of resources namely node, network and peripheral resources.

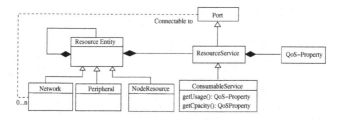

Fig. 5. Distributed infrastructure resource model

A *node resource* represents any computational node in the system that may host potential application components on behalf of the middleware using the adaptive element architecture. This resource type provides services such as memory and CPU used to execute component instances. For the particular case of adaptation domain management, one can distinguish between client (master) and server (slave) nodes. Server nodes can be viewed as grid-like computational server resources, while client nodes represent smaller (e.g. handheld) computers with fewer capabilities and additional limitations (e.g. battery and memory space) which should also be taken into account during the adaptation.

A *network resource* is fundamental to distributed infrastructures which use it to reach to and connect with different remote resources. Particularly, in our mobile setting, a handheld node may have the opportunity to use multiple network connections alternatives (WiFi, Bluetooth, GPRS, etc) between other nodes. This leads the adaptation manager to exploit and to select the appropriate network connections: for example the one with a good bandwidth, the most secure, the one that increases the availability or yet the least expensive connection. In the figure 5, a network connection may exist only between non-network resources and other resources. The implementation of such connections requires composite channel components (proxies, stubs, etc) which are not modeled in the figure. The main common services provided by a network resource are *send* and *receive* where the consumption is qualified using the *throughput* property. Depending on the underlying network technology additional properties such as those related to collision and errors sent or received and signal or noise level (wireless networks) may be considered to perform the adaptation.

A *Peripheral resource* covers the rest of the resources such as remote displays, printers and sensor devices. In our approach, these resource types are handled as application components in the sense that the adaptation manager has to discover the peripheral component services (equivalent to peripheral drivers) and then compose (i.e. connect) them with the application components following the required and provided dependencies.

In our example (see figure 4), the different needed properties of the application components properties (cpu, memory, network, etc.) are used to derive and discover all the exploitable resource types within the user adaptation domain namely the handheld device, the current media server and available networks. All these resources and the services they provide are reified through component.

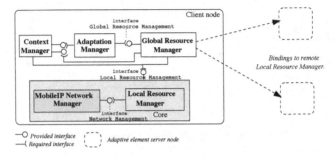

Fig. 6. Distributed resource management architecture

4.2 Distributed Resource Management Architecture

Assuming the above resource model, the resource manager provides a set of services for the exploitation and the management within an adaptation domain. Figure 6 presents the architecture of the distributed resource manager which is plugged to the adaptive element architecture presented in section 3.1. A main principle of the MADAM approach for the management of distributed resources is the separation between the Local and the Global resource manager components.

The local resource manager is part of the core middleware component. It provides a base level of manageability (access, observation and allocation) through the Local Resource Management interface of the local resources entities present in one node (either at the server or the client nodes). It also offers functionalities related to the network detection and connection management by interacting with the Network Management interface provided by the primitive MobileIP network manager component. Although this component hides the underlying heterogeneity by providing uniform resource access, its implementation depends highly on the underlying hardware resource characteristics.

The Global resource manager is only present at the client middleware node to be used by the Adaptation manager. It maintains the distributed resource model by providing a mediation interface, the Global Resource Management, that federates the access and the search for all the available and discoverable resources within an adaptation domain. The following sections present the different services provided by the these different components.

Resources discovery. The preliminary operation before performing any adaptation reasoning is the discovery of the available distributed resources and more generally of the available resource services. The adaptation manager uses the Context manager [7] component to search for remote resources and the Local resource manager to look for the locally available resources. The Context Manager supports plugging different alternative technologies such as TCP/IP, UPnP and Bluetooth for remotely discovering available resources and disseminating information across them. Furthermore, the proposed framework supports configuring the resource discovery to use either a pull or push policy. In the push policy, available resources and services are actively discovered just before an adaptation reasoning process is started. In contrast to this, the pull policy instructs the nodes to periodically disseminate their context information and at the same time always maintain a local model of the distributed context in the environment including resources. This configuration is possible because of the flexibility of the Context Manager which supports both of these strategies. Using either of these two alternatives depends on the state of the system, as the pull policy is more energy efficient (less communication) but less agile compared to the push policy.

The detection of the surrounding network resource types (WLAN, Bluetooth, WiFi, etc) is delegated to the MobileIP network component. Recall that these networks may potentially be used either to join a network (e.g. WLAN), or to be used as protocols for discovering other resources (e.g. Bluetooth devices). Another important discovery feature is the search for the different network paths between two given nodes. As already discussed, this leads the adaptation manager to select the different connections between the distributed component so that to maximise the user utility.

Resources allocation/releasing. Resources sharing between different adaptive applications and potentially between many adaptation domains involve mainly reserving and releasing operations. These operations are provided at both levels the local resource manager and the global resource manager components interfaces.

The Adaptation Manager calls such operation after the planning has been performed, the required resources types (including remote nodes) have been selected, and the amount of resources has been calculated. This operation invoked on the Global Resource Manager uses then the local resource managers of the different remote resources for the registration of the allocation or the releasing resulted from the new selected configuration. The Adaptation manager exploits resources information provided during the discovery, including theirs location (e.g. IP adresses), to establish remote bindings with the remote Local resource managers provided interfaces. For that, a binding framework (see deliverable D2.3 [3]) similar to the one presented in [9] has been adopted. The local resource manager maintains the different reservations per resource service and client ID. Including the client ID allows the local resource manager to release all the reserved resources for a given client in case of the client node, i.e. the mobile user, becomes unreachable.

Resources observation. The Local resource manager allows adding and removing resource listeners so that they are notified of resource usage changes that may trigger the adaptation process. The context manager is responsible for the management of the pool of context listeners, including resource listeners, and for delegating these changes to the adaptation manager.

Network management. The network management facilities are provided by the the MobileIP network component tailored for mobile mobile in IP networks. This component provides mainly operations for seeking for surrounding networks as already discussed and also the management of the connections (and disconnections) to (or from) a given network. When a given network has been selected, the adaptation manager connects to that network. Conversely, if the node was already connected to one different network type, then the adaptation manager should disconnect the node from this network before switching to the newly selected one. Note that in the current specification and implementation of the MobileIP Network Manager, a node is only connected to one network type at any given time.

Resources configuration. Our framework exhibits also configuration methods that allow setting new properties values to certain resources. In some MADAM scenarios (see D1.2 [3]), some adaptations are simply implemented by tuning resource parameters.

5   Distribution Adaptation Reasoning

When replanning is triggered, the adaptation manager uses the application model, the user needs model and the resource model to select the combination of application variants and their deployment on the available resources that best fits the current context. This involves the execution of the following pseudo algorithm:

---

v: represents an application variant from the search space V. It associates for each component type an implementation and a node where to be deployed.
U: is the utility function that takes as input the variant properties and the different contexts information including resources.

1: **begin**
2:     reserve and get resources // *interaction with the Global resource manager*
3:         **for each** variant v from V
4:             aggregate resource needs of v
5:             **if** the resource needs of V can be satisfied with available resources **then**
6:                 compute the utility $U(v)$
7:                 **if** $U(v)$ is better that the utility of the best variant set found so far **then**
8:                 keep v
9:     release and allocate resources // *interaction with the Global resource manager*
10: **end**

The resource needs of a variant set are expressed as dependencies on resource types, and in an adaptation domain there may be several instances of each type. For example there may be several servers and several networks with different capacities. Therefore the adaptation manager must also decide a mapping. As long as resource needs are fixed, i.e. given as constants, this is trivial. All mappings that satisfy the resource needs are valid and have the same utility, so the first one found that satisfies the needs is selected.

However, fixed resource needs is not always an adequate model of an application variant (or component. In many cases a range given as a minimum and a maximum amount is a better model. The variant needs at least the minimum amount to execute properly, but if more resources are available the provided Qos will improve until the maximum amount. Allocating more resources than the maximum amount does not improve the provided QoS. The MADAM application modelling support such open specification of resource needs.

In the presence of open resource needs, the utility of a variant set i) depends on how its components are deployed on alternative nodes of the same type, ii) on how remote connections are mapped on available networks, and iii) how resources are distributed between the components deployed on each node and the connections mapped on each network.

Since on the class of computing infrastructures that we are targeting, cpu and network resources tend to be distributed between competing programs on a fair share basis and memory on a first come first serve basis, all outside our control, we have to base the computation of the utility on an educated guess of how resources will actually be allocated.

6   Implementation Status

The resource and the adaptation framework presented in this paper have been implemented as part of the MADAM adaptation middleware. The MADAM middleware is programmed in Java and runs both on Windows XP on ordinary PCs and on Windows Mobile on HP iPAQ handheld computers. The monitoring and control of network resources (i.e. the MobileIP Network Manager component) is based on the Birdstep[2] Mobile IP product which supports most of the existing networks. The middleware is being used in the development of two pilot applications by the industrial partners of Madam.

The Middleware can be started in either master or slave mode. Slave nodes basically only manage resources and monitor other context information and perform reconfiguration operations in response to reconfiguration requests from a master. Adaptation domains are formed by nodes sending regular multicast messages informing potential neighbours about their presence. This limits an adaptation domain to a local area network. The communication between the master and its slaves is based on RMI.

The adaptation scenario used in the example is present in both pilots, along with a number of other scenarios exercising both distribution and other forms of adaptation. A previous version of the middleware, without support for distribution adaptation but built on the same adaptation approach, has been used successfully in several pilot applications and confirms that the general approach is feasable and quite satisfactory (see deliverables D5.2 and D6.2 [3]).

7   Discussion and Related Work

What makes our work different is primarily the scope of the targeted adaptation in a mobile environment and the variability-based approach used to implement these adaptations. As a result, the proposed resource management framework is tailored towards offering specific functionalities to enable distributed adaptation planning in the MADAM middleware. In addition, the proposed architetcure is flexible and configurable. Firstly, the resource management is not bound to a particular resource type but deals with arbitrary resource types. Indeed the presented resource model is uniform and generic, implying that there is no inherent limitation in the resource model with respect to the range of resource types the resource model can represent. The properties which characterise these resource types enable the adaptation reasoning to affect and compose resource

---

[2] www.birdstep.com

types to a given application components so that the required behaviour is preserved. Secondly, the modularity of the resource management framework makes it configurable in the sense that its components may be deployed and configured to handle different requirements. For example, when there is no requirment for distribution (standalone mode), the resource management framework can be configured with the Local Resource Manager only, as in this case there is no need for the Global Resource Manager and the MobileIP Network Manager. In this configuration, the Adaptation Manager is able to locally adapt the application without involving distributed third parties. Finally, another token of flexibility of our framework is that it can be configured to support both push and pull resource discovery strategies.

Within the context of mobile environment, several systems and middlewares have been proposed to target the management of the adaptiveness of mobile applications. However, from our knowledge, most of them either are centralised or do not provide an explicit architecture of the resource management eventhough they support distribution (e.g. Aura [10]). For example, [11] proposes a resource model that is the basis of a framework for the development and deployment of adaptable applications. This resource model is used to model and declare the resources required by an application and the ones supplied by the hosting environment. To reason on the goodness of a resource set allocated to satisfy a given adaptation a utility function is used as in our approach. While this work target similar adaptations, the proposed model does not support distribution and does not address the management concern. Also, application resources needs are specified for each possible adaptation. This constitues another limitation of this model to be viable in our work since compositional and planning-based adaptation may lead to a huge number of possible adaptations.

In the context of Grid computing, many active researches have focused on designing resource management architectures such as Globus [12] and GridKit [13]. Theirs approach exhibits some similarities with ours in the sense that they distinguish between the local and the global resource managers for the management of distributed resources. Furthermore, from an architectural point of view, our framework has similarities with the GridKit architecture [13] which also proposes a flexible and configurable framework. However, all these systems do not target and consider adaptation types related to mobile applications such as those related to the resource limitations of handheld device and the support of multiple network connection alternatives between different nodes.

It is to be clarified that the computational complexity of distributed (re)deployment is not addressed in this paper. It is well known that this problem is NP-Hard [14] and therefore scalability is a serious concern. However, so far, our experience indicates that the mobile applications and environments that we target are sufficiently constrained both in term of the number of software variation points and the number of nodes and adaptations within an adaptation domain, that acceptable performance can be achieved. Indeed, for example the complexity – i.e. the adaptation reasoning – of our pilot application still inside what we found could be handled in our experiments with the previous centralised version (1000 variants gave adaptation times around 1 s). However, the "heartbeat" messages and the RMI calls for communicating between the master and the slaves seems to be expensive and particularly from the handheld device side. Therefore, further code optimisations and experiments are needed to improve the current implementation. Furthermore, we are also considering other technologies than RMI for new experiments.

8 Conclusion

In this paper we have discussed a general approach for distributed adaptation and subsequently a distributed resource model and management tailored for deployment of adaptive services in a mobile environment. Furthermore, we have presented middleware level mechanisms neccesary for maintaining an up-to-date model of the resources available in the run-time environment of a mobile device. The resulting resource framework has been realized as part of the MADAM planning-based middleware. The framework is configurable and extensible and can be customised and tailored to specific needs through support for middleware configuration. Furthermore, this framework identifies and covers new functionalities and features related to mobile computing which are not common and not covered in the classical grid-like resource management. The use of the resource management in adaptation planning was demonstrated through a real adaptive application that has been implemented on top of the MADAM middleware.

As part of the ongoing projects, two research directions are considered. Firstly, we plan to extend our approach to cover adaptation in ubiquitous computing environments. Secondly, we plan to study the possibilities of projecting and porting the proposed adaptation approach into the context of service oriented computing. This leads us to address the problem of decentralised planning in the presence of many autonomous adaptation domains. This will most likely also require the consideration of more elaborate resource management features that handle complex planning approaches such as those based on market-based and learning automata mechanisms.

Acknowledgements

This work is part of the MADAM project and the authors would like to thank all involved partners.

References

1. Amundsen, S.L., Lund, K., Eliassen, F.: Utilising alternative application configurations in context- and QoS-aware mobile middleware. In: Eliassen, F., Montresor, A. (eds.) DAIS 2006. LNCS, vol. 4025, pp. 228–241. Springer, Heidelberg (2006)
2. Poladian, V., Sousa, J., Garlan, D., Shaw, M.: Dynamic configuration of resource-aware services. In: Proceedings of the 26th International Conference on Software Engineering (ICSE) (2004)
3. Madam Consortium: Mobility and ADaptation enAbling Middleware. Delivrable are open here http://www.ist-madam.org/consortium.html
4. Floch, J., Hallsteinsen, S., Stav, E., Eliassen, F., Lund, K., Gjrven, E.: Beyond design time: using architecture models for runtime adaptability. IEEE Software (2006)
5. Bruneton, E., Coupaye, T., Leclercq, M., Quema, V., Stefani, J.B.: The fractal component model and its support in java: Experiences with auto-adaptive and reconfigurable systems. Softw. Pract. Exper. 36(1112), 1257–1284 (2006)

6. Coulson, G., Blair, G., Grace, P., Joolia, A., Lee, K., Ueyama, J.: A component model for building systems software. In: Proceedings of IASTED Software Engineering and Applications (SEA'04) Cambridge, MA, USA

7. Mikalsen, M., Paspallis, N.J., Floch, E.S., Papadopoulos, G.A., Ruiz, P.A.: Putting context in context: The role and design of context management in a mobility and adaptation enabling middleware. In: 7th International Conference on Mobile Data Management (MDM'06), Nara, Japan, IEEE Computer, Washington, DC (2006)

8. Alia, M., Eide, V.S.W., Paspallis, N., Eliassen, F., Hallsteinsen, S., Papadopoulos, G.A.: A utility-based adaptivity model for mobile applications. In: The IEEE International Symposium on Ubisafe Computing (UbiSafe07), IEEE Computer Society Press, Washington, DC (2007)

9. Parlavantzas, C.G., Blair, G.: An extensible binding framework for component-based middleware. In: Proceedings of 7th international conference on enterprise distributed objects computing, IEEE computer society, New York (2003)

10. Sousa, J., Garlan, D.: Aura: An architectural framework for user mobility in ubiquitous computing environments (2002)

11. Mancinelli, F., Inverardi, P.: A resource model for adaptable applications. In: SEAMS '06. Proceedings of the 2006 international workshop on Self-adaptation and self-managing systems, pp. 9–15. ACM Press, New York (2006)

12. The Globus Project : Resource management: The globus perspective, presentation at globusword, available at http://www.globus.org/ (2003)

13. Cai, W., Coulson, G., Grace, P., Blair, G.S., Mathy, L., Yeung, W.K.: The gridkit distributed resource management framework. In: EGC, pp. 786–795 (2005)

14. Musunoori, S.B., Horn, G., Eliassen, F., Alia, M.: On the challenge of allocating service based applications in a grid environment. In: Proceedings of the International Conference on Autonomic and Autonomous Systems, vol. 43, IEEE Computer Society Press, Los Alamitos (2006)

DOLCLAN – Middleware Support for Peer-to-Peer Distributed Shared Objects

Jakob E. Bardram and Martin Mogensen

Department of Computer Science, University of Aarhus
Aabogade 34, DK–8200 Aarhus N., Denmark
{bardram, spider}@daimi.au.dk

Abstract. Contemporary object-oriented programming seeks to enable distributed computing by accessing remote objects using blocking remote procedure calls. This technique, however, suffers from several drawbacks because it relies on the assumption of stable network connections and synchronous method invocations. In this paper we present an approach to support distributed programming, which rely on local object replicas keeping themselves synchronized using an underlying peer-to-peer infrastructure. We have termed our approach *Peer-to-peer Distributed Shared Objects* (PDSO). This PDSO approach has been implemented in the DOLCLAN framework. An evaluation demonstrates that DOLCLAN can be utilized to create a real distributed collaborative system for ad-hoc collaboration in hospitals, which demonstrates that the approach can support the creation of non-trivial distributed applications for pervasive computing.

1 Introduction

Support for distributed computing in contemporary production OO languages is based on the remote-procedure call (RPC) paradigm [8] where methods on single-copy objects are accessed remotely from other objects. Both Java RMI and .NET Remoting are examples of this approach. A fundamental challenge to this paradigm is its inherent assumption of a reliable infrastructure. Object registration and lookup is primarily done through initialization, since remote object invocation assumes that objects stay on a stable host machine with reliable networking connections. Remote object invocation is furthermore done synchronously with blocking method calls. When programming applications for pervasive computing environments these assumptions do no longer hold. Such an infrastructure is completely different, consisting of a heterogeneous set of more or less stable host devices with intermitted network connections. Using RPC, RMI or similar under these circumstances leads to highly unstable applications, unless the programmer goes through a lot of work of manually handling all sorts of networking and runtime exceptions.

In order to provide a more resilient programming environment for this unstable runtime infrastructure we propose a new approach for distributed programming, which rely on local object replicas keeping themselves synchronized using an underlying peer-to-peer infrastructure. We have termed our approach *Peer-to-peer Distributed Shared Objects* (PDSO), which has been implemented in the DOLCLAN framework. In this approach, each participating peer maintains a local copy of the object and executes

J. Indulska and K. Raymond (Eds.): DAIS 2007, LNCS 4531, pp. 119–132, 2007.

processes that keep these replicas coordinated in real time. This approach has a range of advantages. First, it keeps applications responsive because the applications are much more robust with respect to network latency. Second, applications can continue to run when disconnected from the network. Third, computational and network load is distributed across the whole network of clients and is no longer tied to the machine hosting the remote object. Fourth, finding and joining a network may be simplified since all participating clients can function as the gateway to the network. There are, however, also a range of drawbacks to this approach, mainly associated with the overhead of distributing and managing the placement, synchronization, and replication of data, as well as handling the underlying communication technology and topology. The purpose of DOLCLAN is to help the programmer handle this real-time object synchronization of distributed objects.

The main contribution of DOLCLAN is a novel peer-to-peer distribution mechanism for object sharing which is especially suited for the creation of collaborative applications in a pervasive computing environment. This object sharing mechanism provides optimistic synchronization strategies, easy deployment of distributed applications, and support for different delivery guarantees – all of which can be accessed by the application developers, if needed.

1.1 Related Work

Different suggestions to improve on the shortcomings of existing RPC-style interaction with remote single-copy objects in RMI, CORBA, .NET Remoting, and DCOM have been suggested. For example, asynchronous RPC [30,18], and CORBA Event and Notification Services [22]. One specific approach to improve Java RMI is to support dynamic caching of shared objects on the accessing nodes, as done in Javanaise [13]. Research has also been done within asynchronous method invocation [18,30], tuple spaces [10,19], or more generally with publish-subscribe interaction styles [21]. All of these approaches mitigate the challenges of intermitted network connections, and lack of scalability and performance in RPC. But they do not support object replication and reconciling, and therefore does not allow the application to continue to access and update the distributed objects while disconnected from the network. In certain tuple spaces, a *global virtual data structure* is achieved by letting each device hold a local copy of a tuple space which is transparently shared with the tuple space of the connected devices [23,9]. By accessing its local tuple space, each component has efficiently access to the global tuple space. Hence, actions that are perceived as local actually has global effects. This approach is similar to distributed objects but does not as such support distributed object-oriented programming, and is not designed to disconnected work since it does not provide support for reconciling work done while disconnected.

Orca [4,3,2] is an object based programming language and distributed shared memory system (DSM). Orca is based on distributed coherent objects, e.g. Orca does not invalidate objects on write, but propagates the write to all copies of the object. This is done by sending all writes to a primary copy of an object called *the object manager*, which then updates all copies. Coherence is ensured via a two-phase commit protocol and by sending operations using totally ordered group communication, so all updates are executed in the same order at all machines. To a certain respect, our work extends the principles of Orca, including using a write-update protocol rather than a write-invalidate protocol to address the core consistency challenge in object replication. Our infrastructure also relies on totally ordered group communication. Our work, however, is different in at least two ways. First, we rely on direct object-to-object data synchronization and do not use specialized object managers counting read and write operations. This significantly simplifies program development and deployment. Second, our language support is part of the widely used C# language and does not require a specialized language like Orca.

Globe [1,15] is an object oriented framework for developing wide area distributed applications using distributed shared objects (DSO). On the one hand, the Globe DSO lets the application programmer concentrate on implementing business logic and not worry about distribution and communication. On the other hand, Globe recognizes the need to be able to implement object specific policies on issues such as distribution, replication, and concurrency controls. By implementing a 'replication sub-object', the programmer can create a specific replication policy. Depending on the implementations of the sub-objects, the local object will function as a proxy object, forwarding requests to a real object. Alternatively, the local object can carry out calculations on a local copy of the object state and – depending on the implementation of the replication sub-object – the new state can be propagated to other instances of the distributed shared object. This possibility to override default functionality by implementing specific sub-objects yields a flexible, highly extensible, and scalable framework for creating distributed applications. The approach, however, comes with a huge overhead for the programmer who has to design and implement replication policies in the replication sub-objects.

Our work is situated within this line of research on distributed shared objects and makes contributions primarily in three aspects: (i) we provide language support for a widely used OO language (as compared to special languages like Orca), (ii) we have a simple peer-to-peer distribution and synchronization mechanism for shared objects, and (iii) we support an optimistic synchronization strategy based on user-defined merging methods in write-update protocols.

2 Peer-to-Peer Distributed Object Sharing

The fundamental principles behind the design of our *peer-to-peer distributed shared object* approach are:

Physical distribution. Instead of viewing a distributed object as an entity running on a single host with others accessing it remotely, we physically distribute a copy of the object to all hosts using this object in an application. Hence, applications access and use objects as local objects which ensures fast responsiveness. Objects are distributed on creation (remote instantiation) and removed from the local address space on deletion (distributed garbage collection).

Synchronized objects. The state of the distributed shared object is kept synchronized in real time, if possible. Hence, state changes are propagated to all object replicas. State synchronization is handled by the underlying infrastructure, but the objects themselves are involved in potential conflict resolution, using domain specific conflict resolution algorithms.

Peer-to-peer update. Physically distributed objects rely on a peer-to-peer – or object-to-object – synchronization strategy. Hence, no central entities like an object broker or an object registry are involved in object registration or lookup. Each object is responsible for looking up and synchronizing with its replicas. This principle makes distributed programming simple from the developers point of view since there are no configuration overhead associated with the development and deployment of a distributed application.

Responsive. Objects are used in highly interactive applications and needs to embody a fast update protocol. This rules out pessimistic concurrency control which typically uses some kind of distributed transactional scheme [27,26] or distributed locks [17].

Distribution-aware. Objects are distribution-aware. This means that a shared object must be declared as distributed, must handle potential conflict resolution, and must consider the kind of delivery guarantees wanted in the network transport layer. These issues are normally shielded from the application programmer but, as explained above, we deliberately want these things to surface in the language support for distributed programming.

The principles involved in peer-to-peer distributed object sharing is illustrated in figure 1, showing a set of distributed objects with replicas in four different address spaces (A1–A4), using object-to-object communication pathways to keep the replicas synchronized and sending remote instantiation and garbage collection events.

The main idea is that a distributed object, called a Peer-to-peer Distributed Shared Object (PDSO) consists of several local replicas that keep their state synchronized.

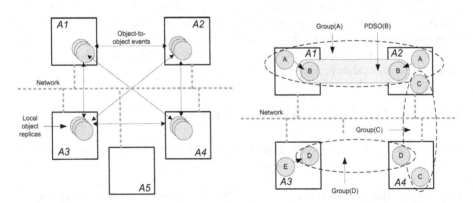

Fig. 1. A set of peer-to-peer distributed shared objects (PDSO) distributed over four address spaces (A1–A4). Each address space holds a local replica of the object which is synchronized by object-to-object eventing. Address space A5 does not currently participate in the object sharing but may join one or more of the objects.

Fig. 2. Five PDSOs (A–E) distributed over four address spaces (A1–A4). Each address space hold a local replica of the PDSOs in the groups the peer is member of.

Each local replica is identified by an Object Identifier (OID). A PDSO consists of the set of local replicas with the same IOD. A set of PDSOs can be tied together by use of distributed variables; we call such a set a group.

To be more precise, we are using the following terms:

OID Object Identifier. The OID is used to name a single instance of a local object replica. Several local object replicas can have the same OID, but not within the same namespace.

$PDSO$ Peer-to-peer Distributed Shared Object. A set of local object replicas, that keep their state synchronized. A $PDSO$ is defined as the set of local object replicas named by the same OID. I.e. $PDSO(s) = \{local\ replicas\ x | OID(x) = s\}$

$Group$ A set of $PDSO$s, defined by the transitive closure of a specified $PDSO\ x$. I.e. all PDSOs in the object graph that can be reached from x.
$Group(PDSO(x)) = \{PDSO(y) | there\ is\ a\ path$
$from\ PDSO(x)\ to\ PDSO(y)\ in\ the\ object\ graph\}$.

Figure 2 shows five PDSOs distributed over four address spaces. The PDSOs are named A, B, C, D, and E respectively. Each distributed object is comprised of several local replicas, all named with the same object identifier (OID). The local replicas comprising the PDSO named B have been highlighted. Also shown in the figure are three groups, namely $Group(A)$, $Group(C)$, and $Group(D)$. The groups are the transitive closure of the named PDSO. $Group(A)$ is therefore comprised of $PDSO(A)$ and $PDSO(B)$, whereas $Group(D)$ equals $PDSO(D)$ because the edges in the object graph are directed. Notice also that two peers, address space A2 and A4, are members of more than one group. Groups are used as a scoping mechanism enabling peers to join only a subset of the object graph.

With respect to delivery guarantees from the transport layer we make a key differentiation between what we have termed *accountable* and *ephemeral* events [5]. In replicated collaborative architectures concurrency control between events on distributed clients is absolutely central in order to maintain correct behavior of the distributed system [24]. We use the term 'accountable' for this kind of distributed events, because the system needs to be accountable for the correctness and timing of these events in order to create a well-behaved collaborative system. Examples of accountable events are the classical text insert, move, and delete commands in collaborative editors or the state changes in general purpose frameworks like Corona [26] or GroupKit [25,12]. An IP-based infrastructure would use TCP or reliable multicast to distribute such events. There are, however, a range of other kinds of events which are not subject to the same kind of accountability. Such events are typically absolute values, independent of previous and subsequent events, and may even be missing or dismissed if needed. We call these events 'ephemeral' because they are short-lived and transient. Examples of such events are telepointer events, voice events, and other collaborative awareness events like the ones in the MAUI Toolkit [14]. An IP-based infrastructure would typically use multicast datagrams to distribute such events.

We argue that giving the application developer access to these low-level transport issues in distributed computing is important since he can make appropriate judgments on the choice of delivery guarantees based on application-specific concerns. Such concerns are not present in contemporary language support for remote objects, like Java RMI, CORBA, .NET Remoting, and DCOM[1].

2.1 An Example

The PDSOs can be used to construct a model for a distributed application, by connecting objects via distributed fields within the objects. Such distributed fields can be declared by using either the *accountable* or *ephemeral* keywords, supported by the language constructs implemented to support the PDSO scheme[2]. A simple example could be a model for a distributed eater or Pacman game. The game consists of a game controller and a game model, which will be used to distribute state between the participating peers. The model is comprised of a game name, a score, a position of the eater and a list of stones visible on the board. Figure 3 shows the model represented as an UML diagram.

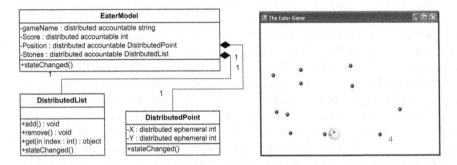

Fig. 3. UML diagram showing the presented part of the EaterModel

Fig. 4. 'The Eater Game' showing the Pacman, stones, and the score

The game's name and the score is modeled as distributed accountable properties. This enables us to intercept flow control every time the fields are set, and notify the view and the other participating peers of the change. The position of the eater is modeled by the `DistributedPoint` class, which contains two distributed ephemeral properties. Each property corresponds to the X and the Y position of the eater. The choice of using ephemeral variables emphasizes speed of delivery rather than delivery guarantees in changes of the eater position. Finally, the model contains a list of stones, which are visible on the game board. The stones are kept in a `DistributedList`, which is a list created using distributed accountable variables inside PDSOs for holding satellite data.

When a peer starts an instance of the eater game, it will first obtain a local replica of the `EaterModel` and the PDSOs in the transitive closure of this PDSO. After joining

---

[1] It is, however, interesting to note that in SUN RPC the implementer has the choice of using either UDP or TCP for transporting remote procedure calls and for broadcasting remote procedure calls [8].

[2] The language constructs is beyond the scope of this paper, but has been presented elsewhere [20].

the game, the state of the model will be replicated between the different local replicas. This is done, by assigning new values to the distributed variables. If a peer for instance moves the eater, new values will be assigned to the distributed properties X and Y in the DistributedPoint object. The infrastructure will intercept flow control and propagate the new values around the network. When the new values reaches the designated local replicas in the other address spaces, it will be set on the corresponding objects. This will cause the objects to fire the stateChanged event on the objects, which in turn, will fire the stateChanged events on the local replicas of the EaterModel and the different views can be updated. The same is true for changes in any stone or the score. Notice also, that if any of the distributed variables is assigned the null value, this value will also be propagated around the network. When this is done, the object which was previously referenced by the distributed variable might become subject to garbage collection.

If a peer becomes disconnected for a period of time, subsequently reconnecting to the network, the state of the peer and the state of the network might diverge. In such a case domain specific conflict resolution methods, specified by the programmer, will be used to handle conflicts bringing the network back to a consistent state.

3 Infrastructure Support

The proposed concepts presented have been implemented in the DOLCLAN[3] infrastructure [20], which uses a pure peer-to-peer architecture and supports object distribution, state synchronization, object discovery, peer joining, event ordering, and concurrency control. This section describes the system and network architecture (section 3.1) and the architecture supporting this infrastructure on each participating peer holding the object replicas (section 3.2).

3.1 System and Network Architecture

Communication between peers can be carried out in several ways. Events and messages can be either unicasted or multicasted, and both reliable and unreliable communication channels can be utilized. In our current implementation we have chosen to utilize the possibilities of multicasting since many peers will have to receive the same information. Point-to-point connections are possible but would require a quadratic number of unicast connections between peers or the utilization of a sophisticated routing scheme, which would impose an extra performance penalty and delay messages. Even though many peers will have to receive the same information, this is not true for all peers. Therefore the infrastructure has a control channel for reaching all peers and individual channels for smaller groups.

Peer-to-peer Distributed Shared Objects require three things of the underlying system infrastructure: (i) service discovery which enables a peer to find existing PDSOs, (ii) peer joining which enables a peer to join a group and get the state synchronized, and (iii) synchronous object state replication amongst connected peers.

---

[3] Distributed Objects in Loose Coupled Local Area Networks.

Service Discovery. To find other peers in the network, the joining peer multicasts a HELLO message on the control channel. This indicates that the peer is looking for another peer which can help it join a group. If one or more peers exist on the network able to serve the new peer, these peers reply with a HELLO_ACK message unicasted to the joining peer. The message contains information about how to reach the sending peer and also information about which channels the events for the shared objects are propagated on. This enables the new peer to start listening for events on the event channels while the state is synchronized via an existing peer. The joining peer now chooses the peer from which it first receives a reply as its *serving peer*. It is possible to pick any peer replying to the HELLO message, as all peers replying will have the same state. The picked peer will with high probability be a peer residing close to the joining peer in terms of network latency, thereby optimizing on network latency overhead in the synchronization of the new peer.

Peer joining. After the service discovery phase, the joining peer will need to synchronize the state between itself and one or more groups. The joining peer may or may not contain state of its own state.

If the joining peer contains no state information, then it needs to obtain the shared state from the serving peer. This is done by a process called 'Just-in-time-eventing' (JITE) where the joining peer first receives a snapshot of the replicated state while collecting events from the other peers during the process. After setting the state of the new peer to the snapshot, the peer also commits the collected events in the correct order [11,29]. If the events were not collected, then the snapshot approach needs to stop any work on the shared object until they were synchronized. This would greatly reduce the responsiveness of the collaborative applications using the infrastructure.

If the joining peer contains state information then the states must somehow be merged. Such a joining peer with state information may be a peer which has been disconnected for a period of time while the user has continued working. The merging or conflict resolution of state based on the local state and the state from the network is highly domain specific. In some cases it makes sense to use the most recent state, in other cases it makes sense to merge the two states, and sometimes the merge is based on the semantics of the application. The joining peer obtains the network state (using the JITE approach) and this state is then given to a conflict resolution method implemented by the application programmer. This enables the programmer to create application specific conflict resolution algorithms.

Synchronous Object State Replication. Synchronous object state replication keeps the replicated objects synchronized, while peers are modifying them. The design should consider basic state change situations, but also be able to handle situations, where two or more peers modify the same component concurrently.

In order to reduce implementation complexity, maximize end-user responsiveness, and minimize communication overhead, the infrastructure utilizes an optimistic concurrency control mechanism based on absolute state events. Event ordering and concurrency control is managed by an extended version of the Lamport clock algorithms [16]. The algorithm uses a logical clock and adds the identity of the sending peer process into the event. Each event is stamped with a timestamp consisting of (time, peer, process) which eliminates the possibility that two events should be stamped with the same logical timestamp. When using this timestamp on each state change event, consistency on fields can be ensured by applying all events with a higher timestamp than the latest committed. If an event is received out of order, the event is simply dismissed. Note that dismissing of events, that is received out of order, will have no influence on the state of the object because only absolute (and not delta) values are sent.

The biggest problem with this design is the case where an event message disappears in the network because of unreliable communication channels. This problem could be eliminated, by using a reliable protocol, but this might imply a huge performance penalty due to the increased communication, as for instance the case with reliable multicast. Sometimes an application may need delivery guarantees and hence pay this penalty, and in other cases the application might not care about reliable delivery but is more focused on speedy delivery. This is precisely the difference between accountable and ephemeral events as introduced earlier and in Bardram et al. [5].

3.2 Peer Architecture

Figure 5 illustrates the peer architecture which consists of three layers. The *application layer* contains the application which is typically programmed according to the model-view-controller pattern. Part of the model uses distributed shared objects, which are located in the *distributed model layer*. This layer contains the distributed part of the model, which consists of distributed objects and nothing else.

The *communication layer* implements the network architecture described in section 3.1 and is responsible for the distribution of state changes to other peers and for managing incoming state changes. This layer is also responsible for the communication between peers holding replicas of distributed objects. This layer keeps track of communication (I/O), event ordering, naming services, and the state of the distributed objects.

Closest to the physical network there are three *I/O Controllers* controlling one form of communication each: TCP unicast, ordinary IP multicast, and reliable multicast. A controller is capable of sending a message to a specified connection point and listening for incoming messages from other devices. The *Communication Controller* manages the I/O controllers and new I/O controllers can be added to support other network protocols.

Management of state change is done by three processes. The *JITE Controller* controls the Just-In-Time-Eventing mechanism explained above. The JITE controller handles a state change event if such an event arrives and no object that corresponds to the event is bound in the naming service. When a new object is created from a remote location, the object is handed to the JITE controller which checks if it contains any events that should be applied to the object. If such events exist they will be applied and the state of the object is up to date. The *Naming Service* is responsible for mapping distributed objects to names and names to distributed objects and it contains methods for looking up an object by name and vice versa. The naming service is used by the distributed object controller. The *Logical Time Tracker* is responsible for keeping track of the logical time by updating the time on both incoming and on outgoing messages.

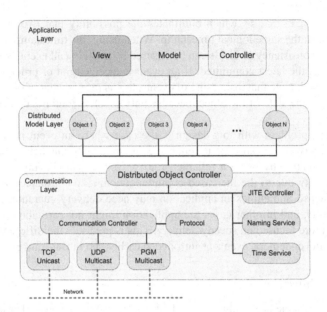

Fig. 5. The architecture of each peer (host) participating in peer-to-peer distributed object sharing. The architecture is divided into three layers: application layer, distributed object model layer, and the communication layer.

The *Distributed Object Controller* works as a facade between distributed objects and the communication layer. When a state change occurs in the distributed objects, the controller will propagate this change to the other participating peers. When a state change arrives from a remote peer, the controller updates the distributed object.

4   Implementation and Evaluation

The infrastructure supporting the proposed PDSOs and a pre-compiler enabling the language support has been implemented. The implementation has been subject to extensive evaluation including completeness of expressiveness, complexity of use, run-time performance, and concept utility. Due to the focus of this paper, presenting the concepts of PDSOs, we shall only present a part of the evaluation focusing on performance and concept utility.

4.1   Performance

Performance evaluation of the DOLCLAN infrastructure has been reported elsewhere [20]. This shows that the infrastructure performs well – both with regard to response time and memory footprint. In this context, we would however like to highlight one particular performance measurement, namely the performance penalty introduced by initiating the propagation of a variable value change.

Figure 6 shows the performance penalty introduced by initiating the propagation of a variable value change. The test measures the time it takes before variable changes have

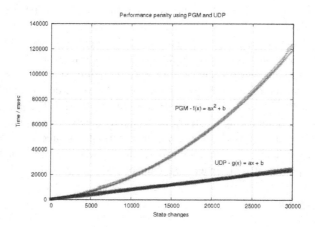

Fig. 6. Performance penalty as a function of number of variable state changes. The graph shows the time it takes to push the state change event into the network asynchronously.

been sent asynchronously into the network. Note that this test does not say anything about the time it takes before the remote peers have received the changes. As reliable multicast protocol we used the Pragmatic General Multicast Protocol (PGM) specified in RFC 3208 [28]. It is clear from the diagram, that there is a significant difference between using reliable and unreliable multicast, even if all communication is done asynchronously. The performance penalty using unreliable multicast has been matched as a linear relationship, while the performance penalty using reliable multicast has been matched with a polynomial relationship. One of the arguments in this paper, is that the application developer should be aware of such differences and have the possibility to make the decisions. This test supports our idea of the need to distinguish between ephemeral and accountable field types.

4.2 Utility

The PDSO concept and the infrastructure described in this paper, has been used to create support for ad-hoc collaboration in the activity-based computing (ABC) framework [5,6]. Previously, the ABC framework was designed according to a client-server architecture and collaboration took place via the activity server. Now, peer-to-peer collaboration can be initiated between two peers with no access to an activity server and activities are replicated on the local peers. This has yielded a higher responsiveness in real-time collaboration and has created support for disconnected work.

In the ABC-framework collaboration is modeled as a number of activities referencing a number of services. The activities represent work tasks and the services represents applications used in the work tasks. To enable ad-hoc collaboration, we used the existing model, but turned the local representation of an activity into a distributed object containing several distributed slots. The same was done with the local representation of a service. This instantly gave us the communication and synchronization between the different participating peers for free.

The effort of extending the ABC framework to support ad-hoc collaboration was limited, counting days rather than weeks or months. Moreover, it showed that the PDSO concepts and the supporting infrastructure are well suited to support the creation of more complex distributed application tasks that just a simple game. The technology is now part of the ABC framework and we are currently creating support for activity-based computing in a hospital setting, by integrating to a Picture, Archiving, and Communication System (PACS) and an Electronic Health Record (EHR). The plan is to deploy the ABC Framework including the distributed shared objects in a hospital. The support for ad-hoc collaboration implemented using the distributed shared objects will enable clinicians to initiate a real-time collaborative session between a surgeon in the operating room and an expert located elsewhere in the hospital.

5 Conclusions

One of the key features of the peer-to-peer distributed shared objects presented in this paper is their support for ad hoc object sharing in loosely coupled networks. The peer-to-peer – or object-to-object – discovery and synchronization makes it simple to create, lookup, and join the distributed objects with their shared data. You can simply look up the object, join it, get a replica, and start to use it as another local object. This indeed makes distributed programming simple while maintaining awareness about the distributed nature of the application.

Furthermore, to support distribution in a pervasive computing environment, the PDSO infrastructure supports intermitted network connections. A peer continues to work while disconnecting and may re-join the network and the PDSOs set of objects later. This applies equally well for smaller network interruptions and for disconnected use. In the former case the user would most likely not even notice the small glitch since all distributed objects are available locally. In the latter case, the user is able to continue working on his local object model and upon reconnect he can re-join the shared network model potentially being involved in some conflict resolution.

The notion of distributed shared objects have been receiving increasing attention because this approach addresses some of the core challenges in existing RPC-based remote method invocation schemes, and it holds the potential to ensure large-scale distribution while ensuring local responsiveness in applications. This paper have suggested one approach to create infrastructure support for such distributed shared objects and should hence be seen as one contribution in this line of research. In our future work we plan to improve on the infrastructure, especially focusing on making support beyond a local area network, and to continue making pervasive computing applications using these distributed shared objects in C#. The latter would also include creating support for e.g. the Pocket PC platform in the .NET compact framework.

Acknowledgments

Jonathan Bunde-Pedersen provided valuable feedback on the ideas and language support presented in this paper. This work is partly funded by the Competence Centre ISIS Katrinebjerg. The ABC project is funded by the Danish Research Council under the NABIIT program.

References

1. Bakker, A., van Steen, M., Tanenbaum, A.S.: From remote objects to physically distributed objects. In: FTDCS '99: Proceedings of the 7th IEEE Workshop on Future Trends of Distributed Computing Systems, p. 47. IEEE Computer Society, Washington, DC (1999)
2. Bal, H.E., Bhoedjang, R., Hofman, R., Jacobs, C., Langendoen, K., Ruhl, T., Kaashoek, M.F.: Performance evaluation of the orca shared-object system. ACM Trans. Comput. Syst. 16(1), 1–40 (1998)
3. Bal, H.E., Kaashoek, M.F., Tanenbaum, A.S.: Orca: A language for parallel programming of distributed systems. IEEE Trans. Softw. Eng. 18(3), 190–205 (1992)
4. Bal, H.E., Tanenbaum, A.S.: Distributed programming with shared data. In: IEEE CS 1988 International Conference on Computer Languages, pp. 82–91. IEEE Press, Piscataway (1988)
5. Bardram, J.E., Bunde-Pedersen, J., Mogensen, M.: Differentiating between Accountable and Ephemeral Events in the ABC Hybrid Architecture for Activity-Based Collaboration. In: Proceedings of the IEEE International Conference on Collaborative Computing (CollaborateCom 2005), pp. 168–176. IEEE Press, Orlando, Florida (2005)
6. Bardram, J.E., Bunde-Pedersen, J., Soegaard, M.: Support for activity-based computing in a personal computing operating system. In: CHI '06: Proceedings of the SIGCHI conference on Human factors in computing systems (To appear), ACM Press, New York (2006)
7. Beaudouin-Lafon, M., (ed.): Computer Supported Cooperative Work. John Wiley and Sons, New York (1999)
8. Birrell, A.D., Nelson, B.J.: Implementing remote procedure calls. ACM Trans. Comput. Syst. 2(1), 39–59 (1984)
9. Cugola, G., Picco, G.: Peerware: Core middleware support for peer-to-peer and mobile systems (2001)
10. Gelernter, D.: Generative communication in linda. ACM Trans. Program. Lang. Syst. 7(1), 80–112 (1985)
11. Geyer, W., Vogel, J., Cheng, L.-T., Muller, M.: Supporting activity-centric collaboration through peer-to-peer shared objects. In: GROUP '03: Proceedings of the 2003 international ACM SIGGROUP conference on Supporting group work, pp. 115–124. ACM Press, New York (2003)
12. Greenberg, S., Roseman, M.: Groupware toolkits for synchronous work. In: Beaudouin-Lafon [7], pp. 135–168
13. Hagimont, D., Boyer, F.: A configurable rmi mechanism for sharing distributed java objects. IEEE Internet Computing 5(1), 36–43 (2001)
14. Hill, J., Gutwin, C.: The MAUI Toolkit: Groupware Widgets for Group Awareness. Computer Supported Cooperative Work 13(2), 539–571 (2004)
15. Homburg, P., van Steen, M., Tanenbaum, A.S.: An architecture for a wide area distributed system. In: EW 7: Proceedings of the 7th workshop on ACM SIGOPS European workshop, pp. 75–82. ACM Press, New York (1996)
16. Lamport, L.: Time, clocks, and the ordering of events in a distributed system. Commun. ACM 21(7), 558–565 (1978)
17. Lipkind, I., Pechtchanski, I., Karamcheti, V.: Object views: language support for intelligent object caching in parallel and distributed computations. In: OOPSLA '99. Proceedings of the 14th ACM SIGPLAN conference on Object-oriented programming, systems, languages, and applications, pp. 447–460. ACM Press, New York (1999)
18. Liskov, B., Shrira, L.: Promises: linguistic support for efficient asynchronous procedure calls in distributed systems. In: PLDI '88. Proceedings of the ACM SIGPLAN 1988 conference on Programming Language design and Implementation, pp. 260–267. ACM Press, New York (1988)

19. Matsuoka, S., Kawai, S.: Using tuple space communication in distributed object-oriented languages. In: OOPSLA '88. Conference proceedings on Object-oriented programming systems, languages and applications, pp. 276–284. ACM Press, New York (1988)
20. Mogensen, M.: Distributed objects in loose coupled local area networks. Technical Report, Computer Science Department, University of Aarhus (2005)
21. Oki, B., Pfluegl, M., Siegel, A., Skeen, D.: The information bus: an architecture for extensible distributed systems. In: SOSP '93. Proceedings of the fourteenth ACM symposium on Operating systems principles, pp. 58–68. ACM Press, New York (1993)
22. OMG. Corba services: Common object services specification, chapter 4: Event service (March 2001)
23. Picco, G.P., Murphy, A.L., Roman, G.-C.: LIME: Linda meets mobility. In: International Conference on Software Engineering, pp. 368–377 (1999)
24. Prakash, A.: Group editors. In: Beaudouin-Lafon [7], pp. 103–134
25. Roseman, M., Greenberg, S.: Building real-time groupware with groupkit, a groupware toolkit. ACM Trans. Comput.-Hum. Interact. 3(1), 66–106 (1996)
26. Shim, H.S., Hall, R.W., Prakash, A., Jahanian, F.: Providing Flexible Services for Managing Shared State in Collaborative Systems. In: Rodden, T., Hughes, J., Schmidtk, K. (eds.) Proceedings of the Fifth European Conference on Computer Supported Cooperative Work, Lancaster, UK, pp. 237–252. Kluwer Academic Publishers, Boston (1997)
27. Smith, D.A., Kay, A., Raab, A., Reed, D.P.: Croquet - a collaboration system architecture. In: C5 2003. Proceedings. First Conference on Creating, Connecting and Collaborating Through Computing, pp. 2–9. IEEE Press, New York (2003)
28. Speakman, T., Crowcroft, J., Gemmell, J., Farinacci, D., Lin, S., Leshchiner, D., Luby, M., Montgomery, T., Rizzo, L., Tweedly, A., Bhaskar, N., Edmonstone, R., Sumanasekera, R., Vicisano, L.: PGM Reliable Transport Protocol Specification. RFC 3208 (Experimental) (December 2001)
29. Vogel, J., Geyer, W., Cheng, L.-T., Muller, M.J.: Consistency control for synchronous and asynchronous collaboration based on shared objects and activities. Computer Supported Cooperative Work 13(5-6), 573–602 (2004)
30. Yonezawa, A., Briot, J.-P., Shibayama, E.: Object-oriented concurrent programming abcl/1. In: OOPLSA '86. Conference proceedings on Object-oriented programming systems, languages and applications, pp. 258–268. ACM Press, New York (1986)

Peer-to-Peer Based QoS Registry Architecture for Web Services*

Fei Li, Fangchun Yang, Kai Shuang, and Sen Su

State Key Lab. of Networking and Switching, Beijing University of Posts and
Telecommunications
187#,10 Xi Tu Cheng Rd.,Beijing,100876, P.R.China
`pathos.lf@gmail.com`, {`fcyang, shuangk, susen`}`@bupt.edu.cn`

Abstract. Web service QoS (Quality of Service) is a key factor for users to
evaluate and select services. Traditionally, run-time QoS of web services stores
in centralized QoS registry, which may have performance and availability
problems. In this paper, we propose a P2P (Peer-to-Peer) QoS registry
architecture for web services, named Q-Peer. Q-Peer is an unstructured P2P
system. Query of QoS is naturally achieved by getting QoS address from
corresponding service description. Q-Peer has a replication based mechanism to
ensure load-balance of the whole architecture. The architecture takes advantage
of P2P systems to ensure its availability, performance and autonomy. We are
currently implementing Q-Peer and planning to test it on Planet-Lab.

1 Introduction

Using web service technology to integrate business applications is one of the major
trends of distributed computing. It is a widely known procedure that service[1]
requesters discover services by functional description and select services by non-
functional properties. Because service function is relatively stable throughout service
lifetime, while service QoS can change frequently with time, load, network condition
and many other factors, maintaining the two types of information has different system
requirements and design considerations. Thus, the 2 steps are often accomplished on 2
entities respectively, called *service registry* and *QoS registry*. Centralized QoS
registry has been proposed and researched before [1][2], but they are sharing some
common shortcomings of centralized systems, like scalability, performance and single
point failure. More importantly, because of business boundary, system scale and other
limitations, centralized system may not be able to support global scale B2B
interoperations. As far as we know, only Gibelin. and Makpangou [3] have considered

---

* This work is supported by the National Basic Researchand Development Program (973
program) of China under Grant No.2003CB314806; the Program for New Century Excellent
Talents in University (No:NCET-05-0114); the Program for Changjiang Scholars and
Innovative Research Team in University (PCSIRT); the Hi-Tech Research and Development
Program (863 Program) of China under Grant No.2006AA01Z164.
[1] In this paper, we use *web service* and *service* interchangeably.

J. Indulska and K. Raymond (Eds.): DAIS 2007, LNCS 4531, pp. 133–138, 2007.

distributed QoS registry architecture but no detailed design is presented and the hash-table based QoS indexing approach is inefficient.

In past several years, peer-to-peer paradigm has gained considerable momentum as a new model of distributed computing. P2P system is created for file sharing at first, like Napster, Gnutella[4], Kazaa[5] and so on. For their scalability, autonomy and robustness, they are introduced into distributed storage and information retrieving[6]. Some applications of P2P have already contributed to web service research, as distributed service discovery[7].

In this paper, we propose our ongoing work--P2P QoS registry architecture, named Q-Peer. Q-Peer is a service QoS information storage architecture. It provides large scale QoS collecting, retrieving and monitoring services. It can work with centralized or decentralized service registry like UDDI or other P2P service discovery system. Q-Peer solving the QoS query problem by adding QoS address information into service registry, so that it does not need a query routing mechanism internally. QoS information of similar or identical services is clustered together. This makes the retrieving and comparison of service QoS very efficient. An autonomous replication mechanism is applied on all peers to adjust load and improve availability.

The rest part of this paper is organized as follows: Section 2 introduces the general model and design consideration of Q-Peer. Section 3 presents how to disseminate QoS and load information in Q-Peer. Section 4 proposes the load balancing approach in Q-Peer. The paper concluded in Section 5 with our future work.

2 System Model

Q-Peer is a peer-to-peer database system for storing QoS information of web services. QoS data is stored in XML documents. Common P2P database has a general requirement that system has to provide an efficient mechanism to query and locate objects, while this requirement can simply be satisfied in Q-Peer by utilizing service registration information. Because no service user cares about service quality without known its function, to query certain QoS metrics without service description is meaningless. Thus, Q-Peer is not an independent P2P database----it has to work with certain service registry system. We organize QoS storage by service description, so that QoS items can simply be located when querying service description. For every service, service registry stores its description and a QoS address list (for replicas). Users retrieve QoS by directly access one of the addresses. In fact, the query mechanism in Q-Peer is similar to the most original P2P system—Napster, by a centralized index server cluster.

QoS can be divided to several classes because same or similar services have same QoS metrics[10]. Functional identical services' quality information is stored at one peer at first, but they could be replicated as a whole when needed. Storing a class of QoS together can improve efficiency because users often retrieve QoS of same service's different implementation to compare and select from them. Different service selection algorithm can be deployed on peers to assist users[1][8]. If a service stores its QoS information at a certain peer, the peer acts as its run-time monitor. Peer updates service QoS periodically. The update process can include certain authentication and evaluation mechanism so that services can not submit fake QoS to Q-Peer.

We do not use super-peer based architecture because super-peer intends to improve query efficiency, which is not a problem in our system. All peers are equal in Q-Peer. Peers employ a replication based load sharing policy which utilizing spare resource on light loaded peers. Every QoS classes can have several replicas on different peers. Service registry has a list of candidate peers for every service and chooses a random one when user request to retrieve QoS. The random peer choosing approach can be substituted with other more sophisticated approach. Every peer has load information about its neighbors for load-balance and backing up each other. The detailed mechanisms will be presented in the following section.

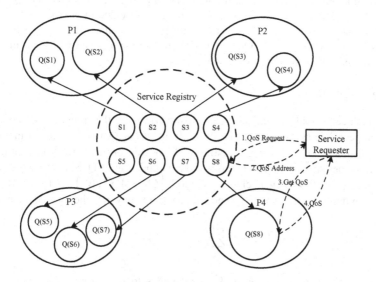

Fig. 1. General model of Q-Peer

Fig.1 illustrates a sample Q-Peer system containing 4 peers and 8 classes of services. Replicas are hided for illustrating our model clearly. Service registry in the figure can be either centralized or decentralized architectures. S_i is a service set which contains a number of same or similar service description. The QoS of a service set S_i is $Q(S_i)$. Each peer stores several sets of $Q(S_i)$. Every service description contains the address of its QoS, like a pointer. When a service requester needs to query QoS of a certain service, it sends a QoS request to service registry, then the registry will reply with a QoS address. Service requester can get QoS by direct accessing the address.

3 Information Dissemination

In Q-Peer, two types of information change frequently which should be constantly updated and properly disseminated in the system. The first is service QoS. The second is load status of peers.

3.1 QoS Update

For a newly registered service *s*, which belongs to service class *S*, it has 2 parts of information to be registered, service description *D(s)* and QoS of the service *Q(s)*. If no service of *S* has been registered before, service registry will choose a random peer to store its QoS information. If *S* has been registered, QoS of the service *Q(s)* is added to the peers storing QoS of the class *Q(S)*. As soon as a peer is informed that it will store a new service's QoS, it contact with the service and get current QoS for the first time.

We have mentioned that for sharing load and improving availability, any *Q(S)* may have several replicas (the replication mechanism is presented in next section). One of the storage peers for a QoS class is the main peer, the others are replication peers. Every time service update its QoS, it update to the main peer first. Then the other replicas are passively updated by the main peer.

3.2 Load Update

In Q-Peer, peer's load and capacity are characterized by the frequency of accessing QoS on a peer. We assume every peer has infinite storage space for cost of increasing storage is much lower than increasing CPU power or network bandwidth. QoS accessing comes from 2 major operations: one is updating of QoS; another is query of QoS. For a peer P storing n classes of QoS: $\{Q(S_1), Q(S_2), ..., Q(S_n)\}$, each class has an updating frequency f_i^u and a query frequency f_i^q, the load of the peer is:

$$L(P) = \sum_{i=1}^{n} \left(f_i^u + f_i^q \right) \tag{1}$$

A peer P has a maxim capacity $C^M(P)$ equals to the estimated maxim allowed accessing frequency $f^M(P)$. The available capacity to accept new service is: $C^A(P) = C^M(P) - L(P)$.

Every peer has a list of other peers' address, called Neighbor List (NL). The neighbor list contains a limited small number of peers which can accept a peer's load sharing request. This list is sorted by C^A in descent order. A neighbor item in NL is $N_i = \langle P_i, C^A(P_i) \rangle, (i = 1...m, a \leq m \leq b, 0 < a < b)$, where m is the total neighbor number, a and b are the lower and upper limit of m. Items in NL can be dynamically added and deleted according to peer status. When a new peer P adds to Q-Peer system, it will get a random NL. P periodically sends its own $C^A(P)$ to peers in NL and gets their C^A back from reply messages to update its NL. For any peer received an unknown peer's C^A, if it is better than the last item in their NL, the new peer is inserted. If NL exceeds the maxim number limit b, the last item will be removed. Peers have a lowest capacity limitation l to take a peer as their neighbor. For any N_i which $C^A(P_i) < l$, it will be deleted. If item number in NL is lower than the minimum number limit, peer will initiate a random walk process to find new satisfied peers. The random walk begins from a random peer in its NL, message containing its own C^A for other peers to update NL if satisfied. For any peer walked through, it sends its C^A back to the initiating peer. The random walk will stop for TTL limitation.

By this load updating approach, peers tend to exchange information with light loaded peers, which is more likely to be able to accept replication requests. For peers having less spare capacity which have not been taken as neighbor of any other peers, they still have chance to use other peers' resource. When they have spare capacity again, they will be added to its neighbor's NL. We have to tune parameters in a more practical environment to limit the message overhead in Q-Peer and improve load sharing.

4   Replication and Load Sharing

If a peer found itself in heavy load, it can ask other peers to replicate some of its service class to share its load. We prefer to replicate service classes as a whole rather than replicate some single service. Because our aim of replication is simply to balance load, to replicate single service could not contribute much to load sharing. And to replicate a part of a QoS class will affect the extended functions like service selection. Thus, a class of QoS is the operation unit of replication.

Every QoS class has $r\left(2 \leq r \leq K\right)$ replicas including the original one, where K is the maxim allowed replica number. To improve availability, the first replica is created immediately after the QoS class is created, so any QoS class has at least 2 replicas. If a peer's load is approaching threshold, it sends replicating request to the neighbor which has the most spared capacity. Peer always tries to replicate the most popular QoS class $Q\left(S_i\right)$. If the spared capacity of the first neighbor can satisfy replication requirement and the class has less than K replicas, the first neighbor will be taken as the replication peer. The replication condition is:

$$C^A\left(P_1\right) > f_i^u + \frac{r \times f_i^q}{r+1} \text{ and } r < K \tag{2}$$

In (2), we can find that by replicating a QoS class, replication peer can share $r/r+1$ of the class' query load, but updating load can not be leveraged because all replicas should keep consistency. With the growing of replica number, load sharing by replication can have less and less effect because $r/r+1$ is approaching 1. What's more, keeping more replicas consistent adds more load on the network. Thus the K should be a small number to make the approach effective.

If the spared capacity of first neighbor $C^A\left(P_1\right)$ could not satisfy the replication requirements, the random walk process in previous section will be initiated to rebuild the neighbor list. As soon as a replication peer is found, a replica of $Q\left(S_i\right)$ is transferred to new peer. Service registry is then informed that a new replica can be selected to retrieve QoS.

If all QoS class in a peer has had K replicas and it is still under load pressure, a random QoS class will be chosen to be deleted. Before deletion, service registry is informed so that it will not retrieve the class of QoS from this peer. Main peer of the QoS class is also informed so that it will not update QoS to this peer. If the deleted replica is the main replica of the service class, another replica will be chosen as main replica and related service providers will be informed to update QoS to the new one.

5 Conclusion and Future Works

In this paper, we presented a distributed web service QoS registry—the Q-Peer architecture. The architecture is based on Napster-like unstructured peer-to-peer model. Every QoS item's address is stored in service registry with its service description. Same or similar services' QoS is clustered together to conveniently expand other QoS operation like service selection. Every QoS class has several replicas to improve performance and availability. Replication is based on load status of peers. There is a simple but effective mechanism to exchange load information between peers. Q-Peer architecture is expected to support efficient QoS storage with excellent scalability. It can be used as a QoS infrastructure for global B2B applications.

The design of Q-Peer has just finished and we are currently implementing it. Many detailed design considerations should be tested and adjusted in practical environment. Our future works may include: to design a peer load based replica selection mechanism to help balance load further; to find out a replica deletion algorithm, which will less affect the whole system; to analyze and adjust parameters with experimental results. We will deploy and test Q-Peer on Planet-Lab[9] in near future.

References

1. Liu, Y., Ngu, A.H., Zeng, L.Z.: Qos computation and policing in dynamic web service selection. In: Proceedings of the 13th International Conference on World Wide Web, pp. 66–73. ACM Press, New York (2004)
2. Yu, T., Lin, K.J.: A Broker-based Framework for QoS-Aware Web Service Composition. In: Proceeding of IEEE International Conference on e-Technology, e- Commerce and e-Service (EEE-05), Hong Kong, China (March 2005)
3. Gibelin, N., Makpangou, M.: Efficient and Transparent Web-Services Selection. In: Benatallah, B., Casati, F., Traverso, P. (eds.) ICSOC 2005. LNCS, vol. 3826, pp. 527–532. Springer, Heidelberg (2005)
4. Gnutella Homepage http://www.gnutella.com
5. KaZaA Homepage, http://www.kazaa.com
6. Koloniari, G., Pitoura, E.: Peer-to-peer management of XML data : issues and research challenges. ACM SIGMOD Record, vol. 34(2) (June 2005)
7. Schmidt, C., Parashar, M.: A peer-to-peer approach to Web service discovery. In: Proceedings of the 13th International Conference on World Wide Web, pp. 211–229(2004)
8. Li, F. Su, S., Yang, F.C.: On Distributed Service Selection for QoS Driven Service Composition. In: Proceedings of the 7th International Conference on Electronic Commerce and Web Technologies, EC-Web'06, LNCS, vol. 4082 (2006)
9. Planet-Lab Homepage http://www.planet-lab.org/
10. Maximilien, E.M., Singh, M.P.: A Framework and Ontology for Dynamic Web Services Selection. IEEE Internet Computing 8(5), 84–93 (September 2004)

Migration in CORBA Component Model

Jacek Cała

AGH — University of Science and Technology
Department of Computer Science
jcala@agh.edu.pl

Abstract. Migration of running application code is considered a very attractive and desired mechanism to improve application performance, resource sharing, self-adaptability, etc. This mechanism seems to be even more important nowadays, considering the growing interest in the area of mobile computing and mobile networks.

This paper briefly presents a migration mechanism for a CORBA Component Model platform. We discuss general issues related to migration of running code, further elaborated in the context of CCM. We also propose an extension to the original CCM model which provides interfaces to implement migration.

The paper presents the most important problems which appeared during implementation of a prototype facility and it discusses possible solutions. One of the most fundamental issues related to mobility of running code is the *residual dependency problem*. The intention of the work is not to provide a solution to this (possibly unsolvable) problem, but to propose an approach which would make programmers aware of its existence. Thus, the paper allows readers to make more conscious decisions when designing their components. The paper ends with an evaluation of the prototype implementation on top of OpenCCM, an open source Java implementation of the CORBA Component Model.

1 Introduction

Migration of processes, tasks, objects, components or even whole operating systems during runtime is considered a very attractive and desired mechanism. Since the 1980s, there has been substantial interest in migration but, unfortunately, with very little use in real-world applications [1,2]. Today, however, as systems become more and more distributed in nature and with increasing interest in Component and Service Oriented Architectures (COA and SOA), migration mechanisms are more attractive than ever, since they enable better processing power exploitation, resource sharing, fault avoidance, mobile computing and self-adaptability.

Migration as a mechanism to facilitate dynamic load distribution may increase exploitation of available processing power by shifting a task from an overloaded node to another node, with sufficient CPU resources. It may also substantially reduce costs associated with frequent remote communication, improving effectiveness of a distributed system. Instead of calling remote objects, it is often

J. Indulska and K. Raymond (Eds.): DAIS 2007, LNCS 4531, pp. 139–152, 2007.

more efficient to move one of the communicating sides directly to the other. The same strategy may be used to facilitate better resource sharing. If there is a node with a large amount of memory or specialized hardware devices, it might be useful to move a software component to this node in order to fully leverage its resources.

Moving instances of running code may also positively influence fault tolerance as well as system maintenance aspects. Given a migration facility, system administrators can move a running application to another node to perform maintenance tasks on the original host machine. Moreover, in more autonomous systems one can imagine that migration would be triggered by a fault detection mechanism whenever there is a suspicion of hardware failure.

Migration may also greatly support system self-adaptability, enabling reaction to changes in the environment e.g. appearance of a new mobile node. In addition, it may support deployment of an application according to changes in the environment. This aspect — support for dynamic and adaptive deployment of component-based applications in heterogeneous hardware and software domains — was the primary motivation behind the provision of a migration mechanism for a platform implementing the CORBA Component Model. The presented paper, however, does not focus on the deployment process itself but rather on issues directly related to the design and implementation of a CCM movement facility.

The paper is organized as follows. The following section covers work related to migration mechanisms, not limited to component architectures but more general in scope. Section 3 briefly introduces the fundamentals of migration mechanisms with relation to component environments. The next section presents the proposed extensions to the CORBA Component Model in order to facilitate migration. Section 5 depicts the internals of the adopted approach and presents solutions to the most important issues. In Section 6 we present evaluation tests of the prototype implementation. The work ends with conclusions and future development directions.

2   Related Work

The problem of migration of application code has already been addressed by many previous research projects and works such as [1], which gives a comprehensive report of achievements in this area.

More recent work related to runtime migration of entire operating systems is presented in [2]. The most important advantages of this approach are: reduction of migration time to only several dozen milliseconds, and limiting the problem of residual dependencies between source and destination locations.[1] However, the important requirement is common network-attached storage (e.g. NFS) between the source and destination nodes which have to be parts of the same LAN. Moreover, the problem of residual dependencies remains a burden even when

---

[1] The residual dependencies problem involves the level of dependency of a migrating entity on the source host. It is the main factor which restrains broad use of migration mechanisms as it substantially reduces fault tolerance of the system.

local devices are considered e.g. when the target node does not provide a given device, present at the source.

Another approach to migration was undertaken at the level of OS processes. Significant research was performed in this area, resulting in several OS solutions, such as Sprite [3], Amoeba [4], RHODOS [5] and many others; however, only a few of them are used today [6]. Process migration is not available in modern, popular operating systems such as MS Windows, Linux and UNIXes. This is mainly due to the complexity of the mechanism and undesirable effects of state dispersal which directly result from the problem of residual dependencies.[2]

Yet another level where a migration facility may be introduced is the mobility of objects. Some languages and environments have been created with migration procedures in mind – e.g. Emerald [7] and COOL [8] but it is a far too complex a mechanism to be concealed underneath high-level language notation. Hence, more recent platforms such as CORBA, Java and .NET effectively implement migration [9] but the mechanism itself is not embedded in them.

The presented paper describes an approach to providing migration of CORBA Components which, in the context of growing interest in COA, may be considered interesting. Through balanced granularity — a component is "larger" than an object and usually "smaller" than a process — movement of components remains a flexible and efficient mechanism and may well support adaptation of application performance, which was the primary motivation behind the presented solution. The proposed extension of the CCM model ensures *weak mobility* (as defined in [10]) which is in contrast to *strong mobility*. The former is migration of "a code accompanied by some initialization data" — in this case the code and the state of a component, whereas the latter provides migration of the code and execution state which is generally more flexible but hardly possible to provide at middleware level.

In [10] there is presented a portable serialization mechanism which allows storing the state of a CORBA object and exchange it between different language domains. The mechanism described in this paper do not provide portability across languages, however offers a solution for migrating code of a component during its runtime with respect to the operations invoked on and by the component.

3 Migration Mechanism

Throughout this work the notion of migration is defined according to [11] as follows:

> object migration refers to the ability to move an object from one address space to another (change its physical location) without breaking references to that object currently held by clients.

This definition comes from a paper related to the CORBA platform, but the *object* mentioned above should not be perceived in OO categories. The notion

---

[2] Due to residual dependencies, multiple migration of entities results in the functioning of those entities being dependent on more and more systems.

may well refer to any code running in an environment, which is able to change its location. It is important to note that the presented definition, by stressing preservation of references between a migrating entity and its surroundings, forces the migration mechanism to ensure that following migration, communication with the entity shall progress as before.

The CORBA environment is well suited to resolving issues related to migration of objects. Mechanisms such as *Request Processing Policy*, `ServantLocators`, *Servant Retention Policy*, `ForwardRequest` exception, etc. may well be used to support a migration facility. As shown later in this paper, all of them are also used to provide migration of components, hence in order to clarify how to move a component from one place to another, it is important to analyze how, in general, movement of objects may be performed.

There are several stages which a running object has to go through when migrating from one place to another:

1. **Suspending** the state of the object which is required to store its state consistently. The main issue here is that following suspending the CORBA platform still has to deal with incoming, ongoing and outgoing requests. Section 5.1 presents these problems in more detail.

2. **Storing** the state of the suspended object, alone or together with code. Which action is to be performed depends on the availability of the code at the destination. It is also crucial to answer the question of what state the object is in. If an object is connected with others, we must know whether they need to be copied as well or perhaps accessed remotely (shallow/deep copy problem). To make things even more complicated, storing state may also take into account heterogeneity of the environment and prepare a copy in an easily transferable format. Some of the issues mentioned here are covered in [12,13,14].

3. **Moving** the state between the source and target locations. This step is quite straightforward but in case of problems with transferring data, it should be possible to roll back the whole process and return the system to the state just before the suspension. Migration requires the target location to be ready to accept incoming objects, hence an appropriate infrastructure must be prepared at the destination.

4. **Loading** the state of the object at the destination. This step requires the code of the moved object to be available at the destination. In the case of heterogeneous environments, such as CORBA, this requirement is sometimes hard to fulfill — e.g. movement of a Java implementation of an object to an ORB for C++ language. Loading is much easier if we can assume platform homogeneity, such as that offered by Java or .Net environments.

5. **Reconnecting** of the moved entity in such a way that every other object (or, more generally, client) communicating with the migrating object should not see any change in behavior. There are three possible techniques of referencing a moved object: (1) deep update, (2) chain of reference, or (3) use of a home location agent. More details about this issue are presented in Sect. 5.3.

6. **Activating** the object at the new location followed by destroying it at the previous location. This is the final step which ends the whole process of migration and results in a fully functional system.

A crucial issue when considering migration is to shorten the time required to proceed through all the above stages, guaranteeing a more responsive and reliable mechanism. An important fact is that after suspension and before activation the object must not respond to any requests which can change its state. Otherwise, the stored state of the object would not match the actual state altered by the invocations and this would lead directly to loss of information.

4 Mobility with CORBA Component Model

The CORBA Component Model [15] defines an approach to designing, implementing and assembling component applications in the CORBA environment. By means of a new, extended version of IDL, it provides designers with an easy yet powerful way to define a component. Components may be equipped with several kinds of ports by which they are connected with other components or their execution environment. The model also introduces a new language, the Component Implementation Definition Language (CIDL), to describe implementation details of a component e.g. its lifecycle, persistence details, etc.

The CORBA Component Model does not in itself provide any mechanism which facilitates migration transparency i.e. movement of components between different locations. It is the goal of the presented work to describe steps which were taken to extend the CCM model and verify the extension on one of the available CCM implementations, namely OpenCCM [16].

A component in CCM may be perceived as having two sides:

– external side — visible to clients, defined by means of the IDL3 language which allows creating component definitions with attributes, ports and inheritance details. The basis for this part is the CCMObject interface,
– internal side — visible to a container, defined by means of the CIDL language. The basis for this part of a component is the EnterpriseComponent interface implemented by component executors.

The presented solution extends both sides of the component definition, allowing easy control of the migration mechanisms by an external entity. A prototype, called the *Component Migration Service* (CMS), has been developed for the purpose of evaluating the approach. This prototype is presented in Sect. 6.

4.1 External Interface

As mentioned earlier, migration consists of several stages: *suspending, storing, moving, loading, reconnecting,* and *activating*. In order to control movement of a component by an external entity it is necessary to extend the existing CCMObject interface with suitable operations. As shown in listing below, most of the steps described above have their counterparts in the proposed extension.

IDL definition of CCMRefugee interface, an extension to the original CCMObject interface

```
interface CCMRefugee : ::Components::CCMObject
{
    void refugee_passivate( );

    void refugee_activate( );

    void refugee_store( out Criteria the_criteria );

    void refugee_load( in Criteria the_criteria )
    raises( InvalidCriteria );

    void refugee_remove()
    raises( ::Components::RemoveFailure );
};
```

The meaning of the operations is consistent with the descriptions given in the previous section. The only two missing operations are move and reconnect which are included at the factory level (i.e. CCMHome). This decision is imposed by the fact that in order to move or reconnect a component it is necessary to destroy and create its instances, which is the primary goal of a factory.

4.2 Factory Involvement in Component Migration

In order to move a component to a new location, the destination must be prepared to accept the component. The presented solution does not introduce any special entities which carry out creation of a migrant at the destination. The CCM model provides a standard factory interface for every component, namely CCMHome, which may be simply extended to fulfill the requirements associated with accepting migrants. As shown in the following listing the CCMRefuge interface has four operations supporting movement of components.

Extensions to the factory interface are twofold:

- required at source location: refugee_freeze, refugee_moved and refugee_unfreeze operations. The aim of the first is to prepare a component and the infrastructure for movement. The second is responsible for reconnection of the moved component at the source location. The last extension is to be called in case of movement failure, when there is a need to reverse passivation of a component and return the system to the state from just before suspension,
- required at destination location: refugee_accept is invoked to ask the target to accept a migrating component. The operation returns a newly created incarnation of the component, used further by CMS to reconnect references. In case of problems, the operation throws an InvalidCriteria exception to signal the CMS to roll back the whole migration attempt.

IDL definition of CCMRefuge interface, an extension to CCMHome interface

```
interface CCMRefuge : ::Components::CCMHome
{
    Criteria refugee_freeze( in CCMRefugee refugee_here )
    raises (::Components::CCMException);

    CCMRefugee refugee_accept( in Criteria refugee_state )
    raises (InvalidCriteria);

    void refugee_moved(
        in CCMRefugee refugee_here, in CCMRefugee refugee_there);

    void refugee_unfreeze( in CCMRefugee refugee_here )
    raises (::Components::CCMException);
};
```

The presented enhancements are used by CMS as depicted in Fig. 1. From the point of view of CMS, migration consists of three basic stages: (1) freezing the state of the component, (2) moving the component to the target location, and (3) reconnecting the component at the target location.

At any stage following passivation of a component, a failure may occur. In such a case migration shall be immediately abandoned and the system shall be restored to its original state as fast as possible. Then, instead of reconnecting by means of **refugee_moved** it is necessary to invoke the **refugee_unfreeze** operation which reactivates the component at the source location.

4.3   Extended Component Lifecycle

Apart from the extensions which enable migration control, some enhancements are required at the internal side of the component, namely its executors. They provide a way to inform the programmer about component state changes.

The operations included in **RefugeeComponent**, which is a basis for executors of movable components, reflect directly operations published in **CCMRefugee**. This is because **CCMRefugee** delegates requests to the appropriate executor, implementing the **RefugeeComponent** interface. Operations of this interface indicate changes in components' lifecycle and should be used by a component developer to control resource usage, progress in communication, internal state of the component, etc. For this reason it seems worthwhile to describe the exact meaning and proposed use of each operation:

- **ccm_refugee_passivate** — is called just before passivation of the component. The developer shall use this indicator to prepare the component for the storing phase, i.e. the component should interrupt any activities which may change its state during migration. As discussed later in Sect. 5.1, the range of activities which the developer should perform during this call depends on the way the component is implemented,

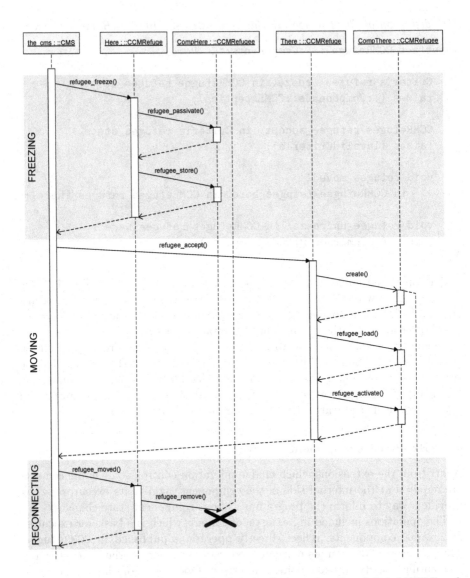

Fig. 1. Sequence diagram of successful migration between locations labeled HERE and THERE

- `ccm_refugee_store` — is called to store the state of the component. Although some languages, such as Java and .Net, can serialize classes automatically by means of the reflection mechanism, in this work a manual approach is adopted in order to preserve greater portability of the CORBA environment,

- `ccm_refugee_load` — is opposite to `ccm_refugee_store` and shall be used by developers to restore the state of the component. Once this operation is invoked, it is certain that the component is located on the destination host.
- `ccm_refugee_activate` — may be called in two cases. Firstly, following successful migration the operation is called on the newly created component at the target location to indicate that the component is going to be activated and has to be ready to resume work. Otherwise, when migration fails, `ccm_refugee_activate` is called at the source location to indicate that the component returns to its normal operation.
- `ccm_refugee_remove` — is called on the component at the source location whenever the migration attempt is successful. The aim of this operation is to indicate that the component should release all resources acquired during its work at the source host.

5   Migration Internals

The interfaces presented above provide a convenient way to control migration of components. However, in order to successfully move a component it is necessary to consider some crucial issues such as processing of requests, reconnection and resource usage. The last issue is particularly important as it imposes some constraints on how resources can be used by a mobile component. The following sections provide a brief discussion about these problems.

5.1   Dealing with Requests on Suspension

As far as migration is concerned, one of the major issues is dealing with requests which an object is or should be involved in. This problem arises when the object is going to be suspended in order to preserve the consistency of its state, but it is still entangled in some operation. In general, three possible cases are relevant here: (1) *incoming requests* invoked on the object during suspension state, (2) *outgoing requests* invoked by the object before suspension, and (3) *ongoing requests* invoked on the object before suspension.

The solution to the first case is to collect all incoming requests until the object is again reactivated. In the case of successful migration, all these requests are redirected to a new location using the CORBA `ForwardRequest` exception.

The second case is more troublesome. It is important for the passivation of the object to be performed if all outgoing invocations are already dealt with. Otherwise, the returning result could introduce some inconsistencies between the stored and real state of the object. In order to deal with such cases automatically, Container Portable Interceptors (COPI) are required. Unfortunately, the COPI specification has only been adopted recently and it is yet not widely implemented by CCM platforms. Without COPI there is no easy way to determine the number of outgoing requests on the middleware level. In the proposed extension the solution to this issue is left to developers who need to be aware of all outgoing requests whenever the `ccm_passivate` operation is called.

Container Portable Interceptors may also be a very convenient and elegant way to deal with the third problem i.e. ongoing requests. In this case, however, their functionality may be easily overtaken by a `ServantLocator`. Two operations of the servant manager — `preinvoke` and `postinvoke` — are used to count the number of ongoing operations. The locator ensures that passivation does not occur until all the operations are finished and, by collecting all incoming requests, guards the object from being bothered. Unfortunately, such a simple solution may sometimes impose substantial delays in suspending a component and developers should take that into account.

An important fact is that the solutions proposed above do not protect the component from all state consistency-related problems. For example, if the component interacts with the environment by means other than CORBA, there is no easy way to provide a general solution at the level of the CCM container.

5.2   Constraints on Resource Usage

As mentioned above, whenever a CCM component communicates with the environment by means other than CORBA it may create problems with state and communication consistency. The very same problem occurs when dealing with a local filesystem, local devices, threads running on a source host and all other local resources which are not accessible in the address space of the destination host.

Nevertheless, in order to give developers substantial freedom of using software and hardware platforms for component hosting it is not desirable to limit access to local resources or native communication technologies. Instead, the lifecycle of a component has been extended, providing programmers with means to be aware of oncoming migration. There are two important cases to be considered: (1) departure from a source host, and (2) arrival at a destination host.

Successful departure is signaled by two operations: `ccm_refugee_passivate`, and `ccm_refugee_remove`. Passivation means that a component should cease all activities which might change its state. Obviously, this may have an important impact on communication, thread usage and sometimes resource allocation. The second operation indicates the moment to free all gained resources, destroy all local allocations, etc. This operation means that the component has been effectively transferred to a new location and may be completely destroyed at the source.

Signaling component arrival at a destination host is done with the use of the `ccm_refugee_activate` operation which should have semantics similar to both the `configuration_complete` and `ccm_ activate` operations originally called by a CCM platform when the component was instantiated.

5.3   Reconnection

Another very important problem related to migration is reconnection between the migrated component and all other clients, objects and components which it interacts with. As mentioned earlier, there are three possible techniques of resolving this issue: (1) deep update, (2) chain of reference, and (3) use of a home location agent.

The first technique requires all clients of the component to update their references following migration. This is very expensive approach and, in fact, not a viable one in distributed environments such as CORBA, since the clients may not yet exist when migration occurs [11]. The second technique assumes that after movement the component leaves a trace at the previous location which points to its new incarnation. From the point of view of a client, this is much more convenient, however, each movement makes the chain longer and longer, eventually introducing significant inefficiencies in communication and being more prone to failures (vide residual dependencies).

The last approach seems to be the most appropriate for resolving the problem of referencing. On the one hand, clients can refer to the moving component through a persistent reference of its home location agent. On the other hand, the home agent is the only entity that should be informed about location changes. This guarantees that consecutive migrations of the component do not incur any additional delays in request processing.

The use of the home location agent has its drawbacks. Firstly, it also introduces the problem of residual dependencies, although to a far lesser extent than the chain-of-reference method. Secondly, use of a separate home location object introduces additional costs even when the movable object is managed by the same object adapter as the home agent. To reduce this overhead a `ServantLocator` extension is proposed, which, by maintaining an additional *migratory table*, becomes the home agent itself. The `ServantLocator`'s `preinvoke` operation is responsible for searching through the migratory table and returning a `ForwardException` if the received request is directed to a component which has migrated away.

6   Evaluation of Efficiency

Despite all the potential advantages stemming from introduction of a migration mechanism to the CCM platform, it is not surprising that its use incurs additional delays on processing requests which, in consequence, lowers the overall throughput of an application. Irrespective of how efficiently migration is performed, the source of the loss of efficiency is at least twofold.

Firstly, it is connected directly with the means by which requests are processed. Clients which use a reference of a moved component have to submit requests twice: first to the home location to get the current reference of the component, and then again, using the acquired reference, to the component itself. This overhead is usually substantially reduced by an ORB which caches references returned in the first step, ensuring that all consecutive requests are sent directly to the new location. Nevertheless, for the first invocation following migration the overhead still persists.

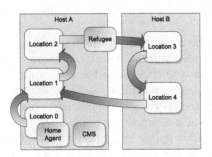

Fig. 2. Migration of a refugee in a testbed used to evaluate overhead of the migration mechanism

The other and more severe reason for loss of efficiency is the time required to move a component between two locations. In order to perform migration, the component is suspended for the duration required to transfer its state. Obviously, the longer this interval is, the less requests the component is able to process. That is the main reason why optimization of this step is a crucial part of providing a mechanism which would offer acceptable responsiveness of migrating components.

Figure 2 presents the testbed used to evaluate this kind of overhead. There were five **Refuge** locations placed in two hosts, A and B, connected with a 100 Mb/s LAN network. Location 0 hosted the Home Agent of a moving component which migrated between locations 1–4.

The testbed was used to evaluate migration of different kinds of components. Table 1 lists the duration required by migration between the locations in relation to the complexity of the component.

Table 1. Time [ms] required to perform migration in relation to complexity of the component

	$L1 \rightarrow L2$	$L2 \rightarrow L3$	$L3 \rightarrow L4$	$L4 \rightarrow L1$
No ports, no data	**109**	**142**	**183**	**147**
One facet	125	157	194	160
One receptacle	108	143	188	151
Some data	114	145	186	151
Five facets	127	168	222	175

Basing on the data presented in the table, it is worth to point out two interesting facts. First, moving a component with a facet or event sink consumes more time than moving a component with only a receptacle or event source. This is because facets and event sinks are CORBA objects and have to be stored together with the state of the migrant in order to reconnect it properly. Second, as can be seen, migration between locations 3 and 4 yielded the worst results, whereas movement between locations 1 and 2 proved fastest. The reason for this is that, originally, the components were placed on host A at location 0, hence local updates of the Home Agent from location 1 and 2 were faster than network communication between locations 3 and 4 and the agent. Additionally, the location of CMS, which was placed on host A, was also important. This, again, resulted in better performance if migration involved locations 1 and 2.

The results collected in the table convey important information. They provide an order-of-magnitude assessment of the time consumed by component migration. The most important case is the one when a component does not have any ports and data. It shows pure migration overhead while other results are distorted by serialization and transfer of code over the network. The results should also be taken into consideration to estimate the number of operations per second which the moving component is able to perform reliably. However, the exact performance of the component highly depends on many factors such as the length of the ORB's request queue and the implementation of lifecycle operations described in Sect. 4.3.

7 Conclusions and Future Work

The presented work describes extension of the CORBA Component Model with a migration facility. The adopted approach does not provide a fully transparent solution which, due to the important problem of residual dependencies, seems to be unattainable. Instead, we propose an extension of component lifecycle, providing programmers with an interface to deal with migration in a proper way. This is consistent with the approach proposed by the original CCM model where a component is notified about configuration completion, activation, removal, etc. Moreover, making programmers aware of component mobility does not impose substantial constraints on the range of resources and communication technologies used. The cost is that the programmer is responsible for manual preparation of a component for a migration attempt. However, at the level of middleware, it seems hard — if indeed possible — to automatically generate the whole required migration infrastructure for a component. The container is responsible for CORBA communication only, and any other technologies are out of its scope.

This situation would improve if the CCM platform implemented the *Streams for CCM* specification [17]. Local resources could then be accessed by means of sink and source ports, allowing for better detachment a component from its execution environment and, in consequence, more transparent migration. This area is a potential direction for further research.

The proposed migration mechanism is a prototype working with **session** components only. It is necessary to develop and test a mechanism suitable for **process** and **entity** component categories, as well as components with multiple segments. Unfortunately, OpenCCM, the platform used as the development environment, does not support components of other types than session, hence this direction of work is currently hampered.

Other possible development directions are related to integration of the migration mechanism with CORBA services, especially Persistent State Service and Transaction Service, as well as better integration with OpenCCM code generation tools. Nonetheless, the mechanism presented in this paper allows for further work concerning adaptive deployment and execution of applications. The migration facility, as one of the executive mechanisms, plays there an important role giving an Adaptation Manager a chance to control component arrangement of an application.

References

1. Milojičić, D., Douglis, F., Paindaveine, Y., Wheeler, R., Zhou, S.: Process migration. In: ACM Computing Surveys, pp. 241–299 (2000)
2. Clark, C., Fraser, K., Hand, S.: Live migration of virtual machines. In: Proceedings of 2nd Symposium on Networked Systems Design and Implementation (2005)
3. Douglis, F.: Transparent Process Migration in the Sprite Operating System. PhD thesis, University of California at Berkeley (1990)
4. Mullender, S., van Rossum, G., Tanenbaum, A.: Amoeba: A distributed operating system for the 1990s. IEEE Computer 23(5), 44–53 (1990)
5. de Paoli, D., Goscinski, A.: The RHODOS migration facility. The. Journal of Systems and Software 40(1), 51 (1998)
6. (openMosix project) Web site at http://openmosix.sourceforge.net
7. Hutchinson, N., Raj, R., Black, A., Levy, H., Jul, E.: The Emerald programming language. Technical report, Institution (1987)
8. Habert, S., Mosseri, L., Abrossimov, V.: COOL: Kernel support for object-oriented environments. In: Meyrowitz, N. (ed.) Proceedings of the Conference on Object-Oriented Programming Systems, Languages, and Applications (OOPSLA), pp. 269–277. ACM Press, New York (1990)
9. Tröger, P., Polze, A.: Object and process migration in.NET. In: Proceedings of the Eighth International Workshop on Object-oriented Real-time Dependable Systems, pp. 139–146 (2003)
10. Fuggeta, A., Picco, G., Vigna, G.: Understanding code mobility. IEEE Transactions on Software Engineering 5, 342–361 (1998)
11. Henning, M.: Binding, migration, and scalability in CORBA. Communications of the ACM 41(10), 62–71 (1998)
12. Killijian, M.O., Ruiz-Garcia, J.C., Fabre, J.C.: Portable serialization of CORBA objects: a reflective approach. In: OOPSLA, Seattle, USA, pp. 68–82 (2002)
13. Object Management Group, I.: Externalization Service Specification. Object Management Group, Inc. Version 1.0 (2000)
14. Object Management Group, I.: Life Cycle Service Specification. Object Management Group, Inc. Version 1.2 (2002)
15. Object Management Group, I.: CORBA Components. Object Management Group, Inc. Version 3.0 (2002)
16. (OpenCCM — the open CORBA components model platform) Web site at http://openccm.objectweb.org
17. Object Management Group, I.: Streams for CCM. Object Management Group, Inc. Draft Adopted Specification (2002)

A Serialisation Based Approach for Processes Strong Mobility

Soumaya Marzouk, Maher Ben Jemaa, and Mohamed Jmaiel

ReDCAD Laboratory
National School of Engineers of Sfax
BPW 3038 Sfax Tunisia
Soumarzouk@yahoo.fr, Maher.benjemaa@enis.rnu.tn,
Mohamed.Jmaiel@enis.rnu.tn

Abstract. We present in this paper a generic approach for process transformation into strong mobile entity. Our approach is based on processes *Serialisation* using source code transformation, which generates the source code of a strong mobile process. Our approach is suitable for transforming distributed applications into mobile applications where every process can be migrated independently any time. We applied our approach to Java Thread by designing a grammar describing the generated mobile process code. The evaluation results of generated mobile Threads shows good performances.

Keywords: Strong Mobility, Source code transformation, Serialisation, Distributed systems, Java Thread.

1 Introduction

Process strong mobility represents an efficient mechanism for solving many problems like fault tolerance [GBB05] and load balancing [BSA05]. Moreover, process strong mobility contributes for managing pair to pair and grid based systems [CB06],[GYHP06].

In fact, process strong mobility allows the transfer of an executing process from a source site to a distant site, where it resumes its execution starting from the interruption point. Thus, strong mobility requires the capture of the process execution state which is a complicated task since programming languages do not allow direct access to the process execution stack.

Generally, there is a trade off between efficacity and portability in most works dealing with strong mobility. Indeed, solutions suggested to solve this problem are either non portable solutions but offering good performances like those which are implemented on operating system level [BSA05],[BHKP04],[DO91], and solutions operating on virtual machine level [BHKP04],[SBB+00],[ZWL02], or more portable solutions but not very powerful like those which operate on compiled code level [GBB05],[TRV+00],[SSY01], or solutions which operate on process source code level [BN01],[CWHB03],[Fun98],[CLG05].

J. Indulska and K. Raymond (Eds.): DAIS 2007, LNCS 4531, pp. 153–166, 2007.
© IFIP International Federation for Information Processing 2007

In this paper, we present a solution for process strong mobility which is: generic, user transparent, offering a great portability, and rather powerful. Our solution is based on process serialisation. Object Serialisation consists in saving current values of its attributes. In case of process serialisation, it consists in saving the process execution context. This makes it possible to have an image reflecting the instantaneous process execution state to resume the execution later by carrying out a deserialisation. Our solution consists in simulating the process execution context with an artificial stack saving a portable image of its execution state and which does not depend on the used programming language. This solution is made by a syntactic transformation of the source code, thus ensuring, the maintenance of the process execution state, while preserving its original semantics. Therefore, the process migration consists in (1) serialising the process on the source site, (2) transferring the serialized process towards the new execution site, (3) deserialising the process and resuming its execution. We applied our transformation approach for Java Thread by implementing a precompiler which transforms a Java Thread into a Mobile Thread. This transformation ensures that restarting Thread after migration is enough to continue its execution starting from the interruption point.

Our approach is distinguished from others in the way that it is completely transparent since it does not need any changes on the original process code, and programmer has not to fix interruption points prealably in the process code. In addition, our approach keeps the instantaneous process state value, so, there is no need to do periodic checkpointing and rollback to resume a suspended process. Moreover, the process migration is dynamic and can be repeated an arbitrary time. Our evaluation tests show that our approach minimizes the execution time overhead due to codes additions, and keeps a proportionally acceptable execution time compared to the initial one. Moreover, the generated Thread is totally portable, thanks to its artificial execution context structure, and it preserves the semantic of the original Thread.

This paper is organized as follows. We will present in the second section the related works. Next in the third section, we present a description of our code transformation approach. Then, in the fourth section, we will present the evaluation results of our approach applied to Java Threads. Finally, we conclude and present perspectives of our works.

2   Related Work

Many works dealt with the process strong mobility problem. We classify this works in four classes according to their action's level.

First, works which operate on **Operating System level** [BSA05], [DO91]. These techniques are characterized with a short response delay since all treatments are integrated into the operating system functionalities. However, these approaches have the disadvantage of forcing all participating nodes to use the particular operating system. Therefore, the use of this type of solutions can be done only in a network with homogeneous operating systems. Thus, such a solution will not be applicable on the grid, for example.

Second class of work act on **Virtual Machine level** [BHKP04], [SBB⁺00], [ZWL02]. Generally, these solutions were particularly proposed for the Java language. They consist in JVM extension to support process strong mobility. These solutions grant the independence with the operating system layer. However, they reduce the application portability since they can be executed only on the extended JVM. This problem is not major if the user work on a local area network but it becomes significant if he wants to distribute the execution over the Internet.

Other solutions operate on **Compiled Code level** [GBB05], [TRV⁺00], [SSY01], [SSY00]. Most of them choose the Java language as target and transform process byte codes. These solutions increase the portability of a mobile application since it is independent from the operation system and the JVM. However, such techniques do not allow forced migration by external Thread but only the Thread itself can initiate its migration. Thus, this solution is not adapted to carry out load balancing or fault tolerance strategies.

Finally, other solutions act on **Source Code level** [BN01], [CWHB03], [CB06], [DR98], [GYHP06],[Fun98], [CLG05], [SMY99]. This approach has the advantage, to be independent of the operating system, to not modify neither the interpreter, nor the programming language. Thus it is more portable than the first three solutions. However, many works adopting this kind of solution reduce the application portability. In fact, many works use a specific platform [CWHB03], [CB06], or impose the use of a procedural language [BN01], or MPI based program [GYHP06], [CLG05]. Others do not allow a forced migration made by an external application [Fun98], [SMY99], or specifies static checkpoints in the process source code [DR98].

Table 1. Classification of Work Treating Strong Mobility

	References	Specific Platform	Forced Migration	Language
Operating System	[DO91][BSA05]	x	v	x
Virtual Machine	[SBB⁺00][BHKP04]	x	v	Java
	[ZWL02]	Multi Agent	v	
Compiled Code	[GBB05][TRV⁺00] [SSY00][SSY01]	x	x	Java
Source Code	[DR98]	x	Static checkpoint	C++
	[GYHP06][CLG05]	x	Static checkpoint	MPI
	[Fun98][SMY99]	x	x	Java
	[BN01]	x	v	procedural Language X-Klaim
	[CWHB03][CB06]	Aglet	v	C++

In *Table 1*[1] we summarize related works dealing with strong mobility. We consider in this classification many criterias like action level, use of a specific platform, the initiator of migration, etc.

Our approach can be classified under the source code modification class, but differs from the others in that it is a generic approach since it is independent of the programming language. It provides a portable solution since it does not depend on a specific platform. In addition, it is transparent because no manual changes must be done to the original process code.

We note that [CWHB03] is the most close solution to the present paper, but our work is distinguished by its portability. Indeed, our pre-processor is needed only at compilation time, and it doesn't introduce any restriction on the executing site configuration. However, in [CWHB03] the mobile agent can be executed only on a site lodging the agent platform, which restrict the mobility and do not motivate the use of this solution in a grid environment.

Moreover, our solution offer forced migration which is a very important characteristic of a process strong mobility approach. In fact, non forced migration signifies that only the process it self can initiate the mobility operation, which implies that migration is pre-programmed in the process code. For example, in a load balancing system, process migration is initiated when the execution host becomes overloaded, which cannot been known in advance. In this case, migration call cannot be written explicitly in the process code but must be initiated instantly by an extern application which is in this case the load balancing system.

3   Transformation Approach

Our approach consists in transforming a process into a strongly mobile entity. This transformation must guarantee

- Persistence: Allowing to save / restore the process execution state at any execution time,
- Repetitivity: The possibility of repeating the migration operation several times during process execution,
- Transparency: The original process code does not need any changes
- Portability: The generated mobile process can be run on any machine, whatever is its software or hardware configuration,
- Genericity: independency of the programming language.

Actually, a process does not have the persistence character (it is not serialisable). To make it serialisable, we will use a source code precompiler which transforms a traditional process into a strong mobile one.

Our approach consists in designing transformation rules of process source code written in an object-oriented language while providing several functionalities. First, generated code simulates the instantaneous process execution state by an artificial structure. Second, it updates this structure while the process execution

---

[1] v : supported; x : unsupported.

progresses. Finally, it ensures the resumption of the process execution while preserving its execution semantics.

In the following, we will present details of our process transformation approach including modelling process execution context, capturing and re-establishing process state and transformation rules of process code instructions.

3.1   Capturing and Reestablishing Process State

To ensure process strong mobility, we propose two mechanisms: Capturing and Re-establishing process state mechanisms.

Capturing process state mechanism serves to store an instantaneous image of process execution progress. It requires modelling and updating process execution context. Thus, we propose to add to the process source code an attribute simulating the process execution progress, and instructions updating the process execution state.

Explicitly, to model process execution state we propose a generic model called process artificial execution stack. This latter includes the execution progress state (method entry point) of each called method. Process artificial execution stack is build by pushing a method entry point for each called method. In fact, an entry point is an object storing method execution progress state. This object will include attributes saving the current values of method input data, local variables, and the position of the next instruction to be carried out by the method. Since the number and types of these attributes depend on methods data, we generate, for each called method (process methods or object methods), a class (method model class) having as attributes the method input data, local variables, and the position of the next instruction.

In addition, the capturing mechanism includes updating process execution state. Therefore, we propose to add, for each called method, instructions updating the method entry point with current method data values. Explicitly, we propose to add at the beginning of each called method (1) instructions which instantiate the method model class generated to create an entry point corresponding to the method call, (2) instructions which pop the entry point on the process artificial stack, and (3) instructions initializing the entry point attributes corresponding to the method input data and local method variables by their initial values. In addition, in the end of each method, it is necessary to add an instruction which pop the entry point from the artificial execution stack. Moreover, updating process execution state requires method instructions transformation which will be detailed in the next section. Thus, the current state of each method is stored in the artificial execution stack, so the capture of the current process state consists in suspending the process execution and serialising it.

The second mechanism involved in process strong mobility is Reestablishing process execution state mechanism. It serves to resume process execution after migration. Thus, reestablishing process execution state requires integrating the process execution state captured by the first mechanism in the new process execution instance, and resuming process execution starting from the interruption point.

In order to integrate captured state in the new process execution, each method has to reference its captured entry point. In fact, we propose to add, in the beginning of each called method, instructions which refer to the captured method entry point if it is the reestablishing step.

In addition, reestablishing process state mechanism must ensure that execution resumption starts always from the interruption point. Thus, we modified process code by adding instructions ensuring that each method execution restart from the instruction having the position of the next instruction stored in method entry point attributes. Doing so, we propose to supervise every method instruction execution by a test on its position ensuring that the executing instruction is always the one which has the position of the next instruction.

3.2   Code Transformation

In order to achieve the process transformation into a strongly mobile entity, we define transformation rules which we will apply to code instructions. To do this, we classify code instructions into three categories:

- Simple instructions: they are elementary instructions, which include assignments, inputs/outputs instructions, calls of method belonging to the process, etc.
- Composed instructions: they are blocks of code containing loops or control structures.

In the following subsections, we will define for each type of instruction, corresponding transformation rules. We describe also code transformations of Shared object(remote object used by many process) and we propose optimizations for our transformation rules.

Transformation of Elementary Instructions. Simple instructions transformation serve to ensure execution state updating and execution resumption while preserving execution semantics. Process execution state updating is ensured by replacing all occurrences of local variables and input data of the method with references to the attribute of the corresponding entry point. Moreover, after each instruction execution, the value of the next instruction position to be executed must be updated. Therefore, after each instruction of the transformed code, we propose to increment the position value of the next code instruction to be carried out. For example, if the following instruction belongs to a method called m_1 : x = y ;
Where x is a local variable and y a method input data, it will be then replaced with:

```
Entry_Point_m_1.x = Entry_Point_m_1.y ;
Entry_Point_m_1.position++ ;
```

In addition, to ensure resuming process execution after migration, every code instruction must be supervised by testing the value of its position. Consequently, the instruction x = y ; will be replaced with:

```
if(Entry_Point_m_1.position==current_position) {
    Entry_Point_m_1.x = Entry_Point_m_1.y ;
    Entry_Point_m_1.position++ ;  }
```

Besides, we must be sure that the execution interruption will not take place after the instruction execution and before the position update. Therefore, we propose to consider the transformation result of an instruction as an atomic operation which can't be interrupted by serialisation. The transformation of the instruction: x = y ; will be as follows :

```
Lock_Serialisation();
if(Entry_Point_m_1.position == current_position) {
    Entry_Point_m_1.x = Entry_Point_m_1.y ;
    Entry_Point_m_1.position++ ;
} Unlock_Serialisation();
```

Thus, these transformations applied for simple instructions, guarantee process execution state updating, as well as reestablishing after migration, while preserving its execution semantics.

Transformation of code with Loops and controls structures. The difficulty which arises for the case of loops and control structures is the update of position of next instruction to be carried out.

In fact, the code transformation has to preserve the execution semantics, whatever the interruption position is, during loop or control structure execution. Next, we will study the case of the structure while (while(cond) Bloc;) *"Fig1"* and if-else (if(cond) Bloc1; else Bloc2;) *"Fig2"*.

```
while ((pc >= inPc(Bloc_transformed)) && (pc <= outPc(Bloc_transformed))) {
        if (pc == inPc(Bloc_transformed) && !cond) {
        // condition not verified
                pc = outPc(Bloc_transformed)+1;
                break;
        }
        Bloc_transformed;
        if (pc == outPc(Bloc_transformed))
                pc = inPc(Bloc_transformed);
}
```

Fig. 1. Transformation of while loop

```
if (((pc >= inPc(Bloc1_transformed)) && (pc <= outPc(Bloc1_transformed))) ||
(pc == Pc(If) && cond)) {
          Bloc1_transformed;
          if (pc == outPc(Bloc1_transformed)) {
          // end of the block if: jump the block else.
                    pc = outPc(Bloc2_transformed) + 1;
          }
} // if the condition is not verified: enter to the block else
else {
          if (pc== inPc(thisIf))
                    pc = outPc(Bloc1_transformed) + 1;
}
if ((pc>= inPc(Bloc2_transformé)) && (pc <= outPc(Bloc2_transformed))) {
          Bloc2_transformed;
}
```

Fig. 2. Transformation of if - else structure

with:

- Bloc1_transformed represent the transformation result of Bloc1.
- outPC(Bloc_transformed) represent the first position in Bloc_transformed.
- inPc(Bloc_transformed)represent the last position in Bloc_transformed
- Pc(if) represent the position of the if instruction. Indeed, we attribute to the if instruction a position to ensure that the if condition will be evaluated only once.

The code given above preserves the initial semantics whatever the execution stop point in this code.

Transformation of Shared Objects. In this step, we extend our transformation to support dependent process. Indeed, we propose to transform distributed applications including dependent process using shared object on mobile application where every component can be moved from a site to another at any execution moment. All transformations presented above remain valid including transformation of shared object methods. Nerveless, if a process migrates while executing shared object method, the execution coherence may be lost. Thus, we propose to add an artificial lock to a shared object which interdicts the execution of a method belonging to a shared object used by a migrating process. That is, if a process migrate while executing a shared object method, it must lock the shared object until resuming the interrupted method. In addition, every process trying to execute a shared object method must verify if this object is unlocked before calling the method. Thus, every call of a shared object method in the process code must be supervised by a test on the shared object artificial lock.

Optimizing the transformed code. In order to optimize the transformed code, we propose to affect a position number for blocks containing more than one instruction. Thus, an instructions block, with the update instruction of its corresponding position, will form an atomic operation during which a serialisation is not authorized. This makes it possible to reduce the size of the code added compared to the initial code, and consequently to reduce the execution time of the transformed process. This modification requires several rules for the choice of blocks.

First, blocks should not contain the headings of controls structures or of loops of the original code. This case can generate compilation errors, since it causes crossed loops.

Second, the method call must be an elementary block or in extreme cases, must be at the beginning of a block. Otherwise, if a serialisation starts during the method execution, block instructions which are before the method call will be re-executed after migration.

Third, the block size must be quite selected not to be, neither too large causing the delay of the serialisation operation, nor too small causing the increase of the size of the generated code compared to the original code.

We propose also another optimization, which consists in not applying transformations concerning loops and control structures in all cases. Indeed, if the code carried out by a loop or a control structure is simple (without imbricated structures, without call of object methods), we propose to assign to this structure only one position number, and thus to authorize the serialisation only at the end of the execution of all the structure code. For the case of loops, this solution remains valid if the total number of instructions to be carried out by the loop is not very large. Otherwise, in general case, we propose to allow the serialisation at the end of each iteration.

4   Performance Evaluation

In order to evaluate performances of the generated mobile process, we apply our transformation rules to Java Threads. Thus, we designed a grammar describing the Java syntax of the mobile Thread transformed code, and we implement a source code transformer which takes a java Thread as entry and generates the equivalent mobile Thread.

In order to evaluate our solution performance, we present the evaluation results of our transformed process execution times, compared to the original processes execution time. We used a mobile computer equivalent processor Centrino 1,7 GHz and having a 1Go size of RAM.

We evaluate the execution time increase, due to the code portions added by our transformer. Moreover, the evaluation of our solution will be based on several criteria:

– Criteria related to the original process: code complexity, code size.
– Criteria related to the transformation: maximum size of the elementary instruction block.
– Criteria related to the execution: data size.

We can notice that the transformation overhead is relatively big for an execution with small data size "Fig3" This can be explained by the fact that the added code can be classified in two classes. First, the initialization code which has a constant size and which is carried out only once at the beginning of each method. Second, the updating code which has a variable size according to the original code size, and which can be carried out several times, according to the size of the input data.

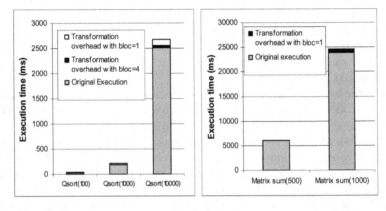

Fig. 3. Transformed Thread Execution time compared to the original Thread execution time

Thus for small size data or for processes having small methods size, and for the same complexity, the overhead of the transformed process execution time compared to that of the original process is proportionally big, since the initialization code is of constant size. This also explains, the overhead increase, for the same code, when the data size increases "Fig3". Indeed, since the data size increases, the iteration number also increases, and consequently the iteration execution number of added code increases too. Moreover, the increase in the maximum block size of atomic instructions causes the decreases of the transformation overhead. This phenomenon happen because the atomic instructions blocks number decrease induced that the added code became smaller than the original one.

We also stress that the overhead is increasingly big, when the number of overlapping loops increases, and especially when the loop code is of small size, a typical example is the multiplication of two matrices. In this case, the added code size becomes large compared to the original code, and considering the great iteration number and the code complexity, the transformed code execution

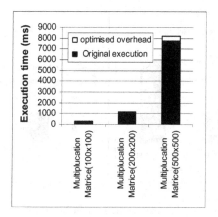

Fig. 4. Execution time of Mobile Thread having an Optimized code

becomes very heavy. To cure this type of behaviour, we presented an optimization in section 3.2.4. The results relating to this optimization are presented in *"Fig4"*.

Following, we aim to evaluate the serialisation/deserialisation operation. Thus, we will use Matrice Multiplication 500X500 Thread, without taking into account the process transfer cost, which depends on the network conditions. Presented results in *"Fig5"* correspond to the Thread execution time stopped at the instant "interruption time", serialized, deserialized, and resumed on the same execution site. These results show that the serialisation/deserialisation operation of process has a weak cost. Consequently, the integration of the execution context operation which requires a partial re-execution of the process code is not an expensive operation.

Next, we aim to evaluate the cost of migration of a process belonging to a distributed application. In this context, we use a producer/consumer application. This application involves a producer mobile process, a consumer mobile process and a Remote Object representing the Buffer.

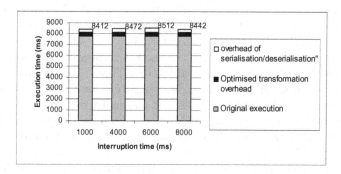

Fig. 5. Execution time of Multiplication matrix Thread (500X500) with serialisation/ deserialisation operation

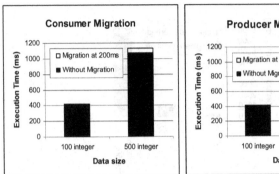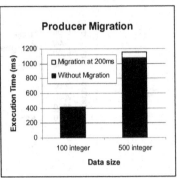

Fig. 6. Overhead introduced by process migration of producer/consumer application

In *"Fig.6"* we represent the overhead caused by the migration of the producer process and the consumer process at different execution moment and for different data size. We notice that the overhead introduced by the migration of producer or consumer process is very small.

5   Conclusion

In this paper, we proposed a generic solution for the processes strong mobility, with great portability, completely transparent and rather powerful. Indeed, our approach consists in transforming process into a serialisable object. Throughout its execution, our mobile process could migrate several times from a site to another, at any execution time, without losing its execution state, nor the semantics of the original process. Our approach is novel in that it was designed to be completely transparent to the programmer, requiring no changes to the original application code. Moreover, our approach makes it possible to generate completely portable mobile processes. Indeed, our approach is independent of the used platform and there are no software or material constraints on the migration participating sites. In addition, our approach makes it possible to force the process migration starting from an external application, which allows its use to implement load balancing, fault-tolerance, peer to peer or grid based systems. We apply our transformation approach for Java Thread. Indeed, to achieve the process migration, it suffies to apply the transformation to the original process code, to compile the generated classes and to launch the Mobile Thread execution from any host lodging the JVM. Thread can be stopped and migrated towards any host lodging the JVM, at any moment of its execution and an ar number of times for the same execution.

Our work perspectives consist in providing solutions to the problem of resource sharing (file, socket) between mobile processes. Indeed until this stage, the Thread migration using a shared resource does not preserve execution semantics. We aims also to validate our code transformer, in order to affirm that the transformation is purely syntactic and that the mobile process always preserves the original process semantics. Another prospect consists in using this approach of mobility for the implementation of a load balancing system or fault tolerant grid based applications. Doing so, an execution environment should be developed.

References

[BHKP04] Bouchenak, S., Hagimont, D., Krakowiak, S., Palma, N.: Experiences implementing efficient java thread serialization (2004)

[BN01]   Bettini, L., De Nicola, R.: Translating strong mobility into weak mobility. In: Picco, G.P. (ed.) MA 2001. LNCS, vol. 2240, pp. 182–197. Springer, Heidelberg (2001)

[BSA05]   Barak, A., Shiloh, A., Amar, L.: An organizational grid of federated mosix clusters. In: CCGRID '05. Proceedings of the Fifth IEEE International Symposium on Cluster Computing and the Grid (CCGrid'05), vol. 1, pp. 350–357. IEEE Computer Society, Washington, DC (2005)

[CB06]   Chakravarti, A.J., Baumgartner, G.: Self-organizing scheduling on the organic grid. International Journal of High. Performance Computing Applications 20(1), 115–130 (2006)

[CLG05]   Cao, J., Li, Y., Guo, M.: Process migration for mpi applications based on coordinated checkpoint. In: ICPADS '05. Proceedings of the 11th International Conference on Parallel and Distributed Systems (ICPADS'05), pp. 306–312. IEEE Computer Society, Washington, DC (2005)

[CWHB03] Chakravarti, A.J., Wang, X., Hallstrom, J.O., Baumgartner, G.: Implementation of strong mobility for multi-threaded agents in java. icpp, 00, pp. 321 (2003)

[DO91]   Douglis, F., Ousterhout, J.K.: Transparent process migration: Design alternatives and the sprite implementation. Software - Practice and Experience 21(8), 757–785 (1991)

[DR98]   Dimitrov, B., Rego, V.: A portable threads system supporting migrant threads on heterogeneous network farms. IEEE Transactions on Parallel and Distributed Systems 9(5), 459 (1998)

[Fun98]   Funfrocken, S.: Transparent migration of java-based mobile agents. In: Mobile Agents, pp. 26–37 (1998)

[GBB05]   Garbacki, P., Biskupski, B., Bal, H.E.: Transparent fault tolerance for grid applications. In: EGC, pp. 671–680 (2005)

[GYHP06] Gao, Q., Yu, W., Huang, W., Panda, D.K.: Application-transparent checkpoint/restart for mpi programs over infiniband. In: ICPP '06. Proceedings of the 2006 International Conference on Parallel Processing, pp. 471–478. IEEE Computer Society, Washington, DC (2006)

[SBB+00] Suri, N., Bradshaw, J., Breedy, M.R., Groth, P.T., Hill, G.A., Jeffers, R.: Strong mobility and fine-grained resource control in nomads. In: Kotz, D., Mattern, F. (eds.) MA 2000, ASA/MA 2000, and ASA 2000. LNCS, vol. 1882, pp. 2–15. Springer, Heidelberg (2000)

[SMY99]   Sekiguchi, T., Masuhara, H., Yonezawa, A.: A simple extension of java language for controllable transparent migration and its portable implementation. In: Coordination Models and Languages, pp. 211–226 (1999)

[SSY00]   Sakamoto, T., Sekiguchi, T., Yonezawa, A.: Bytecode transformation for portable thread migration in java. In: ASA/MA, pp. 16–28 (2000)

[SSY01]   Sekiguchi, T., Sakamoto, T., Yonezawa, A.: Portable implementation of continuation operators in imperative languages by exception handling. In: Romanovsky, A., Dony, C., Knudsen, J.L., Tripathi, A.R. (eds.) Advances in Exception Handling Techniques. LNCS, vol. 2022, p. 217. Springer, Heidelberg (2001)

[TRV⁺00]   Truyen, E., Robben, B., Vanhaute, B., Coninx, T., Joosen, W., Verbaeten, P.: Portable support for transparent thread migration in java. In: Kotz, D., Mattern, F. (eds.) MA 2000, ASA/MA 2000, and ASA 2000. LNCS, vol. 1882, pp. 29–43. Springer, Heidelberg (2000)

[ZWL02]   Zhu, W., Wang, C.-L., Lau, F.C.M.: Jessica2: A distributed java virtual machine with transparent thread migration support. In: IEEE Fourth International Conference on Cluster Computing, Chicago, USA (September 2002)

Parallel State Transfer in Object Replication Systems

Rüdiger Kapitza[1], Thomas Zeman[1], Franz J. Hauck[2], and Hans P. Reiser[3]

[1] Dept. of Computer Science 4, University of Erlangen-Nürnberg, Germany
rrkapitz@cs.fau.de, sithzema@cip.informatik.uni-erlangen.de
[2] Institute of Distributed Systems, Ulm University, Germany
franz.hauck@uni-ulm.de
[3] LASIGE, Departamento de Informática, University of Lisboa, Portugal
hans@di.fc.ul.pt

Abstract. Replication systems require a state-transfer mechanism in order to recover crashed replicas and to integrate new ones into replication groups. This paper presents and evaluates efficient techniques for parallel state transfer in such systems. These techniques enable a faster integration of replicas and improve overall service availability. On the basis of previous work on distributed download in client-server and peer-to-peer systems, we obtain parallel state-transfer mechanisms for replicated objects. Our algorithms support static and dynamic distributed download of state without a priori knowledge about the state size. A non-blocking transfer minimises the time of service unavailability during state transfer. In addition, partial state capturing is presented as an additional technique that improves the parallel transfer of large states.

1 Introduction

Replication is an established way for building reliable distributed applications. In any replication system, state transfer is required for initialising new replicas as well as for updating and recovering existing replicas. With the ongoing trend towards self-organising, dynamic distributed systems, state transfer is becoming an essential aspect of system performance and availability. For example, if the membership in a replica group changes frequently, the efficiency of the state transfer plays a non-negligible role in total system performance. In addition, synchronising the state transfer with state modification usually requires suspending the application for at least part of the duration of the transfer. This suspension time reduces system availability.

Current replication systems often use a very simple strategy for transferring the state from an available replica to the new replica. In this paper, we analyse ways to improve the performance of state transfer in replica groups. Non-blocking state transfer minimises the suspension time during the transfer, and parallel transfer from multiple state-providing replicas to a target avoids bottlenecks in the network. We evaluate the impact of various state-transfer techniques on the performance and availability of the running application.

This paper is structured as follows. The next section analyses the challenges of state transfer in object replication system and discusses related work. Section 3 presents the non-blocking and parallel variants of state transfer in our architecture. Section 4 gives a detailed experimental evaluation and Section 5 concludes.

J. Indulska and K. Raymond (Eds.): DAIS 2007, LNCS 4531, pp. 167–180, 2007.

2 Background and Related Work

The transfer of the state of an application raises the following basic questions:

- The internal application state needs to be serialised, i.e., be converted into a location-independent representation that can be transferred over the network.
- The state transfer (or, more precisely, the serialisation process) needs to be coordinated with the normal operation of the replicated application.
- The state needs to be transferred over the network.

In our prototype, the serialisation is delegated to the application. The replicated object needs to implement two methods: a `getState` method serialises the object's state into a byte stream, and a `setState` method sets the object's state on the basis of data read from a byte stream. The infrastructure provides these streams; different variants of the stream implementation can, for example, read/write directly from/to a network socket or from/to a file on a local disk. This streaming approach allows concurrency between the serialisation and the actual remote transfer, and it avoids the necessity of fully storing the serialised state. Thus, it perfectly qualifies for transferring large states.

This paper focuses on the other two questions. While most replication infrastructures need to suspend an application before state transfer and resume it afterwards, we minimise this suspension time. In addition, while current systems use a simple transfer from a single node to another, we analyse strategies for parallel state transfer from multiple up-to-date replicas to a target replica. In the following, we first discuss basic approaches to state transfer, then extend the discussion to parallel transfer mechanisms.

2.1 Basic Approaches to State Transfer

In an object replication system, the state transfer needs to be coordinated with the execution of object methods. The state has to be captured atomically, without concurrent modifications. Furthermore, the state must be captured at a specific point of time. For example, if a new replica joins a group of actively replicated objects, it needs the current state at the moment of the membership change.

The state transfer can be made in a *blocking*, *non-blocking*, and *checkpoint-based* way. Most systems support state transfer at the group-communication level. Cabaas and Mestras [1] give an overview of existing approaches to state transfer in replication frameworks, and discuss the coordination of state transfer with system operation.

In a blocking transfer, a replica resumes the execution of client requests only after the state is fully transferred to the target node. Arjuna [2] and Electra [3] support an automatic state transfer when a new member joins a replication group and block the whole system during the transfer. Phoenix [4] blocks only the members involved in the state transfer. All three systems block at least some of the group members for the complete duration of the state transfer. For large application states, this can lead to long response times [5].

In a non-blocking transfer, it is necessary only to capture the state atomically. The captured state can, for example, be stored in memory for small states, or written to hard disk for larger states. The node can resume execution while the captured state is afterwards transferred to the target over the network. Systems such as JGroups [6] and

Eternal [7] provide such a non-blocking solution. However, both systems target at the transfer of small application states that can be stored in main memory.

A checkpoint-based approach is a third variant for state transfer, used for example by Mishra et al. [8] and Castro [9]. In this approach, every replica makes periodic checkpoints and records all client requests after the last checkpoint to a log. For state transfer, the existing checkpoint and log can be transferred to the target, without the need for explicit state serialisation at the moment of state transfer.

In the domain of replicated database systems, existing work covers the recovery of replicas using the coordination support offered by group communication frameworks [10,11]. Unlike the approaches discussed above, these systems primarily target the recovery of replicas by using system properties of databases. Thus, the proposed concepts can not be directly applied to object replication systems.

This paper targets at improving and extending non-blocking as well as blocking approaches for direct state transfer in the context of object replication systems. Some of the proposed techniques can also be applied to the checkpoint-based state-transfer approach, but this is not addressed further.

2.2   Parallel Transfer

Parallel transfer of state is not popular in object replication system, but it is a standard technology in other domains such as distributed download and peer-to-peer file-sharing systems.

Rodriguez, Kirpal and Biersack [12] propose two methods for parallel download named *history-based TCP* parallel access and *dynamic TCP* parallel access. Both approaches require a dedicated unicast connection from the client to each of the providing servers. The first approach adapts the packet size depending on the available bandwidth of the accessed servers, estimated on the basis of bandwidth information gathered in earlier accesses. According to the authors, history based TCP parallel access produces good results if the network and server conditions are constant, but lead to poor performance otherwise. The dynamic TCP parallel access does not rely on potentially outdated history information. A file that is to be downloaded is divided into N blocks of equal size. The client requests a different block from every server. If a client has completely received a block, it requests a new, not yet downloaded block from that server. This simple approach assigns more blocks to faster servers, but fully loads all servers. Rodriguez et al. [13] discuss the problem that a server has an idle phase between the end of transmission of a block and the reception of a succeeding request. They suggest *request pipelining* to avoid these inter-block idle times. A new block should be requested at least one round-trip-time (RTT) before the current block is fully received.

Vazhkudai [14] proposes similar parallel access approaches, but targets at downloads of large data sets in a grid infrastructure instead of focusing on clients that access small and mid-size documents. The simplest proposed approach is *brute-force co-allocation*, in which a file is divided in n equal parts that are downloaded in parallel, with n corresponding to the number of state-providing servers. This approach takes advantage of all servers, but the time to transfer the whole file depends on the slowest connection and server. Another scheme proposed as *predictive co-allocation* corresponds to the *history based TCP* approach. Third, Vazhkudai describes two variants of a dynamic approach that takes server and network conditions into account: *conservative load balancing* and *aggressive load balancing*. The first variant is equivalent to dynamic TCP without pipelining. The second variants uses heuristics to increase the amount of data requested from fast servers, and reduce the amount requested from slow servers or even exclude them from download altogether.

3   Decentralised State-Transfer Algorithms

In the following, we adapt the terminology of Xu et al. [15], who classify state-transfer approaches as *static-equal*, *static-unequal*, and *dynamic*. In contrast to previous work, we present an implementation that is adapted to fit the needs of distributed state transfer in active object replication. Our infrastructure provides two variants: The first variant is *static equal*, which assigns equal shares to all state-providing servers and uses small blocks to enable a continuous data flow. The second variant is *dynamic* and can be compared to dynamic TCP [12] and brute-force co-allocation [14]. In contrast to those systems, we support novel approaches for runtime optimisation that are beyond the typical mechanisms in distributed download applications.

The first issue in object replication systems is that the size of the transfer data is not known in advance. The transfer data is the result of an application-specific serialisation process, and thus it will be created "ad-hoc" at the moment the state transfer is requested. Theoretically, it is possible to first acquire the complete state from the application and then start the transfer. This is inefficient in terms of transfer time (the network transfer is delayed instead of being started in parallel to the state serialisation) and in terms of resource usage (if the state is transferred during serialisation, it is not necessary to store the full serialised state in memory or on disk). Thus, we propose algorithms that do not require the state size to be known a priori.

The second key issue is related in terms of resource usage: At the target of the state transfer, it is desirable to pass the serialised state data directly to the deserialisation process. This way, the need for storing a full copy of the serialised data in parallel to the deserialised data can be eliminated. Such functionality, however, requires that state data arrive in correct order. Some buffers for temporarily storing out-of-order data can be provided, but we want our algorithms to provide flow-control mechanisms that limit the size of such temporary storage. As a result, our approach ensures a low resource demand.

3.1   Terminology

In our system, the state data is transferred from a set of *state providers* to a single *transfer target*. The transfer protocols are defined by the exchange of *data requests* from the transfer target to state providers and *data replies* in the opposite direction. We use the following terminology:

- S is the set of state providers (servers).
- D is the state data to transfer. The size $|D|$ is not known in advance.
- A data request is defined by a tuple $< s_i, start, end >$; $s_i \epsilon S$, $start$ represents the first byte and end represent the last byte of a requested byte sequence.

– A data reply is defined as $< start, B >$, in which $start$ determines the absolute position in the state data and B represents a transmitted byte sequence, which we call a *block*.

If the requested block starts beyond the end of the state data ($start > |D|$), a state provider will indicated this fact with an empty response ($B = \{\}$). It is possible that a transfer target requests blocks beyond the end, as $|D|$ is not known in advance.

3.2 Parallel Transfer: Static Equal

The most simple strategy for distributed file transfer is *static equal*. The transfer data is split into n pieces of equal size, with n being the number of servers hosting a replica. Each replica thus has to provide a part of the state data. If the size of the transfer data is known in advance, it can easily be split into n pieces, like is done by Vazhkudai [14] and Gkantsidis et al.[16].

Without such knowledge, we must use a different approach. Each server should provide an equal amount of the state. The solution that we propose is to divide the state into small blocks of static size and to organise the transfer in rounds. In each round, the target sends a request to each server in a round-robin way, requesting a new block that has not been transferred yet. We assume that the block size $|B|$ is defined at transfer start. In round n ($n \in \mathcal{N}_0$), the requests can be constructed as follows: $< i, nr + (i - 1)|B|, nr + i|B| - 1 >$, where $i = 1, ..., |S|$ designates the target of the requests. A round transfers $r = |B||S|$ of data.

As the state size is not known in advance, we define $start_{max} = +\infty$. If a response a with $D = \{\}$ is received, we compute $start_{max} = min(start_{max}, start_a)$. Now, all requests $start = nr + (i - 1)|B| > start_{max}$ can be discarded. As there might be out-of-order transmissions, one has to wait for all pending requests with $start \leq start_{max}$. On the server side, the first request b that arrives with $start_b \geq |D|$ causes the server to send a response $B = \{\}$. All subsequent messages requesting data behind the end of D can be ignored. The server still has to continue participating in the state-transfer protocol, as requests for blocks before the end position might arrive out of order.

Requesting small blocks is expensive in terms of control messages, as for every block a request message has to be sent. We use *batching* to reduce the number of control messages. Instead of requesting only one block at a time, the set of all blocks of a configurable number of rounds p is requested from a state provider with a single message. Batching can easily be combined with pipelining, as suggested by Rodriguez and Biersack [13]. With pipelining, the requests for a new batch round are sent before the previous requests has fully been answered, thus reducing or eliminating the idle time of the servers between requests.

Instead of batching, two other ways might be used to reduce the cost of control messages. First, using a large block size could reduce the number of requests. Unfortunately, this strategy defeats our goal of providing a continuous stream of data that can directly be fed to the deserialisation process and thus would increase the resource usage at the receiver side. Second, the sequence of blocks could be assigned statically to each state provider at the transfer start. This way, each server would start to transfer every n-th block triggered by a single start message. This strategy leads to problems if the relative speed of the servers differs. Again, parts of the state of very different positions might arrive at a time, requiring large buffering and thus causing resource consumption at the receiver side. Consequently, there is a need for flow control, and using explicit requests for each block (or set of blocks) automatically provides such a control mechanism.

3.3 Parallel Transfer: Static Unequal

Some existing approaches to parallel file transfer use a technique called *static unequal* by Xu et al. [15]. The difference to static equal is the addition of a phase that estimates the transfer speed from the replicas. This estimation is later used to distributed the size of the state portions that are transferred according to the relative speed. This way, faster nodes are statically assigned a larger part than slower ones.

Theoretically, this principle could also be applied to parallel state transfer, using the same extensions as for static equal. The disadvantage of static unequal, however, is the addition of the estimation phase that delays the actual phase. A similar estimation can be obtained from the transfer of the first blocks in the subsequently described dynamic approach. The dynamic approach, however, is able to adjust the distribution of blocks dynamically, and, especially if flow control is used, adds no overhead compared to static unequal. Thus, we consider only the dynamic approach.

3.4 Parallel Transfer: Dynamic

While the static-equal algorithm assigns an equal part of the work to each server, *dynamic* adapts the request strategy at runtime, taking network and server condition into account. Our algorithm uses a novel approach to runtime adaptation and, in addition, introduces batching for optimisation.

The basic idea of the algorithm is to request a new block from a server each time the previously assigned block has been fully transferred. This ensures that servers which are less loaded and have a better connection (i.e., higher bandwidth and smaller round-trip time) transmit more data. As a result, the overall transfer time no longer depends on the slowest server, as it is the case for static equal. Similar to our static-equal approach, we obtain a continuous data stream with only minimal signalling overhead with a batching technique.

Our dynamic algorithm adapts the batch size individually for each server. A new batch is requested immediately after the first block has been successfully received, as shown in Figure 1. The key idea is to find an optimised batch size. If too much data is requested, this leads to bad performance in case that the state provider or the corresponding network connection slows down. On the other hand, if too few blocks (in the extreme, only one block) are requested, this causes undesirable idle times at the state provider. The ideal is to compute the batch size in a way such that a new batch request reaches the server when the last block of the previous batch has been fully transmitted. As this is not possible due to the unpredictable behaviour of the network and the server load, an estimation is used. We use a strategy inspired by Rodriguez and Biersack [13], who suggest to estimate an upper bound of the RTT and use this as a mark for submitting the next request.

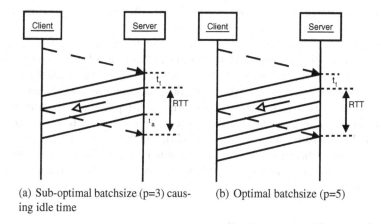

(a) Sub-optimal batchsize (p=3) caus-   (b) Optimal batchsize (p=5)
ing idle time

Fig. 1. Static Dynamic request scheme with adaptive batch size

Figure 1(a) shows an idle time, t_a, that should be avoided by adjusting the batch size. As shown in Figure 1(b), the batch size should be as big as it is necessary to keep the state provider busy until the next requests arrives. The value of t_a can be computed as $t_a = RTT - t_t(p - 1) = RTT - \frac{b}{C}(p - 1)$. In this formula, t_t is the transfer time for a single block, b denotes the block size, p is the batch length, and C is the transfer speed of the network. In the optimal case we require $t_a = 0$, and thus we can compute $p = RTT\frac{C}{b} + 1$. The value of p depends on runtime conditions. An estimate of C can be determined by measuring the time t_t and computing $C = \frac{b}{t_t}$. The RTT can be measured in a straightforward way. As both values depend on runtime measurements that might temporarily fluctuate, an exponential moving average is used to eliminate outliers and to include previous values, but give more recent ones more impact. If the computed batch length is very short, the benefit of batching vanishes, causing a high request overhead. To compensate this fact, we introduce a configurable minimal batch length (e.g., 3).

3.5 Partial State Capturing

In a non-blocking state transfer, the serialised state data is temporarily stored at the state providers. If the state size exceeds the available memory, disk storage has to be used. Writing the state to disk is a bottleneck that limits the performance of the state acquisition, and thus also determines the period of unavailability during state serialisation. Moreover, starting the network transfer of the state in parallel to the state serialisation causes concurrent read and write operations on the same disk, which further decreases the performance.

The performance penalty of writing state data to disk can be reduced in a parallel download strategy by writing only a partial state to disk at each state provider. This requires a coordination between state capturing and state transfer. In case of the static equal approach, the parts of the state that a replica has to transmit are known at transfer start, and thus the state acquistion process at node s_i only has to write the corresponding parts of the state, which are the blocks $s_i + n|S|$ $(n \in \mathcal{N}_0)$.

Using the same approach with the dynamic transfer strategy is more difficult, as there is no fixed rule that defines the blocks that are requested from a replica. Instead, the blocks are defined at run-time. If all replicas write disjunct parts of the state, only a static equal transfer can be used. Using partial state capturing with dynamic transfer can, however, be used with a more relaxed rule. All replicas can write overlapping parts of the state (for example, by letting every replica write half of the state). The writing strategy must be defined at transfer start, and the request algorithm must take into account the availability of blocks at each state provider. The amount of overlap is a trade-off between being able to redistribute load and being able to reduce the cost of state capturing.

4   Experimental Evaluation

This section gives a brief overview of our prototype implementation and evaluates the parallel state-transfer strategies discussed in the previous section in a homogeneous LAN environment and a heterogeneous WAN setting. Finally, the impact of a non-blocking state transfer on service availability is investigated.

4.1   Implementation Overview

The proposed algorithms and mechanisms have been implemented as a protocol layer of the Java-based JGroups [6] group communication framework, which is used for replication support in our Aspectix middleware [17]. JGroups has a modular protocol stack that is configured at start-up time. An application accesses the framework via a *channel* that provides a socket-like communication endpoint. A channel provides a local unique address and enables an application to exchange unicast messages with single members and multicast messages with all members connected to the channel. Each protocol can be configured via properties during the stack initialisation. There are essentially two kinds of transmission units named *events* and *messages*. Events represent a signalling mechanism for corresponding protocol layers. Messages are application-dependent transmission units.

The message sequence diagram in Figure 2 outlines the basic signalling of the non-blocking variant of our distributed state-transfer protocol. Initially, an application requests its current state via GET_DSTATE. The *distributed state transfer protocol (dstp)* layer immediately returns a Java InputStream to the application, which uses this stream to deserialise the state. Next, the dstp layer sends a NEED_CURRENT_STATE message to all members including the local node. This event causes all members to enqueue all subsequent messages and a GET_APPSTATE message is forwarded to the replicas. This message includes a Java OutputStream, which the application uses to serialise the state. All members of the group that reply by sending an event named STATE_VIEW. If there is already an ongoing state transfer, this message and all other actions are suppressed. The joining node will be informed by STATE_TRANSFER_DONE that an earlier initiated state transfer has finished and can restart its state request by resending NEED_CURRENT_STATE. If there is no active state transfer, the requesting node will receive the STATE_VIEW message events of all group members. Collecting these messages provides the information about all fully-functional nodes, enabling the requesting node to compute the request strategy. For example, assuming a non-blocking state transfer with partial state writing and the dynamic algorithm, not every node can provide every part of the state. Consequently, this has to be taken into account when requesting parts of the state. After reception of the STATE_VIEW message, the joining node can request the state according to the request strategy by sending dedicated DATA_REQUEST messages, which are answered by DATA_RESPONSE messages. As soon as the requesting node has received the whole state, the state transfer is finished by sending a STATE_TRANSFER_DONE.

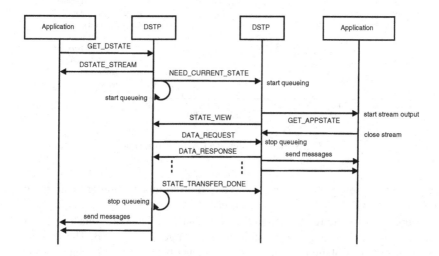

Fig. 2. Message Exchange of the Non-Blocking Distributed State Transfer Protocol

4.2 State Transfer in a Homogeneous LAN Environment

Group communication and active replication of objects often takes place in a homogeneous cluster environment. Thus, the following measurements have been made on a set of PCs with a AMD Athlon 2.0 GHz CPU and 1 GB RAM, using Linux kernel 2.6.17, SUN Java SDK 1.5.0_09, and connected by a 100 MBit/s switched Ethernet network.

We measured the time to do state transfer of state sizes between 0 and 200 MB for replication groups using the static equal and the dynamic state transfer algorithm. As the impact of parallel state transfer depends on the number of state providers, we varied the group size from one to four state-providing nodes. In all experiments, we used a fixed batch length of 10 and a block size of 16 kB. In order to compare our prototype implementations with existing state-transfer protocols, we did the same measurements with two state-transfer protocols provided by the JGroups group communication framework. The first variant, implemented by JGroups version 2.3, supports a non-blocking state transfer that requires the application to provide the state as a byte array that is transferred to the joining node. The second variant has recently been made available in

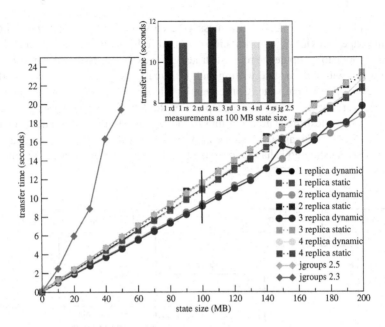

Fig. 3. State transfer in a LAN environment

the preview version of the future JGroups 2.5. It offers an API similar to our prototype and supports a blocking streaming state transfer.

Figure 3 shows the results of the measurement. The old state transfer protocol of JGroups 2.3 is not suitable for transferring states larger than 50 MB. The JGroups 2.5 state transfer protocol implementations scales better, but is not as efficient as any of our parallel state-transfer variants. The static equal parallel transfer produces very similar results for any number of state providers. The dynamic transfer offers a slight speed-up with 2 and 3 state providers, compared to only a single one. However, the performance drops back again with 4 providers. We assume that this is due to a network saturation at the link to the target and the overhead for sending requests to an increasing number of state providers.

All streaming state transfer variants produced good results that are close to each other. The dynamic variant performed slightly better than the static one, but the difference is very small. This matches our expectations, as a static equal distribution of state-transfer tasks on all nodes should be well-suited for the given homogeneous environment.

In practice, a LAN or cluster environment often is not dedicated to a single application. Thus, in a second experiment we evaluated the impact of CPU load at one of the state providing replicas. We implemented a simple load generator to produce a predictable and reproducible load. During the whole experiment, the selected node had a system CPU load between 2 and 3. We chose a group size of three replicas and a fourth node that joins the group. Again, we increased the state size from 0 to 200 MB in steps of 10 MB.

Figure 4 shows the strong impact on the state streaming Jgroups implementation. The state transfer time roughly doubles in comparison to an unloaded system. Both the dynamic and the static implementation perform better, as the state transfer is split among all state-providing replicas. The dynamic variant in general outperforms JGroups 2.5 and static equal state transfer.

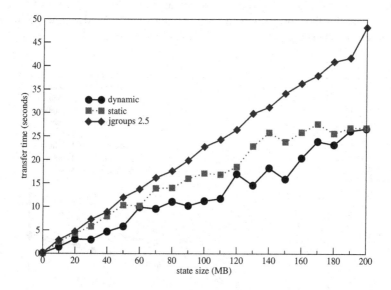

Fig. 4. State transfer in a LAN environment with load injection

In summary, the two experiments have shown that the introduction of parallel download techniques accelerates the transfer of large application states. While the benefit is only small in an idle environment, a significant speed-up is obtained in an environment with high CPU load. In both cases, the proposed dynamic state transfer algorithm outperforms the streaming state transfer offered by JGroups 2.5 and the parallel static equal algorithm.

4.3 State Transfer in a Heterogeneous WAN Environment

For evaluating the proposed techniques in a heterogeneous WAN environment, we chose a set of four different nodes. Two nodes are located in the same sub-network at the FAU Erlangen-Nuernberg, a third node *faui00a* is located in a different sub-network also at the campus of the FAU. Finally the fourth node *schirk* is located more distant at Ulm University.

In the experiment we set up a group of three replicas and let the fourth node join the group. We chose two scenarios: One time one of the machines at FAU faui00a joined the group and another time schirk the node located at Ulm University entered the group (cf. Figure 5).

Again the state transfer protocol of JGroups 2.3 did not scale and had memory problems especially when the distant node joined the group. The JGroups 2.5 protocol produced better results than the implementation of JGroups 2.3 and, as expected, requires
more time for state transfer if the node at Ulm University joins the group. The transfer
values of static equal are very close together, independent of the location of the joining node. Static equal is in general better than JGroups 2.5 if the distant node joins the
group, but slower if the joining node is located at FAU. This is to be expected, as static equal waits for the slowest node to start another round. The dynamic parallel state
transfer performs best regardless of the location of the joining node.

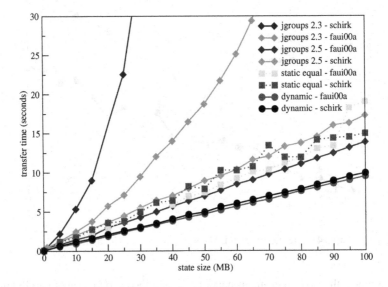

Fig. 5. State transfer in a WAN environment

4.4 Non-blocking State Transfer

This experiment does not target the reduction of the state transfer time, but instead
evaluates the reduction of service unavailability caused by a state transfer.

We set up a replication group of two nodes. One node sending probe message every
100 ms to all group members. Every node that receives a probe message immediately
replies to the probe and the sender records the round-trip time. Again we let a third node
repeatedly join the group and raised step-wise the state size from 0 to 200 MB. During
this process the joining replica recorded the time to acquire the state and the providing
nodes logged the time to hand over the state to the group-communication framework.
As Figure 6 details by the strong red and black lines, far less time is required to provide
the state to the framework than to transfer the whole state. This is achieved as the state
is temporarily saved on disk. Directly after the state provision, the application is able to
respond to requests, as the second set of curves shows.

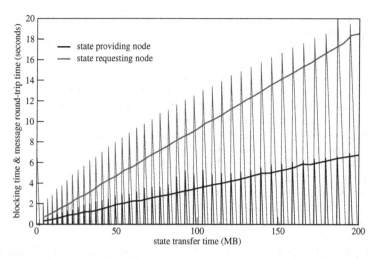

Fig. 6. The impact of a non-blocking state transfer on blocking time and message delay

5 Conclusions

This paper has presented and evaluated concepts for parallel state transfer in object replication systems. First, this paper presented and evaluated the implementation of parallel state transfer in an object replication system. While parallel download has previously been used with success in client-server systems as well as in decentralised peer-to-peer systems, it is currently not used in general infrastructures for object replication. Second, we have defined parallel state-transfer algorithms that work with an object state of unknown a priori size. In our application domain, the size of the serialised state of the replicas is usually unknown; this differs from the situation in other parallel download scenarios, in which files of known size are transferred. Third, we have presented partial state capturing as a technique that enables efficient non-blocking parallel transfer of large application states by generating only a partial state copy on disk.

An experimental evaluation has given important information about which state-transfer strategies are most important, depending on the size of the application state and the distribution of the system. We have particaluary shown that a dynamic parallel transfer enables a highly efficient state transfer. Besides minimising transfer time, our approach also minimises the time that replicas are unavailable because of suspension during state transfer.

References

1. Peña Cabañas, L., Pavón Mestras, J.: PODDP 2000 and DDEP 2000. LNCS, vol. 2023. Springer, Heidelberg (2000)
2. Parrington, G.D., Shrivastava, S.K., Wheater, S.M., Little, M.C.: The Design and Implementation of Arjuna. Computing Systems 8(2), 255–308 (1995)
3. Maffeis, S.: Adding Group Communication and Fault-Tolerance to CORBA. In: Proc. of the Conf. on Object-Oriented Technologies (Monterey, CA) USENIX, pp. 135–146 (1995)

4. Malloth, C.P.: Conception and implementation of a toolkit for building fault-tolerant distributed applications in large scale networks. PhD thesis, EPFL (1996)
5. Birman, K.: Building secure and reliable network applications. Manning Publications Co., Greenwich (1997)
6. Ban, B.: Design and implementation of a reliable group communication toolkit for Java. Technical report, Dept. of Computer Science, Cornell University (1998)
7. Narasimhan, P., Moser, L., Melliar-Smith, P.M.: State Synchronization and Recovery for Strongly Consistent Replicated CORBA Objects. In: DSN, pp. 261–270 (2001)
8. Mishra, S., Peterson, L., Schlichting, R.: Consul: a communication substrate for fault-tolerant distributed programs. Distributed Systems Engineering 1(2), 87–103 (1993)
9. Castro, M.: Practical Byzantine Fault Tolerance. Ph.D., MIT, January 2001, Also as Technical Report MIT-LCS-TR-817 (2001)
10. Kemme, B., Bartoli, A., Babaoglu, Ö.: Online Reconfiguration in Replicated Databases Based on Group Communication. In: DSN '01. Proc. of the 2001 Int. Conf. on Dependable Systems and Networks, pp. 117–130. IEEE Computer Society Press, Washington, DC, USA (2001)
11. Jiménez-Peris, R., Patiño-Martínez, M., Alonso, G.: Non-Intrusive, Parallel Recovery of Replicated Data. In: SRDS '02. Proc. of the 21st IEEE Symp. on Reliable Distributed Systems (SRDS'02), p. 150. IEEE Computer Society Press, Washington, DC, USA (2002)
12. Rodriguez, P., Kirpal, A., Biersack, E.W.: Parallel-access for mirror sites in the Internet. In: INFOCOM 2000. Nineteenth Annual Joint Conf. of the IEEE Computer and Communications Societies. Proc. IEEE, vol. 2, pp. 864–873 (2000)
13. Rodriguez, P., Biersack, E.W.: Dynamic parallel access to replicated content in the internet. IEEE/ACM Trans. Netw. 10(4), 455–465 (2002)
14. Vazhkudai, S.: Distributed Downloads of Bulk, Replicated Grid Data. J. Grid Comput. 2(1), 31–42 (2004)
15. Xu, Z., Xianliang, L., Mengshu, H., Chuan, Z.: A speed-based adaptive dynamic parallel downloading technique. SIGOPS Oper. Syst. Rev. 39(1), 63–69 (2005)
16. Gkantsidis, C., Ammar, M., Zegura, E.: On the Effect of Large-Scale Deployment of Parallel Downloading. In: WIAPP '03. Proc. of the The Third IEEE Workshop on Internet Applications, pp. 79–89. IEEE Computer Society Press, Washington, DC, USA (2003)
17. Reiser, H.P., Kapitza, R., Domaschka, J., Hauck, F.J.: Fault-tolerant replication based on fragmented objects. In: Proc. of the 6th IFIP Int. Conf. on Distributed Applications and Interoperable Systems (DAIS 2006) (2006)

MARS: An Agent-Based Recommender System for the Semantic Web*

Salvatore Garruzzo, Domenico Rosaci, and Giuseppe M.L. Sarné

DIMET, Università Mediterranea di Reggio Calabria
Via Graziella, Località Feo di Vito
89122 Reggio Calabria, Italy
{salvatore.garruzzo, domenico.rosaci, sarne}@unirc.it

Abstract. Agent-based Web recommender systems are applications capable to generate useful suggestions for visitors of Web sites. This task is generally carried out by exploiting the interaction between two agents, one that supports the human user and the other that manages the Web site. However, in the case of large agent communities and in presence of a high number of Web sites these tasks are often too heavy for the agents, even more if they run on devices having limited resources. In order to address this issue, we propose a new multi-agent architecture, called MARS, where each user's device is provided with a device agent, that autonomously collects information about the local user's behaviour. A single profile agent, associated with the user, periodically collects such information coming from the different user's devices to construct a global user profile. In order to generate recommendations, the recommender agent autonomously pre-computes data provided by the profile agents. This recommendation process is performed with the contribution of a site agent which indicates the recommendations to device agents that visit the Web site. This way, the site agent has the only task of suitably presenting the site content. We performed an experimental campaign on real data that shows the system works more effectively and more efficiently than other well-known agent-based recommenders.

1 Introduction

An overwhelming amount of different recommender systems [5,9,10] has been proposed in the last years to support users' Web navigation. They can provide users with useful suggestions, as the most promising pages to visit in a Web site, the items that could meet the user's interest in an E-commerce site, etc. Generally, recommender systems are partitioned in: (*i*) *Content-based*, that recommend to a user the objects which appear similar to those he already accessed in the past; (*ii*) *Collaborative Filtering*, that search similarities among users and consequently suggest to a user some objects also considered by similar users in the past; (*iii*) *Hybrid*, that use both content-based and collaborative filtering

---

* This work has been partially supported by the MIUR–"Italian Ministry of Education, University and Research", under the Research Project Quadrantis.

J. Indulska and K. Raymond (Eds.): DAIS 2007, LNCS 4531, pp. 181–194, 2007.

techniques to generate recommendations (e.g., a Web site can generate suggestions considering user's personal interests and user's commonalities among other known users). In these situations, hybrid recommender systems have been usually recognized as the most promising solution. Generally, these systems exploit in their recommendation algorithms an internal representation (profile) of the user. In order to construct such a user profile, many recommender systems proposed the use of *software agents*. Specifically, each user is associated to a software agent which monitors his Web activities. When the user accesses a Web site, his agent exploits the profile interacting with the site (e.g., through another software agent associated with the Web site). Finally, the site can use both content-based and collaborative filtering techniques to provide recommendations to the user agent by adapting the site presentation. In this scenario, an emerging issue is that nowadays users navigate on the Web using different devices as desktop PCs, cellular phones, palmtops, etc. Each of these devices presents: (*i*) its own interface characteristics (e.g., display capability), (*ii*) a different cost of Internet connection, (*iii*) different storage space and computational capability. These differences can influence the user's preferences; for example, when he accesses to a site with a cellular phone, he could desire a light site presentation. Consequently, we suppose that, for each user, there should be constructed a different profile for all the devices he uses. Furthermore, the issue (*iii*) leads us to argue that a user should be provided with a different and suitable agent for each device typology he exploits. Moreover, since the user's interests change with the exploited device also the recommender system should be adaptive with respect to the device [1,7].

We have recently proposed [8] an agent-based recommender system, called Multi Agent System Handling Adaptivity (MASHA), that tackles this important issue. MASHA provides each device with an autonomous *client agent* to collect into a local profile the information about the user's behaviour associated to just that device. This local profile is continuously updated by a *server agent* that manages a global user profile that collects the information provided by the different devices exploited by the user. The third component of this architecture, called *adapter agent*, is capable to generate a personalized Web site representation. This representation contains some useful recommendations derived by (*i*) an analysis of the user profile and (*ii*) the suggestions coming from other users that exploit the same type of device. The main limitation of MASHA is the significant computational cost of the adapter agent activities, due to the execution of the recommendation algorithm. More in detail, let n be the number of site visitors and m be the number of objects present in the site. The computational complexity of the MASHA technique is $\mathcal{O}(m \cdot n^2)$ in the worst case, since it compares the profile of each visitor with those of the other visitors and considers up to m concepts for each visitor.

In this paper we present a *Multi-Agent Recommender System* (MARS) that is an evolution of the MASHA architecture. The main contribution of this work consists in proposing a new recommendation algorithm that takes into account both the visitor profile and the exploited device, and presents a smaller computational cost with respect to MASHA. The MARS architecture (see Figure 1)

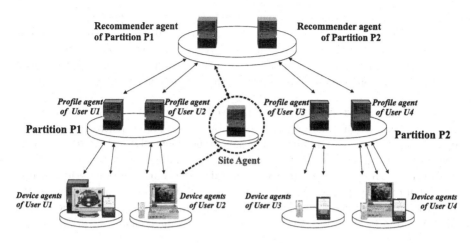

Fig. 1. The MARS Architecture

maintains the three MASHA agent typologies: (*i*) *device agent*, associated with each device, (*ii*) *profile agent*, associated with each user, and (*iii*) *site agent*, associated with each Web site. Differently from MASHA, the recommendations are not autonomously generated by the site agent, but they are the result of a collaboration between the site agent and a new agent type, called *recommender agent*. Indeed, the basic idea underlying MARS is that of partitioning the profile agents in clusters of users having similar global profiles, where each cluster is managed by a recommender agent. As a consequence, when a visitor accesses a Web site, the associated site agent does not have to make any onerous task, but it simply contacts the recommender agent that is associated with the cluster which the user belongs to. Each recommender agent r internally stores the following elements: (*i*) the profiles of the agents that belong to the partition of r; (*ii*) the catalogue of the objects of each site that has interacted in the past with r; (*iii*) the profiles of the past visitors of the site. Each of this profiles, associated with a past visitor v, collects the objects of the site that has been considered interesting by v. A significant advantage of this approach, is that a site agent that is contacted by n visitors, delegates the task of generating both content-based and collaborative filtering recommendations to the associated recommender agents. This way, the computational cost on the site agent side is $\mathcal{O}(m \cdot p)$ (where p is the number of different clusters) that results significantly lower than MASHA. Differently from other recommender systems [3,6,11], MARS presents three original characteristics, namely:

1. In order to construct the global user profile, it takes into account the different devices exploited by the user.
2. It generates the recommendations using the collaboration of the recommender agent, that runs on a server machine and pre-computes most of the necessary data. This way, the task of the site agent becomes very light.

3. It simplifies the task of the device agent, which does not perform neither the construction of the whole user's profile and the generation of the recommendations. Indeed, the user's profile is constructed by the more powerful profile agent running on a server machine, and the recommendations are generated by the site agent in conjunction with the recommender agent.

These characteristics make MARS more effective and more efficient when generating recommendations with respect to other systems, especially in presence of very large agent communities. We have experimentally evaluated MARS by comparing it with other recent profile-based recommender system approaches, and observing a significative improvements of the recommendation performances. The plan of the paper is as follows. In Section 2 we provide an overview of the MARS architecture; Related work is examined in Section 3; some experiments are presented in Section 4. Finally, in Section 5, some conclusions are drawn.

2   MARS Architecture

In this section we describe the MARS architecture that supports (i) the user in his Web navigation by generating personalized suggestions and (ii) the site manager to generate a site presentation in a format suitable for the device currently exploited by the user. To these purposes MARS exploits a suitable user profile. In order to define the notion of user profile, we have to preliminarily introduce the notion of agent *ontology*. We mean as agent ontology a dictionary of the terms used by the agents of the multi-agent system when interacting with each other. We call *concept* a term of an ontology. Here we assume that all the agents in MARS uses the same common ontology and consequently share the same concepts. Moreover, we also assume that all the objects present in the Web sites of MARS can be described by using the concepts of the common ontology. For instance, if an e-commerce site contains a given product (e.g. the book "Anna Karenina"), this product can be considered as an instance of the concept *book* (supposing that this concept is contained in the ontology). Therefore, when in some cases along this paper we say that a Web site contains concept instances, we mean that it contains actual objects. Differently, when we refer to concepts of a Web site, we deal with the concepts of the common ontology which the objects of the site belong to. For each concept of a given Web site visited by the user, the profile stores a value that represents the time spent on the instances of that concept. This time value is considered as a rough measure of the user's interest about the concept and it is strictly related to the characteristics of the exploited device. MARS uses four types of agents, described in detail below. As shown in Figure 1, each user's device is associated with a *device agent* that monitors the user and builds a local user profile. Then, each user is associated with a *profile agent*, running on a server machine, that constructs a complete profile of the user's interests. To this purpose, the profile agent collects the local profiles provided by the different device agents. Profile agents associated to different users, are grouped in partitions, each of them characterized by a specific domain of interest (e.g. sport, travels, etc.). Each profile agent can belong to different partitions if its associated user is interested in different domains. In its turn, each partition is associated with a *recommender agent* that runs on a server machine and that is able of determining similarities between the agents of the partition. Furthermore, for each Web site of the MARS community, a recommender agent contains a complete list of the concepts of the site and, for each agent of the associated partition, a list of the concepts of the site accessed by that agent. These information are provided by a *site agent* associated to each Web site.

The recommender system works as follows. When the user U accesses a Web site W, the device agent of U interacts with the site agent of W and sends to it some information about the U's preferences. These preferences are relative to the presentation format desired by U when exploiting that device. Next, the site agent contacts the recommender agents of the partitions which U belongs to. These recommender agents pre-computed the concept instances of the site that best match with the device profile of U, to support content-based recommendations. Moreover, recommender agents also pre-computed the concept instances accessed by other users similar to U and that exploit the same device of U, to support information filtering recommendations. Then, these concept instances are transmitted to the site agent of W that generates recommendations for U with a suitable site presentation.

Note that the common ontology O exploited in MARS is realized as an XML-Schema document, where each element represents a *concept*. We suppose that all sites are XML sites that contains instances of concepts that belong to O. We also suppose that each Web page contains some *hyperlinks* represented by pairs (s, d), where s and d are instances of concepts. A hyperlink (s, d) in a page p can be clicked by a user that is visiting p, and the click leads to another page that visualizes d.

2.1 The Device Agent

We associate a device agent DA_i with each device D_i exploited by the user U. During a Web session, the device agent stores some device information and locally updates the user's profile based on the visited concepts. We describe below both the data structure and the behaviour of the device agent.

Device Data Structure. The data structure of DA_i can be described by two data structures, namely the *Device Setting* (DS_i) and the *User Profile* (UP_i). DS_i contains the following parameters:

- $RIDSet$, that is the set of recommender agents associated to the partitions which U belongs to;
- $MSSet$, that is the *Maximum Size Set*, containing three parameters that represent the maximum sizes (in Kbyte) of text, audio and video contents that U desires to handle when using D_i;

- $\rho_1, \rho_2, \rho_3 \in [0,1]$, associated to the actions performable by U (i.e., visiting, storing or printing a Web page);
- T, that is an integer coefficient used to evaluate the U's interest in a concept instance;
- P is the *attenuation period* expressed by the number of days between two consecutive U's actions after which the interest for an unvisited concept decreases;
- ψ, that is a function used to decrease each P days the U's interests relative to the associated concepts that are no longer accessed;
- k, z and r, that are parameters exploited by DA_i in its interaction with the site agent of each visited site (see Section 2.3). In particular, k, z and r respectively represent the number of: (i) interesting concepts belonging to the visited site that U desires to be considered in the site presentation; (ii) similar agents that U desires to be considered in collaborative filtering recommendations; (iii) recommendations to be considered for each similar agent.

UP_i stores the profile of U, based on the whole navigation history and updated on the basis of the hyperlinks that U clicked when exploiting D_i. More in detail, UP_i is a set of tuples $\langle c, IR_i, LU_i \rangle$, each one associated with a concept $c \in O$, where IR_i (*Interest Rate*) is a measure of the U's interest in c by using D_i and LU_i (*Last Update*) is the date of the last IR_i update. Analogously to the approaches [3,6], in order to set a coefficient, belonging to the interval $[0,1]$, that reaches the maximum value when $t > T$, we define the measure of interest in c by using the actual time t spent by U when visiting the page containing c. Moreover, U can store, print or simply read the Web page that contains c, and this is taken into account by weighting IR_i with a coefficient ρ_a for each action a (where $a = 1, 2, 3$). More formally, for each new update, IR_i is computed as follows:

$$IR_i = \begin{cases} (IR_i + \frac{t}{T} \times \rho_a)/2 \,, \text{ if } t \leq T \\ (IR_i + \rho_a)/2 \,, \text{ elsewhere} \end{cases}$$

In other words, IR_i is computed as the mean value between the previous value of IR_i and the current value $\frac{t}{T} \times \rho_a$, where the ratio $\frac{t}{T}$ is fixed to 1 if $t > T$. Besides, the function ψ is periodically used to decrease the interest rate of the unvisited concepts, based on the temporal distance from the last update.

Device Agent Behaviour. DA_i supports U as follows: (i) in order to construct UP_i, DA_i monitors U's Web navigation sessions considering the concepts visited by U and his behaviour when accessing them (note that accessed concepts not yet occurring in UP_i require new elements to add into UP_i). DA_i periodically sends UP_i to its profile agent. (ii) When U visits a Web site, DA_i sends to the site agent the parameters relative to the exploited device to generate a personalized presentation of the Web site for U. (iii) In order to take in account the "age" of the interest rate, each P days DA_i updates the interest rate coefficient ($IR_i = \psi(IR_i, LU_i)$) associated to each concept c .

2.2   The Profile Agent

Each user U is associated with a profile agent (PA) that collects by each U's device agent the information about the concepts visited during U's Web activities. These information are sent to the recommender agents of the U's partitions. This is an important feature of MARS, since the device agents live on the associated devices and could have limited computation and storage capability. The contribution of PA, which runs on a more equipped machine, is fundamental to provide U with an off-line collector of all the information obtained by the different device agents that monitored the U's navigation. Below, both the data structure and the behaviour of PA are described.

Profile Data Structure. The data structure of PA contains two elements, namely the *Profile Setting* (PS) and *Global User Profile* (GUP). In its turn, PS stores the following parameters:

- n is the number of device agents associated to PA;
- m is the number of parameters necessary to compute the global interest rates of the various concepts (see below);
- PM is a matrix having n rows and m columns, where each element PM_{ij} is the j-th parameter associated to the i-th device. This matrix is necessary to compute the contribution of DA_i to the computation of the global interest of a concept (see below). It is possible to use as PM_{ij} parameter several characteristics of the D_i connection, for instance the price per byte transmitted, the exploited bandwidth etc.;
- f is a function that accepts as input a PM row and computes as output the contribute of DA_i to the global interest of a concept.

The *Global User Profile* (GUP) stores a global representation of U's interests relative to the concepts visited in his whole navigation when exploiting his devices. It is represented by a pair (IR, GC), where IR is a list of pairs (c, IR_i) such that c is a concept and IR_i is its interest rate computed by DA_i. GC is described by a tuple of the form $\langle c, GIR \rangle$, where c identifies a concept visited by U and GIR is its *Global Interest Rate* shown by U. GIR is the weighted mean of all the interest rates for the concept c. Each weight of IR_i is evaluated by the *weighting function* f by using as input parameters the i-th row of the matrix PM. That is:

$$GIR = \frac{\sum_{i=1}^n f(PM_{i,1}, PM_{i,2}, .., PM_{i,m}) \times IR_i}{\sum_{i=1}^n f(PM_{i,1}, PM_{i,2}, .., PM_{i,m})}$$

Profile Agent Behaviour. The behaviour of PA consists in updating GUP by exploiting the data that each U's device agent periodically sends to PA. These data consist, for each concept c visited by U with the device D_i, of a pair of the form $\langle c, IR_i \rangle$. If c also occurs in the GUP, IR_i is stored in IR and it is immediately exploited to update GIR; elsewhere, if c is a new concept, for the first time visited by the user, a new element is added both in IR and in the set of the global coefficients GC.

2.3   The Recommender Agent and the Site Agent

Two other types of MARS agents are the *recommender agent* (RA) and the *site agent* (SA). Each RA is associated with a set of users that are interested in the same domain. We denote by n the number of users associated with RA. Each SA is associated with a Web site in order to manage the site content.

Below, the data structure of RA and the behaviours of recommender and site agents, that interact together, will be briefly described. We omit to describe the structure of the site agent since it contains only the site catalogue.

Recommender Data Structure. The data structure of RA is composed of three elements called *Site Catalogues* (SG), *Global Profile Set* (GPS) and *Profile Collector* (PC). SG contains, for each site W that interacted with RA in the past, a copy of the catalogue C_W that stores all the concept instances present in W. Each catalogue C_W is periodically updated by the corresponding site agent of W. GPS contains the global profiles of all the users associated to RA. The *Profile Collector PC* contains several data sections, each one relative to a site W of the MARS community and denoted by DS_W. In its turn, DS_W contains a list $PSet_W$ containing the profiles associated to the n_W past visitors of W. We denote by $P_{q,i}$ each of these profiles, associated to a given user q and his device i. In particular, $P_{q,i}$ is described by the pair (DP_i, L) that contains both the device profile DP_i and a list L. The elements of L are pairs (c, IR) where c is a concept instance, that q considers interesting in W, and IR is the interest rate of the associated concept. Note that $P_{q,i}$ denotes the profile of a visitor q using a specific device, and not his global profile. Both the information DP_i and L of each visitor profile $P_{q,i}$ are provided to RA by the site agent of W when q terminates its visit.

Recommender and Site Agent Behaviours. Each Web site W is associated with a site agent SA. Suppose that the user U visits S by exploiting a device D_i; then the device agent of U sends to the site agent SA the device profile DP_i. Moreover, suppose that U's profile belongs to a partition associated to the recommender agent RA. In this case, SA contacts RA, that has pre-computed personalized recommendations for U, and sends to RA the device profile DP_i of the device D_i. In order to generate content-based recommendations, RA has built a list CB that contains those concept instances of W whose concepts belong to the global profile of U (this global profile is contained in the Global Profile Set of RA). Then, RA orders CB in a decreasing fashion based on the coefficient IR of each concept and maintains only the first k concepts deleting the remaining ones. Remember that k is a parameter contained in the Device Profile DP_i. Moreover, in order to generate collaborative filtering recommendations, RA_j compares the device profile $P_{U,i}$ contained in the data section DS_W, with each profile $P_{q,i} \in PSET_W$ of each other user q, that has visited W in the past and that has exploited the same device. As a result, a list CF of the concepts accessed by the z visitors mostly similar to U is obtained. Remember that also z is a parameter contained in DP_i. The similarity between $P_{U,i}$ and that of another agent considered in PC is computed as the sum of all the contributions $(1 - d_j)$, with $j = 1, .., l$, where d_j is the difference, in absolute value, between the l instance rates of each concept common to both U and the other agent.

3   Related Work

Many recommender systems using software agents have been proposed in the last years. Below we present a qualitative comparison between some well-known agent-based recommender systems and MARS, pointing out differences and similarities. Other quantitative comparisons will be presented in the next section.

SUGGEST [11] supports user Web navigation dynamically generating links to pages (also belonging to dynamic Web sites) that are unvisited by a user and potentially interesting for him. In order to carry out its task, SUGGEST builds and maintains historical information about the user behaviour by means of an incremental graph partitioning algorithm. Navigational patterns information are extracted by SUGGEST modelling them as a complete graph $G = (V, E)$. The set V of vertices contains the identifiers of the different pages hosted on the Web server. The set of edges E is weighted by the relation: $W_{ij} = N_{ij}/max\{N_i, N_j\}$, where N_i, N_j and N_{ij} are the numbers of sessions (each one identified by the cookies stored on the client side) containing the page i, j or both, respectively. In order to find groups of strongly correlated pages, G is partitioned using a clustering algorithm, and a suggestion list is constructed in a straightforward manner, by finding the cluster which has the largest intersection with the page window correspondent to the current session.

C-Graph [2] proposes an agent model to support a Web user navigation, monitoring his behaviour and learning his preferences, to provide him with a set of recommendations. The user knowledge is modelled into an ontology as a rooted labelled direct graph $\langle N, A \rangle$, where: N is the set of nodes representing the set of concepts of interest for the user U; A, with $A \subseteq N \times N$, is the set of arcs encoding semantic relationships among concepts perceived by U, where the associated arc labels define a number of properties linked to the relationships containing also the model dependency by U. More precisely, an arc (s, t) is provided with a $label(s, t) = \langle d_{st}, r_{st}, h_{st}, \tau_{st} \rangle$, where $d_{st}, r_{st} \in [0, 1]$, h_{st} is a non negative integer and τ_{st} is a real number. The four *label coefficients* above are related to different properties computable by analyzing the visited documents and expressing some kind of relationships among concepts. The approach defines two functions ψ and ρ encoding the structural closeness and the user preferences, respectively. In order to summarize both structural and behavioural components, a function γ is defined to measure the "subjective" semantic closeness of two concepts. The user can set, in computing the semantic closeness, the degree of importance he gives to the structural preference with respect to the behavioural one, by setting an internal parameter k. More in detail, the semantic closeness between two concepts s and t is $\gamma(s, t) = k \times \psi(s, t) + (1 - k) \times \rho(s, t)$.

X-Compass [3] is an XML-based agent model that supports a user U in his Web activities by monitoring the behaviour in the Web pages access to automatically construct and manage an his profile. X-Compass exploits such profiles to provide content-based and collaborative filtering recommendations, as an example, the next page to visit. In particular, each user U is supported by an agent $Ag(U)$ having the following data structures: (i) a *user profile* $P(U)$ that stores U's interests and two relationships existing among them in a rooted graph, in which each node represents a concept of interest for U and has associated an attraction degree $DAttr$ and a key set $KSet$ of the semantics of the interest relative to that node; while each $P(U)$ arc represents both is-a relationships and associative rules, extracted by using data mining techniques (namely: *is-a relationships*, organize such interests in a generalization hierarchy; *associative relationships*, link U's interests appearing distant in the is-a hierarchy but closed from the analysis of the user behaviour); (ii) a list *history* $H(U)$ of elements, each one associated with a Web page access performed by U, ordered on the basis of the temporal access; (iii) an *aggregated history* $AH(U)$, that is a list of elements, each one representing the whole past U's history in visiting the associated Web page. During each Web session, $Ag(U)$ monitors each U access to a Web page to: extract the necessary information, and to update H, AH and $DAttr$ of the node representative of the currently visited page.

CBCF [4] (Content-Boosted Collaborative Filtering) uses a content-based predictor to enhance existing user data, to exploit collaborative filtering to generate personalized suggestions. The content-based approach views content information as text documents, and user ratings as one of six class labels. The collaborative filtering component uses a neighborhood-based algorithm, where a subset of users similar to the active users, and a weighted combination of their ratings is exploited to generate recommendations for the active user.

Similarities and differences with MARS Similarly to MARS, all the aforementioned systems exploits an internal profile to store information relative to the user. The main difference with MARS is that such a profile is stored in a unique agent that supports the user and manages his profile. Differently, in MARS the profile is managed by the profile agent and is built on the basis of the information provided by the device agents associated with the different user's devices. As a result, the device agents only collects information about the user, while the profile construction is performed by the profile agent. Moreover, in MARS recommendations are not generated by the only site agent, but they are the result of a collaboration between the site agent and the recommender agent that pre-computes most of the necessary data. This way, the task of the site agent becomes very light. Finally, none of the above described systems considers the effect of using different devices in the profile construction and, consequently, in the recommendation algorithm. Instead, MARS uses this information providing personalized content-based and collaborative filtering recommendations.

4   Experiments

In this section, we present some experiments devoted to evaluate the capability of MARS to perform both content-based and collaborative filtering activities by compare its performances in generating suggestions with all the systems previously described. We have chosen X-COMPASS, C-GRAPH and CBCF since they are, similarly to MARS, both content-based and collaborative filtering and exploit a user profile. They are, at the best of our knowledge, three of the most performative recommender systems. Moreover, to analyze separately the contribution of the content-based and the collaborative filtering algorithms, we have chosen also the content-based system SUGGEST, that is one of the most performative in this context. For our experiments, we have built 30 different XML Web sites by using a common ontology represented by a unique XML Schema; therefore each page has only instances of this XML schema. Furthermore, we have monitored 97 real users in their Web sites navigation, without using any recommendation support. For each user, a log file has recorded his choices in a list of 700 elements $\langle s, d, t \rangle$, relative to 700 different clicks performed by him during 15 days, where s (resp. d) is the identifier of the *source* (resp. *destination*) concept instance, and t is the time of his choice to go from s to d via a hyperlink.

We have also realized eight different types of device agents, developed by using JADE (Java Agent Development Framework) and JADE/LEAP (JADE Lightweight Extensible Agent Platform) for devices, as palmtop and cellular phones, with limited resources. Four of these agent types are MARS agents (namely device, profile, site and recommender agents) that implement our approach of generating user suggestions. The other four agent types are client agents built by following the recommendation-based approaches called SUGGEST, C-GRAPH, X-COMPASS and CBCF, that we have presented in Section 3 and that we compare in this section with our approach.

MARS Device Agents. We have three device agents associated with three different devices, namely a desktop PC, a palmtop and a cellular phone. We have set their parameters (described in Section 2.1) as shown in Table 1. However, we remember that the interest for a concept has been assumed as "saturated" if the visit time of the concept is higher than T seconds. While, the coefficient ρ_1 (resp. ρ_2, ρ_3) weights the user's interest in a concept in the case the user simply visits (resp. stores, prints) a page containing an instance of that concept. Moreover, the attenuation period P is equal to 3 for each device agent; this means that the interest for a concept that has not been visited for three consecutive days is decreased by using the coefficient $\psi \in [0, 1]$. Finally, for each client agent the parameter k is equal to 4, thus showing to the user all the instances of the four most interesting concepts.

Other Client Agents. The SUGGEST, C-GRAPH, CBCF and X-COMPASS device agents are built by following the descriptions of the relative data structures and recommendations algorithms proposed in [2,3,4,11], respectively. In particular, relatively to the C-GRAPH agent, we have used a coefficient $k = 0.5$ to give the same importance to both the structural and semantics closeness.

Table 1. The setting of the MARS device agents

device agent	T (sec.)	ρ_1	ρ_2	ρ_3	P	ψ	k
desktop PC	200	0.6	0.8	0.9	3	0.90	4
palmtop	120	0.6	0.9	1.0	3	0.95	4
cellular phone	60	0.5	0.9	1.0	3	0.95	4

MARS Profile Agents. Each user is associated with a profile agent. All the profile agents adopt the same parameters values: (*i*) $n = 3$, having only three types of device agents for each user. (*ii*) $m = 1$, since we have decided to use, as unique parameter to weight the contribution of the interest rate coming from each client agent, the *price per Mega Byte* (estimated for each adopted device typology). In this case, the matrix PM becomes a vector $[PM_1, PM_2, PM_3]$. The prices per Mbyte (in euro cents) that we have considered are: $PM_1 = 0.9, PM_2 = 1.4, PM_3 = 1.8$. (*iii*) We use the identity function $f(PM_i) = PM_i$ as weighting function. Thus the formula for computing the global interest rate GIR is:

$$GIR = \frac{\sum_{i=1}^{3} PM_i \times IR_i}{\sum_{i=1}^{3} PM_i}$$

4.1   Description of the Experiments

In our experiments we monitored the users in their Web visits. We denote with a triplet (s, d, t) the transition of the user, that visits the instance s of the concept c_s, to the instance d of the concept c_d at time t. Initially, in order to allow the users' agents to build their user profiles, for each user we have collected the first 450 triplet (s, d, t) as training-set. Other 300 triplet have been used as test-set to evaluate the recommendation algorithm used by the site agent. That is, for each user, in correspondence of each triplet (s, d, t) belonging to the test-set, we have generated a recommendation $R(s)$, for each of the five algorithms MARS, X-COMPASS, C-GRAPH, CBCF and SUGGEST. Each recommendation $R(s)$ is a list of recommended concept instances. We have checked if d belongs to $R(s)$ in order to measure the effectiveness of the different approaches and we have stored the result in a value $c(s)$. Formally $c_s = \begin{cases} 1 \text{ , if } d \in R(s) \\ 0 \text{ , otherwise} \end{cases}$

The average precision Pre of each recommender method is defined as the average of the $c(s)$ values on all the triplets (s, d, t).

The first row of Table 2 presents the results obtained in this experiment comparing the five approaches. In terms of Average Precision MARS has resulted the best of the other approaches chosen for the comparison (the CBCF in all the occurrences), measuring about a 21, a 48 and a 35 percent better than CBCF, respectively. We argue that this very good performance that MARS obtains as recommender systems, than the other considered approaches, it is due to the fact that MARS considers, in determining its suggestions, also the devices exploited by the user. To confirm such an influence, we have repeated the above

Table 2. Performances of different recommendation algorithms

	MARS	X-COMPASS	C-GRAPH	CBCF	SUGGEST
Global	0.270 (0.189)	0.183	0.178	0.198	0.148
Content Based	0.196	0.139	0.140	0.156	0.148
Collaborative Filtering	0.139	0.086	0.081	0.100	-

comparisons, by using the only PC MARS device agent (already used in the previous experiment), instead of three different clients. In this way, the effect of the different devices, exploited by the user in the past, is not taken in account in the generation of the MARS recommendations. Result of this experiment is shown in round parenthesis in Table 2. In this conditions, MARS approach shows performances comparable with, but no higher than those of the other approaches. This confirms that the main advantage of MARS is in the introduction of different device agents associated to each devices exploited by the user. To understand more precisely how such a device consideration improves the recommendation performances, we have repeated the experiment considering separately the content-based and the collaborative filtering components of the experiments. That is, we have generated the recommendations of MARS, X-COMPASS, C-GRAPH, CBCF and SUGGEST only taking in account the concepts deriving from the similarity between the visitor profile and the site content, without considering the concepts suggested by the other users. Since SUGGEST is only a content-based recommender, the suggestions so generated are in this case the same than those of the previous experiments. The results of this experiment are reported in the second row of Table 2 and show that the performances of MARS is about a 26 percent higher than the best of the other systems. This confirms the supposition that taking into account the device exploited in accessing the concepts leads to model more precisely the user preferences, and this positively influences the suggestion performances. Furthermore, we have repeated the experiments with only the three approaches that act also as collaborative filtering methods, those concepts deriving from the suggestions of the other users, without taking into account the content-based component. The result of this latter experiment (reported in the third row of Table 2) shows that the performances of MARS are in this case significantly improved (about 39 percent higher than the other three approaches). We argue that this is the effect of having considered, in generating collaborative filtering recommendations for a user, only those users that exploited his same device.

5 Conclusions

In this paper we have presented a recommender system architecture, called *Multi-Agent Recommender System* (MARS), designed to generate recommendations on the basis of both user profile and exploited device. More specifically, our system is based on the following two ideas. The first is that a device agent monitors a user that is exploiting a fixed device to build a light profile just for that device, while a profile agent constructs off-line a complete user profile. This leads to make more simple the task of the device agent, that often has limited resources and, on the other hand, to take into account the different exploited devices in constructing the user profile. The second is that each group of agents interested in the same domain is associated with a recommender agent. It computes off line the similarity between these agents and recording the behaviours of the agents in accessing the Web sites of the community, in order to support both content-based and collaborative filtering recommendations. This leads to generate very effective recommendations, taking into account also the exploited devices, and leaving to the site agent the only task of generating the graphical presentation. We have performed some experiments for evaluating the performances of our systems, in comparison with other four agent-based recommender systems, and the obtained results show a significative improvements of the suggestions. It is worth to point out that, besides these performance improvements, the main advantage of the system is, in our opinion, the particular lightness of both the device agent and the site agent that make very efficient the navigation of the agents through the Web sites.

References

1. Anderson, C.R., Domingos, P., Weld, D.S.: Adaptive web navigation for wireless devices. In: 17th Int. Joint Conf. on Artificial Intelligence, pp. 879–884 (2001)
2. Buccafurri, F., Lax, G., Rosaci, D., Ursino, D.: A user behavior-based agent for improving web usage. In: CoopIS/DOA/ODBASE, pp. 1168–1185 (2002)
3. Garruzzo, S., Modafferi, S., Rosaci, D., Ursino, D.: X-Compass: An XML Agent for Supporting User Navigation on the Web. In: Andreasen, T., Motro, A., Christiansen, H., Larsen, H.L. (eds.) FQAS 2002. LNCS (LNAI), vol. 2522, pp. 197–211. Springer, Heidelberg (2002)
4. Melville, P., Mooney, R.J., Nagarajan, R.: Content-boosted collaborative filtering for improved recommendations. In: AAAI/IAAI, pp. 187–192 (2002)
5. Montaner, M., López, B., de la Rosa, J.L.: A taxonomy of recommender agents on the internet. Artif. Intell. Rev. vol. 19(4) (2003)
6. Parsons, J., Ralph, P., Gallagher, K.: Using viewing time to infer user preference in recommender systems. In: AAAI Workshop on Semantic Web Personalization, San Jose, USA, pp. 52–64 (July 2004)
7. Peñalvo, F.J.G., Paternò, F., Gil, A.B.: An adaptive e-commerce system definition. In: 2nd Int. Conf. on Adaptive Hypermedia and Adaptive Web-Based Systems
8. Rosaci, D., Sarné, G.M.L.: MASHA: A Multi Agent System Handling User and Device Adaptivity of Web Sites. User Modeling and User-Adapted Interaction: The Journal of Personalization Research, vol. 16(5)
9. Sarwar, B.M., Karypis, G., Konstan, J.A., Riedl, J.: Analysis of recommendation algorithms for e-commerce. In: 2nd ACM Conference on Electronic Commerce (EC-00), Minneapolis, USA, October 2000, pp. 158–167. ACM Press, New York (2000)
10. Schafer, J.B., Konstan, J.A., Riedl, J.: E-commerce recommendation applications. Data Mining and Knowledge Discovery 5(1/2), 115–153 (2001)
11. Silvestri, F., Baraglia, R., Palmerini, P., Serranò, M.: On-line generation of suggestions for web users. J. of Digital Information Management 2(2), 104–108 (2004)

An HTML Fragments Based Approach for Portlet Interoperability

Jingyu Song, Jun Wei, and Shuchao Wan

Technology Center of Software Engineering
Institute of Software, Chinese Academy of Sciences
Beijing, 100080, P.R.China
{songjy, wj, wsc}@otcaix.iscas.ac.cn

Abstract. Presentation level integration now becomes an important and fast growing trend in enterprise computing and portals are the mainstream to realize it. However, there is not yet a definitive mechanism to achieve interoperability between the basic components of a portal i.e. portlets, whereby HTML data flows smoothly from one portlet to a neighboring one. This paper proposes an HTML fragments based approach to achieve portlet interoperability. Fragments are a block of HTML elements, which are generated by portlets and are used to aggregate a portal page. We first construct a presentation component, which is named as ShadowComponent, for each portlet involved in a portlet interoperation using its fragments, then define a data flow process between ShadowComponents using ECA rules, and finally drive such a process by creating events to fulfill data flow between ShadowComponents. As the fragments of a portlet are synchronized with their corresponding Shadow Component, such a process enables the portlet interoperation. Experimental results show that the proposed approach is effective in achieving portlet interoperability in portals.

Keywords: Portal, Porlet Interoperability.

1 Introduction

Presentation level integration now becomes an important and fast growing trend in enterprise computing [9] and portals are the mainstream to realize it. Portals enable the aggregation of interactive interfaces of different applications as components on the same web page [1]. Portlet is the basic component of a portal, which represents an interactive web mini application and is deployed on a portal server [7].

A portal typically decorates the HTML fragment returned by a portlet with a title and several buttons, such as minimize, maximize and edit etc., then aggregates all fragments together into a portal page. Though such unconstrained aggregation is useful since applications are simultaneously rendered in the same page and users see comprehensive information in a more convenient way, further integration capability is surely desired. Information contained in a portlet may be required as the input in other portlets. The information has to be manually copied from source to target portlets. Such manual interactions may lead to frustration, low productivity, and inevitable

J. Indulska and K. Raymond (Eds.): DAIS 2007, LNCS 4531, pp. 195–209, 2007.

mistakes. Therefore, an effective mechanism for portlet interoperation is needed. Unfortunately, currently available standards such as JSR168[7] and WSRP[11] support no further integration of portlets than being displayed on the same page.

This paper proposes an HTML fragments based approach to achieve portlet interoperation in portals. Rather than resorting to back-end solutions, we support a pure front-end approach. A presentation component, which is named as ShadowComponent, is constructed for each portlet involved in an interoperation using the fragments produced by the portlet. Then an interoperation process, which uses ShadowComponents as its nodes, is defined using event-condition-action (ECA) rules. An ECA rule defines when and how the input/output data of a ShadowComponent are received from or sent to a shared data space. Because the fragments are synchronized with their corresponding ShadowComponents, such a process achieves the interoperation between portlets. As the approach is based on the fragments generated by portlets only, there is no need of modifications for portlets to take part in an interoperation.

The rest of this paper is organized as follows: Section 2 presents related work. Section 3 defines the requirements concerning portlet interoperation in portals based on a typical scenario first, and then analyzes the inefficiencies and drawbacks of the approaches that implement interoperation at different layers of a portlet based on a general portlet architecture and points out that using fragments to achieve portlet interoperation is a more reasonable solution. Our approach is proposed and discussed in detail in section 4, 5 and 6. A practical example is also discussed in section 6. Finally conclusions and future work are given in section 7.

2   Related Works

A variety of mechanisms for portlet interoperation have been proposed, which can be classified as application-based, datasource-based and annotation-based.

The application-based approach, which is proposed by JSR168[7], introduces the notion of "portlet application" that allows distinct portlets to share a common piece of information to achieve portlet interoperation. However, a portal normally frames portlets from distinct portlet applications, which prevents the data from being exchanged.

Both approaches presented by Roy-Chowdhury et al.[14] and Weinreich et al.[16] can be classified as datasource-based since the authors propose the use of a custom JSP tag library or XML descriptions to enable a portlet to be a data source. The target portlet is defined in a WSDL file with a custom extension to describe the actions, which can consume data transferred from other portlets. However, the description-based approach may cause compatibility problem, as there is no agreement yet on how to standardize this mechanism.

Diaz et al. propose an annotation-based portlet interoperation approach that supports semantic data transfer[2]. In that approach, portlets are characterized by their ontology. Then portlet fragments extend their markups with information about the supported process. Portlet interoperability is achieved through the mapping of the ontology concepts. However, this approach relies on the cooperation of the markup producer who has to embed the underlying information structure into the fragments in the development phase. Moreover, the approach further requires that the operation defined in the specification should be extended.

Furthermore, in many scenarios, a portal is used to integrate existing web-based applications. An application may be integrated into a portal without modifications because of maintenance, cost, or technical reasons. Therefore, a portlet interoperation should also be achieved without modifications to the corresponding applications. In such situations, though all above three approaches provide some kinds of mechanisms to transfer data between portlets, the portlet may not use them because the portlets or back-end applications were not designed and developed to be used in an interoperation context, which makes interoperation hard to be achieved.

3   Problem Statement and Analysis

3.1   A Scenario

We use the following scenario to analyze portlet interoperation requirements. Consider a marketing department of a motor corporation. Three are three applications developed and deployed: Order Management System(OM), Customer Relationship Management System(CRM) and Business Intelligence System(BI). Each application has been wrapped into a portlet, OMPortlet, CRMPortlet and BIPortlet respectively using the method proposed in [3].

To analyze the market situation of cars and to find out the potential customers, the marketing manager built a Market Analysis portal page containing the above three portlets. The marketing manager has to interact individually with each portlet on the page and key in data manually. For example, to get the customer details of an order, the manager must copy the CustomerID of specified order from the OMPortlet to the CRMPortlet's entry textbox, and submit the query by clicking on the "Submit" button. If the manager needs further to do a data mining to find out the sale status of such a car model in the community with the same occupation as the customer in this month, he/she has to copy the ProductID, Date from OMPortlet and Occupation from CRMPortlet to BIPortlet's corresponding entry textbox again. As shown in Fig.1, the whole process is very fussy and error prone, which affects the fluency of analysis process greatly.

According to the IEEE Standard Computer Dictionary, interoperability means "the ability of two or more systems or components to exchange information and to use the information that has been exchanged"[6]. The essential function of portlet interoperation is to provide a mechanism that would facilitate portlet

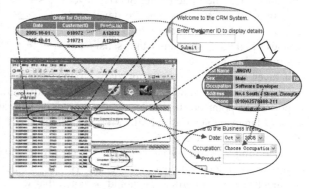

Fig. 1. A scenario of portlet interoperation

interactions by enabling easy transfer of compatible data between portlets. Given the above example, a better data flow is shown as follows: by one click in OMPortlet, the CustomerID is transferred to CRMPortlet; then CRMPortlet submits a query request automatically with the received CustomerID; and then the Occupation in the response page and Date, ProductID in OMPortlet are transferred to BIPortlet automatically; again a request is submitted. With such an automated mechanism, all required information could be displayed in the three portlets simultaneously only by one mouse click.

Thus, we can define the basic requirements of portlet interoperation as follows.

1. A portlet need not to be modified to take part in an interoperation. That requirement enables interoperation between portlets within one portlet application, portlets of different portlet applications and even remote portlets.
2. Supporting multiple outputs and 1:n communication. A portlet may have a set of output candidates. In such a case, a user can choose which output data is used. Data from one portlet may be simultaneously sent to a number of destination portlets.
3. Supporting portlet wiring. An interoperation process can be started automatically or manually. Portlets involved in an interoperation are loosely coupled and can be decomposed and re-composed easily.

To make it a general and platform independent approach, one additional requirement is defined as follows:

4. Support standards based implementation. The use of standards allows reuse of standard compliant portlets and enables the independency from a particular portal.

3.2 Achieving Interoperability at Different Layers of a Portlet

Usually, portlets employ a similar layered architecture as general web applications, as shown in Fig.2. The architecture consists of four layers: resource layer, service layer, orchestration layer and presentation layer.

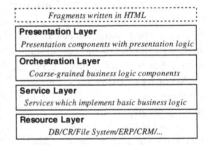

Resource layer contains the resources that a portlet uses, such as database, content repository, and file system, etc. Service layer consists of basic services that are developed on top of resource layer, which represent business logic software units that satisfy the enterprise business requirements. Orchestra-

Fig. 2. Layered Portlet Architecture

tion layer assembles services to coarse-grained business components. Presentation layer creates the graphical view of the portlet, and interacts with portal users. It is important to point out that presentation layer is not the user interface presented by markup language such as HTML. Presentation layer is a part of a portlet. It has its own model and process logic.

According to the analysis of section 3.1, the problem we concerned with is how to achieve the association and transfer of HTML elements, which are located on fragments, between portlets. It should be noted that we could achieve such a goal by working on all these four layers. That is because the four layers of a portlet are related with each other. When the model or data of a lower layer change, the data or model of the layer above it will also change. However, the approach implemented on each layer has some deficiencies or drawbacks that are list as follows:

1. Achieving portlet interoperability at resource, service and orchestration layer are indirect solutions to the problem. To use these solutions, the portlet designers have to consider interoperation requirements, such as which HTML elements in a fragment are involved in the interoperation, besides the requirements of each layer at design time, which increases the problem complexity.
2. Whatever layers we used to implement portlet interoperation, we have to know the technical details of the portlet. For example, to implement interoperation at resource layer, we have to know the data schema details of the resource the portlet used. That also increases the complexity of portlet interoperation. Moreover, not all information of each layer of a portlet is accessible in enterprise environment, e.g. a portlet may be produced by wrapping an existing web-based application.
3. There are currently no acceptable and standard methods to invoke or to share the components of the orchestration and presentation layer of a portlet, which makes it difficult to achieve portlet interoperability at these two layers directly.

Thus, we have to find out another approach beyond such layers. Noted that all portlets use HTML to describe their fragments and our goal is also to achieve the association and transfer between HTML elements, we hope to find out a method based on such HTML fragments that are produced by each portlet. Such an approach at least has the following two merits:

1. It is a general and platform-independent solution. Because only HTML fragments are employed, the approach can be used in different scenarios, no matter which applications the portlet belongs to, how the portlet is designed and developed. That makes possible that the approach can be implemented on different portal servers.
2. There is no need of the knowledge of the technical details of the portlets involved in the interoperation. The approach does not care about the technical details such as service interfaces, how to invoke a component, etc. That is also to say, there is no need to modify a portlet to make it involved in an interoperation.

There are mainly two key problems in such an approach: how to describe the user interfaces of a portlet i.e. the fragments produced by the portlet; how to define associations and how to transfer data between HTML elements. We will propose our approach to portlet interoperation based on the answer of these two questions.

4 Reference Model for Portlet Presentation Layer

Moreno et al. proposed a reference model for portlet[10]. In such a model, the presentation layer consists of six main sub models: Conceptual, Navigation, Presentation, User, Context and Adaptation, as shown in Fig.3a. The Conceptual model encapsulates the information handled by the rest of the models at the presentation layer. The Navigation model describes the application navigational requirements building the navigational structure of the portlet. The Presentation model captures the presentational requirements in a set of HTML elements. The User model describes and manages the user characteristics. The Context model deals with device, network, location and time aspects. The Adaptation model is used to obtain appropriate web content characteristics and target markup.

For modeling the presentation layer of a portlet, we need at least its Conceptual, Presentation, and Navigation models. However, as we do not know the exact internal details of a portlet, we can only reconstruct the presentation components using fragments by a reverse engineering way. So we propose a simplified presentation model in our approach, which describes the most important characteristics of the presentation layer of a portlet, as shown in Fig.3b. The simplified presentation model consists of three sub models: **Element**, **Location** and **Interaction**. Element is a simplified Conceptual model, which describes what types of elements are located on the fragments. Location is a corresponding model to Presentation, which defines the locations for each elements described in Element. Interaction is a simplified Navigation model, which defines the interactive relationships between elements, e.g. a customer's name can be obtained by submitting a *CustomerID*.

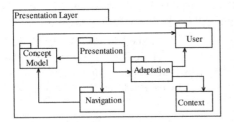

Fig. 3. (a) Presentation model of a portlet   **Fig. 3.** (b)Simplified presentation model

5 Portlet Interoperation Model

Papadopoulos et al.[13] and Malone et al.[8] gave the basic model of coordination.

Definition 1. A coordination model can be viewed as a triple (E, L, M), where **E** represents the entities being coordinated, **L** the media used to coordinate the entities, and **M** the semantic framework the model adheres to.

In this paper, we propose a portlet interoperation model based on the above generic coordination model, as shown in Fig.4.

Definition 2. A portlet interoperation model is the coordination model in a portal context, it is defined as a tuple (PF, SC, SD, O, R), where **PF** is the set of fragments of the portlets that participate in an interoperation. **SC** is the set of ShadowComponents corresponding to PF. **SD** provides a shared data space for portlet interoperation. **O** represents the ontology used in the interoperation. **R** represents the ECA rule set that defines the conditions about when and how to execute a data flow. From a coordination model point of view, SC is the entity of the semantic coordination model, O and R together form the semantic framework of the portlet interoperation model, and SD is the data coordination media.

A ShadowComponent is constructed for each portlet, which takes part in an interoperation, using its fragments. A ShadowComponent usually has several slots that represent the HTML elements located in portlet fragments. The ShadowComponent keeps synchronized with its corresponding portlet fragments during the whole interoperation process. Each slot has its type that maps to a concept of the ontology, which achieves semantic data type match between slots. Finally, ECA rules define a data flow process, which uses ShadowComponent as its nodes. An ECA rule specifies when and how a ShadowComponent receives matched data or sends data to shared data space.

Because the portlet fragments are synchronized with the corresponding ShadowComponent, the execution of such a data flow process transfers an HTML element value on a portlet fragment to a neighboring one, thereby achieving portlet interoperability.

In the following subsection, the detailed definitions of Shadow Component, Operation Primitives and ECA rule are presented. Then, we will further explain the proposed interoperation model by discussing the implementation of such a model in a real portal server.

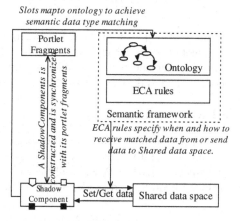

Fig. 4. Portlet interoperation model

5.1 ShadowComponent

Definition 3. A slot represents an HTML element in a given portlet fragment FP, it is a triple (path, type, value) where **path** is the information extraction path, which we proposed in [15], of the element in FP. An information extraction path is a concatenation of node identifiers along a path from the root to the specified element, thereby specifying the location of an element. **type** represents the slot type with its value constrained to the concept set defined in the ontology, **value** stores the current value of the slot.

Definition 4. A ShadowComponent is a component constructed using portlet fragments and is synchronized with the fragments of the portlet. A ShadowComponent is defined as a tuple (triggerSlot, IS, OS, inputProperty, outputProperty, status) where Both **IS** and **OS** are slot set, representing input and output data of the ShadowComponent. **triggerSlot** is a special slot whose value is a URL, which indicates the interaction relationship between IS and OS. Usually the URL represents a "submit" or "click" action that returns output data using current input data. **InputProperty**∈{MANUAL,AUTO,TRIGGER} and **outputProperty**∈{MANUAL, AUTO}, which decide the data process policy of the ShadowComponent. The descriptions of these values are showed in table 1. **status** is a BOOL variable, which is used to indicate if all input data needed could be obtained from a shared data space.

Table 1. A summary of input/output properties

Property	Summary(Input)	Summary(Output)
MANUAL	A user decides when the data are loaded from Shared data space	A user decides when the data are sent to Shared data space
AUTO	Data are loaded from Shared data space as long as all input data needed is ready	Data are sent to Shared data space automatically if they are available in fragments
TRIGGER	Data are loaded if all input data needed is ready, then a request is submitted automatically after the fragment is displayed in the client side browser	/

ShadowComponent is the realization of the simplified reference model of a portlet presentation layer, which is proposed in section 4. The types of input and output data form the Element model; the paths of input data and output data form the Location model; whereas the triggerSlot, IS and OS together form the Interaction model.

5.2 Operation Primitives

The operation primitives in portlet interoperation model consist of two parts: slot operation primitives and ShadowComponent operation primitives. Slot operation primitives include GetValue and SetValue. ShadowComponent operation primitives include Import, Export and SetStatus. Table 2 gives the detail.

Table 2. Descriptions of Operation Primitives

Operation Primitive	Belongs to	Description
GetValue	Slot	Load matched data from Shared data space
SetValue	Slot	Send current slot value to Shared data space
Import	ShadowComponent	Invoke GetValue action of all IS slots of the ShadowComponent
Export	ShadowComponent	Invoke SetValue action of all OS slots of the ShadowComponent
SetStatus	ShadowComponent	Set the status of the ShadowComponent

Table 3. Descriptions of Events

Event	Para Table	Description
SlotDataReady	(slot)	There is a match data for the given slot in Shared data space
TriggerOutput	(ShadowComponent)	A user starts a request to output data manually
InputDataReady	(ShadowComponent)	Data for all input slots of a ShadowComponent sc is ready
AskForInput	(ShadowComponent)	A user starts a request to input data from Shared data space

5.3 ECA Rules

We employ an event-based architecture[5] to define data flow process between ShadowComponents.

Definition 5. ECA rule is the fundamental metaphors for defining and enforcing data flowing logic, it is a tuple (event, condition, action) where the possible values of **event** include SlotDataReady, TriggerOutput, InputDataReady and AskForInput. Each event has parameters indicating to whom the event is oriented. Details of each event are shown in table 3. **condition** is a logic expression that is composed of inputProperty and outputProperty of a ShadowComponent. **action** is composed of ShadowComponent operation primitives. condition could be *null*, which indicates the action should be executed as long as the event occurs. When an action consists of several operations, the operations should be executed serially. For example, the ECA-rule

ON InputDataReady(sc1) [IF sc1.inputPorperty = = TRIGGER]
DO sc1.Import, sc1.SetStatus(TRUE)

indicates that when an event InputDataReady happens, if the inputProperty of the corresponding ShadowComponent is TRIGGER, the ShadowComponent will first import data, then set status to TRUE.

6 Implementation

We have validated our approach by extending OncePortal portal system of ONCE platform[12]. OncePortal is a JSR168 and WSRP compatible portal, which can integrate different resources and aggregate them into personalized page. Since our implementation is based on the Portlet and WSRP specifications, it can be easily migrated to any JSR168 compatible portal server.

6.1 Constructing ShadowComponents

The key to construct a ShadowComponent is slot definition. The information extraction path used to define a slot is specified in the context of a fragment. Because there are usually several fragments returned by a portlet during the whole interoperation process, we have to consider in which fragment the slot is defined. We use the following two methods in our implementation:

- In default, we assume that the slots of IS and triggerSlot of a ShadowComponent are defined in the first fragment produced by a portlet. If a ShadowComponent has no input slots, then slots of OS are defined in the first fragment. In most practice scenarios, these assumptions can be satisfied, whereas they decrease the implementation complexity greatly.
- Adding fragment marks. If the above assumption cannot be satisfied, then we need to do some modification to the portlet, which adds marks to the fragment to indicate that it has IS or OS slots. Such marks can be simply added as the properties of an HTML element on the fragment or provided as HTML annotations.

A ShadowComponent can be constructed visually by specifying some portions on the portlet fragments to work as IS/OS slots through mouse operations or can be pre-configured using configuration file.

6.2 InteroperationFilter

InteroperationFilter is one of the most important components in our approach. Fig.5 gives the location of InteroperationFilter during the whole interoperation process.

When a user submits a request in a browser, it is received by portal servlet. We define two types of portal request in a portlet interoperation process: normal request and interoperation request..

For a normal request, portal servlet uses a pre-defined user page profile to find which portlets are needed to build the requested page. It then forwards the request to the corresponding portlets. Each portlet returns a fragment, which is aggregated with a general page frame and the fragments returned from the other portlets to form the final portal

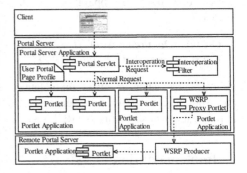

Fig. 5. Portlet interoperation process

page. In common portals, the page will be returned to the browser and waiting for next request at this time. However, to achieve portlet interoperability, we first transfer the fragments returned by each portlet to InteroperationFilter, which rewrites each fragment based on the interoperation related information. Then portal servlet uses such modified fragments to assemble the final page and returns it to the browser. Based on the fragment and the input/output properties of the corresponding ShadowComponents, there are two types of process:

1. **There are output parameters on the fragment, the value of outputProperty is MANUAL.** In such a case, InteroperationFilter modifies the fragment so that to insert icons before each output parameter. By clicking on an icon, a user can output a parameter or the whole of the parameters that the portlet provides. From technical point of view, such a click submits an interoperation request, which embeds the output parameters as its request parameter.
2. **There are output parameters on the fragment, the value of outputProperty is AUTO.** InteroperationFilter informs the ShadowComponent to export its output parameters to Shared data space. The value of outputProperty is not allowed to be AUTO, if the ShadowComponent has an output parameter whose path has variable, preventing the situation that which parameters to be used cannot be decided.

After finishing the process, new data are added or updated to Shared data space, which may create new events, such as InputDataReady, etc. Such events then trigger certain actions, which may start the three types of process for input parameters:

1. **There are input parameters on the fragment and the value of inputPorperty is MANUAL.** In such a case, if all input parameters of the ShadowComponent can be

obtained from Shared data space, then inserts an icon into the fragment, which will submit an interoperation request when it is clicked on.

2. **There are input parameters on the fragment and the value of inputProperty is AUTO.** In such a case, InteroperationFilter retrieves data from Shared data space and fills the input slots of the ShadowComponent automatically. Different with the process when inputProperty value is MANUAL that an icon will be inserted only when all input parameters are ready, InteroperationFilter will try to fill each slot as long as a matched data can be obtained from Shared data space for it.

3. **There are input parameters on the fragment and the value of inputProperty is TRIGGER.** In such a case, the process is similar to the case when inputProperty is MANUAL i.e. it is only be processed when all input parameters needed are ready in Shared data space. After the input parameters are filled into the fragment, a block of JavaScript is further added to the element that is specified by triggerSlot of the ShadowComponent, whose function is to submit the page automatically after the page is displayed in the browser.

On the other hand, an interoperation request is processed by InteroperationFilter directly. InteroperationFilter creates events according to the request, which ultimately results in the data flowing between ShadowComponents and Shared data space based on ECA rules. There are two types of interoperation request:

1. **A user outputs data manually** i.e. a user clicks the icon that is inserted by InteroperationFilter for the fragment whose corresponding ShadowComponent's outputProperty is MANUAL during the process of normal request. In such a case, InteroperationFilter creates event TriggerOutput that results in the execution of Export operation of the ShadowComponent, which exports data to Shared data space. Also, other events may be created because the adding or updating of data.

2. **A user requires to fill data manually** i.e. a user clicks the icon that is inserted by InteroperationFilter for the fragment whose corresponding ShadowComponent's inputProperty is MANUAL. In such a case, InteroperationFilter creates event AskForInput, which results in the execution of Import operation of the ShadowComponent, thereby loading data from Shared data space.

The definition information for ShadowComponents is stored in portal page profiles for each user, while not the portlet related profiles, so that to ensure that given the same portlet, a user can decide whether that portlet takes part in an interoperation process and how the interoperation happens.

Whatever type of a request that is received, InteroperationFilter initializes ShadowComponents or synchronizes the ShadowComponents with corresponding fragments, i.e. to update the input/output parameters using the received fragment, based on current interoperation definition information. After all event and action are processed, another synchronization from ShadowComponents to fragments is processed i.e. to update the fragments using current input/output data of the corresponding ShadowComponents. Moreover, fragments are cached to ensure the interoperation request can be processed by InteroperationFilter only.

6.3 Interoperation Process

InteroperationFilter is the only component that interacts with portal servlet. However, the whole interoperation process is supported by several components together.

Besides InteroperationFilter, other important components include ECA rule engine, Shared data space, ShadowComponent instances, etc. The collaboration diagram is shown in Fig.6.

InteroperationFilter receives fragments and user portal page profiles from portal servlet and then initializes ShadowComponents and ECA rules based on such information. New events are created by InteroperationFilter and Shared data space. When receiving these events, ECA rule engine sends actions to certain ShadowComponents based on current ECA rules.

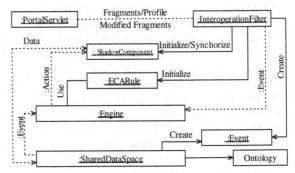

Fig. 6. Collaboration Diagram of Portlet Interoperation

The events created by InteroperationFilter are mainly related to user interactions such as TriggerOutput, AskForInput, whereas the events created by Shared data space are mainly data-related such as InputDataReady, SlotDataReady. The execution of an action may create new events that result in new actions. When there is no event created, InteroperationFilter does the synchronization from ShadowComponents to fragments and decides if scripts should be added to fragments based on their properties such as if status is TRUE. All modified fragments and other cached fragments that are not involved in the interoperation then are returned to portal servlet to aggregate the final portal page. InteroperationFilter will wait for next request.

For the scenario described in 3.1, the events and actions sequence of an interoperation process is depicted in Fig.7. OmSC, CrmSC and BiSC are corresponding ShadowComponents for OMPortlet, CRMPortlet and BIPortlet. Comprehensive information are displayed in a portal page only by one mouse click.

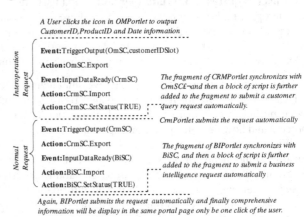

Fig. 7. Sequence of events and actions of an interoperation

6.4   A Practical Example

Our framework opens a new vista to the integration of applications and services in portal context, which makes possible portal-based composite applications.

Fig.8 shows a composite application that is constructed in OncePortal using our proposed portlet interoperation approach. The composite application is composed of three portlets: TripSchedule, WeatherForecast and FlightSearch. The Trip-Schedule portlet is an internal information system that shows the user's trip schedule in the near future. The Weather Forecast portlet provides weather information for a given city and the FlightSearch portlet provides flight information from the user's current city to a destination city. They are constructed by wrapping two Internet web sites: eLong Flight[4] and Yahoo Weather [17] using the approach proposed in [3].

We configure the ShadowComponents for the three portlets manually by defining the configuration file. The corresponding

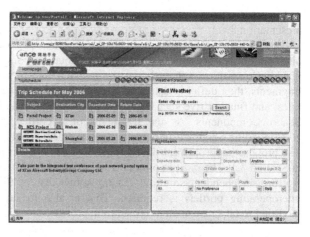

Fig. 8. (a)Trigger a portlet interoperation

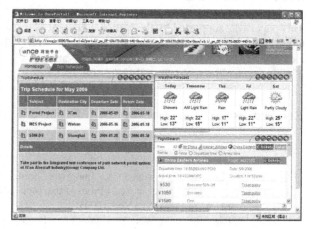

Fig. 8. (b) After the portlet interoperation

ShadowComponent of TripSchedule has two output parameters: DestinationCity and DepartureDate. WeatherForecast has one input parameter: City. FlightSearch has two input parameters: DepartureDate and DestinationCity. When a user clicks on the icon before each row of the trip schedule table, which is generated automatically by InteroperationFilter, and chooses OUTPUT All (Fig.8a), WeatherForecast and FlightSearch portlets will receive DepartureDate and DestinationCity from TripSchedule, and show the weather and flight information for the specified city and date (Fig.8b).

7 Conclusion

Portals provide presentation level integration capability. Portlet interoperability makes possible portal-based composite applications, which enable users to easily fuse data and processes from multiple existing stove-piped systems into a unified solution at presentation level.

This paper describes an HTML fragments based approach for portlet interoperability. We first construct a presentation component, which is named as ShadowComponent, for each portlet involved in a portlet interoperation using its fragments, then define a data flow process between ShadowComponents using ECA rules, and finally drive such a process by creating events to fulfill data flow between ShadowComponents. As the fragments of a portlet are synchronized with their corresponding ShadowComponents, such a process enables the portlet interoperation. The proposed approach fulfills all functional and non-functional requirements defined in Section 3.1. The most important features of our approach are: (1) it is a general and platform-independent solution; (2) no knowledge of the internal workings of the interoperating portlets is required. That is also to say, a portlet need not to be modified to take part in an interoperation process.

Acknowledgments

This paper was supported by the National Natural Science Foundation of China under Grant No.60673112; the National High-Tech R&D Plan of China under Grant Nos.2006AA01Z19B, 2006AA01Z161; the National Key Technology R&D Program of China under Grant No. 2006BAH02A08.

References

[1] Clarke, S.: Standards for Second-Generation Portals. IEEE Internet Computing 8(2), 54–60 (2004)
[2] Díaz, O., Iturrioz, J., Irastorza, A.: Improving portlet interoperability through deep annotation. In: Ellis, A., et al. (ed.) Proc. of the 14th Int'l Conf. on World Wide Web, pp. 372–381. ACM Press, NewYork (2005)
[3] Díaz, O., Paz, I.: Turning Web Applications into Portlets: Raising the Issues. In: Proc. of the 2005 Symposium on Applications and the Internet, pp. 31–37. IEEE Computer Society, Washington, DC (2005)
[4] eLong Flight (2006) http://www.elong.net/flights
[5] Geppert, A., Tombros, D.: Event-based Distributed Workflow Execution with EVE. In: Davies, N., et al. (eds.) Proc. of the IFIP/ACM Int'l Conf. on Distributed Systems Platforms and Open Distribued Processing(Middleware), The Lake District, pp. 427–442. Springer, Heidelberg (1998)
[6] Institute of Electrical and Electronics Engineers: IEEE Standard Computer Dictionary: A Compilation of IEEE Standard Computer Glossaries, New York (1990)
[7] Java Community Process. JSR 168 Portlet Specification (2003) http://www.jcp.org/en/jsr/detail?id=168
[8] Malone, T.W., Crowston, K.: The Interdisciplinary Study of Coordination. ACM Computing Surveys 26(1), 87–119 (1994)
[9] McDonough, B.: Enterprise Portal Survey. An Examination of Business Processes Driving Adoption (2004) http://www.marketresearch.com/map/prod/1045547.html.(2004)

[10] Moreno, N., Romero, J.R., Vallecillo, A.: Incorporating Cooperative Portlets in Web Application Development. Workshop on Model-driven Web Engineering (MDWE 2005) (2005)

[11] OASIS. Web Services For Remote Portlets Specification (2003) http://www.oasis-open.org

[12] Once Platform (2005) http://www.once.com.cn

[13] Papadopoulos, G., Arbab, F.: Coordination Models and Languages. In: Zelkowitz, M. (ed.) Advances in Computers, vol. 46, pp. 329–400. Academic Press, New York (1998)

[14] Roy-Chowdhury, A., Ramaswamy, S., Xu, X.: Using Click-to-Action to Provide User-Controlled Integration of Portlets (2002) http://www7b.software.ibm.com/wsdd/library/teacharticles/0212_roy/roy.html

[15] Song, J., Wei, J., Wan, S., Huang, T.: Extending Interactive Web Services for Improving Presentation Level Integration in Web Portals. Journal of Computer Science and Technology 21(4), 620–629 (2006)

[16] Weinreich, R., Ziebermayr, T.: Enhancing Presentation Level Integration of Remote Application and Services in Web Portals. In: Proc. IEEE Int'l Conf. on Services Computing(SCC05), pp. 224–236 (2005)

[17] Yahoo Weather (2006) http://weather.yahoo.com

Scalable Processing of Context Information with COSMOS

Denis Conan[1], Romain Rouvoy[2], and Lionel Seinturier[3]

[1] GET/INT, CNRS Samovar
9 rue Charles Fourier, 91011 Évry, France
Denis.Conan@int-evry.fr
[2] University of Oslo, Department of Informatics
P.O.Box 1080 Blindern, 0316 Oslo, Norway
rouvoy@ifi.uio.no
[3] INRIA-Futurs, Projet Jacquard/LIFL
Université des Sciences et Technologies de Lille (USTL)
59655 Villeneuve d'Ascq, France
Lionel.Seinturier@inria.fr

Abstract. Ubiquitous computing environments are characterised by a high number of heterogeneous devices that generate a huge amount of context data. These data are used to adapt applications to changing execution contexts. However, legacy frameworks fail to process context information in a scalable and efficient manner. In this paper, we propose to organise the classical functionalities of a context manager to introduce a 3-steps cycle of data collection, interpretation, and situation identification. We propose the COSMOS framework, which is based on the concepts of *context node* and *context management policies* translated into software components in software architecture. This paper presents COSMOS and evaluates its efficiency throughout the example of the composition of context information to implement a *caching/off-loading* adaptation situation.

Keywords: Mobile computing, context, architecture, component.

1 Introduction

Ubiquitous computing environments are characterised by an high number of mobile devices, wireless networks and usage modes. Distributed applications for such environments must continuously manage their execution context in order to detect the conditions under which some adaptation actions are required [6]. This execution context contains various categories of observable entities, such as operating system resources, user preferences, or sensors. Data coming from these entities are often related and aggregated to provide a high-level and coherent view of the execution context. Besides, the management of such a view

J. Indulska and K. Raymond (Eds.): DAIS 2007, LNCS 4531, pp. 210–224, 2007.

is under the responsibility of a context manager, which is furthermore in charge of identifying situations where applications need to be adapted.

Two categories of approaches exist in the literature for context management: The ones that are "user-centred", and those based on "system" supervision. This paper wishes to reconcile both by proposing a component-based framework for context management.

With the "user-centred" approach, context includes the user terminal, nearby small devices, such as sensors and devices reachable through a network. Existing works in the literature [6,10,17] divide context management into four functionalities: *Data collecting, data interpreting, condition-for-change detection*, and *adaptation usage*. The central point of existing frameworks consists in computing high-level abstract information about the context from some low-level raw data. In our opinion, two weak points can be identified in these frameworks: *(i)* the difficulty for composing context information and *(ii)* scalability, either in terms of the volume of processed data and/or in terms of the number of supported client applications.

The "system" supervision approach has been studied thoroughly in the past [15]. This approach is gaining again some attention as clusters, grids [2,4] and ubiquitous computing [7,9] are becoming mainstream. Existing solutions consist in instrumenting operating systems and collecting data. The weak point of frameworks in this approach is often that the collected data are numerical and too low-level for being used efficiently by adaptation policies.

This paper proposes COSMOS (*COntext entitieS coMpositiOn and Sharing*), which is a component-based framework for managing context data in ubiquitous environments. The applications we are targeting are, for example, tourist computer-based guides with contextual navigation or applications with contextual annotations, such as multi-player games. The context management provided by the COSMOS framework is *(i)* user and application centred to provide information that can be easily processed, *(ii)* built from composed instead of programmed entities, and *(iii)* efficient by minimising the execution overhead. The originality of COSMOS is to combine component-based and message-oriented approaches for encapsulating context data, and to use an architecture description language (ADL) for composing these context data components. By this way, we hope to foster the design, the composition, the adaptation and the reuse of context management policies.

This paper is organised as follows. Section 2 motivates the definition of the COSMOS framework for composing context information. Section 3 presents the design of the COSMOS framework, starting from the concept of a context node, and then proceeding by presenting the design patterns that are proposed for composing context nodes. Section 4 presents the case study of a *caching/offloading* adaptation situation. Sections 5 and 6 reports on the implementation of the COSMOS framework and evaluates its performances, respectively. Section 7 presents some related work. Finally, Section 8 concludes this paper and identifies some perspectives.

2   Overview and Motivations

This section proposes a general overview of COSMOS, which is our framework for context management. The architecture of the COSMOS framework is illustrated in Figure 1. COSMOS is divided into three layers: the Context collector layer, the Context processing layer, and the Context adaptation layer.

The lower layer of the COSMOS framework defines the notion of a context collector. Context collectors are software entities that provide raw data about the environment. These pieces of data come from operating system probes, network devices (*e.g.*, sensors), or any other kind of hardware equipment. The notion of a context collector also encompasses information coming from user preferences. The rationale for this choice is that context collectors should provide all the inputs needed to reason about the execution context.

The middle layer of COSMOS defines the notion of a context processor. Context processors filter and aggregate raw data coming from context collectors. The purpose is to compute some high-level, numerical or discrete, information about the execution environment. The status of the network link (*e.g.*, strongly connected, weakly connected, or disconnected) is an example of the piece of information outputted by a context processor. Data provided by context processors are fed into the adaptation layer.

The upper layer of COSMOS is concerned with the process of decision making. The purpose is to be able to make a decision on whether or not an adaptation action should be planned. The adaptation layer is thus a service that is provided to applications and that encapsulates the situations identified by context nodes and processors.

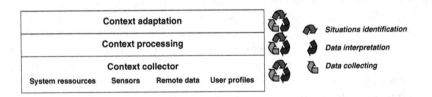

Fig. 1. Architecture of a COSMOS context manager

To provide a scalable context processing framework, the design of COSMOS has been motivated by three founding principles: *separation of concerns, isolation* and *composability*. We elaborate on these principles in the next paragraphs.

The notion of separation of concerns promotes a clear separation of functionalities into different modules. In the case of the COSMOS framework, the activities we want to separate are related to the grabbing of context information, the interpretation of this information, and the decision making process. The actions undertaken in these three cases correspond to three separate software engineering domains. The context collector layer addresses issues that are related to network technologies with solutions, such as UPnP for discovering and connecting devices, to distributed systems with, for example, data consistency protocols and network failure detectors, and to operating systems for information about hardware devices. Although separate, these three domains (network, distributed systems and operating systems) are close. The context processor layer addresses issues that are quite different. The techniques used to aggregate, filter, and reason about context data are related to domains, such as software engineering, databases, or information systems. One can also envision case studies where inference engines are used to implement the process of decision making. Finally, the context adaptation layer is directly related to the application being developed. The adaptation scenarios which are handled by this layer are domain-specific. The fact that all these concerns are quite different motivated the definition of the three above-mentioned layers.

The second principle which motivated the definition of a 3-layers architecture for the COSMOS framework, is to isolate the part that interacts with the operating system, from the rest of the framework and of the application. Although adaptation actions should not be too frequent, processing context information is an activity that must be conducted more often, while data gathering is a third activity that must be continuous. Thus, we have three different activities with different frequencies. We decouple as much as possible these activities in order to obtain a non-blocking and usable framework. Each activity is conducted in one of the three layers, which has its own autonomous life cycle: Each layer performs a 3-steps cycle of data collection (from its lower layer), processing, and decision making (for its upper layer). This principle is illustrated on the right side of Figure 1.

Composability is the third principle that motivated the design of the COSMOS framework. We want to obtain a solution where context information can be easily assembled. By being able to compose context information, we hope to foster the reuse of context management policies. For this, we adopt a component-based software engineering approach: As explained in the next section, context information is reified into software components. By connecting these components, we define assemblies that gather all the data needed to implement a specific policy.

3   Building Context Management Policies from Context Nodes

In this section, we present the composition of context information with COSMOS. Sections 3.1 and 3.2 introduce the concept of context nodes, their properties and parameters. Next, Section 3.3 defines the generic architecture of context nodes. Finally, Section 3.4 is focused on the design of the overall architecture of COSMOS, that is the relationships between the context nodes.

3.1   Concept of Context Node

The basic structuring concept of COSMOS is the *context node*. A context node is a context information modelled by a component. Context nodes are organised into hierarchies with the possibility of sharing. The graph of context nodes represents the set of context management policies defined by client applications. The sharing of a context node (and by implication of a partial or complete hierarchy) corresponds to the sharing (of a part or the whole) of a context management policy.

COSMOS provides the developer with pre-defined generic context nodes: *Elementary nodes* for collecting raw data, *memory nodes*, such as averagers, translation nodes, *data mergers* with different quality of service, *abstract or inference nodes*, such as additioners, thresholds nodes, etc. Note that in a classical context manager architecture the first nodes constitute the collectors, most of the other ones are part of the interpretation layer, while the last thresholds based ones serve to identify situations. In COSMOS, each class of nodes can be used in every layers, hence leveraging the expressiveness power of context policies.

3.2   Properties of a Context Node

Passive vs. active. A passive node obtains context information upon demand. A passive node must be invoked explicitly by another context node (passive or active). An active node is associated to a thread and initiates the gathering and/or the treatment of context information. The thread may be dedicated to the node or be retrieved from a pool. A typical example of an active node is the centralisation of several types of context information, the periodic computation of a higher-level context information, and the provision of the latter information to upper nodes.

Observation vs. notification. The observation reports containing context information are encapsulated into messages that circulate from the leaves to the root of the hierarchies. When the circulation is initiated at the request of parent nodes or client applications, it is an observation. In the other case, this is a notification.

Blocking or not. During an observation or a notification, a node that treats the request can be blocking or not. During an observation, a non-blocking context node begins by requesting a new observation report from each of its child nodes, and then updates its context information before answering the request of the parent node or the client application. During a notification, a non-blocking node computes a new observation report with the new context information just being notified, and then notifies the parent node of the client application. In the case of a blocking node, an observed node provides the most up-to-date context information that it possesses without requesting child nodes, and a notified node updates its state without notifying parent nodes. In addition, a node can be configured for a unique observation or notification if its state is immutable. Finally, the observation of a node can raise exceptions, for instance when the physical resource is not present or in case of a configuration problem. On demand, the thrown exception can be masked to parent nodes or client applications, and default values can be provided in that case.

3.3   Architecture of a Context Node

The architecture of a context node is component-based. This architecture is implemented with the FRACTAL component model [3] and its associated tools: the FRACTAL ADL architecture description language, and the DREAM [13] message-oriented component library. We take advantage of the two main characteristics of FRACTAL which are to provide a hierarchical component model with sharing. However, nothing is specific to FRACTAL in our design and COSMOS could be implemented with any other component model supporting these two notions.

Each context information is a context node which extends the composite abstract component ContextNode (see Figure 2). Pull and Push are interfaces for observation and notification. A ContextNode contains at least an operator (primitive abstract component ContextOperator), and is connected to the message-oriented communication service provided by the DREAM framework. The properties introduced in Section 3.2 become component attributes of ContextOperator. By default, nodes are passive (isActiveXxx $= false$), non-blocking (xxxThrough $= true$), and the observation reports are mutable (xxxOnlyOnce $= false$). The attributes nodeName and catchObservationException serve to name the context node, and to specify whether the exceptions which may be thrown must be forwarded to parent nodes (the default value is $false$), respectively.

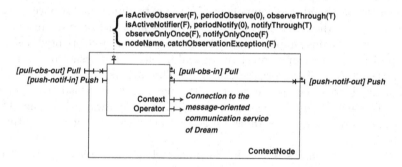

Fig. 2. Abstract Composite ContextNode

Context nodes are then classified into two categories. Leaves of the hierarchy import context information from a lower layer of the context management architecture. This lower layer may be the operating system or another framework, built with COSMOS or not, component-oriented or not. For instance, a WiFi resource manager can obtain the corresponding context information directly from the operating system (through system calls) or can encapsulate a (legacy) framework dedicated to the reification of system resources. Nodes of the graph that are not leaves, contain one or several other context nodes. For instance, a context node may compute the overall memory capacity of a terminal by encapsulating two other context nodes, the first one computing the average free memory and the second one computing the average free swap.

3.4   Architecture of COSMOS

COSMOS proposes three design patterns to compose context nodes. These are architectural design patterns which organise the collaboration between context nodes to implement the context management policy. The four patterns that are used by COSMOS are: Composite, Factory method, Flyweight and Singleton.

The hierarchical composition of context nodes is achieved with the "Composite" [11] design pattern. This design pattern homogenises the definition of the architecture and allows defining elements composed of several sub-elements, which may be themselves either composite or primitive elements. Hierarchies built in COSMOS take advantage of nodes composition for inferring higher-level context information. The Composite pattern simplifies the composition of context nodes and the management of their dependencies.

Each node of the hierarchy encapsulates a particular treatment on the information provided either by child nodes or by encapsulated primitive components in the case of leaves. The context nodes apply a component-oriented version of the design pattern "Factory method" [11]. The skeleton of a context node is defined as the assembly of a context operator (extension of ContextOperator) with, on the one hand, the components for the extra-functional services and on the other hand, the child nodes. Thanks to this approach, the definition of a context node remains simple. In addition, the internal object-oriented design of the primitive component ContextOperator also follows the design pattern "Factory method" (the object-oriented version). Through its server interfaces, this component defines generic (resp. abstract) methods to overload (resp. implement). The algorithms for observing and notifying are always the same. Thus, the skeletons of theses algorithms are generic and delegate specific treatments to sub-classes.

The system resources reified in the nodes of the hierarchy can be shared by several context nodes since the leave nodes may contain lots of elementary context data. This is precisely the purpose of the design pattern "Flyweight" [11] to efficiently share numerous fine-grained objects. By applying a component-oriented version of this design pattern, context nodes in COSMOS can efficiently share any child node of the hierarchy.

4   Case Study

In this section, we assess the expressiveness and the quality of context composition using COSMOS with a scenario from the domain of ubiquitous computing: Caching/off-loading (see Section 4.1) which is implemented with context nodes (see Section 4.2).

4.1   Caching/Off-Loading Scenario

The scenario of the case study follows. We assume that the user of a mobile terminal executes a distributed application while roaming. The WiFi connection of the mobile terminal is subject to disconnections. In order to tolerate such disconnections, the middleware platform can be augmented with the capabilities of importing/caching application entities into a software cache. Another issue is the capability of exporting/off-loading application treatments on (more powerful) hosts of the wired network. In order to choose between caching and off-loading, the context manager computes the memory capacity as the sum of the average free memory plus the average free swap. The context manager also monitors the connection to the WiFi network. It detects disconnections and computes the adjusted bit rate (average bit rate during periods of strong connectivity). When the memory capacity is sufficient, but the adjusted bit rate low, caching is preferred. When the memory capacity is low, but the adjusted bit rate sufficient, off-loading is preferred. In the two other cases, the end-user or the middleware platform give their preferences (caching or off-loading). Once the decision is taken, connectivity information is used to detect the activation instants for caching/off-loading when the connectivity mode changes (from strongly connected to disconnected and *vice versa*).

4.2   Implementation with COSMOS Context Nodes

The implementation with context nodes of the above described scenario is illustrated in Figure 3. Every node is given an intuitive name expressing the context operator it contains. The edges of the graph model the composition and the sharing relationships. When the value of a property differs from the default case, this value is indicated next to the node: Active observations and notifications, blocking or non-blocking, etc. In the example, most of the actives nodes are observers; only the nodes that detect state changes (User preference's change detector and Connectivity detector) and decision changes (Decision stabilisation) notify their changes to parent nodes. Note that the Connectivity detector node is shared by two parents, one of them being not a direct parent. The WiFi manager is shared by three parent nodes. This is a blocking node. This choice has been made to avoid emitting system calls too frequently and thus to avoid freezing the user device.

The decision When caching/off-loading? requires a graph of approximately twenty context nodes. In COSMOS, developers have at their disposal raw numerical data: Swap size, free swap, free memory, WiFi link quality, etc., plus composition facilities that help in declaratively composing these data. The resulting solution is thus reusable for other use cases. Furthermore, developers are assisted in the management of extra-functional concerns: These tasks prove to be cumbersome, and indeed even not completely manageable. The strength of COSMOS thus lies into the separation of concerns: Separation of business concerns (relevant raw data and inference treatments) from extra-functional ones (system resource management for performance).

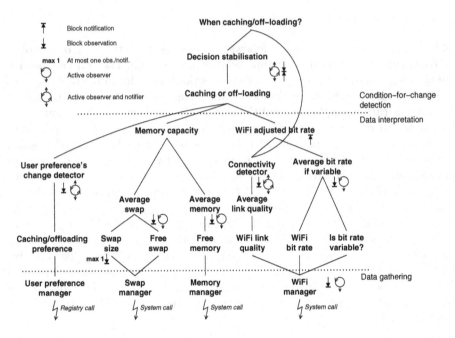

Fig. 3. Example of Composition of Context Nodes

5   Implementation of COSMOS

The implementation of the COSMOS framework is based on three existing frameworks: FRACTAL, DREAM, and SAJE. FRACTAL [3] is the component model of the ObjectWeb consortium for open-source middleware. FRACTAL defines a lightweight, hierarchical and open component model (see http://fractal.objectweb.org). We use the Julia [3] version, which is a Java implementation of FRACTAL. We also take advantage of the numerous tools available for this component model, such as FRACTAL ADL, FPath, and Fraclet (a lightweight programming model). DREAM [13] is a library composed of several FRACTAL components. DREAM allows the construction of message-oriented middleware (MOM) and the fine-grained control of concurrency management with thread pools and message pools. Finally, SAJE [5] is a framework for gathering data from system resources, either physical (battery, processor, memory, network interface, etc.) or logical (sockets, threads, etc.). SAJE supports several operating systems: GNU/Linux, Windows XP, Windows 2000 and Windows Mobile 2003.

Implementing context adaptation policies with COSMOS consists in conducting two activities: (i) developing FRACTAL components for the context nodes that are resource managers linked with SAJE and for the context operators, and (ii) composing these components by using the FRACTAL ADL language. Furthermore, as described in Section 3.2, context nodes are defined to be highly configurable through numerous attributes (about ten attributes). The inherent drawback is the complexity of the configuration of a graph of context nodes, such as the one presented in the example of Section 4.2 which contains about twenty nodes. To address this complexity, we use FPath, a language inspired from XPath and dedicated to the navigation into hierarchies of FRACTAL components.

A first version of COSMOS is available under the GNU LGPL license and can be downloaded from http://picolibre.int-evry.fr/projects/cosmos.

6   Performance Evaluation of the Prototype

The objective is to confirm experimentally the appropriateness of the component-based approach. Therefore, we make the distinction between the costs introduced by the reification of system resources by the framework SAJE and the costs due to the composition with COSMOS.

We have conducted performance measurements on a laptop PC with the following software and hardware configuration: 1.8GHz processor, 1GB of RAM, Compaq IEEE 802.11b WL110 card at 11Mbps, GNU/Linux Debian Sarge with the kernel 2.6.15, Java Virtual Machine Sun JDK 1.5 Update 6, and FRACTAL implementation Julia 2.1.3 (none of the execution optimisations activated). The results are presented in Table 1. Each test was run 10,000 times in order to obtain meaningful averages. A garbage collection and a warm-up phase occurred before each run. The unit of measure is the millisecond. When the measured values are less than one millisecond, the iterations number becomes 1,000,000. The configuration is the default one: passive nodes and non-blocking observations.

Table 1. Performances of SAJE and COSMOS

				Observation (ms)
a	SAJE Free memory	Memory		0.038
	COSMOS Memory manager	PeriodicMemory		0.045
b	SAJE Quality of the WiFi link	WirelessInterface		14.0
	COSMOS WiFi manager	PeriodicWireless		33.8
c	COSMOS Example of Figure 3	WhenCachingOffloading—default config.		163.7
	COSMOS Example of Figure 3	WhenCachingOffloading—Figure 3 conf.		4.7

The first series of measurements (see Table 1-a) concerns the extraction of the free memory information. With SAJE, the observation of the Memory object corresponds to an access to the Unix /proc file system (present in RAM) and to the initialisation of the data structures storing the information, that is to say less than 1ms. The differences between the observations with SAJE and with COSMOS (PeriodicMemory), which is evaluated to approximately $7\mu s$, is the sum of (1) the cost of the calls to FRACTAL components (crossing the membrane and interception by controllers), (2) the extraction of context information from the SAJE object, and (3) the filling of the DREAM message chunk via the message manager component.

The second series of measurements (see Table 1-b) concerns the extraction of the quality of the WiFi link. The observation of the WirelessInterface SAJE object lasts longer than the observation of the Memory SAJE object because the data of the WiFi interface are not present in RAM, but must be read from the network device. The observation of a PeriodicWireless component lasts longer since the context node extracts automatically all the available atttibutes (more than 30).

The last series of measurements (see Table 1-c) is the observation of the example of Figure 3 (component WhenCachingOffloading). It takes 163ms in the worst case: Every component is non-blocking. If the components are configured as presented in Figure 3, since the child components of WhenCachingOffloading block the observations, the observation time of WhenCachingOffloading becomes neglible (less than 5ms). This concludes that the component-based composition of context data not only pertinent but also efficient while preserving the context information accuracy.

7   Related Work

In this section, we compare COSMOS with the legacy frameworks dedicated to context monitoring, such as Phoenix and LeWYS. Then, we compare COSMOS with several middleware frameworks for context management.

Phoenix is a software framework for the observation of system resources for distributed applications deployed on clusters [2]. The architecture of Phoenix is composed of four parts: Observation agents, probes, broadcast primitives (into local networks), and a tool library. Observation agents can configure the observation frequency and multiplex the observations (by adjusting the frequency to the lowest requested value). Phoenix provides a dedicated language for describing an observation: Observable resource identifiers, comparison operators, first order logic and DELTA operators to measure the amplitude of variations. Phoenix provides only elementary operators: No memory or threshold operators, format translation, data merging, etc. However, the dedicated language approach for expressing observation requests could be used in the future evolution of COSMOS. In addition, Phoenix does not support the easy introduction of new operators.

LeWYS is a middleware framework for the supervision of clusters [4]. Its architecture encompasses probes that are deployed on all the computers of the cluster and a distributed system for notifying events. Even if LeWYS is built using FRACTAL, it does not support the composition of context data. For example, all the data retrieved by the probes are propagated without being filtered.

Context Toolkit is one of the first work on context management that was based on event programming and widget concepts introduced by GUI (*Graphical User Interfaces*) [10]. In the same framework, all the following functionalities are grouped: The interpreter for composing and abstracting context information, the aggregator for the mediation with the application, the service for controlling application actions performed on the context, and the discoverer that acts as a registry. Following the same philosophy, interpretation and aggregation functionalities have to be programmed in monolithic blocks: One interpreter and one aggregator per application, independently of the number of widgets and the level of abstraction requested by the application. Finally, the management of system resources consumed by treatments is not addressed.

MoCA Context Service architecture [8] defines an access interface, an event manager, a context-type manager, and a context repository. The event manager design highlights the need for technical services, called orthogonal services, to improve performance. In addition, context data are typed and described using an XML-based model that builds a type system implemented as Java objects. Similarly to our work, the authors describe the need for using meta-information in order to leverage performance and scalability. However, since the authors transpose an ontology-based approach to an object-oriented one, the MoCA architecture does not separate the context management functionalities. For instance, the source of context data (local or remote) is described via an attribute rather than being described in the architecture. Contrariwise, with COSMOS, we apply the component-oriented approach both at the context manager architecture level and at the context node definition level. The XML-based model of MoCA is similar to a component descriptor with its attributes. But, since COSMOS uses an ADL, the specification becomes explicit and benefits from the expressiveness of the language and its tools. Finally, the authors propose to partition the context data space into views for improving the performance. In a component model with hierarchy and sharing, this feature is automatically available.

MoCoA provides an environment for building context-aware applications for ad hoc networks based on sentient objects [16]. Sentients objects have most of the characteristics of components. The low-level inference treatments are organised as data merging pipes. MoCoA only allows notifications, contrary to COSMOS that add observations. Pipe treatments are complemented with inference ones with facts and rules, which are inspired from artificial intelligence. The pipes are logically enclosed in sentients objects, including for the control of system resources' consumption. But, contrary to COSMOS, MoCoA neither details nor provides any means to externally specify these controls. Finally, the authors of MoCoA express the useness of an ADL to describe the composition of pipes and sentients objects as we propose in COSMOS.

The context manager of Draco [14] is organised around a database and an ontology broker. The component-based approach is chosen for its ability to dynamically adapt the context management system to changing conditions of applications' requirements and context devices. The objective is to deploy / undeploy on demand functional context management components, such as filtering, history or transformation. The drawback of this use of the Singleton design pattern for functional context management services is that it does not scale. On the contrary, in COSMOS, these fine-grained functional services are replicated and integrated into context nodes when necessary. Concerning the ontology orientation, the evaluation concludes *(i)* to the difficulty to define an optimal deployment due to the difficulty to estimate of the processing time for all context management activities, and *(ii)* to the difficulty to use an ontology broker on small devices.

In *Le Contexteur* [7], *Contexteurs* are software entities similar to data components, and their meta-data (describing the data quality) as well as their controllers (modifying the configuration) are available for both inputs and outputs. A *Contexteur* is a Java class that is associated to an XML descriptor. Thus, the software framework builds, in an *ad hoc* manner, a container around the *Contexteur* component. This *ad hoc* component model is implicit and not configurable (*e.g.*, for managing system resources). For each *Contexteur* using at least an activity, the local resource consumption can not be controlled. Furthermore, the sharing of context nodes supported by COSMOS is not addressed by *Le Contexteur*. In addition, *Contexteurs* exchange control information in order to ask to stop or force the data notification for example. However, given that there is no explicit component model, it is impossible to introduce new configuration possibilities, such as some new attributes or control modes. In COSMOS, the structure and the life-cycle of components is finely managed by the FRACTAL controllers.

Last but not least, RCSM [17] is an object-oriented framework with an architecture similar to ours. Every context source (users, sensors, operating system, remote hosts) is separated. But, the authors do not tackle the issues of the synchrony of the treatments or of the control of system resources for context management. PACE [12] presents a different architecture in which context data are stored in a database. The meta-data (temporality, quality, etc.) are added either to context data or to relations between them. The authors indicate clearly that they did not have a look at issues such as scalability or performance. Concerning context modelling, the same authors prone the object or the ontology orientations as the two acceptable alternatives among the myriad of modelling methods. With COSMOS, we add the component orientation, which raises a limitation of the object orientation: A more formal specification of the dependencies between context entities thanks to the usage of an ADL.

8   Conclusion

Ubiquitous environments put some constraints on the design and the implementation of applications. Among other requirements, applications for such environment must be highly adaptable. Before adapting, the decision making process that leads to adaptation is a difficult issue for which few efficient solutions exist. This process is based on gathering, analysing and treating vast amount of physical and logical data produced by the execution environment. In this article, we propose the COSMOS framework for managing such context information.

The COSMOS framework introduces the notions of context nodes and context policies (see Section 3). Context nodes are designed and implemented as software components, and can be composed and assembled to form complex context management policies. The goal of such an assembling is to drive the adaptation of an application.

The COSMOS framework is architectured around three principles: the separation of context data gathering from context data processing, the systematic use of software components, and the use of software patterns for composing these components. The first principle allows proposing new scalable context management architectures with several levels of cycles, each one being composed of successive "gathering / interpretation / situations identification" phases. The second principle, software components, allows reusing more easily context nodes and the processors in the context nodes. The third principle allows composing rather than programming context management policies. For that, we have selected, in Section 3.4, three well-know design patterns [11] that are recurrently used when designing adaptation policies: the Composite, the Factory method, the Flyweight and the Singleton design patterns. The novelty of our approach is to use these patterns for composing software components which represent context nodes and context processors.

Scalability has been a driving factor for the design of COSMOS. We believe that several elements participate to this result: the composability brought by software components, the fact that COSMOS is divided in three independent layers, the fact that components can be shared and can have different properties to reduce their intrusiveness (see Section 3.2) and that the execution overhead have been kept as low as possible (see Section 6). The COSMOS framework is implemented on top of the FRACTAL [3] component model and the DREAM component library [13].

As a matter of future work, we plan to adopt three directions. First, we believe that the COSMOS framework is one of the main services that lies at the core of a platform for adapting distributed applications in a mobile environment. We could therefore think of integrating COSMOS in such a platform. A second direction concerns the composition of context management policies. The issue is to be able to address situations where two or several policies have to cohabit in a same platform for a same set of applications. As the intersection between these policies may not be empty, it is then necessary to provide tools to detect and solve the conflicts that arise between these policies. A direction that can be investigated consists in defining a type system [1] such as the one existing for the DREAM component library [13]. A related issue consists also in the possibility of setting up repositories for context collector components in order to facilitate their sharing. Finally, a third research direction consists in defining a domain specific language (DSL) for designing the composition of context nodes and context processors. Such a DSL could reuse ideas from the WildCAT [9] framework.

Acknowledgements

The authors wish to thank the anonymous reviewers and (in alphabetical order) Djamel Belaïd, Sophie Chabridon, Bertil Folliot, Pierre Sens and Chantal Taconet for their detailed reading and their numerous remarks on this paper.

References

1. Bidinger, P., Leclercq, M., Quéma, V., Schmitt, A., Stefani, J.-B.: Dream Types: A Domain Specific Type System for Component-Based Message-Oriented Middleware. In: 4th ESEC/FSE Workshop on Specification and Verification of Component-Based Systems, Lisbon, Portugal (September 2005)
2. Boutros Saab, C., Bonnaire, X., Folliot, B.: PHOENIX: A Self Adaptable Monitoring Platform for Cluster Management. Cluster Computing 5(1), 75–85 (2002)

3. Bruneton, É., Coupaye, T., Leclercq, M., Quéma, V., Stefani, J.-B.: The FRAC-TAL Component Model and Its Support in Java. Software—Practice and Experience, special issue on Experiences with Auto-adaptive and Reconfigurable Systems 36(11), 1257–1284 (2006)
4. Cecchet, E., Elmeleegy, H., Layaïda, O., Quéma, V.: Implementing Probes for J2EE Cluster Monitoring. Studia Informatica 4(1), 31–40 (2005)
5. Courtrai, L., Guidec, F., Le Sommer, N., Mahéo, Y.: Resource Management for Parallel Adaptive Components. In: IEEE IPDPS Workshop on Java for Parallel and Distributed Computing, pp. 134–141, Nice, France (April 2003)
6. Coutaz, J., Crowley, J., Dobson, S., Garlan, D.: The disappearing computer: Context is Key. Communications of the ACM 48(3), 49–53 (2005)
7. Coutaz, J., Rey, G.: Foundations for a Theory of Contextors. In: 4th International Conference on Computer-Aided Design of User Interfaces, pp. 13–34. Kluwer Academic Publishers, Dordrecht (2002)
8. da Rocha, R., Endler, M.: Context Management in Heterogeneous, Evolving Ubiquitous Envrionments. IEEE Distributed Systems Online, vol. 7(4) (April 2006)
9. David, P., Ledoux, T.: WildCAT: a generic framework for context-aware applications. In: 3rd International Workshop on Middleware for Pervasive and Ad-hoc Computing, pp. 1–7, Grenoble, France (November 2005)
10. Dey, A., Salber, D., Abowd, G.: A conceptual framework and a toolkit for supporting the rapid prototyping of context-aware applications. Special issue on context-aware computing in the Human-Computer Interaction Journal 16(2–4), 97–166 (2001)
11. Gamma, E., Helm, R., Johnson, R., Vlissides, J.: Design Patterns: Elements of Reusable Object-Oriented Software. Addison-Wesley, London (1994)
12. Henricksen, K., Indulska, J., McFadden, T., Balasubramaniam, S.: Middleware for Distributed Context-Aware Systems. In: 7th International Symposium on Distributed Objects and Applications, Agia Napa (Cyprus). LNCS, Springer, Heidelberg (2005)
13. Leclercq, M., Quéma, V., Stefani, J.-B.: DREAM: a Component Framework for the Construction of Resource-Aware, Configurable MOMs. IEEE Distributed Systems Online, vol. 6(9) (September 2005)
14. Preuveneers, D., Berbers, Y.: Adaptive context management using a component-based approach. In: 5th IFIP WG 6.1 International Conference on Distributed Applications and Interoperable Systems, Athens (Greece), vol. 3543, pp. 14–26. Springer-Verlag, Heidelberg (2005)
15. Schroeder, B.: On-Line Monitoring: A Tutorial IEEE Computer, pp. 72–78 (June 1995)
16. Senart, A., Cunningham, R., Bouroche, M., O'Connor, N., Reynolds, V., Cahill, V.: MoCoA: Customisable Middleware for Context-Aware Mobile Applications. In: 8th International Symposium on Distributed Objects and Applications. LNCS, vol. 4275, pp. 1722–1738. Springer, Heidelberg (2006)
17. Yau, S., Karim, F., Wang, Y., Wang, B., Gupta, S.: Reconfigurable Context-Sensitive Middleware for Pervasive Computing. IEEE Pervasive Computing 1(3), 33–40 (2002)

Experiences from Developing a Distributed Context Management System for Enabling Adaptivity

Nearchos Paspallis, Avraam Chimaris, and George A. Papadopoulos

Department of Computer Science, University of Cyprus
P.O. Box 20537, Postal Code 1678, Nicosia, Cyprus
{nearchos, cspgha, george}@cs.ucy.ac.cy

Abstract. Today, one can observe an ever increasing trend in the use of mobile systems. This change inevitably affects the software running on such devices by necessitating additional functionality such as context awareness and adaptive behavior. While some developers design their systems to be fully self-reliant with regard to context awareness, others aim for more synergistic approaches by allowing context sharing across devices. This paper describes our experience with first designing and implementing a basic context management system, and then with extending it to allow context distribution. In the proposed architecture, the developers define the context dependencies for their software independently of the availability of context information in their corresponding devices. An automated mechanism is then used to match these needs to the corresponding providers, even when those reside across distributed devices. This approach enables them to utilize shared context information at runtime thus reducing both development efforts and hardware costs.

Keywords: Context-awareness, Middleware, Distributed architectures.

1 Introduction

Today, one can observe an ever increasing trend in the use and proliferation of mobile systems. This change has inevitably affected the design and the implementation of software running on such devices. For instance, additional functionality in terms of context awareness and adaptive behavior is now a common feature desired and frequently found in such systems. While the adaptive-behavior implies the capability of a system to run in a number of different configurations or modes, context-awareness refers to its ability to dynamically perceive the characteristics of its surrounding environment. The ultimate benefit is provided in mobile systems which are capable of monitoring and exploiting the contextual information, and infer decisions on choosing the optimal adaptation. This process is guided by the aim for maximizing the quality of the service as it is perceived by the users.

In this work it is assumed that an adaptive, mobile system monitors its environment and dynamically chooses an optimal configuration, thus adapting itself on demand. While the context information which is monitored can be theoretically of unbound variability, in practice only a small fraction of the available context data is delegated as input to the adaptation decision-making component. Naturally, the more context

J. Indulska and K. Raymond (Eds.): DAIS 2007, LNCS 4531, pp. 225–238, 2007.

information is available to such a decision maker, the better the decision can be. In most context-aware systems, acquired information is retrieved from sensors or the client side of services. Consequently, the available context information types are restricted by the limited mobile device size and resources which render the hosting of unlimited context sensors intolerable. This limitation highlights the importance of enabling sharing of context information between distributed sources. In this way, the distributed context sources can further eliminate the related costs (e.g. battery consumption, memory use, etc.) while providing mobile nodes with richer context information which otherwise would be impossible to have access to.

This paper describes the architecture of a distributed context management system which is used to drive the adaptation reasoning process in the *mobility and adaptation enabling middleware* (MADAM) [1, 2]. Besides the architecture design this paper's contributions also include a review of requirements for the design and implementation of such a system, as well as a list of related experiences and findings.

The rest of this paper is organized as follows: First, section 2 describes the basic aspects of context-aware systems, followed by section 3 which analyzes a number of requirements for distributed context management systems. Then the proposed architecture is analyzed in section 4, along with a description of its implementation. Following that is a discussion of experiences and related work presented in section 5, and finally, section 6 concludes with a review of the contributions of this paper.

2   Context Awareness

Context-aware computing is an area which studies methods and tools for discovering, modeling and consuming contextual information. Such information can include any information affecting the interaction of a user with a system, such as user location, time of day, nearby people and devices, user activity, light or noise conditions, etc. A more formal and widely used definition specifies context as *"any information that can be used to characterize the situation of an entity; an entity is a person, place, or object that is considered relevant to the interaction between a user and an application, including the user and application themselves"* [3, 4].

Context can also be classified in more fine-grained categories: *physical, computing* and *user* context information types [5]. The physical context type is related to environmental factors which can usually be evaluated by using specialized hardware mechanisms. The light, noise, and temperature are examples of physical context data types. The computing context refers to the information which describes the resources available in the computing infrastructure. This includes information such as the network connectivity and its characteristics (e.g. bandwidth, latency, etc.), nearby resources (such as printers, video projectors, etc), and details concerning the memory availability, the processor use, etc. Finally, the user context refers to the user's profile by focusing on the user needs, preferences, mood, etc. For example these can include information concerning the user's occupation (e.g. driving, studying, etc.) or the user's choice for preferring, say, to use a desktop computer rather than a PDA while at work.

Furthermore, it is argued that any system that aims to be minimally intrusive must be context aware, in the sense that it should be cognizant of its user's state and environment [6]. In other words, context-aware mobile systems are expected to utilize such information in order to adapt their behavior, based on a predefined set of adaptation rules. These rules are usually monitored by a system which dynamically adapts the system's operation based on the contextual information sensed.

In this paper, the context awareness is treated as an independent concern, where the applications can separately and independently register for particular context change events, without having to be involved in the collection or management of contextual information. Because of this separation of concerns, it is possible to treat the context awareness support mechanism independently of the adaptation mechanism. I.e. from a developer's point of view, the two mechanisms can evolve independently, thus improving on both the development and the maintenance effort required.

3   Requirements for Distributed Context Management

The main responsibilities of a context-aware, adaptive mobile system include acquiring context information, reasoning on the acquired information, and performing adaptations as a result of these changes. In many cases the acquired information is retrieved locally (e.g. through attached sensors) but frequently this information is insufficient for performing the required adaptation reasoning. In a distributed context management system, additional context information can be shared among a set of distributed mobile devices. This enhances the process of making adaptation reasoning decisions by offering context information which would otherwise not be accessible.

3.1   General Requirements

The implementation of a distributed context-aware framework should address many of the requirements of traditional distributed systems such as *heterogeneity, mobility, scalability,* and *tolerance* to system and network failures. Heterogeneity is required because systems are inevitably developed by different teams and target many different platforms. However, these systems are still expected to collaborate with each other and share context information. Distributed context management systems are also naturally expected to enable mobility, and thus it should be possible to disseminate context information independently of the communication protocols, the underlying network infrastructure or the location of the nodes. The requirement for scalability is a natural consequence of the distributed nature of the desired context management system. This requirement dictates that the performance of the system is not severely downgraded as the number of participating nodes increases. Finally, and although not critical from a functional point of view, the *ease of deployment and configuration* is also an important requirement for such a system. These requirements were considered in our implementation, as it is discussed in sections 4 and 5.

3.2   Requirements for the Distribution of Context

Typical context management systems adhere to the publish/subscribe model, where providers asynchronously provide their information, and clients subscribe for notification when such events occur. This approach however, is further extended in the case of distributed systems, as the providers and the subscribers can reside on different, network connected nodes. The additional requirements are:

Service Discovery: The service discovery requirement refers to the need for discovering context providers (i.e. nodes capable of sharing context information). Suitable approaches include two main categories: centralized and ad-hoc service discovery. Centralized approaches include services which provide context at well known locations (e.g. a URL), or advertise their capabilities in directories. Contrary to these, ad hoc approaches utilize services which dynamically form partnerships for context exchange. Their communication can be realized by using combinations of infrastructure-based, wireless and ad hoc-based networks.

Modeling and Semantics: The context modeling refers to the requirement for formatting the information so that it encapsulates both the required data and metadata. Context modeling is important for guaranteeing compatibility among the possibly heterogeneous devices (i.e. mobile nodes, context sensing mechanisms, etc.). This is particularly important in ad-hoc configurations, where the nodes participate to context exchanges without being *a priori* aware of each other, and consequently of the methods they use to abstract (model) and interpret (semantics) context information.

Scope and Privacy: When sharing context information in a distributed environment, it is important to define its scope. For example, context information which is limited to local use should be prevented from being generally distributed. Rather, suitable methods should be used to limit its dissemination within a local area in which it is more likely to be valid. As most of the context information is expected to be of local interest only, this requirement seeks to ensure that an explosion of context information is prevented and rather a form of localized scalability is enabled. On the other hand, the dissemination of context information should also be controlled so that no sensitive information can be leaked to the wrong hands. Similar to the context scope, the privacy is another important parameter which must be taken into account when defining the access to context information. In particular, the access to sensitive context information must be explicitly defined so that only the context information which is intended to be public is shared with other devices.

4   The Architecture of the Context Management System

The main concept of the implemented architecture is the separation between *context clients* and *context providers* [7,8]. In this respect, all nodes act as both context providers and context consumers, as part of a membership group which is formed using a loosely coupled protocol. Furthermore, while individual nodes are free to access context information from any possible provider (i.e. even context servers located at remote geographical locations), it is nevertheless assumed that in most cases context sharing is limited to a local area only. In this respect, the locality refers to groups formed by nodes which can directly communicate with each other, e.g. over a wireless link by forming an ad-hoc WiFi or Bluetooth network (i.e. a piconet).

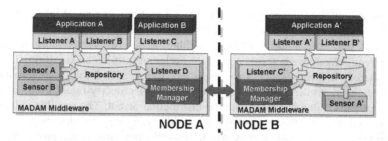

Fig. 1. Distributed Context Management System Architecture

This approach has the important advantage of assigning higher importance to local context and consequently enabling localized scalability [6]. The first one refers to the fact that it is more likely that two neighboring nodes will share a common interest on the same context as opposed to nodes at different geographical locations. This is true for example in most pervasive computing applications where applications aim to utilize the infrastructure which is embedded in the surrounding environment. In another example, it would be more likely that an application would be more interested in the temperature information provided by nearby nodes (and thus residing in the same environment) as opposed to the temperature information provided by distant nodes. Second, localized scalability is achieved by preferring local sources (and respectively consumers) for sharing context information with. In this approach, the use of mainstream links is avoided as most of the communication is carried out over local (i.e. direct) network links. The following paragraphs describe the basic ideas of this approach, along with the algorithms required to support it.

4.1 Context Management in Centralized Environments

As it has already being mentioned, the implemented architecture is based on the separation of roles between context *providers* and *consumers* [7]. Even if all nodes can interchangeably act as both clients and producers, at the underlying layer there are specialized architectural components which can either support context production or consumption. These components are the Context Sensors that are used to *produce* context, and the Context Listeners which can be registered to *listen* for context changes (Fig. 1). When the monitored context type changes, the listeners inform the linked applications (e.g. *Application A* is informed for context changes for the monitored context of *Listener A* and *Listener B*). The Context Sensors generate context elements that are stored in local repositories. This centralized architecture is quite simple and is based on the requirements defined in the context-aware section.

4.2 Membership and Distributed Context Management

In a distributed context-aware system the intention is for the information in the local repositories to be shared between nodes. In order to enable this, we implemented a loosely coupled communication protocol between the distributed nodes which is based on the transmission and handling of *heartbeat* messages. This architecture is based on the requirements that were identified in section 3. In the analysis of the required communication protocol we discovered that not all context information was suitable for sharing. For example, context information describing the battery status of a device is generally useless to other, neighboring devices. Furthermore, as per the privacy requirement, we detected a need for excluding some context information from being shared. In this respect, two *properties* were defined for characterizing the context element types: *scope* and *privacy*. The first property refers to whether the context element value is appropriate for distribution or not. The possible values that can be assigned to this property are: *public* (i.e. can be distributed without restrictions), *local* (i.e. useful only within a small range around the providing node; such information is typically directly communicated across devices) and *private* (meaningful only within the device itself). The *privacy* property describes how sensitive is the context information and consequently whether it is suitable for sharing or not. This property can be assigned two values: *public* (i.e. the information can be shared unrestricted), and *private* (i.e. the information is not subject to distribution outside the local device).

Once the context information is appropriately annotated with properties, the next step is to define an appropriate mechanism to first enable the dynamic discovery of nodes, and second to physically enable information sharing among them. In this work, we have purposely aimed for a completely ad-hoc approach, which has the benefit of not requiring the set-up of context servers and, additionally, it provides better access to neighboring information which is much more likely to be relevant to collaborating nodes. The used protocol is based on a loosely coupled method, which is enabled by periodically broadcasting and handling heartbeat messages. Furthermore, the overall system is based on a push/pull hybrid approach. While pull approaches attempt to retrieve context information without *a priori* being aware if the requested data is available or not, push approaches proactively communicate context information to peer nodes regardless of whether the context was requested or not. In our hybrid approach, the distributed context is transmitted (pushed) from the providing nodes to the requesting ones. Additionally, the requesting nodes do not keep track of the remotely provided context, but rather they notify nearby nodes of their needs.

The distributed context needs are defined inside the heartbeat messages which are broadcasted by the underlying network layer. The broadcasted messages also encode the types of the desired context data. When received, the context data is decoded to form a list of the required values by all nodes in the neighborhood. Then, from an individual node's point of view, requested context types that are available are subsequently broadcasted to the local network (push approach) also by being encoded in the corresponding heartbeat messages that are periodically broadcasted. On the receivers' side the heartbeats are decoded and the corresponding context values are used to generate a local context change event, as if the changes were sensed locally.

In practice, the push mechanisms are more efficient than their pull counterparts, as the pull mechanisms need local meta-data in order to select the proper provider to request for, and to construct the request message. In push architectures, there is no need to keep local information about remote providers because as soon as a nearby node receives a context request an appropriate heartbeat message is immediately constructed and communicated back to the requestor.

We argue that this architecture satisfies the detected required features. The use of a broadcasting mechanism for the heartbeat messages reduces the communication overhead (especially as the required context information is piggy-backed into these messages). Another alternative would be to have nodes announcing their offered context information, but this imposes significant overhead for updating local tables mapping context offerings to context requestors. Instead, in the proposed architecture there is no need for storing such information because the requests are handled directly by context producers. Consequently, this architecture provides the benefits of better scalability and consistency, while at the same time requiring fewer resources.

This architecture is heavily based on the periodic broadcast of special heartbeat messages which serve two purposes: first they are used to update the membership status of the individual nodes and they communicate basic information about context required by the sender. Additionally, the heartbeat messages are used for transmitting context change events from providing nodes (using the discussed push approach) to the requesting nodes. This approach also enables a loosely-coupled synchronization method which is based on periodic broadcast of heartbeat messages. These messages are intended to both form and maintain a *membership group*, as well as to update the individual nodes of the context information required by the senders. Similar protocols have also been proposed and tested in commercial environments (e.g. the Bonjour [9] and the Bluetooth technologies [10]). In the proposed approach however, the aim is specialized on the exchange of context information rather than of general data.

The membership manager: In this architecture, the most important component is the *Membership Manager* (see Fig. 1). The Membership Manager is part of the context management system of the MADAM middleware. Its main responsibility is to periodically multicast the heartbeat messages and to handle the received ones.

The periodic multicast of heartbeats aims at achieving mainly two goals: first, to enable the formation of a loosely coupled membership group, and second, to inform the neighboring nodes (i.e. the group) about possible context needs which cannot be locally satisfied. Additionally, the heartbeats are also used to encapsulate context data so that they can be shared with other nodes. On the receiving side, the membership manager exploits this information exactly for forming this loosely coupled group and for decoding possible context change events which are of interest to the local node.

The membership manager's functionality is supported by two table-like data structures: the *membership table* which is used for managing the membership status and the *context requestors table* to maintain the context requests from the remote nodes. When a heartbeat message is received, the membership table is updated with the provided information. For example if the heartbeat was sent by a node which is not already present in the membership management table, a new entry is created for it. At the same time, an event is generated indicating the addition of the new member. If the node is already present in the membership table, then its context requirements are examined for changes, and appropriately update the context requestors table. In this way, the requesting nodes notify the nearby context-provider nodes of their newly required context in order to adjust their remote context listeners.

In order to detect when a node has left the membership, a simple algorithm is also used which is based on a predefined, globally agreed timeout period: the *heartbeat interval*. In simple words, this algorithm periodically checks the table with the current members and ensures that all members have a recent heartbeat timestamp. When a

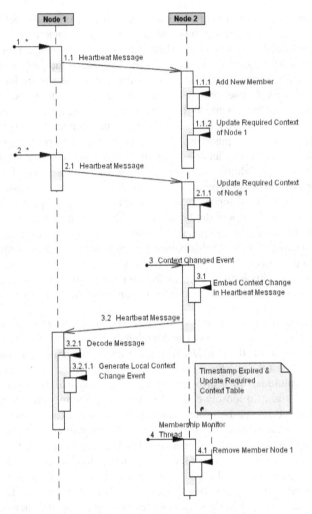

Fig. 2. Sequence diagram of a typical message interchange in a group membership

member misses a predefined number of consecutive heartbeats, it is assumed to have left the group. At that point, an appropriate event is generated indicating the fact that the member in question has left the group. Because the departed node was possibly also included in the context requestors table, an appropriate update takes place there too, so that all context entries requested by that node only, are removed.

As a result of the heartbeat messages, two main events are triggered by the corresponding membership management mechanism: the *new member added* event and the *existing member left* event. An additional event concerning context updates (pushed context changes) can also be raised: the *context updated* event. All events encapsulate information about the identity of the node involved, as well as information on its requested context. To better explain the used algorithm, the following paragraphs explain how these events are handled by the context manager:

- **New member added event:** This type of event is generated when a heartbeat message is received from a node not previously registered with the membership manager. Once detected, the new node is also automatically considered for its needed context. For each remote requestor, a local context listener counterpart is instantiated. This listener automatically pushes context information to the remote requesting node when the respective context changes (sequence 1 in Fig. 2).
- **Existing member left event:** This event is triggered when a node is detected to have left the membership group. Each heartbeat timestamp is updated whenever a heartbeat message is received from the specific node. In this way, when the heartbeat timestamp of a node in the context providers table is found to be outdated, the corresponding node is assumed to be disconnected. At that time, the listeners that are pushing information to this remote node are considered obsolete, and thus are removed from the table (sequence 4 in Fig.2).
- **Context requirements updated event:** Finally, a context change event occurs when an existing node is found to have changed its needed context. In that case, the membership manager iterates through the context requestors table and updates the corresponding entries (i.e. removes obsolete entries and add newly required ones). This is depicted by sequence 3, in Fig. 2.

Besides generating these events, the membership manager also reacts on them, by adding and removing context listeners (to itself). The actual context information is communicated through the heartbeat messages, as piggy-backed context information. Thus, beyond updating the membership status when a heartbeat is received, the membership manager also parses the heartbeats and passes possible context change events to the context repository (see Fig. 1) for further distribution.

4.3 Implementing the Architecture

The described architecture was designed and implemented as part of a broader adaptation enabling middleware (MADAM). The system was implemented in the Java language and tested on both a laptop computer running the Windows XP operating system and an iPAQ PDA computer running the Windows Mobile operating system. Regarding the JVM, in the first case we used the mainstream implementation provided by Sun Microsystems, while in the case of the PDA we used the CreMe JVM by NSI.com. Finally, the MADAM middleware provides a context visualizer (a simple context client) which allows a user or a developer to dynamically monitor and edit (simulate) the context information (shown in Fig. 3, when deployed on a PDA).

During the implementation, some of our main goals were interoperability, platform independence, and extensibility. To facilitate the first two goals, we used the Java system while refraining from using *native* (i.e. platform dependent) libraries. However, lower-level layers of the MADAM middleware (and especially the resource management component) do extensive use of native libraries, which are platform-dependent (e.g. two different implementations are made available by the MADAM consortium targeting both Windows-based PCs and PDAs). However, extensive coverage of the resource management layer is beyond the scope of this paper. The interested readers are rather referenced to the MADAM website [1].

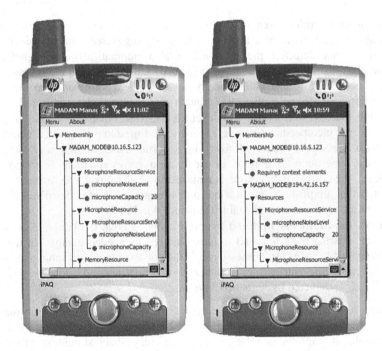

Fig. 3. The left diagram depicts the context view in the case of a single node, while the right diagram depicts a situation where two individual nodes form a membership

For the extensibility goal, we used an approach which allows to interchangeably selecting different networking technologies. In this respect, we defined a *Broadcast Service* interface which provides methods for *broadcasting* generic, serializable messages and for subscribing (and unsubscribing) for the reception of such messages. The membership manager is only aware of this interface, thus allowing a developer to provide different implementations.

At this time, we have tested a default implementation of the broadcast service which has successfully demonstrated message broadcasts on both wired and wireless networks, on both Windows XP and Windows Mobile-based systems. Furthermore, we developed a simulated version of this service, which uses plain TCP communication messages and a simulation hub, with the intention of enabling the middleware to function even behind firewalls or simply when on devices which do not support multicasting. Finally, a Bluetooth-based implementation is also underway.

5   Experiences from the Development of the Context System

The process of first designing a basic context management system and then extending it to enable distributed context sharing has provided us with many valuable insights that we attempt to document in the following paragraphs:

Non-functional nature of context should remain as such: When designing context aware systems, the aim is usually to optimize the operation of the system, rather than extend its capabilities. For example, an intelligent agenda could exploit GPS information so that when a "lunch at 12pm" entry is activated, a list of nearby restaurant options, compatible with the user's taste, are automatically displayed to inform the user about them. However, in this case the availability of context information (i.e. GPS coordinates) is completely optional and does not prevent the software from performing its basic goals. Rather, it simply limits its functionality to some extent, with also a possible decrease in the quality of the offered service. It has been our experience with the development of the context management system, but also with the development of the MADAM adaptation-enabling middleware, that the context information should be used as such and never being allowed to become a part of a *critical path*, i.e. its absence should never cause a system to stop functioning. In this respect, the MADAM middleware suggests the designers to provide a set of possible adaptations (i.e. configurations) for their applications, along with a set of *properties* and *utility functions* which always allows the computation and the selection of a minimal configuration, regardless of the availability or absence of (possibly distributed) context information. This experience is in accordance to a common distributed computing fallacy[1]: *the network is reliable.*

Modeling of context should provide support for distribution: While designing the basic context management system, one can be easily mislead to the assumption that the context information is both generated and consumed at the same node. However, in real distributed systems, sharing of context information imposes additional requirements for identifying both the nature and the origin of the context information. For example, information about the memory availability of a node becomes useless, unless the actual node association is explicitly or implicitly defined. This also implies that unless the context information is generated and consumed by the same system (e.g. the MADAM middleware), then a set of semantics metadata must accompany the actual context data to allow for better optimization of the context data (e.g. the metric system used for the measurements, the methods used to acquire the data, and even the accuracy of the communicated information). Last but not least, distributed dissemination of context data requires that the distributed peers *trust* each other and they are capable of securing that the communicated data is handled as it is intended.

Plug-and-Play architecture support for context sensors: Assuming that a device will require a constant set of context information types is erroneous. In practice, different applications are dynamically started and stopped. Additionally, in the case of adaptive, component-based applications different variants of the same application might impose different context requirements. Having the maximum context information provided at all times is not an optimal solution, especially in mobile systems where resource consumption is an important concern! In this respect, the design of a plug-and-play architecture enables dynamic reconfiguration of the context manager's architecture, which can greatly improve the system's efficiency and autonomy. In our context system's architecture, we maintain a dynamically updated list with the registered context listeners (consumers) along with their corresponding

---

[1] http://en.wikipedia.org/wiki/Fallacies_of_Distributed_Computing.

needs. This allows the system to periodically and dynamically evaluate the situation which concerns the need for context information and dynamically activate and deactivate the corresponding context sensors. Additionally, while some of the sensing functionality (such as the memory and CPU monitoring) can only be embedded in the middleware system, others depend on software and hardware sensors, both native to the device and newly added ones. For example, a system might be originally designed with a GPS device only, but in the future it might be equipped with a temperature and barometer sensor as well. Such an addition should not require any updates to the middleware, but simply the addition of new software context sensors which would make the new information available to the middleware as well. This is combined with the general middleware's pluggable architecture which allows dynamic loading and unloading of applications and components together with the corresponding (software) context sensors and reasoners. In effect, this enables the context system to extend its domain of covered context information at runtime while at the same time conforming to the actual needs of the hosted applications.

6 Related Work and Conclusions

A plethora of related work studies both centralized and distributed issues of context management. This section discusses a number of achievements established already, but also detects open problems which are not addressed by existing approaches yet.

Centralized context-aware systems use a local service which provides applications with contextual information. Such infrastructures encapsulate these services as part of a middleware which acquires raw contextual information from sensors and provides interpreted context to applications via a standardized API. Furthermore, the middleware is assigned to monitor particular context changes and dispatch relevant events to interested applications when required.

In contrast to centralized approaches, distributed context-aware applications allow the generation of context information at several locations, thus avoiding potential bottlenecks and unnecessary hardware duplication. Despite the fact that decentralized architectures increase the communication cost, they are more resilient to errors as they do not require a central server to maintain the context information.

An approach which is partly based on message multicasts is described in [12]. In this approach clients broadcast their location queries to all the members of a group and interested parties anonymously listen to the queries. When they match a query and their privacy policy allows it they reply to the query. Just like in our approach, the main disadvantage lies in the increased computation and communication cost. Unlike that approach though, our proposed mechanism aims at limiting the communication cost by minimizing the heartbeat message size. Furthermore, both the computation and communication costs can be minimized by increasing the heartbeat interval if that can be tolerated by the applications. Finally, the computation cost is further limited by using the context update timestamp which prevents the nodes to perform unnecessary computations when there are no context changes encoded in the heartbeat.

The Context Toolkit [13] provides a component framework for acquiring and handling context using three key abstractions: widgets, interpreters, and aggregators.

The context widgets are the most important components of this framework because they provide applications with access to the context information while hiding the details of context sensing. The context interpreters convert or interpret context to higher level information and the context aggregators collect context relevant to particular entities. Similar to our approach, the Context Toolkit provides support for storing historical context data, and then reusing them to estimate their value trend.

Other systems, like Jini [14], use coordination model infrastructures to implement well-formed shared repositories. This technology is usually used in the background, such as for example in the Smart Map project [15], which enables position-aware applications by using the Jini technology for implementing a registry. The registry is used by service providers to register themselves for context availability and the service consumers use the registry to discover them. The Context Fusion Networks (CFN) [16] project is implemented as a context-aware middleware which handles context information by realizing sources, sinks and channels. The context sensors are represented by sources because they are responsible for constructing contextual information. The applications which use this information are represented by sinks. Furthermore, more recent approaches exist which aim at enabling generic data sharing between neighboring devices. A notable approach is described in [17] where support is provided for developing efficient solutions for sharing data in the neighborhood.

In contrast to most of these approaches, which do not explicitly tackle fault tolerance, our approach provides limited fault tolerance. As the context manager has a minimum state, any failures can be tolerated by simply re-instantiating the context manager and allowing some time for the corresponding context producers and consumers to recover by processing their periodic messages. However, our approach is not tolerant to malicious attacks such as message flooding, which is a common limitation of broadcasting-based approaches. Finally, unlike most other works, our approach implements and promotes localized scalability as an effective measure to optimize the consumption of resources and maintain the system performance.

In conclusion, this paper proposes a distributed context management mechanism which aims at driving the decision making in the *adaptation enabling middleware* (MADAM). We have detected a number of both general and more specific requirements imposed by the distribution aspect. In this respect we have proposed an approach which is based on the periodic communication of heartbeat messages for forming loosely coupled membership groups and for advertising their required context. We argue that this approach satisfies the detected requirements to a great extend. Furthermore, this architecture has been implemented, tested, and evaluated in real pilot applications, on both resourceful (laptops) and small (PDAs) computers, with significant success. Further work is underway, aiming at specifying a more structured context model, as well as extending its application domain to ubiquitous computing (i.e. embedded in addition to mobile devices).

Acknowledgments. The authors would like to thank their partners in the MADAM-IST and the MUSIC-IST projects and acknowledge the financial support given to this research by the EU (6th Framework Programme, contract numbers 4169 and 35166).

References

1. IST MADAM (Mobility and Adaptation Enabling Middleware), http://www.ist-madam.org
2. Floch, J., Stav, E., Hallsteinsen, S., Eliassen, F., Gjørven, E., Lund, K.: Using Architecture Models for Runtime Adaptability. IEEE Software 23(2), 62–70 (2006)
3. Dey, A.: Providing Architectural Support for Building Context-Aware Applications, PhD Thesis, College of Computing, Georgia Institute of Technology, pp. 170 (2000)
4. Dey, A.: Understanding and Using Context. Personal Ubiquitous Computing 5(1), 4–7 (2001)
5. Chen, G., Kotz, D.: A Survey of Context-Aware Mobile Computing Research, Technical Report: TR2000-381 Dartmouth College, Hanover, NH, USA (2000)
6. Satyanarayanan, M.: Pervasive Computing: Vision and Challenges, IEEE Personal Communications Magazine, pp. 10–17 (2001)
7. Mikalsen, M., Paspallis, N., Floch, J., Stav, E., Papadopoulos, G.A., Ruiz, P.A.: Putting Context in Context: The Role and Design of Context Management in a Mobility and Adaptation Enabling Middleware, International Workshop on Managing Context Information and Semantics in Mobile Environments (MCISME'06). In: conjunction with the 7th International Conference on Mobile Data Management (MDM'06), Nara, Japan, May 9-12, 2006, pp. 76–83. IEEE Computer Society Press, Washington, DC (2006)
8. Paspallis, N., Papadopoulos, G.A.: An Approach for Developing Adaptive, Mobile Applications with Separation of Concerns. In: 30th Annual International Computer Software and Applications Conference (COMPSAC 2006), Chicago, IL, USA, Sept. 17-21, 2006, pp. 299–306. IEEE Computer Society Press, Washington, DC (2006)
9. Bonjour: Connect Computers and Electronic Devices Automatically without any Configuration http://images.apple.com/macosx/pdf/MacOSX_Bonjour_TB.pdf
10. Draft Bluetooth Core Specification v2.1 + EDR https://www.bluetooth.org /spec/
11. Want, R., Schilit, B., Adams, N., Gold, R., Petersen, K., Goldberg, D., Ellis, J., Weiser, M.: An Overview of the PARCTAB Ubiquitous Computing Experiment. IEEE Personal Communications 2, 28–43 (1995)
12. Spreitzer, M., Theimer, M.: Providing location information in a ubiquitous computing environment. 14th ACM Symposium on Operating Systems Principles, Asheville, NC, USA, December 5-8, pp. 270–283. ACM Press, New York (1993)
13. Dey, A., Salber, D., Abowd, G.: A conceptual framework and a toolkit for supporting the rapid prototyping of context-aware applications. Human Computer Interaction 16(2-4), 97–166 (2001)
14. Sun Microsystems, Jini Network Technology, http://www.sun.com/software/jini/
15. Urnes, T., Hatlen, A., Malm, P., Myhre, O.: Building Distributed Context-Aware Applications. Personal Ubiquitous Computing 5(1), 38–41 (2001)
16. Chen, G., Li, M., Kotz, D.: Design and implementation of a large scale context fusion network. 1st Annual International Conference on Mobile and Ubiquitous Systems: Networking and Services (MobiQuitous), Cambridge, MA, USA, Aug. 22-25, 2004, pp. 246–255. IEEE Computer Society Press, Washington (2004)
17. Lachenmann, A., Marrón, P.J., Minder, D., Saukh, O., Gauger, M., Rothermel, K.: EWSN 2007. LNCS, vol. 4373, pp. 1–16. Springer, Heidelberg (2007)

Towards Context-Aware Web Applications

Po-Hao Chang and Gul Agha

University of Illinois at Urbana-Champaign,
201 North Goodwin Avenue, Urbana IL 61801, USA
{pchang2, agha}@cs.uiuc.edu

Abstract. In order to guarantee certain levels of QoS, a Web application needs to adapt itself to different execution contexts. However, because of the lack of coordination support in Web platforms, service providers respond to the challenge by simply providing multiple versions of a Web application, one for each context. We argue this top-down approach is neither efficient nor scalable: developing a context-specific application requires considerable effort and expertise while the ever-changing Internet never stops generating interesting contexts which can be exploited for better deployment. As an alternative, we propose a three-layer, bottom-up approach to building context-aware Web applications. At the bottom layer, we characterize a context-specific Web application with a particular *component distribution plan* which provides details for composing individual objects. In the middle layer, recursively defined *configurations* provide a bridge which relates high-level context features to low-level component distribution properties, where a configuration is a combination of configurations and/or component distribution properties. At the top level, a *context management system* selects desirable configurations according to the execution contexts.

1 Introduction

Evolving from its original mission of content delivery, the Web has become a gateway of assorted interactive applications: people access emails, shop online, trade equities, manage accounts and even remotely control home appliances using various Web applications. Unlike its typical standalone and distributed peers, a Web application encounters heterogeneous execution environments and numerous, unpredictable circumstances in its deployment. From the early days of the Web, developers identified the need to differentiate execution contexts: it was common for a Web application to have one version with *HTML frames* and another without. Context differentiation has become more critical as the Web has evolved: new crop of context-specific versions such as *broadband, JavaScript-enabled, HTML only* and *low graphics* can be found in many Web applications.

In most cases, these versions are built in a top-down fashion: that is, given a context, the programmer exploits its features and develops a specific version accordingly. However, the development and maintenance cost of multiple versions is always expensive, and in the case of Web applications, this approach is fragile in two ways:

J. Indulska and K. Raymond (Eds.): DAIS 2007, LNCS 4531, pp. 239–252, 2007.
© IFIP International Federation for Information Processing 2007

1. Web applications are usually evolutionary in their life cycles. A minor change in the application requirement may result in a re-evaluation of features to be exploited in the contexts of interest.
2. The domain of interesting contexts is changing. Some contexts have fallen into disuse and others are gaining sufficient momentum to require particular attention. Since the future trend is hardly predictable, not much of existing code can be readily reused.

We believe a bottom-up approach is a more feasible way to build and manage a context-aware Web application. This is motivated by the following observation: no matter how many versions the application supports, there are some elements in common, such as its core application logic. We model a Web application as a composition of distributed objects: the composing structure and the functions of individual objects characterize the application. Instead of building a monolithic context-specific version from scratch, the developer picks and/or adapts composing objects with desired attributes, for example, implementation technology, execution location and deployment policy, to fit for the context of interest. The idea is similar to Web styling sheets [13, 7]: a customized presentation of a document can be achieved by supplying a specific style sheet.

The ability to customize a Web application through object annotations is just on the halfway to context-aware Web applications: the customizable application requires human intervention (meta-programming) to adapt into contexts. To be truly context-aware, the application needs assistance from a context management system to automate this process. The goal of the system is to generate detailed deployment plans based on the context features at runtime. However, using straight-forward reasoning from context features to desired object attributes complicates policy-design and suffers similar difficulties to those described above. We use modularity to address the problem: a full deployment plan is decomposed into sub-plans, each of which determines a set of closely-related object annotations, and a policy associates a context feature to one or more sub-plans only. A full deployment plan can be decided as the context management system applies the policies applicable to an incoming context.

In this paper, we describe a software system to support context-aware Web applications. Our system follows the bottom-up approach and enables a Web application to adapt its component distribution to different execution contexts. The rest of this paper is structured as follows: Section 2 provides a comprehensive background of the problem and an overview of our strategies. Section 3 introduces a component framework supporting customizable Web applications through annotating composing objects. In section 4 we present a structural and parameterized representation of related annotations akin to potential context features. Section 5 describes a context management system which follows user-defined policies to generate context-specific deployment plans from applicable object annotations – and thus makes Web applications context-aware. We conclude the paper with a discussion in the final section.

2   Overview

Web applications are inherently distributed: they require cooperation between a server and a client in order to accomplish their tasks. We argue that component distribution, and particularly execution location and loading policy, has a strong impact on the performance of Web applications in different contexts. Therefore, we propose enabling a Web application to adapt its distribution to the execution context. We first motivate the problem, discuss related work, and outline design strategies.

2.1   The Need for Context-Aware Web Applications

The goal of Web applications is to be accessible regardless of the platform a client is executing on. However, limitations in the capability of a client restricts what object distributions it can support: for example, a thin client cannot perform complex computing tasks and has limited control over application loading. The limitations posed by a thin client simplify the problem of object distribution: there are no choices to be made in determining the component distribution. However, as more and more clients support *AJAX* [8] Web applications–which require a full-fledged computing platform in the client–component distribution becomes an important factor in ensuring certain levels of QoS. The examples below illustrate how an execution context may favor certain distribution plans.

Location: For computing components which require no input from the server and consume few CPU cycles, such as a unit converter or a mortgage calculator, it is preferable to deploy them in the client both for a faster response time and to create less workload in the server. In other cases, the best location is not always clear: a CPU-intensive component which takes input from a backend data source is usually better allocated in the server because JavaScript is not an efficient way to do the computation and bringing data across the Internet is a significant overhead; however, in cases where the server CPU is extremely busy but the server is less stressed in I/O and bandwidth, it is better to shift the component to the client. A case of this sort that we have seen in practice is a component which extracted excerpts of documents based on a user's query. The computation consumes many more CPU cycles than searching and fetching the documents, although it still finishes in milliseconds when the server is lightly loaded. When the server is busy doing multiple tasks (e.g., processing other requests or indexing documents), it can take dozens of seconds to return the excerpts; in such a context, it is more efficient to deploy the component in the client.

Timing: Many user interface controls, such as layered menus, list boxes and detailed information panels, have multiple levels of presentation. These components can be *preloaded* as their containers load, or loaded *on demand* when a user's action explicitly requires it. Preloading client components provides better response time but wastes bandwidth: some of these components are never used. We have investigated the effect on a TV listing application; preloading all the detailed information consumed double the bandwidth compared to loading on demand. A smarter solution is to exploit the user's profile: if certain preference can be identified, the application preloads only frequently used components. In this case, the preferable distribution depends on the current network utilization and identifiable usage patterns.

2.2   Problem Analysis and Related Work

It is desirable to make Web applications context-aware. Specifically, these applications require:

- The ability to *adapt* themselves to specific contexts of their deployment.
- The potential to *evolve* under widespread change in both execution environment and patterns of usage.

There are quite a few systems supporting context-aware applications under specific assumptions. Although their design concepts and principles can be applied to Web applications, there are several difficulties in using these systems in the domain of Web applications. We describe the difficulties below.

A key element of context-aware applications is adaptability. The execution environment of Web applications is heterogeneous: clients and servers usually employ incompatible technologies and assume different roles, which complicates the process of adaptation. Several research projects [15, 2, 19, 14, 9, 17, 16] have been able to support location-transparent application development in distributed platforms; some of them are targeted to Web applications. One limitation in these systems is that the adaptability is restricted to component execution location: component distribution timing, which is crucial in many Web applications, is missing.

Another common limitation is in the mechanism to express and enforce deployment plans. Some systems [15, 2, 19] require *metaprograms* [11] (separate programs which manipulate programs) to control the distribution at runtime. This approach is not feasible in Web platforms because of the lack of rich runtime support. In [14, 9] the adaptivity is embedded in the library design: developers have to provide and use different libraries to reconfigure applications. *XML11* [17, 16] supports customization through separate specifications because the components are truly portable in various platforms natively; however, it is not clear yet how to construct specifications systematically.

Conceptually, the deployment plans contain information about component distribution *aspects*–concerns that are orthogonal to the application logic–and thus principles akin to *Aspect-Oriented Programming* (AOP) [1,5] can be applied as in [10, 18]. We observe that the complexity in aspect design has hindered its acceptance in Web applications: to facilitate fast prototyping and frequent modification, most Web applications are written in a less constrained fashion using scripting languages. In addition, the use of aspect programming results in an over specification of the requirements in a deployment plan and complicates the design of the context management system.

Context-aware software and service adaptation have been extensively studied and have gained success in pervasive computing [12] and multimedia QoS [6] adaptation; however, there are several assumptions in the case of adaptive component distribution in Web applications:

- It is acceptable to have a few bad deployments since there are several factors in the Internet which cannot be observed and predicted, such as actual network condition and client's stability. It is more important to ensure overall efficiency instead of optimal allocation in each execution.
- Resource consumption in a single execution is usually not demanding and the service duration is comparatively short. The pressure on the server system comes from numerous concurrent sessions, not individual sessions. This has two implications:
  - Complex decision-making processes such as negotiation may kill any benefit gained through adaptation.
  - The ability to re-adapt (under context change) during a session is not crucial.
- The Web is an *open system* composed of standards and protocols. A solution requiring extra features in all participating platforms is unlikely to win wide acceptance.

2.3 Design Strategies

From the analysis above, we identify two requirements of context-aware Web applications: *adaptability* and *extensibility*. We follow the principle of *separation of concerns* [4] in design to ensure adaptability, and adopt the paradigm of *generative programming* in implementation to guarantee extensibility. In the bottom layer, component distribution is separated from application logic and thus can be reconfigured according to separate specifications. A generative framework allows new distribution features to be added in the future. In the middle layer, features related to higher-level concepts are abstracted from component distribution rules and new features can be exploited using new transformation processes. In the top layer, context features are rendered into context variables which are used in defining deployment policies. New context features can be imported through new context variables with modules to collect them.

3 Customizable Web Applications

We have designed and implemented a component framework (Figure 1) to support reconfigurable component distribution. The basic idea is to separate component design and distribution features. In our framework, a *prototype* represents a design concept of component; the implementation of a component is synthesized by a generator with the distribution features that have been specified separately. The implementation details and algorithms used for synthesis can be found in [3]. In this section, we describe the extensible specification system which enables customizable Web application through distribution reconfiguration.

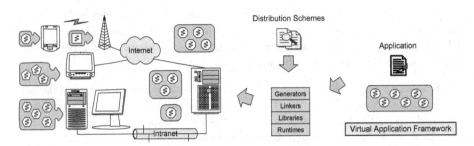

Fig. 1. Distribution transparent component framework

3.1 Component Annotation

Many non-functional concerns, including those we are particularly interested in, can be specified by annotating components. For example, in order to specify the execution location, an attribute **Location** can be defined. However, it is not generally possible to annotate a specific component without knowing its unique identification. Instead of annotating specific individual components, we apply a rule to the set of all components that are created by a prototype. This turns out to be reasonable in the applications that we have looked at. The syntax for specifying that all components created with prototype X have the same *value* of **attribute A** is given below, together with an example of its use:

```
[prototype X]:[attribute A] = value;
```

```
DateValidator:Location = Client;
```

Rules of this form are suitable for large or unique components, but not for small ones which are used for different purposes. For example, `Button` is a common component; however, we expect that buttons have different attribute values in different circumstances.

3.2 Selection by Genealogy

An obvious candidate to further distinguish a component is its creator. We can select a set of components not only by their prototypes, but also by their creators' prototypes. This motivates the second rule for our specification scheme. The syntax to specify that all Y's created by an X share the same *value* of **attribute A** and examples of its use are shown below:

```
[prototype X]>[prototype Y]:[attribute A] = value;
```

```
OrderForm>Button:Location = Client;
InventoryForm>Button:Location = Server;
```

A generalization of the creator relation is to specify a component by its *genealogy*–extending creatorship to more generations. Note that the genealogy can be determined at creation time and remains invariant for a component. For example, the following rule says the attribute value of a component of prototype X_i is decided by examining its genealogy for up to i generations.

```
[X₀]>...>[Xᵢ]: [attribute A] = value;
```

Obviously, examining the rules for more than one generation can lead to conflicting rules for the same attributes. We use the principle that a more specific rule overrides a less specific one. Because the genealogical ordering is linear, this serves to resolve conflicts.

3.3 Discussion

Annotating a set of components of a prototype with specific attributes is useful if the components use a specialized implementation of that prototype which produces components obeying the given specification. Note in our model, a prototype is a "concept of design" instead of an "implementation of design." From another prospective, a specification rule annotates a prototype implementation. Currently we define an attribute controlling the loading policy of prototype **PrototypeLoad** with two possible values *PreLoad* and *OnDemand*:

```
SubMenu:PrototypeLoad = OnDemand;
PricePanel>GridControl:PrototypeLoad = PreLoad;
CalcPanel>GridControl:PrototypeLoad = OnDemand;
```

The current implementation supports the following attributes: **Load** to control the component's loading policy, **PrototypeLoad** to the prototype's loading policy and **Location** to the component's execution location. Although only three attributes are supported, interesting attributes can be defined using supporting generators. For example, to support component mobility at runtime, we can add an attribute value `mobile` to **Location** and implement a generator synthesizing mobile components.

4 Structured Deployment Plans

It turns out that using the specification rules described directly is verbose and error-prone for human developers. Two attribute annotations may be combined in a rule if the target genealogy is the same, but two genealogies must be written in two rules even when they differ in only one generation. In addition, not all attributes are available for a prototype and some attribute values are in conflict with others. For example, the attribute **PrototypeLoad** is only applicable to a client implementation: a component cannot have this attribute with *Server* in **Location**. It is also difficult to manage and reuse individual specification rules. In a specification scheme containing a large number of complex rules, there is a greater chance that it has common building blocks that are reusable.

```
<OrderForm Location="Client">
    <ListControl Location="Client">
        <ListItem Location="Client" PrototypeLoad="OnDemand"/>
    </ListControl>
    <TaxCalculator Location="Client"/>
    <AddressValidator Location="Server"/>
</OrderForm>


OrderForm : Location =  Client;
OrderForm > ListControl : Location = Client;
OrderForm > ListControl > ListItem : Location = Client;
OrderForm > ListControl > ListItem : PrototypeLoad = OnDemand;
OrderForm > TaxCalculator : Location = Client;
OrderForm > AddressValidator : Location = Server;
```

Fig. 2. Using XML to represent specification rules

4.1 Moving to XML

We use XML to organize specification rules: an XML element represents a prototype and multiple rules can be expressed in a tree structure. For example, the XML fragment and rules in Figure 2 are equivalent:

Using XML helps the developer to structure specification rules. Although it is legal to have a rule of a genealogy starting with a sub-component such as SubMenuItem, this makes little sense in practice. Instead, a set of specifications usually starts from a major component, such as OrderForm in our example. Another advantage of using XML is the existence of XML schema validation tools which can check validity and consistency of our specification rules. Note that adopting XML does not sacrifice expressiveness: any specification rule can be expressed in one XML fragment where every node has at most one child.

4.2 Parameterized Specification Blocks

Consider a specification scheme in the first part of Figure 3. The specifications on OrderForm and ProfileForm have a common building block highlighted in the grey areas. The observation immediately leads us to a shorthand representation in the second part of Figure 3. The specification scheme defines an XML Block element containing the common block with an attribute *name*, which can be used to refer the whole block in other specifications. The idea behind this is to make use of XML's tree structure: a node can readily refer to a set of subtrees with a modular representation.

However, using an element to represent a fixed set of subtrees is not as useful as it seems to be. If there is no other rule in Figure 3, it is not necessary to define a Block for ListControl and AddressValidator because OrderForm

```
<OrderForm Location="Client">
    <ListControl Location="Client">
        <ListItem Location="Client" PrototypeLoad="OnDemand"/>
    </ListControl>
    <TaxCalculator Location="Client"/>
    <AddressValidator Location="Server"/>
</OrderForm>

<ProfileForm Location="Client">
    <ListControl Location="Client">
        <ListItem Location="Client" PrototypeLoad="OnDemand"/>
    </ListControl>
    <PhoneValidator Location="Client"/>
    <AddressValidator Location="Server"/>
</ProfileForm>
```

```
<Block name="block1">
    <ListControl Location="Client">
        <ListItem Location="Client" PrototypeLoad="OnDemand"/>
    </ListControl>
    <AddressValidator Location="Server"/>
</Block>

<OrderForm Location="Client">
    <TaxCalculator Location="Client"/>
    <block1/>
</OrderForm>

<ProfileForm Location="Client">
    <PhoneValidator Location="Client"/>
    <block1/>
</ProfileForm>
```

Fig. 3. A common block can be defined by a `Block` element

and `ProfileForm` have the same specification on these prototypes; top-level specifications on `ListControl` and `AddressValidator` are sufficient: `OrderForm` and `ProfileForm` will follow. A reusable block must be parameterized: it does not represent a set of rules (with fixed attribute values), but a group of *selectors*; the actual attribute values of these selectors, *configuration of the block*, can be controlled through a parameter.

We introduce another tag `Configuration` for configurations in a `Block`. Each `Configuration` element in a `Block` has the *name* attribute and contains an XML fragment representing the configuration. To reuse a block, we can set the

```
<Block name="block1">
      <AddressValidator Location="Server"/>
      <Configuration name="conf1">
            <ListControl Location="Client">
                  <ListItem Location="Client" PrototypeLoad="OnDemand"/>
            </ListControl>
      </Configuration>
      <Configuration name="conf2">
            <ListControl Location="Client">
                  <ListItem Location="Client" PrototypeLoad="PreLoad"/>
            </ListControl>
      </Configuration>
</Block1>

<OrderForm Location="Client">
      <TaxCalculator Location="Client"/>
      <block1 configuration="conf1"/>
</OrderForm>

<ProfileForm Location="Client">
      <PhoneValidator Location="Client"/>
      <block1 configuration="conf1"/>
</ProfileForm>

<FriendsList Location="Client">
      <EmailValidator Location="Client"/>
      <block1 configuration="conf2"/>
</FriendsList>
```

Fig. 4. A block can define multiple configurations

configuration attribute to choose the desired configuration in the block. Figure 5
shows the expanded specification from Figure 4. Blocks and configurations can be
constructed recursively: a `Configuration` element can contain other blocks. In
addition, a `Block` element can contain elements other than `Configuration`: these
elements will be included in the block replacement no matter which configuration
is selected. (See `AddressValidator` specification in `block1`.)

4.3   Partial Plans

XML is sufficiently expressive to represent an application's composition structure; XML can also organize cross-cutting concerns: logically unrelated components sharing common properties can be aggregated into a specification block.
For example, a developer can identify those objects whose deployment have great
impact on a certain resource (hence share a common property), such as CPU
cycles and bandwidth, and define a specification block accordingly. The block
then serves as a *partial plan* on condition of the specific resource. The context
management system can reuse partial plans to create a deployment plan for
a new identified context preference. This approach also provides extensibility:
as new resources are taken into consideration, new specification blocks and new
configurations can be designed independently without drastic changes in existing
ones.

```
<OrderForm Location="Client">
     <TaxCalculator Location="Client"/>
     <AddressValidator Location="Server"/>
     <ListControl Location="Client">
          <ListItem Location="Client" PrototypeLoad="OnDemand"/>
     </ListControl>
</OrderForm>

<ProfileForm Location="Client">
     <PhoneValidator Location="Client"/>
     <AddressValidator Location="Server"/>
     <ListControl Location="Client">
          <ListItem Location="Client" PrototypeLoad="OnDemand"/>
     </ListControl>
</ProfileForm>

<FriendsList Location="Client">
     <EmailValidator Location="Client"/>
     <AddressValidator Location="Server"/>
     <ListControl Location="Client">
          <ListItem Location="Client" PrototypeLoad="PreLoad"/>
     </ListControl>
</FriendsList>
```

Fig. 5. The expanded specification of Figure 4

5   Context Management

We have designed and implemented an extensible context management system (Figure 6). The system includes three modules: *context monitors* active collect context information and store context features in *context variables*, which are used by *Adaptation Policies* to generate full deployment plans.

5.1   Context Features

The concept of context is abstract and the available features of a context are evolving. For example in the past service providers had little access to information about the client's *geolocation*, which is widely exploited nowadays for better service and resource allocation. Nonetheless, a context feature can be utilized only if it is quantitative and measurable. In our context management system, a context feature is represented by a *context variable*, and the introduction of a new context variable must come with a variable monitor maintaining the value.

Monitors can be implemented in a variety of forms as long as they update their variables in a timely manner. For example, the system status monitor for System.CPU and System.Bandwidth is implemented with OS system calls; the monitor for client capabilities is implemented with JavaScript detection code; and the user preference monitor reports related variable values by consulting the user profile database.

5.2   Policy Design

Defining an adaptation policy is straightforward: a policy is pair of a condition on context variables and a set of partial plans. When the context management

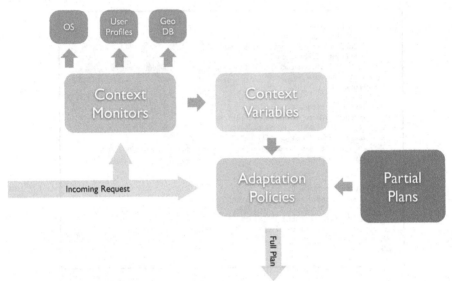

Fig. 6. The context management system

system receives an incoming context, it collects the partial plans in the policies whose conditions are evaluated true and generates the full deployment plan.

Consider the first example in Section 2: we want to deploy the *Highlighter* to the client only under a special context where the CPU cycles are much more precious than the bandwidth, the policy can be written as follows:

```
(System.CPU*[Cost_cpu] > System.Bandwidth*[Cost_bandwidth])
=> <Highlighter Location="Client"/>
```

A cost function can be a constant for the normalization factor or a function of other context variables. In the second example, first we define a specification block **TVListing** with a configuration *FastResponse* which specifies all client components as *PreLoad*. The following policy selects the partial plan for fast response when the client's connection has long latency and the available bandwidth is not in stress.

```
(Client.Latency*[Cost_latency] > System.Bandwidth*[Cost_bandwidth])
=> <TVListing configuration="FastResponse"/>
```

6   Conclusion

We described a new approach for building context-aware Web applications. Using our system, a Web application can adapt to specific contexts through reconfigurable component distribution. Patterns of distribution are extensible: as interesting patterns are identified as useful, developers can define attributes and add new generators that are able to synthesize components with the desired behavior, or just design new specification blocks that realize the patterns. Such extensibility ensures existing Web applications can evolve in the face of widespread change in the Web environment and their users' interaction. The system itself is adaptive: new context features can be integrated by adding the corresponding context variables and monitors, followed by adaptation policies conditioned by these variables.

As future work, we are exploring solutions to automatic policy design and optimization. Currently, good adaptation depends on human design in specification blocks (partial plans) and adaptation policies. As mentioned earlier, a typical Web application is executed numerous times a day and a few bad deployments do not incur much loss. There are great opportunities in mining the performance history and exploring test cases for better policies. We expect future Web applications will adapt themselves automatically by learning their past usage patterns.

References

1. Aspect-Oriented Software Association. http://www.aosd.net/
2. Caromel, D., Henrio, L.: A Theory of Distributed Objects: Asynchrony-Mobility-Groups-Components. Springer, Heidelberg (2005)
3. Chang, P.-H., Agha, G.: Supporting reconfigurable object distribution for customizable web applications. In: SAC '07: Proceedings of the 2007 ACM symposium on Applied computing, pp. 1286–1292 (2007)
4. Dijkstra, E.W.: A Principle of Programming. Prentice-Hall, Englewood Cliffs (1997)
5. Elrad, T., Filman, R.E., Bader, A.: Aspect-oriented programming. Communications of ACM, vol. 44(10) (2001)
6. Fitzpatrick, T., Blair, G., Coulson, G., Davies, N., Robin, P.: Supporting adaptive multimedia applications through open bindings. In: CDS '98. Proceedings of the International Conference on Configurable Distributed Systems, p. 128. IEEE Computer Society, Washington, DC (1998)
7. Gardner, J.R., Rendon, Z.L.: XSLT and XPATH: A Guide to XML Transformations. Prentice-Hall, Englewood Cliffs (2002)
8. Garrett, J.J.: Ajax: A New Approach to Web Applications (February 2005)
9. Google Inc. Google Web Toolkit - Build AJAX Apps in the Java language. http://code.google.com/webtoolkit/
10. Kersten, M., Murphy, G.C.: Atlas: a case study in building a Web-based learning environment using aspect-oriented programming. ACM SIGPLAN Notices 34(10), 340–352 (1999)
11. Kiczales, G., Rivieres, J.D., Bobrow, D.G.: The Art of the Metaobject Protocol. MIT Press, Cambridge, MA (1991)
12. Lum, W.Y., Lau, F.C.M.: A context-aware decision engine for content adaptation. IEEE Pervasive Computing 1(3), 41–49 (2002)
13. Meyer, E.: Cascading Style Sheets: The Definitive Guide. O'Reilly (2000)
14. NextApp, Inc. Echo2. http://www.nextapp.com/platform/echo2/echo/
15. Philippsen, M., Zenger, M.: JavaParty – Transparent Remote Objects in Java. Concurrency: Practice and Experience 9(11), 1225–1242 (1997)

16. Puder, A.: A code migration framework for ajax applications. In: Eliassen, F., Montresor, A. (eds.) DAIS 2006. LNCS, vol. 4025, pp. 138–151. Springer, Heidelberg (2006)
17. Puder, A.: XML11 - an abstract windowing protocol. Sci. Comput. Program 59 (1-2), 97–108 (2006)
18. Tilevich, E., Urbanski, S., Smaragdakis, Y., Fleury, M.: Aspectizing server-side distribution. In: Proceedings of the Automated Software Engineering (ASE) Conference, IEEE Press, New York (2003)
19. Varela, C.A.: Worldwide Computing with Universal Actors: Linguistic Abstractions for Naming, Migration, and Coordination. PhD thesis, University of Illinois at Urbana-Champaign (2001)

A Flexible Architecture for Enforcing and Composing Policies in a Service-Oriented Environment

Tom Goovaerts, Bart De Win, and Wouter Joosen

DistriNet Research Group, Katholieke Universiteit Leuven
Celestijnenlaan 200A, 3001 Leuven, Belgium
{tom.goovaerts,bart.dewin,wouter.joosen}@cs.kuleuven.be

Abstract. Service Oriented Architectures (SOA's) enable powerful application and end user service composition from independently defined services. The effective deployment of such composed services requires adaptation of and interoperability between services. This challenge can be approached by specifying service composition in policies, and by enforcing these policies in a sophisticated run-time architecture.

In this paper, we present an open architecture for enforcing and composing complex policies that can depend on the available services in the environment. Complex polices have typically been studied in the context of policy languages, yet they have never been fully supported in a SOA-based execution environment. We have created a flexible run-time architecture that maximizes interoperability, adaptability and evolution. We have prototyped our architecture on an Enterprise Service Bus and we illustrate how our solution supports realistic and complex policies.

1 Introduction

Services are the fundamental building blocks of software systems when applying the Service-Oriented Computing (SOC) paradigm [17]. Services expose a well-defined behavior in independent units of business logic and are used and deployed in complex compositions to create distributed business applications. The applications that emerge in service oriented architectures can become large and fairly complex, and can be interconnected with services from various organizations and stakeholders. In this context, describing and enforcing acceptable (correct, permitted, manageable, affordable, etc.) compositions have become key challenges.

Policy languages and subsystems that ensure the enforcement of policies have become an increasingly important sub domain in distributed systems and middleware as they deal with the above mentioned challenges. Systems need to be able to comply with an ever growing set of business rules and regulations that are subject to continuous change. Policies are rules that specify choices in the behavior of a system [4]. By specifying these rules separately from the applications, the behavior can be changed dynamically by modifying the policy rules

J. Indulska and K. Raymond (Eds.): DAIS 2007, LNCS 4531, pp. 253–266, 2007.

without affecting any application code. Policy-based systems most often adhere to the XACML dataflow model [16], which consists of policy decision points (PDPs), policy enforcement points (PEPs) and optionally policy information points (PIPs). A PDP focuses on how policy rules are evaluated given a certain state of the system. A PEP handles the provisioning of system state information to the PDP and the execution of the correct semantics of the policy decisions that are returned by the PDP. The PIP provides additional context information to support the decision making process of the PDPs. The most familiar types of policies are probably in the area of authorization. Other examples of policies include user preference policies that govern user-configurable behavior of a system, privacy policies that contain privacy rules and SLA/SLO policies that deal with elements of quality of service.

In most cases, policies are defined and enforced at the level of individual resources such as objects or components. However, a SOA introduces an abstraction layer of services that are indirectly related to the underlying resources. Therefore, new types of policies arise that make use of services. Moreover, the underlying resources that are being interconnected may be implemented on different heterogeneous systems that are unaware of each other. For these reasons, the emerging policies cannot exclusively be enforced at the level of the underlying systems, or at the level of underlying resources.

In other words, the kinds of policies that can be supported by straightforward adoption of existing policy technology are often restricted in several ways. First: it is hard to enforce application-level policies that require information that is contained in multiple distinct services. Secondly, policy enforcement mechanisms are often tightly coupled with both the specific middleware platform and/or with specific policy-related technologies. Due to the openness and very frequent evolution of a service oriented environment, it needs to be able to interface with a range of policy languages, policy servers, message formats and functional services.

This paper addresses the gap between existing message oriented service platforms and known policy systems by offering policy enforcement as a service. A message oriented service platform is a specific type of message oriented middleware that is based on message interception capabilities. Such architecture therefore is agnostic on specific message formats and policy languages. Our architecture maximizes the reuse of policy decision logic and of enforcement logic. Due to its flexibility, the architecture can be used to implement fine-tuned policy enforcement points in multiple operational contexts.

The main contribution of this paper is an open architecture for enforcing and composing complex policies that can depend on the available services in a SOA. To the best of our knowledge, complex polices have typically been studied and supported in the context of policy languages, yet they have never been fully supported in a SOA-based execution environment. We have created a flexible run-time architecture that maximizes interoperability, adaptability and evolution. We have prototyped our architecture on an Enterprise Service Bus (ESB). The prototype demonstrates policy enforcement for SOAP messages in a telecom-centric ESB. We show how our solution improves interoperability and flexible adaptation in a service oriented environment.

The rest of the paper is structured as follows. Section 2 elaborates on the problem domain by presenting some representative policies. Section 3 then summarizes the requirements for a policy enforcement architecture that can manage complex polices. Section 4 presents our solution: the architecture, an illustration of policy enforcement in the architecture and the prototype implementation. We evaluate our solution in Section 5 and compare with related work in Section 6. Then we conclude.

2   Motivating Example

We illustrate the kinds of high level policies that need to be enforced by means of a concrete policy set. Suppose we have a set of three services: an Address Book service that keeps track of a contact list, a Call service that can be used to setup phone calls and a Location service that can be used to lookup the current location of a given user. Consider the following policy set:

1. Everyone can view all address book records, but one can only modify the contact information of its own record.
2. Address book records can only be modified when the user is at its desk. When a user tries to modify its address book record when he/she is at home, deny this and audit the attempt.
3. Only allow calls to someone's work phone during office hours. If someone calls a user on its work phone during office hours, but the user is not located in the office, reroute the call to the user's mobile phone.

The first rule illustrates the fact that policies can be based on the contents of a message. In this case, the message will contain an argument that determines the target record that will be modified. The second rule illustrates the fact that the enforcement of rules that concern one service (in this case the Address Book service) may need information contained in other services (the Location service). Moreover, the second rule illustrates that policies might specify complex results that can contain obligations. Obligations are tasks that need to be fulfilled by the system upon enforcement of a policy decision. The third rule shows that a high level policy rule might actually consist of different kinds of policies that need to be combined. The first part of the policy rule specifies an authorization while the second part is a typical business rule. Therefore, this policy rule will normally be split up (or at least, it may be implemented) in different languages and with different decision mechanisms.

These services are loosely coupled to each other: they could be implemented by a different underlying platform or could even belong to an external party. The implementations of the services are fully unaware that they are being integrated with specific other services. For these reasons, the enforcement of such policies needs to be performed at the level of the platform that hosts the services.

3   Requirements

This section describes the most important characteristics that drive the architectural design of our policy enforcement solution. We assume that policies are contained in *policy services* that support the making of policy decisions and thus function as PDPs.

Advanced policy support. Advanced service-level policies such as the example policies from Section 2 should be supported. What is characteristic for these policies, is that their enforcement might need the invocation of other services. This consists of:

- *Information provisioning* ensures that policy services have access to all the information they need in order to make a policy decision. This information can be contained in the message itself or it can be contained in functional services.
- *Decision execution* is the execution of the decision(s) that are returned by a policy service. In contrast to an authorization decision that declares a binary allow/deny result, the execution of a general policy decision can be a complex operation. Policy decisions can also contain obligations that need to be executed by the system in addition to the decision itself.

Interoperability with policy services and message formats. A SOA interconnects a set of heterogeneous systems that may use different messages and formats. Moreover, it is important that different policy languages and engines can be supported. Therefore, a policy enforcement solution needs to be interoperable with multiple message formats and with multiple policy services.

Flexibility. Because the operational environment is subject to frequent evolution, it is necessary that a policy enforcement solution is able to be adapted to these changes. More specifically:

- *Changing and combining policy services* It should be possible to easily change policy services that are specific to one language. Moreover, it is possible that policy enforcement for one message requires the combination of decisions from multiple policy services. Therefore, an enforcement solution should allow policy services to be changed and combined with each other.
- *Flexible binding with the operational environment* The policy services and their policies should be made independent of all environment-specific aspects. Therefore, it must be possible to change the binding of the policies with the environment. This binding consists both of information sources containing policy-relevant data and of the execution logic of the policy decisions and their obligations.

Performance. Since policy enforcement needs to operate on messages, it may become an unacceptable performance bottleneck. Therefore, the runtime enforcement overhead should be minimized.

The first and last requirements ensure that policy enforcement is possible and feasible in practice. The second and third requirements make sure that the architecture can deal with changes in the environment. These requirements are used as the basis for the architectural design that is discussed in Section 4.

4   Architecture

In this section, the policy enforcement architecture is presented. Since the service is the basic building block in the environment, we have chosen to offer the policy enforcement functionality itself as a service, which we call the 'policy enforcement service' or simply the 'enforcement service'. In Section 4.1, we elaborate on the architectural design that was driven by the requirements from Section 3. In Section 4.2, the architecture is applied to the example policies from Section 2 and in Section 4.3 we discuss our prototype.

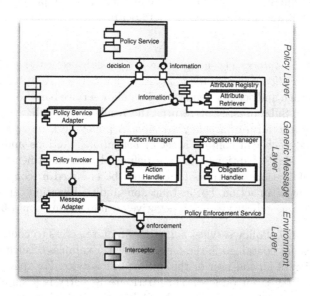

Fig. 1. Overview of the architecture

4.1   Architectural Design

Figure 1 depicts the main structure and the components of the architecture. The architecture is structured in three layers. From top to bottom, the *Policy Layer* focuses on managing and reasoning about policy rules. The *Generic Message Layer*, which is the most important layer of the architecture, is responsible for connecting execution contexts with high-level policy services (by means of a generic message format), for coordinating the invocation of policy services and for executing policy decisions. Finally, the *Environment Layer* represents the operational environment. Since each layer operates with different representations, adapter components are introduced to bridge between the different layers.

From a high-level perspective, the architecture operates as follows. All messages in the environment that require policy enforcement are forwarded to the policy enforcement service by means of an *Interceptor* component. *Policy services* contain the effective policies and return policy decisions over a native protocol. For each relevant policy service, the enforcement service creates a policy request based on the contents of the message, sends it to the policy service and obtains a policy decision. Subsequently, the policy decision is enforced and the next policy service is consulted and so on. The final output of the enforcement service will always be another message, which is usually a transformation of the incoming message.

In terms of the XACML model, the combination of the Interceptor and the Policy Enforcement Service function as PEP, the Policy Enforcement Service functions also as PIP and the policy services function as PDPs. The core components of the architecture, contained in the architectural component as indicated on Figure 1, will now be discussed in more detail.

Policy Layer

Policy Service Adapters. The integration of (possibly external) policy services is enabled by *Policy Service Adapters*. A Policy Service Adapter inspects an incoming message and sends a request to its policy service based on the contents of the message. Subsequently, it returns the result of the policy service to the architecture in the form of a *policy decision*. A policy decision consists of a set of *actions* that each can contain a set of *obligations*. Actions and obligations are abstract task descriptions that are defined by an identifier and a set of arguments. Obligations are tasks that should be enforced in conjunction with the enforcement of an action. For instance, an 'audit' obligation can be attached to a 'deny' action, indicating that a negative authorization should be audited.

Attribute Registry. Policy services sometimes require access to contextual information that is not contained in the message itself. Examples of such information are the location of an end-user or the uptime of a service. For this purpose, the Attribute Registry is introduced. The Attribute Registry is a simple attribute repository that can be queried by the Policy Service Adapters or by Policy Services themselves. It actually binds the abstract information that is used in the policies with the concrete environment. The retrieval logic for a particular attribute is contained in Attribute Retrievers and can be plugged in upon integration with a particular environment.

Generic Message Layer

Generic Message Model. The policy enforcement service needs to bridge a variety of message formats on the one hand, and different types of requests for policy services on the other hand. In order to deal with this N-to-M mapping, a common message representation, the *generic message format*, is introduced. A generic message consists of the subject responsible for sending the message, the action that is being targeted by the message and the target service for the message. For instance, if user 'X' requests an address on an Address Book service, the generic message will consist of subject X, action 'getAddress' and target 'Address Book'. Each of these elements is represented by an identifier and a set of key-value pairs called attributes. The architecture assumes that all messages in the environment at least contain identifiers for these three concepts.[1] The generic message also contains a reference to the original message. Within the architecture, each generic message is wrapped in a *Message Context*, which is used, among others, to maintain state over the invocation of multiple policy services.

Policy Invoker. The Policy Invoker expects an incoming generic message and is responsible for coordinating the invocation of the different policy services. The Policy Invoker holds a sequential chain of Policy Service Adapters to determine the order in which the policy services are consulted and their decisions are enforced. After a Policy Service Adapter returns a decision, the Policy Invoker passes it to the Action Manager. When the actions are enforced, the next Policy Service Adapter gets to process the message and the process is repeated.

If multiple policy services are chained, one policy service might need to use information that has been generated by a decision of a previous policy service. While the architecture does not provide support for the semantics of such metadata, it does allow a Policy Service Adapter to influence the decisions of its successors in the following ways:

1. By modifying the original message. This can result in new or modified attributes of the subject, action or target service of the message.
2. By adding attributes to the generic message. These modifications only live as long as the enforcement service handles the message.
3. Through the Message Context. The Message Context consists of a set of key-value pairs that can contain arbitrary metadata that is not related to the subject, action or target service.

Action Manager & Obligation Manager. Actions and obligations in a policy decision specify *what* functionality needs to be enforced. The architecture needs to know *how* to enforce these actions and obligations in a concrete environment. This is the responsibility of the *Action Manager*. Action execution logic is delegated to *Action Handlers*: the Action Manager associates action identifiers to the Action Handlers that are responsible for executing them. Modification of the original message (e.g., for an 'encrypt' action) is supported through the generic message's reference to the original message. Obligations are handled similarly: an *Obligation Manager* consisting of a set of *Obligation Handlers* executes the obligations contained in each action.

---

[1] While this consideration makes sense at a conceptual level, it is possible that these elements are not explicitly represented in the actual messages. In these cases, adaptations to services or middleware infrastructure should take care of attaching the appropriate metadata to the messages.

Environment Layer

Message Adapters. Messages from the environment layer in a specific format are converted into generic messages by *Message Adapters*. It is possible that the original message is changed by a policy decision. If this happens, the Message Adapter needs to synchronize the generic message with the original message in order to represent the potentially altered subject, action and target attributes.

4.2   Enforcement of Example Policies

We illustrate the architecture by describing the enforcement of the three example policies from Section 2. Figure 2 illustrates the execution flows in the architecture. Since the example policies contain authorization rules as well as business rules, we assume that there are two different policy services. The authorization service returns 'allow'/'deny' decisions (potentially including an 'audit' obligation) and the business rule service returns a 'redirect' decision. Therefore, the Action Manager is configured with 'allow', 'deny' and 'redirect' Action Handlers and the Obligation Manager is configured with an Audit Obligation Handler. Furthermore, the Attribute Registry is configured with two Attribute Retrievers: one that fetches the current time and one that contacts the Location Service for getting the location of a user with a given identifier.

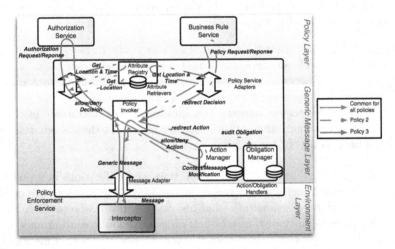

Fig. 2. Execution flow throughout the architecture applied to the example policies

The solid gray arrows show the minimal flow that is followed for enforcing all three policies. First of all, the incoming message from the bus is translated into a generic message by the message adapter. In our case, the target of the generic message can be either the Address Book service or the Call service.[2] Then,

---

[2] The Location service is only used within the policies for gathering the location attribute for the subject.

the generic message is forwarded to the Policy Invoker that contains a chain of two Policy Service Adapters. The generic message is wrapped in a Message Context and is sent to the Authorization Service Adapter. For the first rule, no additional attributes have to be gathered from the Attribute Registry, but both the second and the third rule do require the Attribute Registry. In the example, the adapter fetches these attributes proactively. After the adapter has created and sent a policy request from the generic message, the policy service returns a decision. In this case, the decision will contain either an 'allow' or 'deny' action without parameters and optionally an 'audit' obligation with the audit message as parameter. The decision is returned to the Invoker, which forwards it to the Action Manager. The Action Handlers execute the decision, potentially modifying the Message Context or the message itself. If an obligation is included, the Action Manager invokes the Obligation Manager.

For the third rule, an additional Adapter is required. The invocation of the Policy Service is similar to the previous case, except that the decision can be a 'redirect' action with the new telephone number as argument. Again, the invoker sends this action to the Action Manager which executes it and has the potential to modify the target telephone number in the original message.

4.3   Prototype

We have implemented a prototype of the architecture and we have validated it on an ESB-based telecom service platform in the context of the T-CASE project [9]. An Enterprise Service Bus (ESB) is a message oriented middleware for the integration of enterprise applications that in itself is architected in a service-oriented way. The ESB is used to mediate SOAP messages between a set of simple Web Services, such as an Address Book service, a Jabber service and a Calendar service. The interception logic is implemented by a message routing service that is called the Content-Based Router. The policy enforcement service itself is integrated by means of a SOAP interface.

It is expected that the SOAP messages on the ESB at least contain the following information:

- The authenticated identity of the user represented by a SAML [14] authentication assertion in a WS-Security [15] header.
- The action and the target service are represented in a WS-Addressing [23] header as <Action> and <To> elements respectively.

Since the ESB only mediates SOAP messages, a single SOAP Message Adapter has been implemented. For efficiency reasons, the body of the SOAP message is not processed, but the full SOAP message does get attached to the generic message so that it can be used later on.

Two Policy Service Adapters have been implemented. The first one verifies the SAML assertion that is included with the message. A separate authentication server is used to authenticate users in advance and generate these assertions. The second adapter wraps a rule-based policy service and returns authorization decisions that contain either 'permit' or 'deny' actions. The 'deny' action is enforced by a SOAP-specific Action Handler that replaces the original message by a SOAP Fault message that is directed to the original sender.

The implementation of the Attribute Registry consists of a set of Attribute Retrievers that are responsible for looking up attributes for demonstration purposes. Attribute Retrievers can inspect the SOAP message, for instance to lookup information that is contained in the body.

5   Evaluation and Discussion

In this section each of the requirements of the architecture is evaluated and some interesting points of discussion are put forward.

Advanced Policy Support. The information that can flow to the policy services consists of two categories: information that is pushed towards the policy services and the information that is pulled from the environment. The former is realized by the generic message model and the Message Adapters and the latter is realized by the Attribute Registry. Some information such as the parameters of a message can be pushed as well as pulled. The choice for pulling such an attribute from the Attribute Registry is mainly driven by performance reasons, since pushing an attribute introduces an overhead for every single message.

Interoperability with Policy Services and Message Formats. Interoperability is achieved by inserting the adapter components (Message Adapters and Policy Service Adapters) that translate back and forth between the generic format and native formats. In our prototype, we chose to focus on SOAP messages. However, we are confident that, as long as messages contain the right set of metadata, it is feasible to write a Message Adapter for them. Concerning policy service interoperability, we have implemented one adapter for an authentication policy service and one adapter for a business rule-based policy service.

Flexibility

– *Changing and Combining Policy Services* The combination of multiple policy services is supported by sequentially chaining Policy Service Adapters, which may cause conflicts. The architecture has no explicit support for conflict detection or resolution: we assume that conflicts are solved at the policy layer. If two or more Policy Service Adapters have a large semantic overlap, they should be integrated in a single adapter that is capable of resolving conflicts.
– *Flexible Binding with the Operational Environment* The policy enforcement service effectively binds heterogeneous policy services with functional services by presenting a generic policy-centric view of the environment to the policy services. This view consists of an information part, which is realized by the generic message format and the Attribute Registry, and of an enforcement part, which is realized by the Action Manager and Obligation Manager. Flexibility of the mapping between this abstract view and the concrete semantics – *how* to enforce an action, *how* to retrieve an attribute, etc.

– is supported by isolating this logic in replaceable components (Message Adapters, Attribute Retrievers, Action Handlers and Obligation Handlers). Throughout the development of the prototype, this flexibility proved to be very useful: numerous transitions and additions of logic were made to support new kinds of policies.

If the semantics depend on specific functional services (eg. send a warning message to a user's mobile phone or get the bank account number of a user), new instances of these components have to be written and need to be plugged into the enforcement service. The architecture currently has no support for automating this problem and thus dealing with it in a fully generic way.

Performance. The performance of the prototype has been evaluated at two levels. At a macroscopic level, the average response times have been measured for a set of incoming messages. A set of 4 policy rules of increasing complexity has been created that allowed us to trigger the execution of specific and predictable components. The test has been performed in six phases in which the response times for a specific and known message has been measured. The first two policies have also been tested for a 'deny' decision. The results of the macroscopic test are shown in Figure 3(a). The enforcement of a 'deny' result is slightly more efficient since it does not induce duplication of the original message. The biggest performance hit is introduced by Policy2 and Policy4 and is caused by the introduction of additional Attribute Retrievers.

Figure 3(b) gives an insight into the microscopic performance overhead. The left bar shows the percentage of the total time spent in each of the components during the execution of all six test phases. The major performance overhead is introduced by two components that operate on the SOAP messages: the SOAP Message Adapter and the XPath Attribute Retriever. The second bar zooms in on the lower part of the left bar and shows that the internal components of the enforcement service (including the policy service adapters) only account for less than 5% of the total overhead. This means that there is still much room for improvement for optimized implementations of the adapters and Atribute Retrievers.

The current design of the architecture has some limitations as well, which will be discussed next. Note that addressing these limitations involves a trade-off that depends on the deployment environment, as they increase the complexity and, hence, the execution time of the architecture.

The chaining of Policy Service Adapters only supports the combination of policy services in a static way such that chains cannot be changed dynamically at runtime. The latter could be useful however, among others, to support scenarios in which the outcome of one policy service can have an impact on the other services to be consulted. The support for dynamic policy service combination requires the extension of the Policy Invoker component with a meta-policy that specifies the effective sequence of policy services based on runtime information. The Policy Invoker needs to enforce this meta-policy before each invocation of a Policy Service.

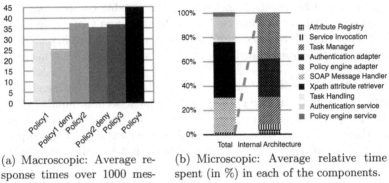

(a) Macroscopic: Average response times over 1000 messages (in ms) for increasingly
complex policies.

(b) Microscopic: Average relative time
spent (in %) in each of the components.

Fig. 3. Performance measurements

Related to this, the composition of policy services is currently purely sequential. Other useful composition strategies exist [11] such as parallel or hierarchical composition. The former could improve the execution speed of the architecture and the latter could be used to support the semantic composition of policy rules. While these strategies are realizable at the level of the enforcement architecture in the Policy Invoker, they are often also supported at the level of individual policy services, in which case they are fully transparent for the enforcement architecture.

6   Related Work

In the field of policy languages, some languages such as Rei [10] and XACML [16] put more focus on the language features itself than on the enforcement aspect. Some notable languages that do consider enforcement in detail are Ponder [4,7] and KAoS [22]. These languages offer excellent support for specifying and combining advanced policies, but they assume that a single policy language governs the whole environment. Our work is capable of integrating multiple languages.

We take a centralized approach to policy enforcement: policies are enforced near the services they govern. Some kinds of policies such as refrain policies [4] require client-side enforcement. If interceptor components can be placed at the client side, these kinds of policies can also be supported. In the context of large scale SOA's such as Web Services or Grid systems, policy enforcement is often decentralized [19,5]: effective properties of an interaction are negotiated at runtime by the semantic matching of client requirements with service offerings. Our architecture can enforce the outcome of these policies at each peer once they are negotiated.

When enforcing security policies for isolated applications, the PDP and PEP are often merged and integrated by instrumenting the application's code [20,1].

While this approach is very efficient, it is difficult to apply it to an open environment where policies and applications evolve rapidly.

Evolution and openness requires the strict separation of PEPs and PDPs. In the access control field, there are two major directions that promote this separation: PDPs can be offered through a uniform API (for example, the Authorization (AZN) API from the Open Group [8] and the Java Authorization Contract for Containers (JACC) [21]) or they can be offered as a distributed service (such as the Resource Access Decision Facility (RAD) [2] and Tivoli Access Manager [12]). Pulling decision logic out of the application increases interoperability and flexibility, at the expense of making it harder to enforce advanced kinds of application-level policies. Our work is a first step towards bridging this gap.

Message interception is a well known technique for separating policy logic from application logic that is generic and flexible (for example, see [3,18]). Other authors have used Aspect-Oriented Programming (AOP) [13] for integrating security and policies with applications [6,24]. AOP is situated at a higher level of abstraction but is less generic, which makes it hard to apply it in a heterogeneous environment.

7 Conclusion

In this paper, we have presented an open architecture for enforcing advanced policies in a service-oriented environment. The architecture can be used to instantiate flexible policy enforcement points; it can handle realistic policies that are required by state-of-the-art Service Oriented Architectures. Our solution supports adaptation and evolution of the platform, the service composition and the specific policies. We have prototyped and validated our architecture on a telecom-centric ESB.

Future work includes further validation of our architecture. More specifically, the interoperability with existing environments and policy languages will be studied in more detail. In addition, the challenge of managing the information flow of policy-relevant data will be studied.

References

1. Bauer, L., Ligatti, J., Walker, D.: Composing Security Policies with Polymer. In: Proceedings of the 2005 ACM SIGPLAN conference on Programming language design and implementation, pp. 305–314 (2005)
2. Beznosov, K., Deng, Y., Blakley, B., Burt, C., Barkley, J.: A Resource Access Decision Service for CORBA-based Distributed Systems. In: Proceedings of the 15th Annual Computer Security Applications Conference, p. 310 (1999)
3. Damiani, E., De Capitani di Vimercati, S., Paraboschi, S., Samarati, P.: Securing SOAP e-services. International Journal of Information Security 1(2), 100–115 (2002)
4. Damianou, N., Dulay, N., Lupu, E., Sloman, M.: The Ponder Policy Specification Language. Lecture Notes in Computer Science 2001, pp. 18–38 (2001)

5. Dan, A., Dumitrescu, C., Ripeanu, M.: Connecting Client Objectives with Resource Capabilities: an Essential Component for Grid Service Managent Infrastructures. In: Proceedings of the 2nd International Conference on Service Oriented Computing, pp. 57–64 (2004)
6. D'Hondt, M., Jonckers, V.: Hybrid Aspects for Weaving Object-Oriented Functionality and Rule-Based Knowledge. In: Proceedings of the 3rd International Conference on Aspect-Oriented Software Development, pp. 132–140 (2004)
7. Dulay, N., Lupu, E., Sloman, M., Damianou, N.: A Policy Deployment Model for the Ponder Language. Integrated Network Management Proceedings, 2001 IEEE/IFIP International Symposium on, pp. 529–543 (2001)
8. The Open Group. Authorization (AZN) API. Open Group Technical Standard C908 (2000)
9. Interdisciplinary Institute for BroadBand Technology. T-CASE Project (Technologies and Capabilities for Service-Enabling) (2005) https://projects.ibbt.be/tcase/
10. Kagal, L.F., Joshi, T.A.: A Policy Language for a Pervasive Computing Environment. Policies for Distributed Systems and Networks, 2003. Proceedings. POLICY 2003. IEEE 4th International Workshop on, pp. 63–74 (2003)
11. Kanada, Y.: Taxonomy and Description of Policy Combination Methods. In: Proceedings of the International Workshop on Policies for Distributed Systems and Networks, pp. 171–184 (2001)
12. Karjoth, G.: Access Control with IBM Tivoli Access Manager. ACM Transactions on Information and System Security 6(2), 232–257 (2003)
13. Kiczales, G.: Aspect-Oriented Programming. ACM Computing Surveys 28, 232–257 (1996)
14. OASIS. Security Assertion Markup Language Specification, Version 1.1 (2003)
15. OASIS. Web Services Security: SOAP Message Security, Version 1.0 (2004)
16. OASIS. eXtensible Access Control Markup Language (XACML) Version 2.0 (2005)
17. Papazoglou, M., Georgakopoulos, D.: Service-Oriented Computing: Introduction. Communications of the ACM, vol. 46(10) (2003)
18. Ritter, T., Schreiner, R., Lang, U.: Integrating Security Policies via Container Portable Interceptors. IEEE Distributed Systems Online, vol. 7 (2006)
19. Schlimmer, J., et al.: Web Services Policy Framework Specification, Draft Version (2004)
20. Schneider, F.B.: Enforceable Security Policies. ACM Transactions on Information and System Security 3(1), 30–50 (2000)
21. Sun Microsystems. Java Authrozation Contract for Containers (JACC) Version 1.0 (2003)
22. Uszok, A., Bradshaw, J., Jeffers, R., Suri, N., Hayes, P., Breedy, M., Bunch, L., Johnson, M., Kulkarni, S., Lott, J.: KAoS Policy and Domain Services: Toward a Description-logic Approach to Policy Representation, Deconfliction, and Enforcement. Policies for Distributed Systems and Networks, 2003. Proceedings. POLICY 2003. IEEE 4th International Workshop on, pp. 93–96 (2003)
23. W3C. Web Services Addressing, W3C Member Submission (2004)
24. De Win, B.: Engineering Application-level Security through Aspect-Oriented Software development. PhD thesis, Katholieke Universiteit Leuven (2004)

Managing Concern Interactions in Middleware

Frans Sanen, Eddy Truyen, and Wouter Joosen

DistriNet, Department of Computer Science, K.U.Leuven,
Celestijnenlaan 200A, 3001 Leuven, Belgium
{Frans.Sanen, Eddy.Truyen, Wouter.Joosen}@cs.kuleuven.be

Abstract. In this paper, we define a conceptual model that describes the relevant information about interactions between concerns that needs to be captured. We have developed a prototype system that, starting from this model, can automatically generate a set of rules that enables software developers to improve their understanding of concerns in middleware and their interactions. This rule-base is the basis for an expert system that can be queried about particular concern interactions and a software engineering tool to support an application development team.

1 Introduction

In this paper, we present a conceptual model that helps a software development team to understand and manage the different interactions between typical concerns in a component-based distributed application. In general, the conceptual model complements methods for building large and complex component-based distributed systems. To demonstrate results, we have focussed on the particular application domain of middleware (see Section 2).

Nowadays, software applications are being increasingly complex and large-scale. This is mainly because of two reasons. First, the number of different implemented concerns has exploded. Concerns are similar to requirements in a broad sense of the word (a more detailed definition of concerns will be given in Section 2). Secondly, and more importantly, there are many (often hidden) interactions between all these different concerns. Concerns are typically not completely orthogonal to each other, but can relate to each other in a variety of different ways: they can either depend upon each other, conflict with each other, exclude each other, etc... This makes it challenging for a development team to understand, sustain, maintain, adapt and evolve contemporary software applications.

There is a wide consensus in the software engineering community that in order to manage large and complex software systems, one must rely on intensive separation of concerns [29] and componentization [1]. Separation of concerns is not easy to achieve however. Software development methods often only achieve a good separation of concerns if sufficient application domain expertise is present within the development team. We therefore believe that application domain expertise should be represented explicitly as part of a conceptual model such that it can be shared and used during the course of system evolution. The conceptual model we propose identifies and describes the different concerns of importance in the middleware domain and provides the foundation for the construction of reusable components.

J. Indulska and K. Raymond (Eds.): DAIS 2007, LNCS 4531, pp. 267–283, 2007.

This paper addresses the following problems. Expertise about interactions between concerns (and therefore components) is seldom made explicit. As a result, this knowledge cannot be shared and used among a development team. In monolithic software, concern interactions are often hidden in the implementation details of components. Yet, we argue that concern interactions and expertise on how to resolve these also forms very important domain knowledge as this leads to a better understanding of the application domain. Despite the fact that modeling techniques exist that explicitly represent concern interactions (e.g. [9,11]), few of these modeling techniques make the link between concerns and implementation components, i.e., they provide no practical support to the software developer for managing the interactions when he/she is in the course of creating, adapting or evolving the component composition of an application. This problem statement will be elaborated upon in Section 2 using some scenarios.

Our contributions are threefold. Next to the conceptual model for representing concern interactions we also propose to use reasoning techniques for detecting interactions in a given concern composition. Third, as a proof of concept, but also as a useful tool, we have implemented a solution in OWL [28] and Prolog [31]. The CIA (Concern Interaction Acquisition) expert system uses Prolog as a reasoning technique for detecting interactions in a given concern composition. The acquisition of the interaction knowledge to be captured in the conceptual model is realized through OWL. We consider this expert system as a backend for various software development tools.

The rest of this paper is structured as follows. Section 2 motivates our research by setting the scene and elaborates on some specific concern interactions in middleware we want to investigate. We explain the proposed conceptual model in Section 3 and illustrate it with a running example. Section 4 discusses the prototype of the CIA (Concern Interaction Acquisition) expert system. Finally, related work is discussed in Section 5. We present a conclusion in Section 6.

2 Background and Motivation

2.1 Background

Management of concern interactions is a general problem that is relevant in many application domains, such as telecommunications, middleware, email, thermo control, policy-based, multimedia and other systems [5,6,7,12,17,20,23,24]. Our work is focused on the domain of *common middleware services* and all example concern interactions and further details within this paper should be interpreted with respect to that background.

Middleware is systems software that resides between the applications and the underlying operating systems [38]. Its primary role is to functionally bridge the gap between application programs and the lower-level and heterogeneous software infrastructure. It is used most often to support complex, distributed applications. It includes web servers, application servers, content management systems, and similar tools that support application development and delivery. Middleware is typically decomposed into four layers [38], which are shown in Figure 1.

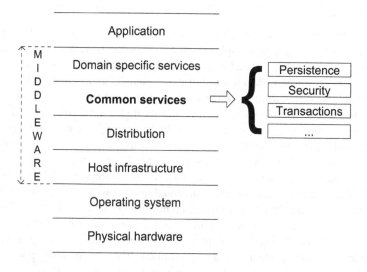

Fig. 1. The different layers in common middleware

- Host infrastructure middleware provides an abstraction layer that shields software in the higher layers from the details of the underlying OS (Operating system). By abstracting away the peculiarities of individual operating systems, many tedious and error-prone aspects of sustaining networked applications via low-level OS programming APIs are eliminated. Widely known examples are Sun's Java Virtual Machine [22], Microsoft's .NET [40] and the ADAPTIVE Communication Environment [39].
- Distribution middleware defines higher-level distributed programming models whose reusable APIs and components automate and extend network programming capabilities encapsulated by host infrastructure middleware [38]. One advantage that is most cited for this middleware layer is that it provides networking transparency to the programmer. CORBA ORB's [26] and RMI [43] are two well-known examples.
- Common middleware services are built upon distribution middleware. They define higher-level domain-independent services that allow application developers to concentrate on programming business logic. Without these services, end-to-end capabilities (such as transactional behavior, security, database connection pooling or threading) would have to be implemented ad hoc by each networked application over and over again. The form and content of these services will continue to evolve as the requirements on the applications being constructed expand. Logical examples here are CORBAservices [27], EJB technology [15] and .NET web services [40].
- Domain-specific middleware services are tailored to the requirements of particular domains, such as telecom, e-commerce, health care, process automation, or aerospace. Unlike the other three middleware layers, which provide broadly reusable horizontal mechanisms and services, domain-specific middleware services are targeted at vertical markets.

2.2 Motivation

What are concerns in middleware? Concerns are similar to requirements in a broad sense of the word, ranging from high-level requirements that are articulated in an early stage of the software project[1] to additional - often more detailed - requirements that are generated when performing detailed design and implementation[2]. Moreover, the various concerns embodied in current middleware can be situated from the lower-level host-infrastructure and distribution software layers to the higher-level common and domain-specific middleware services. For the sake of understanding, we use the term concern throughout this paper both for requirements and the artefacts that realize or implement these requirements in later stages of the software development lifecycle.

Common middleware services such as security, persistence and others correspond naturally to a number of (mostly non-functional) concerns that typically can interact with each other. Notice that there exist different sorts of interactions. We elaborate on a classification of concern interactions in Section 3. We now discuss three motivating examples of concern interactions. We provide some more detail regarding the common middleware services that are involved as it is not our intention to come up with a complete and exhaustive overview of existing common middleware services.

- In most cases, it is useless to have an authorization service without an authentication service. Authentication is the confirmation of a claimed set of attributes or facts with a certain level of confidence by providing sufficient evidence thereof. For example, providing your user name and password to your email client is a possible way to authenticate a person, principal or entity. Authorization refers to (1) the permission of an authenticated entity to perform a defined action or to use a defined service or resource; (2) the process of determining, by evaluation of applicable permissions, whether an authenticated entity is allowed to have access to a particular resource. Authorizing an entity E to perform an action A only makes sense if you are sure that entity E effectively is entity E, i.e. entity E is authenticated. In other words, authorization depends on authentication.
- Audit and confidentiality services are in conflict with each other. An audit service is responsible for maintaining an audit trail, i.e. a record of events, in order to be able to trace the activities and usage of a software system. Confidentiality refers to the state of keeping the content of information secret from all entities but those authorised to have access to it. An often used mechanism to realize confidentiality is encryption, the process of obscuring information to make it unreadable without special knowledge. Suppose data item X has to be kept secret, i.e. is confidential. Is the goal to have only the encrypted version to be logged in case of an event in which the data item X is involved and hence, compromising the readability and usefulness of the audit track? Or should the audit trail just refer to the plain data item X, sacrificing a large part of its confidentiality. Clearly, both middleware services correspond to conflicting concerns. The same conflict also arises between caching and confidentiality. Caching refers to saving recently accessed data in a small fast memory in order to speed up subsequent access to the same data.

---

[1] E.g. the middleware should ensure confidentiality when information is exchanged between two parties.

[2] E.g. decrypted messages should never be cached.

– A transaction and authorization service also possibly conflict. A transaction service handles units of interaction in a coherent and reliable way. Such units of interaction have to happen in an all-or-nothing mode and must be either entirely completed or aborted. An ideal transaction service guarantees all of the ACID (Atomicity, Consistency, Isolation and Durability) properties for each transaction. Suppose an entity starts a transaction. Consider for example the case where an employee starts to update some parts of the personnel database of the company he is working for. As soon as he tries to upgrade his monthly salary, the authorization service halts the execution by indicating the denied permission. The transaction service hence should no longer complete the started unit of interaction and abort.

We propose to explicitly capture this kind of interaction knowledge using a conceptual model that captures the most important concepts for representing concern interactions (see Section 3). The CIA expert system we propose in Section 4 will enable exploiting this knowledge as depicted in Figure 2. First of all, different domain experts incrementally insert new interaction knowledge coming from their domain expertise into the CIA system, based on the conceptual model. This corresponds to arrow (1) in Figure 2.

Fig. 2. Exploiting concern interaction knowledge

Then, the expert system can be used in various composition activities during the software development process, such as for example trade-off analysis [35], component deployment [8] and concern composition. In this paper, we further investigate component composition during application assembly by means of a visual software composition tool. Suppose the user is creating a component composition using a visual composition environment. As the user drags new components on the canvas, the composition tool may query the CIA system about known interactions (see (2) in Figure 2). CIA then uses reasoning techniques to detect the interactions that occur in the given component composition. It will respond to the software composition tool with this list of interactions and tactics for resolving them (3). The composition tool may present then this knowledge to the user in its own notation. In the long run, a component framework that can cope with adding components in a flexible and generic way could interpret these tactics automatically. The internals of the CIA expert system will be discussed in Section 4.

3   Conceptual Model

In this section, we present the conceptual model behind the CIA system. We start with a general overview of the most important and top-level concepts in Section 3.1. In the

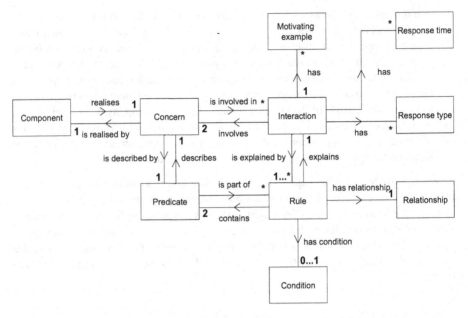

Fig. 3. A conceptual model for describing concern interactions

subsections thereafter, we will provide some more detail on some of these concepts. Throughout the elaboration of our model, we will use our second motivating example from section 2, the conflict between audit and confidentiality services, to illustrate the different concepts and relationships between these concepts.

3.1 Overview

Our conceptual model provides a number of concepts in terms of which knowledge about interactions between concerns can be acquired; it is thus a meta-model. It is aimed at being sufficiently rich to allow all kinds of concern interactions for any kind of component composition to be captured in a precise and natural way. The model for capturing concern interactions knowledge can be represented as a conceptual graph where nodes represent concepts and edges represent structuring links, similar to [11]. Figure 3 illustrates the most important portion of the conceptual model. Roughly spoken, a concern, which is realised through one component, can be involved in one or more interactions. Such an interaction is explained by one or more rules, which essentially are a relationship (indicating the kind of interaction) between a number of predicates that in turn each describe one concern.

Concerns. The central concept in our conceptual model is *concern*. As been said before, concerns are similar to requirements in a broad sense of the word that are realized through one or more components, ideally one. Our model currently only deals with applications that implement a one to one mapping between components of concerns. In the model, concerns are organised based on subconcern refinement relationships into a specialization hierarchy. Hence, under the umbrella of this abstract concept are the more concrete concerns and their subconcerns, in our case the common middleware services and their subservices. Multiple inheritance within this concern specialization hierarchy is inherently supported because of the underlying mechanism we use to implement the conceptual model (see Section 4.2). We will discuss here only a small part of this concern hierarchy in order to illustrate the approach. What is important is that this concern hierarchy has to be based on a lot of domain expertise from within the different domains to reach an as complete as possible state. At the second level (the concern concept forms the root of the concern hierarchy), we distinguish between the different layers in middleware: host infrastructure middleware, distribution middleware, common middleware services and domain-specific middleware layers. In a third level, each of these is further refined. E.g. the common middleware services node is refined to specific common middleware services such as security, persistence, transactions, etc. Additionally, each of these can be again decomposed. As an example, standard security typically breakdowns into an authentication, authorization, audit, confidentiality, integrity and non repudiation service [37]. The discussed part of the concern hierarchy is shown in Figure 4.

Fig. 4. Portion of the concern hierarchy   **Fig. 5.** Classification of concern interactions

Interactions. A concern can be involved in an arbitrary number of *interactions* with one or more other concerns. To structure concern interactions and address their effective management, we have devised a classification that distinguishes between different kinds of interactions. This interaction classification is based on earlier work and intensive workshop discussions [36,3] and is shown in Figure 5. We distinguish between five different classes.

- Dependency covers the situation where one concern explicitly needs another concern and hence depends on it. A dependency does not result in a problem or erroneous situation as long as the concern on which another one depends is ensured to be present in the final component composition. E.g. authorization depends on authentication.
- Conflict captures the situation of semantical interference: one concern that works correct in isolation does not work correctly anymore when it is combined with

other concerns. In other words, a concern influences the correct working of another one negatively. Typically, a conflict can be solved by mediation or performing a trade-off analysis because the concerns, in a sense, are complementary. E.g. confidentiality and audit are conflicting (cfr. Section 2.2).

- Choice defines the interaction between two equivalent concerns. In other words, there is no need to have the components realizing both concerns deployed because their net effect will be the same. However, doing so won't give any problems. E.g. one of multiple authentication services gets chosen.
- Mutex encapsulates the interaction of mutual exclusiveness of concerns. Realizing one of both concerns prohibits the use of the other one. No mediation is possible because the concerns are not complementary: only one of them can be used, the other cannot. E.g. an extensive audit can compromise a certain strong timing constraint.
- Assistance arises when a concern influences the correct working of another concern positively and hence assists it. There can be no doubt that this type of interaction is a positive one. Typically, when a concern assists another concern, extended functionalities become possible and extra support is offered. E.g. caching encrypted data assists confidentiality by improving performance.

Predicates. The third essential relationship for a concern shown in our conceptual model is the fact that a concern will be described by a *predicate*. Predicates enable us to describe the semantics of a specific concern. A predicate always has the format illustrated below. The definition of each predicate consists of two parts: a head, indicating the concern that is being described, and a number of parameters that are used to add all the concepts and values that are relevant for a complete description of a specific concern. Example definitions of the audit and confidentiality concerns in pseudo-code are shown in lines (2) and (3). (2) describes the audit concern in terms of four information items or parameters: entity, action, object and result. At all times, the semantics of the predicate is that all events where an entity `Entity` (e.g. a user) performing an action `Action` (e.g. a read operation) on an object `Object` (e.g. a data item) resulted in `Result` is recorded. Similarly, the confidentiality predicate can used to express that an object `Object` (e.g. a data item) is confidential.

```
(1)  <head> ( <param1>, ..., <paramN> )
(2)  audit ( Entity, Action, Object, Result )
(3)  confidentiality ( Object )
```

An important characteristic of these predicates is their language and technology independence. Moreover, if we start from the observation that for each predicate, including for its head and parameters, an unambiguous definition exists, our approach is very intuitive. On the contrary, a mapping from this conceptual level to a lower language specific level will be needed in future work to ensure that a predicate at all times reflects the correct runtime state of the application components and the middleware environment.

Rules. As depicted in Figure 3, our idea is to have each interaction between concerns explained by one or more *rules*. A rule essentially is a *relationship* between two predicates. It explains the context in which a specific interaction occurs by means of these predicates. Secondly, it also indicates the kind of interaction depending on the relationship a rule is associated with. There are five relationships included in our conceptual model corresponding to the five kinds of interactions we defined:

- depends_on, indicating a dependency,
- conflicts_with, indicating a conflict,
- mutex, indicating a mutual exclusion,
- one_of, indicating a choice, and
- assists, indicating an assistance.

We also take into account the concept of an optional *condition* which enables us to take certain conditions into account when describing an interaction. For example, if a conflict only appears under the runtime circumstances where battery power is low (as in [36]), we can express that. If we now look at our example, the interaction between audit and confidentiality clearly is a conflict, because both services operate correctly in isolation, but when they are composed, mediation is necessary to regulate their coexistence. Therefore, the rule explaining the interaction in pseudo-code is

```
for each Object o: audit(_,_,o,_) conflicts_with confidentiality(o)
```

It states that when certain objects (such as data items) both are required to be confidential and be part of events that need to be audited there is a conflict between audit and confidentiality.

Others. Next to the information elaborated upon above, we obviously are also interested in possible solutions of specific interactions. This information need is reflected into the concepts *time of response* and *type of response*. It is clear that some stages of the software development lifecycle are more appropriate than others when trying to cope with a certain interaction. E.g. dependencies typically will be taken care of during the architecture phase, while conflicts potentially occur at runtime and need to be handled in later stages if they were overlooked during requirements analysis. The type of response concept represents the information definining an appropriate response to a specific interaction into more detail. Both can be considered as a sort of tactics for solving specific interactions. The details for specifying such tactics are subject of ongoing work. For now, a tactic compares to a textual description of the different alternatives to resolve the interaction. The remaining *example* concept is used to illustrate an interaction with a concrete motivating example for a better understanding of a specific interaction.

4 CIA Expert System

In this section, we sketch the main architectural building blocks of the CIA (Concern Interaction Acquisition) expert system, again illustrated with our running example of the confliciting audit and confidentiality services. In Section 4.1, we present the high-level architecture of our expert system. Next, we provide the most important details about the OWL implementation of our conceptual model in Section 4.2. In Section 4.3, we proceed by discussing the use of Prolog for detecting interactions. Finally, we revisit the audit and confidentiality example conflict in Section 4.4.

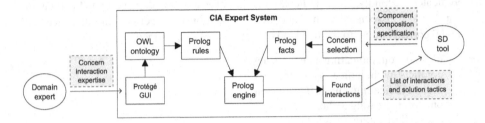

Fig. 6. Architecture of the CIA expert system

4.1   Overview

The expert system is built upon two technologies. Firstly, OWL is used together with the Protégé [32] environment for representing knowledge about interactions. Secondly, we use Prolog for querying and reasoning about knowledge from the database. Note that OWL also provides some form of reasoning that is limited to class and instance inferences, which is not enough to express our interaction rules. Figure 6 shows how these two technologies are used together. Expertise about interactions between concerns is added to the OWL ontology by domain experts who use the Protégé graphical user interface for this. The OWL representation is generated by Protégé. Subsequently, the acquired interaction knowledge is automatically transformed into a set of Prolog rules. Secondly, a software development (SD) tool has to provide a specification of a certain concern composition to be investigated for potential concern interactions. Essentially, this specification consists of a list of the selected concerns. Based on this list, a set of Prolog facts is generated that contains all the predicate definitions that describe the listed concerns. Both the set of Prolog rules and Prolog facts are fed into a Prolog engine that through reasoning can detect all the interactions that occur in the given concern composition. This list of interactions finally is presented back to the software development tool. We consider the available concern interaction knowledge to be rather stable in time while, on the contrary, concern composition specifications can easily vary greatly for different concern interaction acquisition requests. We now zoom into the use of OWL, Protégé and Prolog. Finally, we illustrate the whole on our running example.

4.2   Ontology-Based Representation of Concern Interaction Knowledge

To start with, we implemented the conceptual model under the hood of the CIA expert system as an OWL ontology in Protégé, a widely known open source ontology editor and knowledge-base framework. By definition, an ontology is a data model that represents a domain (in our case concern interactions) and can be used to reason about the objects in that domain and the relations between them. Ontologies are commonly used as a form of knowledge representation for a variety of purposes including inductive reasoning, classification, problem solving techniques and to facilitate communication and information sharing. They are generally made up of concepts (classes), relations between these classes and characteristics of individual classes. OWL stands for Web Ontology Language and it is designed for use by applications that need to process the content of information. OWL facilitates greater machine interpretability of content than that supported by XML, RDF, and RDF Schema by providing additional vocabulary along with a formal semantics [28]. Protégé is capable of automatically generating the OWL representation and it also assists the domain experts as it automatically checks the consistency of the inserted knowledge and also automatically completes it with new inferred knowledge.

4.3 Reasoning

We generate a set of Prolog [31] rules based on the OWL implementation of our conceptual model that serves as our concern interaction knowledge base. We wrote a parser in Java using XPath [44] enabling the transformation of the OWL code[3] into a set of Prolog rules. We explicitly did not opted for existing tools that combine OWL and Prolog, which we motivate in Section 5. Next to concern interaction expertise that is expected from domain experts, the CIA system also requires the specification of a given concern composition from a software development tool. The selection of the concerns to be composed for example can be done by drag and dropping them onto a canvas. The list of all concerns within such a specification is deduced from the knowledge database. Based on this list of concerns, we select the corresponding predicates that describe these concerns out of our ontology. It is exactly this list of predicates that we use as the second input for the Prolog engine. The engine will match the set of facts against the set of Prolog rules. The reasoning then results in the set of interactions that occur within the specified concern composition. Via these interactions, we can again query the OWL ontology for tactics on how to solve the interactions.

4.4 Our Example Revisited

In order to illustrate the steps that allow us to have a set of Prolog rules, we show the example definition of the conflict between audit and confidentiality by providing some snapshots of its OWL representation that is generated by Protégé in Figure 7. Lines 1 – 6 cover the definition of the interaction with as name ConflictBetweenAuditAndConfidentiality. The definition indicates the type of the interaction (line 2) which can be concluded automatically through OWL reasoning based on the relationship of the rule that explains this interaction. This rule is mentioned at line 5 and defined in lines 25 – 31. Lines 3 and 4 reference the concerns that are involved in this interaction. Both, audit and confidentiality, are described respectively in lines 7 – 15 and 16 – 24. Each concern lists the different interactions it is involved in (lines 9 – 10 and 18 – 19), the components it is realised by (lines 11 – 12 and 20 – 21) and the different predicate instances that describe the concern under consideration (lines 13 – 14 and 22 – 23). Notice that the latter ones match with the predicates contained within the description of the rule (lines 29 –30) that explains the original interaction. Finally, lines 32 – 38 give the representation of the audit predicate (the one for confidentiality is similar), indicating the head and the relevant parameter.

---

[3] We used RDF as the syntax for presenting the OWL ontology because it is more structured and consistent than Protégé's standard abbreviated OWL syntax and, hence, simplifies the parsing work.

Our parser will start looking for all known rules that explain an interaction together with their specific relationship and the predicates that are contained within each rule, followed by getting the concerns that are involved in the interaction a rule describes. As a result, the following Prolog code can automatically be generated and matched against the facts based on this OWL code.

```
% ConflictBetweenAuditAndConfidentiality rule
conflicts_with(audit,confidentiality) :-
    audit(_,_,Object,_),
    confidentiality(Object).
% Facts if the audit and confidentiality service are selected
audit(entity,action,object,result).
confidentiality(object).
```

5   Related Work

5.1   Interaction Modeling

Chung et al. [9] have defined the NFR framework for representing and analyzing non-functional requirements (NFRs). The framework provides a goal-oriented approach for dealing with NFRs and is intended to help developers produce customized solutions by considering characteristics of the particular domain and system being developed. An essential part of their approach is the notion of softgoal interdependency graphs. These are graphs that represent softgoals and their interdependencies. Such a graph maintains a complete record of development decisions and design rationale in a concise graphical form. A softgoal corresponds in a way to our concern concept. In their work, the inter-dependencies between softgoals can be of various natures: refinements, contributions, operationalizations, correlations etc. Under the umbrella of their notion of correlations, interactions can be modelled. However, they only take into account conflicts. A NFR type catalogue is another artefact in their work which resembles our concern hierarchy a lot.

Feature models represent hierarchies of properties of domain concepts [33,10]. The properties are used to discriminate between concept instances, i.e. systems or applications within that domain. The properties are relevant to end users. At the root of the hierarchy there is the so-called concept feature, representing a whole class of solutions. Below of this concept feature there are hierarchically structured sub-features showing refined properties. Feature models are used for development and application of software product lines, i.e. for defining products and configurations, for describing possibilities of a product line, and for establishing new products and adding new properties to a product line [18]. Compared to our work, a feature model matches more or less with our concern hierarchy. An instance of the feature model corresponds to a selected set of concerns in our approach. In [4], the authors use an algebraic theory for modeling interactions in feature-oriented designs in which feature interactions are modeled as derivatives.

Work on integrating ontologies and rules also exists. Rules are the next layer of the Semantic Web [41] that is the subject of currently ongoing research. Ontologies form

```
(1)    ...
       <rdf:Description rdf:about="#ConflictBetweenAuditAndConfidentiality">
(2)      <rdf:type rdf:resource="#Conflict"/>
(3)      <involves rdf:resource="#AuditI"/>
(4)      <involves rdf:resource="#ConfidentialityI"/>
(5)      <is_explained_by rdf:resource="#rule4"/>
(6)    </rdf:Description>

(7)    ...
       <rdf:Description rdf:about="#AuditI">
(8)      <rdf:type rdf:resource="#Audit"/>
(9)      <is_involved_in rdf:resource="#ConflictBetweenAuditAndConfidentiality"/>
(10)     <is_involved_in rdf:resource="#..."/>
(11)     <is_realised_by rdf:resource="#auditComponent"/>
(12)     <is_realised_by rdf:resource="#..."/>
(13)     <is_described_by rdf:resource="#AuditPred_23"/>
(14)     <is_described_by rdf:resource="#..."/>
(15)   </rdf:Description>

(16)   ...
       <rdf:Description rdf:about="#ConfidentialityI">
(17)     <rdf:type rdf:resource="#Confidentiality"/>
(18)     <is_involved_in rdf:resource="#ConflictBetweenAuditAndConfidentiality"/>
(19)     <is_involved_in rdf:resource="#..."/>
(20)     <is_realised_by rdf:resource="#confidentialityComponent"/>
(21)     <is_realised_by rdf:resource="#..."/>
(22)     <is_described_by rdf:resource="#ConfidentialityPred_11"/>
(23)     <is_described_by rdf:resource="#..."/>
(24)   </rdf:Description>

(25)   ...
       <rdf:Description rdf:about="#rule4">
(26)     <rdf:type rdf:resource="#Rule"/>
(27)     <explains rdf:resource="#ConflictBetweenAuditAndConfidentiality"/>
(28)     <has_relationship rdf:resource="#conflicts_with"/>
(29)     <contains_predicate rdf:resource="#AuditPred_23"/>
(30)     <contains_predicate rdf:resource="#ConfidentialityPred_11"/>
(31)   </rdf:Description>

(32)   ...
       <rdf:Description rdf:about="#AuditPred_23">
(33)     <rdf:type rdf:resource="#AuditPred"/>
(34)     <describes rdf:resource="#AuditI"/>
(35)     <is_part_of_rule rdf:resource="#rule4"/>
(36)     <head rdf:datatype="http://www.w3.org/2001/XMLSchema#string">audit</head>
(37)     <object rdf:datatype="http://www.w3.org/2001/XMLSchema#string">object</object>
(38)   </rdf:Description>
       ...
```

Fig. 7. Part of the OWL representation of a concern interaction

the highest layer that is sufficient mature and are a first step from adding reasoning to pure domain descriptions. The combination of both promises to offer enhanced representation and reasoning capabilities. SweetProlog [21] is a system for translating web rules into Prolog enabling an integration of ontologies and rules. This is achieved via a translation of OWL ontologies and OWLRuleML rules into a set of facts and rules in Prolog. Antoniou et al. [2] implemented DR-Prolog, a powerful declarative system supporting rules, facts and ontologies together with all major Semantic Web standards. We deliberately chose not to use these systems, because the rules we need are already modelled through our OWL ontology implementation of the conceptual model and hence, can be easily generated from the ontology itself.

5.2 Interaction Detection and Resolution

Wohlstadter et al. [42] have presented GlueQoS, a middleware-based approach to managing dynamically changing QoS requirements (quality of service issues related to non-functional requirements such as security, reliability and performance) of components. They use policies to advertise non-functional capabilities. These policies vary at runtime with operating conditions. GlueQoS also incorporates middleware enhancements to match, interpret, and mediate QoS requirements of clients and servers at deployment time and/or runtime. The latter is their main contribution. In their work, they assume a fixed ontology of features, with all interactions explicitly identified ahead of time. The link with our work here is obvious. Moreover, they also provided a classification of feature interactions. The similarities with our categorization makes us believe both interaction classifications are very close to a sweet spot. Another piece of work on conflicts in policy-based distributed systems management is done by Lupu et al. [24].

In the field of aspect-oriented software development [16], aspect interactions represent one of the biggest remaining challenges. In this context, Pawlak et al. [30] propose CompAr, a language that allows programmers to abstractly define an execution domain, advice codes and their often implicit execution constraints. In our opinion, the high level of abstraction the language offers to specify very generic aspect definitions is their major contribution. Moreover, their language enables the automatic detection and solving of aspect-composition issues (interactions between aspects) of around advices. A number of other approaches with respect to automatic detection and resolution of interactions exist [14,19,34,13]. For example, [14] proposes a language-independent technique to detect semantic conflicts among aspects that are superimposed on the same join point. Their approach is based on a resource-operation model. They argue that a formalization of the complete behaviour of a component is not realistic; we agree. However, they don't motivate that their abstraction mechanism is designed in such a way that it is possible to represent the essential behaviour of an aspect. [19] describes interference (i.e. interactions) between aspects at the semantic level, irregardless of any overlap among joinpoints or variables. Their definition of interference resembles our definition of conflicts a lot. They assume that each aspect already has a specification and is correct with respect to that specification. The specification of an aspect consists of a set of assumptions and guarantees which both are expressed in temporal logic. Based on these specifications, they want to generate proofs that one aspect does not interfere with another one.

6   Conclusion

In this paper, we presented a conceptual model that helps a software development team to understand and manage the different interactions in a component-based distributed application. To demonstrate results, we have focussed on the particular application domain of common middleware services. However, we are convinced that the models and techniques presented here are equally applicable to other domains as well. In general, the conceptual model complements methods for building large and complex component-based distributed systems. We addressed two problems. First, we defined a conceptual model for explicitly representing knowledge about interactions between concerns and how to solve these. As a result, this knowledge can be shared and used in the course of system evolution. Secondly, we provide practical support to the software developer for managing the interactions when he/she is creating, adapting or evolving the component composition of an application. Finally, we discussed our prototype implementation of the CIA expert system that uses a concern composition specification as input for detecting interactions that occur in the given set of concerns.

References

1. Booch, G., Kozaczynski, W.: Component-Based Software Engineering. Software, IEEE, vol. 15(5), pp. 34–36 (1998)
2. Antoniou, G., Bikakis, A.: DR-Prolog: A System for Defeasible Reasoning with Rules and Ontologies on the Semantic Web. IEEE Transactions on Knowledge and Data. Engineering 19(2), pp. 233–245 (2007)
3. Aspects, Dependencies and Interactions Workshop, ECOOP 2006, Nantes, France, http://www.aosd-europe.net/adi06/
4. Liu, J., Batory, D., Nedunuri, S.: Modeling interactions in feature oriented systems, International Conference on Feature Interactions (ICFI) (June 2005)
5. Blair, L., Pang, J.: Feature interactions - Life beyond traditional telephony, FIW, pp. 83–93 (2000)
6. Blair, L., Blair, G., Pang, J.: Feature interaction outside a telecom domain. Workshop on Feature Interaction in Composed Systems (2001)
7. Calder, M., Kolberg, M., Magill, E.H., Reiff-Marganiec, S.: Feature interaction: A critical review and considered forecast. Computer Networks: The. International Journal of Computer and Telecommunications Networking archive 41(1), 115–141 (2003)
8. CAM/DAOP, Component-Aspect Model / Dynamic Aspect-Oriented Platform, http://caosd.lcc.uma.es/CAM-DAOP/index.htm
9. Chung, L., Nixon, B.A., Yu, E., Mylopoulos, J.: Non-Functional Requirements in Software Engineering. Kluwer Academic Publishing, Norwell (2000)
10. Czarnecki, K., Eisenecker, U.W.: Generative Programming. Addison Wesley, London (2000)
11. Dardenne, A., Van Lamsweerde, A., Fickas, S.: Goal-directed Requirements Acquisition. Science of Computer Programming 20, pp. 3–50 (1993)
12. Diaz Pace, J.A., Trilnik, F., Campo, M.R.: How to handle interacting concerns?, Workshop on Advanced for Separation of Concerns in OO Systems, OOPSLA 2000, Minneapolis, USA (2000)
13. Douence, R., Fradet, P., Sudholt, M.: Composition, reuse and interaction analysis of stateful aspects, International Conference on Aspect-Oriented Software Development (AOSD04) (2004)
14. Durr, P., Bergmans, L., Aksit, M.: Reasoning about Semantic Conflicts between Aspects. In: Proceedings of Aspect, Dependencies, and Interactions (ADI) Workshop (2006)
15. Enterprise JavaBeans Technology, http://java.sun.com/products/ejb/white_paper.html (1998)
16. Filman, R., Elrad, T., Clarke, S., Aksit, M.: Aspect-oriented software development. Addison-Wesley, London (2004)
17. Hall, R.J.: Feature interactions in electronic mail. In: Proceedings of the 6th International Workshop on Feature Interactions in Telecommunications and Software Systems, IOS Press, Amsterdam (2000)
18. Kang, K.C., Lee, K., Lee, J.: FOPLE - Feature Oriented Product Line Software Engineering: Principles and Guidelines. In: Pohang University of Science and Technology (2002)

19. Katz, S.: Aspect categories and classes of temporal properties. In: Rashid, A., Aksit, M. (eds.) Transactions on Aspect-Oriented Software Development. LNCS, vol. 3880, pp. 106–134. Springer, Heidelberg (2006)
20. Keck, D.O., Kuehn, P.J.: The feature and service interaction problem in telecommunications systems: A survey. IEEE Transactions on Software Engineering, vol. 24(10) (1998)
21. Laera, L., Tamma, V., Bench-Capon, T., Semeraro, G.: SweetProlog: A system to integrate ontologies and rules. In: Antoniou, G., Boley, H. (eds.) RuleML 2004. LNCS, vol. 3323, pp. 188–193. Springer, Heidelberg (2004)
22. Lindholm, T., Yellin, F.: The Java Virtual Machine Specification. Addison-Wesley, London (1997)
23. Liu, X., Huang, G., Zhang, W., Mei, H.: Feature interaction problems in middleware services. International Conference on Feature Interactions (ICFI) (June 2005)
24. Lupu, E., Sloman, M.: Conflicts in policy-based distributed systems management. IEEE Transactions on Software Engineering 25(6), pp. 852–869 (1999)
25. Meyer, B.: Object-oriented software construction, 2nd edn. Prentice-Hall, Inc., Englewood Cliffs (1997)
26. Object Management Group, The Common Object Request Broker: Architecture and Specification Revision 2.4, OMG Technical Document (2000)
27. Object Management Group, CORBAservices: Common Object Service Specification, OMG Technical Document (1998)
28. OWL Web Ontology Language, Overview, http://www.w3.org/TR/owl-features/
29. Parnas, D.L.: On the Criteria to be Used in Decomposing Systems into Modules, Communication of the ACM, vol. 15(12) (1972)
30. Pawlak, R., Duchien, L., Seinturier, L.: CompAr: Ensuring safe around advice composition. 7th IFIP International Conference on Formal Methods for Open Object-Based Distributed Systems (FMOODS05) Athens, Greece (June 2005)
31. SWI-Prolog's Home, http://www.swi-prolog.org/
32. The Protégé Ontology Editor and Knowledge Acquisition System, http://protege.stanford.edu/
33. Riebisch, M.: Towards a More Precise Definition of Feature Models. In: Riebisch, M., Coplien, J.O., Streitferdt, D. (eds.) Modelling Variability for Object-Oriented Product Lines, BookOnDemand Publ. Co., Norderstedt (2003)
34. Rinard, M., Salcianu, A., Bugrara, S.: A classification system and analysis for AO programs. In: Proceedings of the Twelfth International Symposium on the Foundations of Software Engineering. Newport Beach, CA (November 2004)
35. Sampaio, A., Chitchyan, R., Rashid, A., Rayson, P.: EA-Miner: a tool for automating aspect-oriented requirements identification. In: Proceedings of the 20th IEEE/ACM international Conference on Automated Software Engineering (ASE) (2005)
36. Sanen, F., Truyen, E., Joosen, W., Jackson, A., Nedos, A., Clarke, S., Loughran, N., Rashid, A.: Classifying and documenting aspect interactions. In: Coady, Y., Lorenz, D., Spinczyk, O., Wohlstadter, E. (eds.) Proceedings of the Fifth AOSD Workshop on Aspects, Components, and Patterns for Infrastructure Software, pp. 23–26. Bonn, Germany (2006)
37. Sanen, F., Truyen, E., Joosen, W., Loughran, N., Rashid, A., Jackson, A., Nedos, A., Clarke, S.: Study on interaction issues (2006) AOSD-Europe Deliverable 44 http://www.aosd-europe.net/deliverables/d44.pdf
38. Schantz, R., Schmidt, D.C.: Middleware for Distributed Systems. In: Wah, B. (ed.) Encyclopedia of Computer Science and Engineering (2007)
39. Schmidt, D., Huston, S.: C++ Network Programming: Resolving Complexity with ACE and Patterns. Addison-Wesley, MA (2001)

40. Thai, T., Lam, H.: .NET Framework Essentials. O'Reilly (2001)
41. W3C Symantic Web Activity, `http://www.w3.org/2001/sw/`
42. Wohlstadter, E., Tai, S., Mikalsen, T., Rouvellou, I., Devanbu, P.: GlueQoS: Middleware to Sweeten Quality-of-Service Policy Interactions. In: Proc. of the International Conference of Software Engineering (2004)
43. Wollrath, A., Riggs, R., Waldo, J.: A Distributed Object Model for the Java System. USENIX Computing Systems (1996)
44. XML Path Language, `http://www.w3.org/TR/xpath`

An Improved Genetic Algorithm for Web Services Selection*

Sen Su, Chengwen Zhang, and Junliang Chen

State Key Lab of Networking and Switching Technology
Beijing University of Posts & Telecommunications (BUPT), 187#
10 Xi Tu Cheng Rd., Beijing 100876, China
zwjcbj2007@gmail.com, {susen, chjl}@bupt.edu.cn

Abstract. An improved genetic algorithm is presented to select optimal web services composite plans from a lot of composite plans on the basis of global Quality-of-Service (QoS) constraints. The relation matrix coding scheme of genome is its basis. In this genetic algorithm, an especial fitness function and a mutation policy are proposed on the basis of the relation matrix coding scheme of genome. They enhance convergence of genetic algorithm and can get more excellent composite service plan because they accord with web services selection very well. The simulation results on QoS-aware web services selection have shown that the improved genetic algorithm can gain effectively the composite service plan that satisfies the global QoS requirements, and that the convergence of genetic algorithm was improved very well.

1 Introduction

Web service is a software application identified by an URL. The most-promising aspect of web service is the ability of engaging other web services in order to realize higher-order business transactions. Some interoperation mechanisms [1] are enabled in a service-oriented architecture. The framework of web services creates new possibilities to assemble distributed web services. How to create robust service compositions becomes the next step [15] and there are a lot of researches concentrated on it [8,9,16,17].

A composite service has specific functions that can be divided into some component functions. These component functions are accomplished by component services respectively. If the dependencies among component functions are represented through state charts that were used in [9], there are usually many available paths that can finish the same composite functions. So, web service composition has many scenarios [3], such as probabilistic invocation, parallel invocation, sequential activation and so on. If every component function is signified by a task, an execution path of a composite service can be constructed by a sequence of tasks including an

---

* The work presented in this paper was supported by the National Basic Research and Development Program (973 program) of China under Grant No. 2003CB314806; 863 program of China under Grant No.2006AA01Z164; the Program for New Century Excellent Talents in University of China under Grant No. NCET-05-0114.

J. Indulska and K. Raymond (Eds.): DAIS 2007, LNCS 4531, pp. 284–295, 2007.

initial task and a final task. In the phase of running time, some candidate services with same functions and different QoS attributes are discovered for every task. Thus, for each path, there are various composite plans corresponding to the specific function of composite service. Moreover, since component services with the same functions and different QoS are increasing with the proliferation of web services, the composite size should be larger and larger. For example, there are only one path that accords with the composite functions, 15 component functions in this composite path, and average 10 candidate web services for each component function. In this kind of composition scenario, the composite size should be about 10^{15}. Furthermore, since web services requesters always express both their functional requirements and their global QoS constraints set, it is needed to select which component services will be used in a given composite service in order to maximize user satisfaction, select the best composite plan from numerous plans and satisfy the consumers' global QoS constraints. Hence, web services selection with global QoS constraints plays an important role in web services composition [2, 3]. In the past years, the researches about web services selection have gained considerable momentums.

To figure out web services selection, some approaches are presented with the help of semantic web [4, 5, 6], and the others are based on QoS attributes computation [7, 8, 9, 10, 11, 23]. But the latter approaches are the more suitable solutions satisfying the global QoS requirements of web services selection. It is a combinatorial optimization issue that the best combination of web services is selected in order to accord with the global QoS constraints. Some traditional optimization techniques are proposed in [7, 8, 9, 23]. However, finding a plan for quality driven web services selection is NP-hard [11], so the effective strategies based on Genetic Algorithm (GA) are introduced in [10, 11].

Genetic Algorithm is a powerful tool to solve combinatorial optimizing problems [13]. It solves the formulated optimization problem using the idea of Darwinian evolution. It is an iterative procedure that consists of a constant-size population. Every individual describes a solution. Basic evolution operations, including crossover, mutation and selection operations, make GA be apt to very effectively perform global search. The design of genetic algorithm has the greatest influence on its behavior and performance [12], especially the design of coding scheme of chromosomes, fitness function, evolution operations and selection mechanism will have direct effect on efficiency and global astringency of genetic algorithm. It is necessary for GA to accord with characters of web services composition in order to get global convergence.

In the literatures, a suitable genetic algorithm for web services selection with global QoS constraints has not been taken into account, although the presented genetic algorithms can attain service composition supporting QoS to some extent. They always adopted the one dimension coding scheme that can not represent effectively the composite service re-planning, cyclic paths. The one dimension coding scheme can also not express all paths of assemble service at the same time. They did not think more about how to overcome the premature phenomenon of GA. Therefore, they did not suit effectively the issue about how to select the best composite plan from many plans of many paths in order to satisfy global QoS constraints.

Following the above analyses, we proposed a novel relation matrix coding scheme of chromosomes in [21], the relation matrix coding scheme suits with web service composition with global QoS constraints more than the one dimension coding scheme. In [20], we presented a population diversity handling mechanism. But, the fitness function in [20] is not very fit one for many QoS properties with large quantity difference. Furthermore, the mutation policy should be designed on the basis of relation matrix coding scheme. Aiming at these issues, we discuss how to construct fitness function, mutation policy and present an improved fitness function and an improved mutation policy. Finally, the simulated results show that improved fitness function and improved mutation policy accord with QoS-aware web services selection and relation matrix coding scheme.

The remainder of this paper is organized as follows. After a review of the literature of web services selection in section 2, Section 3 presents the discussion of fitness function and mutation policy in detail. Section 4 describes simulations about fitness functions and mutation policies and discusses results aiming to support the work. Finally, our conclusions are given in section 5.

2 Quality Computation-Based Selection of Web Services

According to Std. ISO 8402 [18] and ITU E.800 [19], QoS may include a number of nonfunctional properties such as price, response time, availability and reputation. Thus, QoS value of a composition service can be achieved by fair computation of QoS of every component web services. In this section, some traditional optimization techniques [7, 8, 9, 23] and Genetic Algorithm (GA) [10, 11] in the literatures are discussed in detail.

The QoS computation based on QoS matrix is a representative solution. [7] ranked web services by means of normalizing QoS matrix, however, it was only a local optimization algorithm but not a global one for services selection. Other works in the area of QoS computation include [8, 9], which proposed local optimization and global planning. The local optimization approach could not take global QoS constraints into consideration. For example, there are only one path that accords with the composite functions, 15 component functions in this composite path, and average 10 candidate web services for each component function. In this kind of composition scenario, the composite size should be about 10^{15}. When the size of composite service is very large, the overhead of global planning is quite enormous. Hereby, both had limitation to some extent. [23] proposed pattern-wise QoS selection, which split the difference between the global planning selection and local optimization selection. Although its execution is faster than a true global planning approach, it misses global perspective. Furthermore, it takes a lot of cost on identifying pattern elements while the composition patterns are very complex. Especially, it will work very badly if the given user-defined QoS requirements go beyond all of offered QoS.

The above means are not able to resolve effectively the issue of web services selection with global QoS constraints belonging to the class of NP-hard [10]. GA is more suitable for this issue. But, GA can play an important role only while the combinatorial size is very large. Some numerical simulations in [22] show that the linear integer programming outperforms GA while the combinatorial size is small. Two different GAs were proposed in [10, 11].

In [10], binary strings of chromosome were proposed for service selection. Every gene in chromosome represented a service candidate with values of 0 and 1. Thereby, the more service candidates or web services clusters were, the longer chromosome was. Since at most only single service candidate could be selected in each of web services clusters, only one gene was "1" and others were "0" in all of genes of every cluster. When the number of component services and the number of candidate services of each component service are all very big, the length of genome will be very long. This kind of manner resulted in poor readability. Further, the authors proposed only coding manner of chromosome for service selection with little further information about the rest parts of genetic algorithm, such as selection mechanism.

In [11], a genetic algorithm was also used to tackle the service selection problem. The one dimension coding way of chromosome was proposed to express services composition, and each gene represented an abstract service of composite service. The value of abstract service was one of concrete services. The length of genome was shorter than the one in [10]. The change of the number of concrete services could not influence the length of genome. Therefore, the stability of genome length was better than [10]. The coding way of chromosome and the fitness function were all of which were proposed in [11], but without more information about the algorithm.

In [20], a genetic algorithm with population diversity handling is presented in order to maximize user satisfaction during composition of web services. Evolution is directed effectively through the conservation of the historical optimal population and the competition between the historical optimal population and the current population.

In [21], a special relation matrix coding scheme of chromosomes is presented. It suits with QoS-aware web service composition more than the one dimension coding scheme. The relation matrix has the ability to represent simultaneously the composite service re-planning, cyclic paths and many web service scenarios.

In addition to coding schemes, the other parts of genetic algorithm should also be taken into account in order to accord into the special points of web services selection with global QoS constraints, for example, fitness function, mutation policy.

3 Improved Genetic Algorithm

In this section, we present an improved genetic algorithm in order to resolve quality-driven selection, mainly including the design of fitness function and mutation policy. The relation matrix coding scheme is firstly reviewed because the mutation policy is based on it.

3.1 Relation Matrix Coding Scheme

In [21], a special relation matrix coding scheme was introduced using neighboring matrix. In the case of that the number of component services and dependencies among component services in every path are different from each other, the relation matrix coding schemes can express all paths of assemble service at the same time. The coding scheme has the function to express not only the relation among tasks but also paths information.

In this matrix, "n" is the number of all tasks in the services composition. The following is the definition of the relation matrix coding scheme.

(1) The g_{ii} is located at the main diagonal of the matrix for the ith locus of the chromosome and presents a task. The possible values of g_{ii} are the following:

a) The number "0" that represents that the pointed task is not included in the special services composition.

b) The number "-1" that represents that the pointed task is implementing while the composite service re-planning.

c) The number "-2" that represents that the pointed task becomes invalid while the composite service re-planning, such as all of candidate services of the pointed task become invalid or the pointed task is canceled for some reasons.

d) The number "-3" that represents that the selected concrete service of the pointed task has some changes while the composite service re-planning. These changes include that the selected concrete service becomes invalid or some QoS constraints of the selected concrete service have some changes.

e) If the number "t" represents that the sum number of concrete services of the pointed task, any number in the range of [1, t] represents that the pointed task is included in the special services composition and one concrete web service is selected.

(2) The g_{ij} represents the direct relation between the ith task and the jth task. Here, $i \neq j$.

Before g_{ij} is defined, four values of k1, k2, k3 and k4 should be defined firstly. The four values are adjustable and represent the different situations of parallel invocations. They are boolean variables coded. They are integer number in hexadecimal idea (they may have values: 100, 200, 400, 800, etc.). The following is the definition of g_{ij}:

a) The number "0" represents that the ith task is not the immediate predecessors of the jth task.

b) The number "p" represents that the ith task is the immediate predecessors of the jth task and the ith task invokes the jth task with probability "p". Here, $0 < p \leq 1$.

c) The number "m" represents that the ith task is the immediate predecessors of the jth task and the ith task invokes the jth task with "m" times. Here, $1 \leq m < Min\{k1, k2, k3, k4\}$.

d) The number "k1" represents that all of parallel invocations of immediate predecessors of the jth task belong to one identical parallel invocations group. The ith task is one of the immediate predecessors.

e) The number "k2" represents that all of parallel invocations of immediate successors of the ith task belong to the same group. The jth task is one of the immediate successors.

f) The number "k3" represents that all of parallel invocations of immediate predecessors of the jth task belong to the different groups. The ith task is one of the immediate predecessors.

g) The number "k4" represents that all of parallel invocations of immediate successors of the ith task belong to the different groups. The jth task is one of the immediate successors.

Obviously, in the case of k3 and k4, it is necessary to seek a table of parallel invocations to find out which parallel invocations belong the same group.

By means of the combination of the values of m, p, k1, k2, k3, k4, many web service scenarios, such as probabilistic invocation, parallel invocation, sequential activation, etc, can be represented by the relation matrix. Additionally, the values of m, k1, k2, k3, k4 should not influence the decomposition of the value of g_{ij}. For example, if value of m is less than 100, values of k1, k2, k3 and k4 can be set as 0x100, 0x200, 0x400 and 0x800. Thus, value of g_{ij} can be decomposed precisely.

Following the definition of the relation matrix, the objects of the evolution operators are all of elements along the main diagonal of the matrix. The chromosome is made up of these elements. The other elements in the matrix are to be used to check whether the created new chromosomes by the crossover and mutation operators are available and to calculate the QoS values of chromosomes.

As stated the above, the abilities of the relation matrix are the following:

(1) The ability to seek simultaneously all of paths: since every locus of the chromosome can randomly be set to value "0", the chromosome has the ability to express all of paths of services composition.

(2) The abilities of the path re-planning and the task re-planning thanks to the introduction of values of "-1/-2/-3" to g_{ii}.

(3) The ability to resolve the cyclic paths thanks to the introduction of values of "m" to g_{ij}.

(4) The ability to represent simultaneously many web service scenarios, such as probabilistic invocation, parallel invocation, sequential activation, etc.

The following is one example of the relation matrix coding scheme.

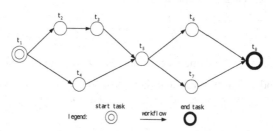

Fig. 1. Statechart of a web services composition

Figure 1 is one example of a web services composition. Its coding scheme is shown in figure 2.

$$\begin{pmatrix} t_1 & 1 & 0 & 1 & 0 & 0 & 0 & 0 \\ 0 & t_2 & 1 & 0 & 0 & 0 & 0 & 0 \\ 0 & 0 & t_3 & 0 & 1 & 0 & 0 & 0 \\ 0 & 0 & 0 & t_4 & 1 & 0 & 0 & 0 \\ 0 & 0 & 0 & 0 & t_5 & 1 & 1 & 0 \\ 0 & 0 & 0 & 0 & 0 & t_6 & 0 & 1 \\ 0 & 0 & 0 & 0 & 0 & 0 & t_7 & 1 \\ 0 & 0 & 0 & 0 & 0 & 0 & 0 & t_8 \end{pmatrix}$$

Fig. 2. Coding scheme

In figure 2, all of numbers at the main diagonal of the matrix will be set at concrete genome.

3.2 Fitness Function

In [20], objective function is defined in (1) and it is named ObjectiveFunction 1(OF1 is its abbreviation):

$$f(g) = \frac{\sum_j (Q_j \times w_j)}{\sum_k (Q_k \times w_k)}.$$ (1)

Where $w_j, w_k \in [0,1]$, and w_j, w_k are real positive weight factors, represent the weight of criterion j and k. By providing w_j, w_k respectively, end users show their favoritism concerning QoS. The sum of all of them is 1. Q_j and Q_k denote values of the jth and kth QoS properties of the individual respectively. All of negative QoS properties (for example, price, time etc.) will be selected for the denominator (k). All of positive QoS properties (for example, reputation, availability etc.) will be selected for the numerator (j).

The formula (1) is not fit for the great quantity difference that QoS properties have. For example, response time and availability have large quantity difference. Furthermore, may be the same QoS properties have huge quantity difference in different web services. So, different QoS properties have not same influence on fitness function. It is not equitable for these QoS properties with low quantity level.

A method should be taken to transform values of all QoS properties into the range of [0,1]. In this way, all of QoS properties will have same influence on fitness function. A proportional fitness function is defined in formula (2) and it is named ObjectiveFunction 2(OF2 is its abbreviation):

$$f = \sum_{i=1}^{m} (w_i \times Q_i')$$ (2)

In formula (2), w_i is the same as formula (1). Q_i' denote the value of the ith QoS property of the individual. For negative QoS properties, values are scaled according to (3). For positive QoS properties, values are scaled according to (4).

$$Q_i' = \begin{cases} \dfrac{Q_i^{max} - Q_i}{Q_i^{max} - Q_i^{min}} & \text{if } Q_i^{max} - Q_i^{min} \neq 0 \\ 1 & \text{if } Q_i^{max} - Q_i^{min} = 0 \end{cases}$$ (3)

$$Q_i' = \begin{cases} \dfrac{Q_i - Q_i^{min}}{Q_i^{max} - Q_i^{min}} & \text{if } Q_i^{max} - Q_i^{min} \neq 0 \\ 1 & \text{if } Q_i^{max} - Q_i^{min} = 0 \end{cases}$$ (4)

In formula (3) and (4), Q_i^{max} and Q_i^{min} are the maximum and minimum of the ith QoS property of all individuals respectively. Q_i is the same as formula (1).

In order to express the difference of negative QoS properties and positive QoS properties further, the formula synthesizing the formula (1) and (2) is provided in formula (5) and it is named ObjectiveFunction 3(OF3 is its abbreviation):

$$f = \frac{\sum_j \left(\dfrac{Q_j - Q_j^{min}}{Q_j^{max} - Q_j^{min}} \times w_j\right)}{\sum_k \left(\dfrac{Q_k - Q_k^{min}}{Q_k^{max} - Q_k^{min}} \times w_k\right)}, \quad \text{if } Q_k^{max} - Q_k^{min} = 0 \text{ then } \dfrac{Q_k - Q_k^{min}}{Q_k^{max} - Q_k^{min}} = 1$$ (5)

In formula (5), positive QoS properties are in the place of numerator and negative QoS properties are in denominator. The fitness function with penalty character is defined in formula (6):

$$Fit = f - \sum_{j=1}^{n} (\lambda_j \times \frac{\triangle P_j}{R_{jMax} - R_{jMin}}) \tag{6}$$

In formula (6), P_j represents the calculation value of a Q_i or some Q_is and these values are limited by a quality constraint. R_{jMax}, R_{jMin} are the maximum value and minimal value of calculation formula of the No.j quality constraint in all of web services composite plans. n is the number of quality constraints. λ_j is the calculation value of a Q_i or some Q_is and these values are limited by a quality constraint. It is a parameter used to adjust the scale of penalty value. The reason why λ_j is used: the higher users show their favoritism is, the bigger the penalty value is. Formula (7) is the definition of $\triangle P_j$:

$$\triangle P_j = \begin{cases} P_j - \min\{R_{jMax}, P_{jMax}\} & if & P_j > \min\{R_{jMax}, P_{jMax}\} \\ 0 & if & \max\{R_{jMin}, P_{jMin}\} \le P_j \le \min\{R_{jMax}, P_{jMax}\} \\ \max\{R_{jMin}, P_{jMin}\} - P_j & if & P_j < \max\{R_{jMin}, P_{jMin}\} \end{cases} \tag{7}$$

In formula (7), P_{jMax}, P_{jMin} are the maximum value and minimal value of the No.j quality constraint respectively.

In section 4, some simulations about these fitness functions will be provided.

3.3 Mutation Policy

Here, some mutation policies are proposed and discussed on the basis of the relation matrix coding scheme.

The first one is named MutationPolicy 1(MP1 is its abbreviation.): The probability of mutation is for the locus. Every locus in every chromosome will be asked whether mutating or not according to mutation probability. The child chromosome must be the same path as the mother chromosome during mutation operation. After the mutation operation, only the chromosome with the biggest fitness values will survive among the mother and child chromosomes. In fact, the mutation operation enhances the ability to search composition plans of every path.

The second one is named MP2: In the standard genetic algorithm, the probability of mutation is for the locus of chromosome. Here, in order to promote the probability to create different paths from the mutated path, the probability of mutation is for the chromosome instead of the locus. The concrete policy is as follows: before mutation operation of every chromosome, the probability of mutation is used to confirm whether the chromosome mutates or not. If mutation, the object path will be confirmed firstly whether it is the same as the current path expressed by the current chromosome. If difference, the object path will be selected from all available paths except the current one. If the object is itself, the new chromosome will be checked whether the new chromosome is the same as the old chromosome. Same chromosome will result in the mutation operation again. If the objects are different paths from the current path, a new chromosome will be created on the basis of the object path. Obviously, it is not necessary to check whether new and old chromosomes are same.

The third one is named MP3: It is similar to MP2. The different point is that the object path of the current path will be selected directly from all of available paths including the current path. This means that the objects are permitted to have the same paths as the current path

The fourth one is named MP4: The probability of mutation is for the locus. During the mutation of one task, the selection probability of every concrete service and the one of the "0" value are equal.

In section 4, some simulations about these mutation policies will be provided.

4   Experiments

To verify the excellence of GA we have proposed, numerous simulation comparisons had been performed on QoS-aware web services selection. All experiments were taken on same software and hardware, which were Pentium 1.6GHz processor, 512MB of RAM, Windows XP Pro, development language JAVA, IDE Eclipse 3.1. Same data were adopted for two compared GAs, including workflows of different sizes, 15-50 concrete web services for each task and 5 QoS data for each web service. A simplified representation of web service was used, including an ID number, some QoS data that were retrieved randomly in the range of defined values.

The following is about how these simulation data are produced. Firstly, there are three simulated compositions in all: the number of component functions is 10, 25 and 30 respectively. Composition state charts are used to represent the dependencies among component functions. Secondly, candidate services for each task are randomly created with one ID and values of five QoS properties. Finally, some global constraints of some QoS properties are provided for every composition. Then, these three composition situations are saved for the use later. Comparisons will be made in the same composition situation. In the three composition situations, the composite size is all very large. For example, there are 64 paths in the case of tasks 30, average 19 tasks in every path and average 15 candidates services for every task. Thus, the composite size is very enormous: 64×15^{19}.

The compared GAs were set up with same population size, crossover operation and probability, mutation probability. QoS model in [9] was used for them. The penalty technique is used for constrained optimization problems in algorithms. These algorithms have same selection mechanism of individuals, that is the "roulette wheel selection".

The fitness function and the mutation policy are the different points among the compared GAs.

4.1   Experiments on Fitness Function

There are three kinds of fitness function comparison between GA with the relation matrix coding scheme (the capital letter "A" represented it) and GA with the one dimension coding scheme (the capital letter "B" represented it). The three kinds of fitness function comparison are based on OF1, OF2 and OF3 respectively.

The following is the experiments of the three kinds of fitness function comparison. Some same parameters are population size 400, crossover probability 0.7, mutation probability 0.1, iterations 500, running times 50. The unit of time is *ms*. As shown in table 1, the statistic data of the average fitness, time and generation of the maximal fitness value were collected.

Table 1. Fitness, time and generation

Tasks Num	Comparison Name	Average Maximum Fitness	Average Time	Average Generation
10	A with OF1 : B with OF1	0.197 : 0.197	216 : 1582	5 : 518
10	A with OF2 : B with OF2	0.672 : 0.631	1298 : 4543	33 : 1027
10	A with OF3 : B with OF3	2.446 : 1.998	332 : 4769	7 : 1077
25	A with OF1 : B with OF1	0.217 : 0.066	3046 : 8891	42 : 8453
25	A with OF2 : B with OF2	0.638 : 0.538	15330 : 16369	188 : 8058
25	A with OF3 : B with OF3	1.658 : 0.601	12202 : 16677	146 : 8149
30	A with OF1 : B with OF1	0.191 : 0.053	6551 : 11361	78 : 16608
30	A with OF2 : B with OF2	0.628 : 0.529	20906 : 22746	219 : 16223
30	A with OF3 : B with OF3	1.515 : 0.541	18981 : 23198	199 : 16414

The above simulations show that GA with the relation matrix coding scheme and Objective Function OF3 is excellent than other GAs at the average fitness, time and generation. In table 1, "A" GA with OF3 can gain higher fitness value than other GAs. "A" GA with OF3 can have faster convergence speed than "A" GA with OF2. The reason is that OF3 express exacter comparison standard than OF1 and OF2.

4.2 Experiments on Mutation Policy

The mutation policy is the only different points between the compared GAs. Clearly, the compared GAs should adopt the relation matrix coding scheme. Some same parameters are population size 400, crossover probability 0.7, mutation probability 0.1, iterations 500, running times 50. The unit of time is *ms*.

The table 2 is the results of experiments among MP1, MP2, MP3 and MP4.

Table 2. Fitness (MP1:MP2:MP3:MP4)

Tasks Num	Average Maximum Fitness
10	0.196:0.191:0.191:0.196
25	0.193:0.165:0.141:0.089
30	0.152:0.132:0.108:0.069

In table 2, the largest fitness value is from MP1. These mean that the MP1 is the most effective mutation policy among MP1, MP2, MP3 and MP4. MP2 and MP3 increase the probability to create the different paths from the mutated path. This is the reason that MP2 and MP3 are better than MP4. If mutation, the probability to hold the mutated path in MP2 is 0.5, but the probability to hold the mutated path in MP3 is the value of 1 divided by the number of all paths. So, MP3 has higher probability to lose the good genetic information from the predecessor populations than MP2. This is why MP2 has better fitness than MP3. The MP1 increases the probability to search more composition paths and only the chromosome with the biggest fitness values will survive among mother and child chromosomes. Thus, the evolution direction is enhanced. These are why MP1 is best one among these mutation policies.

5   Conclusions

The web services selection with global QoS restrictions is an active research area. In this paper, we discuss fitness function and mutation policy of GA on the basis of the relation matrix coding scheme of genome. After discussion, the improved fitness function and mutation policy are proposed. They direct the evolution of GA. They also improve the convergence speed of GA. While GA includes the relation matrix coding scheme and Objective Function OF3, it can gain 30 times fitness value than the GA with one dimension coding scheme and Objective Function OF1. The results of experiments show that genetic algorithm with improved fitness function and mutation policy can get more excellent composite service plan.

To provide adaptive capability of genetic algorithms is an active research area [14]. Therefore, how to design a self-adaptive genetic algorithm for QoS-aware selection is one of our future works.

References

1. W3C.Web Services Architecture (2004) http://www.w3.org/TR/2004/NOTE-ws-arch-20040211/
2. Menascé, D.A.: QoS Issues in Web Services. IEEE Internet Computing 6(6), 72–75 (2002)
3. Menascé, D.A.: Composing Web Services: A QoS View. IEEE Internet Computing 8(6), 88–90 (2004)
4. Tian, M., Gramm, A., Ritter, H., Schiller, J.: Efficient Selection and Monitoring of QoS-Aware Web Services with the WS-QoS Framework. IEEE/WIC/ACM International Conference on Web Intelligence (WI'04) (2004)
5. Soydan Bilgin, A., Singh, M.P.: A DAML-Based Repository for QoS-Aware Semantic Web Service Selection. In: Proceedings of the IEEE International Conference on Web Services (ICWS'04) (2004)
6. Zhou, C., Chia, L.-T., Lee, B.-S.: DAML-QoS Ontology for Web Services. In: IEEE International Conference on Web Services (ICWS'04) (2004)
7. Liu, Y., Ngu, A.H., Zeng, L.: QoS Computation and Policing in Dynamic Web Service Selection. In: Proceedings of the 13th International Conference on World Wide Web (WWW), pp. 66–73. ACM Press, New York (2004)

8. Zeng, L., Benatallah, B., Dumas, M., Kalagnanam, J., Sheng, Q.Z.: Quality Driven Web Services Composition. In: Proc. 12th Int'l Conf. World Wide Web (WWW) (2003)
9. Zeng, L., Benatallah, B., Ngu, A.H.H., et al.: QoS-Aware Middleware for Web Services Composition. IEEE Transactions on Software Engineering 30(5), 311–327 (2004)
10. Zhang, L., Li, B., Chao, T., et al.: On Demand Web Services-Based Business Process Composition. IEEE, pp. 4057–4064 (2003)
11. Canfora, G., Di Penta, M., Esposito, R., Villani, M.L.: A Lightweight Approach for QoS–Aware Service Composition. ICSOC (2004)
12. Ignacio, R., Jesús, G., Héctor, P., et al.: Statistical Analysis of the Main Parameters Involved in the Design of a Genetic Algorithm. IEEE Transactions on Systems, Man, and Cybernetics—Part. C: Applications and Reviews 32(1), 31–37 (2002)
13. Srinivas, M., Patnaik, L.M.: Genetic Algorithm: a Survey. IEEE, pp. 17-26 (1994)
14. Hinterding, R., Michalewicz, Z., Eiben, A.E.: Adaptation in Evolutionary Computation: a Survey. IEEE EC, pp. 65–69 (1997)
15. Curbera, F., Khalaf, R., Mukhi, N., et al.: The Next Step in Web Services. Communication of the ACM 46(10), 29–34 (2003)
16. Milanovic, N., Malek, M.: Current Solutions for Web Service Composition. IEEE Internet Computing, pp. 51–59 (2004)
17. Orriens, B., Yang, J., Papazoglou, M P: Model Driven Service Composition. In the First International Conference on Service Oriented Computing (ICSOC'03) (2003)
18. ISO 8402, Quality Vocabulary
19. ITU-T Recommendation E.800, Terms and Definitions Related to Quality of Service and Network Performance Including Dependability (1994)
20. Zhang, C., Su, S., Chen, J.: Efficient Population Diversity Handling Genetic Algorithm For Qos-Aware Web Services Selection. In: Alexandrov, V.N., van Albada, G.D., Sloot, P.M.A., Dongarra, J.J. (eds.) ICCS 2006. LNCS, vol. 3994, pp. 104–111. Springer, Heidelberg (2006)
21. Zhang, C., Su, S., Chen, J.: A Novel Genetic Algorithm For Qos-Aware Web Services Selection. In: IEEE CEC'06 and EEE'06, USA. LNCS, vol. 4055, Springer-Verlag, Berlin (2006)
22. Canfora, G., Di Penta, M., Esposito, R., et al.: An Approach For QoS-Aware Service Composition Based On Genetic Algorithms, Genetic and Evolutionary Computation Conference (GECCO), Washington DC, USA, vol.1, pp. 1069–1075 (2005)
23. Grønmo, R., Jaeger, M.C.: Model-Driven Methodology for Building QoS-Optimised Web Service Compositions. The 5th IFIP International Conference on Distributed Applications and Interoperable Systems (DAIS), Athens, Greece (June 2005)

A UML Profile for Modeling Mobile Information Systems

Vegard Dehlen and Jan Øyvind Aagedal

SINTEF ICT, Cooperative and Trusted Systems, Forskningsveien 1, 0314 Oslo, Norway
{vegard.dehlen, jan.aagedal}@sintef.no

Abstract. In this paper we propose a framework for modeling mobile information systems. Mobility introduces several challenges and issues that impact the development of mobile systems. As a result, we want applications running on mobile devices to exhibit certain traits; they should be aware of the mobility and be adaptive to the changes that occur due to it. Literature has identified several types of mobility – among them, physical and logical mobility. The former pertains to tangible mobile entities like cars, devices and people, while the latter encompasses mobile software entities. In addition to these, this paper includes the concept of *vertical mobility* – the movement of a network connection between overlapping networks – in a UML profile for modeling mobile information systems. We discuss our experiences from a case study described in [1] , where we modeled a simple mobile information system and transformed parts of the model into code.

Keywords: Mobility, UML profile, model-driven development.

1 Introduction

The introduction of small hand held devices with Internet connection is rapidly changing the way we both work and live, and an increasing number of people are acquiring these devices. In today's society we can identify several mobile devices. Laptop computers, cell phones, PDAs and tablet PCs are all examples of devices that can be used while moving around. Common usage is accessing e-mail, remote databases or the Web, sending faxes and making phone calls, scheduling and document processing [2], in addition to newer usage areas like watching TV or movies, performing video phone calls or downloading music.

The emergence of novel and useful services and applications in a domain is highly dependent on software engineering. The existence of a solid development framework and methodology allows applications to be developed more rapidly and with higher quality, in addition to promote consistency, interoperability and reuse within the community. Such a framework should capture the characteristics and concepts of the target domain. The work in this paper builds upon and expands the previous efforts towards reaching this goal, i.e., representing the mobility domain at the metalevel.

This paper is organized as follows. Chapter 2 gives an analysis of the problem, by analyzing the concept of mobility and what we mean by it and by introducing different types of mobility. In Chapter 3 we list some requirements for a framework for

J. Indulska and K. Raymond (Eds.): DAIS 2007, LNCS 4531, pp. 296–308, 2007.

modeling mobile information systems. Chapter 4 presents our solution to the problem; a mobility metamodel and an accompanying UML profile. Chapter 5 discusses the validity of our solution, before Chapter 6 draws some conclusions and suggests future work.

2 Problem Analysis

2.1 Theory of Mobility

Since its inception, mobile computing has resulted in the introduction of several sub-fields, and today we talk about systems that are context-aware, location-aware, mobility-aware and/or adaptive. In the following, we will further explain our views of mobility and the kind of applications we are interested in modeling.

An adaptive system simply refers to a system with the ability to adapt to different situations and contexts. Adaptation is not a phenomenon exclusive to mobile computing, but it is, as pointed out earlier, identified as the main strategy for coping with the high variability and heterogeneity of the mobile domain [3, 4]. There are several factors an application can adapt to:

1. To its current context or changes in context.
2. To its available system and network resources and changes in these.
3. To changes in location, i.e., mobility.

There are different ways to view mobility. First, we can see it as an entity's ability or willingness to move. Second, we can see it as an entity that is currently moving. Movement patterns can be described by different modalities, as defined in [7]. Third, we can view mobility as a change of an entity's location, where the movement between locations is considered an atomic action.

In the area of context awareness, change of location is interesting due to the changes in context that naturally occur. Location change might entail changes in several environment properties like temperature, nearby people and devices, available printers and ongoing activity - properties a context aware application can take advantage of. In the field of mobility, location change also means roaming between different network cells, requiring seamless handoff and service [8] and session [9] mobility. Some of these issues are handled in the network and middleware layers, but the application can also take advantage of these activities, like employing a new mobile code strategy based on the change in network characteristics. However, in an adaptivity context, these issues alone are not enough to warrant the concept of location as a first class entity, as an application does not need to know of any other than its current location to perceive changes in context and network resources. A system that only considers location change can offer *reactive* adaptation, which means that it can react to the changes that occur because of mobility.

Modeling locations as first class entities is only necessary in an application that needs to know the properties of locations other than its current one, which is enabled by an entity's ability to move. A system can then provide *proactive* adaptation.

There are different ways of representing a location. The abstraction we choose depends on the unit of mobility, where location could be represented by Cartesian coordinates for a mobile device or by a host address for a mobile agent [6]. Optionally, we can choose abstractions that are conceptually related to the world we live in, where a mobile device could be located in the tax free shop at Gardermoen airport in Norway. In the latter scenario, we see that locations are defined within locations. In addition, locations can be mobile. A passenger on a ferry will have a location relative to the boat (being in his cabin, for example), while the boat has a location relative to its previous and destination port. In addition to being nested, locations can be overlapping. An example of this is a road that runs through several areas of a city. One could thus say that, conceptually, an entity has two different locations. However, in practice, we consider the entity to be located in the intersection of the overlapping locations.

Another reason for treating locations as a first class concept is, as identified in [11], that locations may have access restrictions or barriers. A person traveling from one country to another will have to pass security mechanisms at the border, while a mobile agent might have to pass a firewall to access a remote device or administrative domain. These concerns are out of this paper's scope, but the concepts of mobility and locations presented provide a foundation on which security and access control can be modeled and reflected upon.

2.2 Types of Mobility

Physical and Logical Mobility. Literature has long since identified two main types of mobility. Logical mobility (also called mobile computation) deals with the movement of software entities, while physical mobility (mobile computing) deals with the movement of physical entities.

There is a distinct difference between physical and logical mobility. The former is something that occurs in the real world, as people or devices move and change locations. Each location might offer different resources and context, like nearby printers or available networks. An application running on a mobile device might thus continually experience change in available resources and context. A mobile information system cannot control or influence physical mobility, but it can observe location changes and react with different adaptation strategies if necessary. For logical mobility, on the other hand, the situation is the total opposite, as logical mobility is a phenomenon that encompasses software entities that are designed by an application developer. Consequently, while an application reacts to physical mobility, it can employ logical mobility and mobile code as an adaptation strategy – possibly as a reaction to physical mobility.

It is worth noting, however, that logical mobility can exist without physical mobility and vice versa.

These fields are mostly disconnected; logical mobility within the software community and physical mobility within the hardware community. However, [11] argues that the two types of mobility are intertwined, and should be treated in a uniform way.

Vertical Mobility. As time progresses, more and better access points become available in our environment. Especially in high density areas, a device can have several heterogeneous access networks to choose from. These networks might offer different services, coverage, cost and bandwidth, and the mobile device can choose which network to use. Change of access network is thus not only caused by physical mobility, but might also happen while the device remains stationary. This is called vertical handoff. The term vertical refers to overlapping wireless networks and their hierarchical and asymmetric relationship [12]. A device can thus have access to networks that offer low-bandwidth over a wide geographic area to networks that offer high-bandwidth over a narrow geographic area [13]. The opposite is called horizontal handoff, where the handoff occurs between access points in a homogeneous network infrastructure [14]. An example of horizontal handoff is when a mobile phone switches between different access points.

One of the main problems of mobile systems is that a mobile device will have to change access network, which can be divided into three different scenarios:

1. The device leaves the coverage area of its current network, and loses connection.
2. The device leaves the coverage area of its current network, and connects to another available network.
3. The device is stationary, and chooses to connect to another available network.

The first two scenarios are direct results of physical mobility, where mobile nodes move out of their present network coverage. The third scenario, however, is not true mobility, but has the same effect; the system must manage the change in IP routing caused by the vertical handoff [15]. This is what we term *vertical mobility* (or policy mobility, as defined in [15]), where a node can be in an environment of several overlapping networks with different properties and choose freely which network to use. In our definition of vertical mobility we do not require the networks to be heterogeneous, as we would also be interested in the possibility to change between, say, two overlapping WLANs with different properties.

For vertical mobility we define the unit of mobility to be a network connection, which we define as a logical mobile entity that can move between networks. This fits our focus on mobility as an atomic change of location, as identified in the previous section. Subsequently, we view vertical mobility as a type of logical mobility. They both share the characteristic that they can be controlled by the application designer.

3   Requirements for the Modeling Framework

We are interested in providing a framework for modeling mobile information systems. Specifically, we are interested in modeling concepts that are useful when designing applications and that allow us to leverage all the new possibilities that mobility brings. This is also known as *adaptive, mobility-aware* applications.

In our approach, we are interested in an entity's change of location and its ability or willingness to move. Consequently, we can reason about both reactive and proactive adaptation. We do not consider the continuous movement of entities, but only the result of it, i.e., location change. Furthermore, we view location as a defined entity with boundaries that can contain other entities. Following this definition, we do not consider location by satellite positioning, as in location aware systems, to be a location entity, but rather one of several properties that might describe a location.

The framework should separate between the different types of mobility that have previously been identified; physical and logical mobility. In addition, we believe that a framework for modeling mobile information systems should also include the concept of vertical mobility, as change of network is very relevant to mobility and adaptive applications. Our goal is to propose a user-friendly and visual modeling framework that allows developers to reason and communicate about these types of mobility in mobile systems.

We do not have the opportunity to go into a detailed discussion of requirements here, but for a fine-grained list of requirements and the reasoning behind them, see [1].

4   Proposed Solution

4.1   Mobility Metamodel

Grassi et al. [3] define the following issues that need clarification when we want to model mobility:

- Which entities move?
- How do we model the movement of an entity?
- What causes the movement of an entity?

As we defined in the requirements, we view mobility as an entity's willingness and ability to move and the actual location change of these entities. First, we introduce location as a concept. By location we mean any entity that has some concept of a boundary and that can contain other entities. A location can be divided into physical and logical locations. Examples of locations we are interested in separating between are **places, networks, devices** and **execution environments** (such as a virtual machine like JVM), as illustrated in Figure 1.

Second, we need to identify the entities with the ability to change location. Mobile entities are also divided into physical and logical elements, and indicative examples of interest are **devices, people, locations** (e.g. vehicles), **network connections** and **software.** See Figure 2. Our metamodel does not include concepts for detailed modeling of the network topology (like routers, proxies, multiplexes, etc), as we, from an adaptive application's point of view, are only interested the different networks the application has access to and their characteristics.

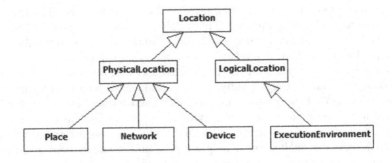

Fig. 1. Location metamodel

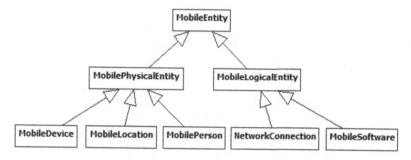

Fig. 2. Mobile entity metamodel

Third, Figure 3 illustrates how these concepts relate. A location is an entity that can contain other entities. These entities can be stationary or mobile in nature. There is a nesting relationship between locations, where one location can contain several other locations. This relationship can effectively model locations at different levels, like a room contained within a building contained in a city. Most entities will have one location. However, some entities might not have a location, e.g. a top-level location, while other entities might have several locations, e.g. a distributed file system. Mobile entities must have at least one location, and they have the ability to move between locations that are connected. The semantics of being connected varies for the different types of mobility, which is explained in the next section.

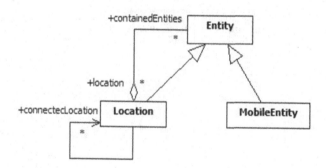

Fig. 3. Mobility metamodel

Several of the entities in our mobility domain can play different roles depending on the selected viewpoint. A mobile device is considered an entity that can change location from the viewpoint of physical mobility, while it has the role of a location that mobile code potentially can move to and from in the context of logical mobility.

Figure 4 shows a conceptual model for vertical mobility, which is somewhat different from general mobility. A network can not contain another network like locations can contain other locations. In addition, vertical mobility does not only involve the mobile entity (network connection) and its container (network), as the device and its location has to be considered as well. A physical location is associated with the available networks at that location, while a device is associated with the network it is currently using. A device is thus aware of its available networks through its location.

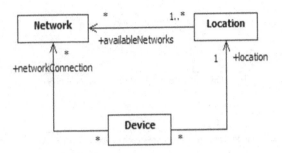

Fig. 4. Vertical mobility metamodel

4.2 UML Profile for Modeling Mobility

The profile presented in Figure 5 is inspired by the profile introduced by Grassi et al. in [3], which is a profile for modeling physical and logical mobility. A detailed discussion of the differences of our approach and that of Grassi et al. is provided in Section 5.2.

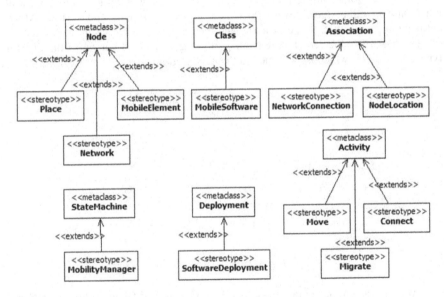

Fig. 5. UML profile stereotypes for mobile systems

The previous section identified the entities we consider for physical, logical and vertical mobility. For devices, users and other physical mobile entities we use the stereotype MobileElement [3]. Furthermore, we introduce the stereotypes Mobile-Software and NetworkConnection. These three stereotypes extend Node, Class and Association, respectively. Consequently, MobileSoftware can be used on both classes and components to denote a piece of mobile software.

Table 1. Profile stereotypes

Stereotype	Extends	Constraints	Description
MobileElement	Node	Can be located in a Place.	Has the ability to be moved between physical locations.
MobileSoftware	Class	Can only be located in a Node.	Has the ability to be moved between nodes.
NetworkConnection	Association	Connects a Device to a Network.	Has the ability to be moved between networks. Can be changed by Connect.
Place	Node		A physical location that can contain other entities.
Network	Node		Networks can span several locations and devices can connect to them through NetworkConnection.
Move	Activity	Locations must be connected.	Moves a MobileElement between two physical locations.
Migrate	Activity	Locations must be connected.	Moves a MobileSoftware between two nodes.
Connect	Activity	Destination Network must be at Device's NodeLocation.	Moves a NetworkConnection between two networks.
NodeLocation	Association	Connects a Node to a Place.	Specifies the location of a MobileElement. Can be changed by Move.
SoftwareDeployment	Deployment	Deploys a Component to a Node.	Specifies the current deployment of a MobileSoftware. Can be changed by Migrate.
MobilityManager	StateMachine		Models the causes and triggers of the movement of mobile entities.

Mobile entities move between locations. The UML2 specification has already defined constructs for the Device and ExecutionEnvironment concepts, which are locations for MobileSoftware. We introduce the stereotypes Place and Network to denote physical locations and overlapping access networks.

Each entity can have a location. NodeLocation is a stereotyped Association that specifies the location of a node. The location of mobile software is modeled through the SoftwareDeployment stereotype.

The movement of mobile entities is modeled by extensions to the Activity metaclass. These are Move, Migrate and Connect for physical, logical and vertical mobility, respectively. A mobile entity can only move if there exists a channel connecting the two locations. This could imply a corridor connecting two rooms for physical mobility, or two nodes being connected to the same network or the Internet for logical mobility. For vertical mobility, both networks have to be available from the device's current location.

As presented in [3], we use the concept of a mobility manager. The MobilityManager stereotype is a state machine for modeling the cause of mobility. The intention is that a system can change its mobility policies by selecting between different mobility managers. It is worth noting that a mobility manager only covers adaptation through mobility. Our profile does not try to cover adaptation in general.

5   Validation

In [1] we validated our profile through a case study. In the following, we present our experiences and lessons learned from the case study, in addition to positioning our profile among related work on the topic.

5.1   Case Study

In [1] we conducted a case study where we used the profile to develop a mobile information system. A PIM was designed before being marked with stereotypes from the UML profile. A part of this design was then transformed from PIM to PSM (platform specific model) and all the way to code. For the PIM to PSM transformation we used the ATLAS Transformation Language (ATL) [16], while we used MOFScript [17] for the PSM to code transformation.

In the case study we designed two deployment diagrams – one with and one without the use of stereotypes from our profile. While the first diagram only models one static scenario, the second diagram represents a snapshot of a possible scenario, while also showing other scenarios that are possible due to physical, logical and vertical mobility.

This type of model can serve two purposes; as a design time and a runtime model. In our case it was used as the former. Applying the profile resulted in a model that describes an important part of the application domain for an adaptive system. The mobility and location of a mobile entity will heavily influence the resources and context available to the system, giving the designers a fuller understanding of the environments the system will run in and needs to adapt to.

An adaptive system can also maintain a runtime version of the model, always keeping track of its current location and context. By analyzing previous mobility patterns or a schedule, the application could also offer adaptation based on future location and context. This area of use has been explored in the FAMOUS project, without seeing realization in the middleware.

We also designed a class diagram of the client application and marked a class as being mobile. Based on the transformation mappings we defined, we transformed the class diagram into a simple mobile code solution for Java Micro Edition (J2ME). The transformations did not result in a running application, but showed how marking a piece of software as mobile at the PIM level can automatically produce application solutions through transformations.

With the use of transformations, development time was naturally significantly shorter than it would have been to manually create all the models and code. In addition, the developer does not need to have any knowledge about the platform. However, developing transformations requires both time and expert knowledge of domains and platforms. As the number of platforms is significant for mobile devices and new devices are introduced at a rapid pace, one must consider the time and resources spent on implementing a MDD approach versus time saved using it.

The last part of the design phase was designing mobility managers for the different types of mobility, which specified the different causes and triggers for the mobility and transitions between the different scenarios modeled in the mobility deployment diagram. The drawback of using state diagrams is that they model state changes based on simple event-condition statements. Sometimes, decision making about which adaptation strategy to use is a complex calculation. In the MADAM middleware, for example, utility functions might draw information from numerous context sources to determine the best adaptation strategy for a given context [18].

5.2 Related Work

The literature contains several approaches to modeling mobility. In the following, we give a brief overview of some of these and show what our approach contributes with.

In [19] UML sequence diagrams are extended to model complex mobility patterns, but this requires a nonstandard extension of UML sequence diagrams. The diagrams provide the possibility to abstract away from irrelevant details. Their semantics is similar to that of ambients in that a mobile object is a location and a mobile process as well [20].

In [20], UML class and activity diagrams are extended, allowing the representation of mobile objects and locations as well as basic primitives such as moving or cloning.

Most relevant for the approach presented in this paper, though, is Grassi et al.'s UML profile for modeling mobile systems [3]. It makes a clear distinction between logical and physical mobility, and these concepts have their own representations.

The most significant difference between the approaches in [3] and this paper is the introduction of metalevel concepts for vertical mobility. The network a device is connected to has significant effects on the context a system experiences and the adaptation strategy it employs. By allowing developers to reason about different, overlapping networks in their models, we believe they will have a better vocabulary for reasoning about mobility and adaptivity in mobile systems.

When it comes to modeling physical and logical mobility, the approaches are similar except for a few differences.

Grassi et al. use the stereotypes MobileElement and its inherited stereotype MobileCode to model physical and logical mobile elements, respectively. They neglect to extend any metamodel classes for these concepts. We remedy this situation in our profile. In addition, we deemed the inheritance relationship as unnecessary and removed it, and renamed MobileCode to MobileSoftware as we think the latter puts less restrictions on the use of the concept.

Place, NodeLocation and MobilityManager are the same in both profiles. CurrentDeployment has been renamed SoftwareDeployment to better reflect the naming convention used for NodeLocation. In [3] the concept MoveActivity is used for moving MobileElements, while this is further specialized into PhysicalMove and LogicalMove in [21]. We used the terms Move and Migrate for the same meaning.

In [3], the authors introduced the stereotyped deployment AllowedDeployment, which is used to model additional constraints, like security and administrative domains, to the mobility of mobile code. We do not, however, see any reason for treating logical mobility any differently from physical mobility in this respect. As security is outside our scope, we chose not to include AllowedDeployment or any similar constructs.

Grassi et al. also specifies a set of Activity stereotypes that supports more fine-grained concepts and operations related to mobility and management of a mobility model; BeforeMoveActivity, AfterMoveActivity, AbortMoveActivity, AllowDeploymentActivity and DenyDeploymentActivity. We have not treated these in this paper.

The following table lists the stereotypes presented in this paper and the corresponding stereotypes in Grassi et al.'s profile.

Table 2. Comparison to earlier work

UML profile for mobile systems	Corresponding concepts in Grassi et al.'s profile
MobileElement	MobileElement
MobileSoftware	MobileCode
NetworkConnection	None
Place	Place
Network	None
Move	MoveActivity/PhysicalMove
Migrate	MoveActivity/LogicalMove
Connect	None
NodeLocation	NodeLocation
SoftwareDeployment	CurrentDeployment
MobilityManager	MobilityManager

6 Conclusions and Future Work

Mobile computing is characterized by a high level of heterogeneity and significant variations in available resources. As a result of this, it is generally accepted that mobile systems should be able to adapt to changes in context and resources.

Based upon earlier work, we presented a UML profile for modeling mobile information systems. The focus has been on modeling mobility as a change of location, and how a mobile system can adapt to its changing environment. The profile differentiates between and provides concepts for physical, logical and, as included in this paper, vertical mobility. Our approach is based on deployment diagrams, where we model the relationships between locations and mobile entities. Mobility managers, as defined in [3], are state machines that drive the mobility of a system. Based on events like location change, change in battery levels or network quality, the mobility managers can decide to employ a mobile code strategy or connect to another network.

In [1] we used our framework to develop a case study application. This provided us with valuable information about the usefulness of the framework and was a basis for its validation. In this paper we discussed the experiences we gained from the case study, before giving an overview over related work on the topic. The major contribution from our profile is the introduction of vertical mobility. To further validate the proposed framework we should perform additional case studies to assess its usefulness in different kinds of and more complex systems.

References

1. Dehlen, V.: Developing Mobile Information Systems. University of Oslo: Oslo, pp. 145 (2006)
2. Chalmers, D., Sloman, M.: A Survey of Quality of Service in Mobile Computing Environments. IEEE Communications Surveys (1999)
3. Grassi, V., Mirandola, R., Sabetta, A.: A UML Profile to Model Mobile Systems, in 2004 - The Unified Modelling Language. SpringeLink, pp. 128–142 (2004)
4. Satyanarayanan, M.: Pervasive Computing: Vision and Challenges. IEEE Personal Communications (2001)
5. Patterson, C.A., Muntz, R.R., Pancake, C.M: Challenges in Location-Aware Computing. IEEE Pervasive Computing 2(2), pp. 80–89 (2003)
6. Roman, G.-C., Picco, G.P., Murphy, A.L.: Software engineering for mobility: a roadmap, in The Future of Software Engineering. Limerick, Ireland (2000)
7. Kristoffersen, S., Ljungberg, F.: Mobile Informatics Innovation of IT Use in Mobile Settings: IRIS'21 Workshop Report. SIGCHI Bulletin, vol. 31(1) (1999)
8. Küpper, A., Spaniol, O.: Evaluation of strategies for supporting personal mobility and service portability, in 2000 IEEE Service Portability and Virtual Customer Environments (2000)
9. Sun, J.-Z., Sauvola, J.: On fundamental concepts of mobility for mobile communications. In: 13th IEEE International Symposium on Personal, Indoor and Mobile Radio Communications. Lisbon, Portugal (2002)
10. Cardelli, L., Gordon, A.D.: Mobile Ambients. In: First International Conference on Foundations of Software Science and Computation Structure (1998)

11. Cardelli, L.: Abstractions for Mobile Computation. , Microsoft Research, Microsoft Corporation (1998)
12. Ylianttila, M.: Vertical handoff and mobility - system architecture and transition analysis, University of Oulu: Finland, pp. 70 (2005)
13. Stemm, M., Katz, R.H.: Vertical handoffs in wireless overlay networks. Mobile Networks and Applications, vol. 3(4) (1998)
14. Bellavista, P., Cinque, M., Cotroneo, D., Foschini, L.: Integrated support for handoff management and context awareness in heterogeneous wireless networks. In: 3rd International Workshop on Middleware for Pervasive and Ad-hoc Computing MPAC '05. ACM Press, New York (2005)
15. Tourrilhes, J.: L7-mobility: a framework for handling mobility at the application level. In: 15th IEEE International Symposium on Personal, Indoor and Mobile Radio Communications (2004)
16. ATLAS Transformation Language (ATL) homepage. http://www.eclipse.org/gmt/atl/
17. MOFScript homepage. http://www.eclipse.org/gmt/mofscript/
18. Paspallis, N., Papadopoulos, G.A.: Distributed Adaptation Reasoning for a Mobility and Adaptation Enabling Middleware. In: 30th Annual International Computer Software and Applications Conference (COMPSAC 2006), IEEE Computer Society Press, Los Alamitos (2006)
19. Kosiuczenko, P.: Sequence diagrams for mobility. in ER/IFIP 8.1 Workshop on Conceptual Modelling Approaches to Mobile Information Systems Development (MobIMod), Tampere, Finland. Springer, Heidelberg (2002)
20. Baumeister, H., Koch, N., Kosiuczenko, P., Wirsing, M.: Extending Activity Diagrams to Model Mobile Systems. In: Revised Papers from the International Conference NetObjectDays on Objects, Components, Architectures, Services, and Applications for a Networked World, Springer, Heidelberg (2002)
21. Grassi, V., Mirandola, R., Sabetta, A.: UML based Modeling and Performance Analysis of Mobile Systems. In: 7th ACM International Symposium on Modeling, Analysis and Simulation of Wireless and Mobile Systems, ACM Press, New York (2004)

A Planning Method for Component Placement in Smart Item Environments Using Heuristic Search

Jürgen Anke[1,2], Bernhard Wolf[1], Gregor Hackenbroich[1], and Klaus Kabitzsch[2]

[1] SAP Research CEC Dresden, Germany
[2] Dresden University of Technology, Institute of Applied Computer Science, Germany
{juergen.anke, gregor.hackenbroich, b.wolf}@sap.com,
kk10@inf.tu-dresden.de

Abstract. Smart item environments consist of networked nodes with heterogeneous hardware equipment and intermittent network connections. Using a common component technology allows for flexible distribution of components for processing of smart item data. Finding a good deployment plan for a new set of components in an infrastructure is called Component Placement Problem. We propose an approach for finding suitable deployment plans for components with special regard to the characteristics of smart item environments. Our method evaluates deployment plans in terms of both resource consumption and availability. From the analysis of the solution space we conclude that the number of network link uses is an important criterion for the quality of a deployment plan regarding both cost and availability. Based on this finding, we have derived a heuristic that creates deployment plans, which have a low number of link uses and are thus more likely of high quality.[1]

1 Introduction

Smart items are physical products that include product embedded information devices (PEIDs), e.g. embedded systems, or RFID tags. For application domains such as Product Lifecycle Management (PLM), enterprise applications benefit from accessing data on smart items. Error-prone manual data input can be replaced with automatic data acquisition to support business decisions, e.g. for maintenance planning, effective recycling, and product design improvements. As it is not reasonable to integrate mechanisms for accessing PEIDs into business applications, this functionality is provided by a middleware. The middleware and the PEIDs form the *smart item environment*, which can be distributed in a network over various nodes. A key characteristic of smart item environments is a high degree of heterogeneity in terms of hardware resources. Typically, there is a powerful middleware server which is contacted by client applications to request smart item data. The requests are then forwarded to other nodes in the field, which translate the requests into a PEID specific protocol. Finally, the PEIDs are embedded systems, which contain the data sources and have very limited resources. In general, available resources are decreasing towards the edge of the network.

[1] Parts of this work are based on the PROMISE project (www.promise.no), which is funded by the European Union IST 6th Framework program, project no 507100.

J. Indulska and K. Raymond (Eds.): DAIS 2007, LNCS 4531, pp. 309–322, 2007.

All nodes in the smart item environment can contain a standardised execution environment, such as OSGi [1] or Jini [2]. This turns the smart item environment into a distributed execution environment, allowing for flexible placement of components that format, analyse, filter, or pre-process the data flows between backend applications and smart items [3]. If a new set of components (a *component composition*) has to be deployed onto the smart item environment, each component has to be assigned to a host. The assignment of a component to a host is called *component placement*, and hence finding a set of good assignments is the *component placement problem* (CPP) [4]. A *deployment plan* is a set of component placements for a given component composition. Previously, we have proposed a method to identify good deployment plans in smart item environments based on the *cost of demanded resources* [5]. The cost of demanded resources is an important evaluation criterion as resources on the various hosts and network links are differently valued in heterogeneous environments.

However, considering the cost of resource demands alone is not sufficient to identify suitable deployment plans. Most products are mobile and therefore communicate with middleware over wireless connections, which influences the *availability* of PEID data. Availability is defined as the degree to which a system or component is operational and accessible when it is required for use [6]. In a distributed component-based system, the availability depends on the placement of components [7,8,9] and hence availability is also a relevant evaluation criterion for deployment plans. Intuitively, the availability increases when the amount of data to be transferred over unreliable connections decreases. This can be achieved by placing components on the PEIDs to perform data analysis locally and transmit only the analysis results. However, this competes with the goal of minimising cost of resource demands as resources on the PEIDs are much more expensive than on other nodes. This trade-off has not been investigated in the context of component deployment planning. Instead, existing approaches use a single evaluation criterion to determine the quality of deployment plans (see section 3).

In this paper, we propose a component deployment planning method, which is applicable for smart item environments. More specifically, we propose an extended system model, evaluation functions for both cost and availability, and methods to determine model parameters. Using a practical application, we found that the number of network link uses is an important driver for the quality of a deployment plan. Based on that finding, we propose a heuristic for creating deployment plans with few network link uses. We show that applying this heuristic leads to good results in very short time.

The remainder of the paper is structured as follows: First, the characteristics of smart item environments are discussed and a set of requirements for deployment planning are derived. Afterwards, we review related work and point out their shortcomings with regard to our problem. In section 4 our solution is presented in an overview. Section 5 contains the core model for the CPP including evaluation functions and constraints. The extension of this model for smart item infrastructures is shown in section 6, where we propose methods to determine availability and resource demands. Finally, in section 7 it is investigated whether the two dimensions cost and availability are competitive, i.e. form a trade-off. Furthermore, we show that the number of network link uses is a major driver for the quality of deployment plans and present an algorithm, which creates deployment plans based on this heuristic.

2   Problem Analysis

Smart item environments have some characteristics which place special requirements on deployment planning methods. Here, these characteristics are briefly discussed to derive requirements from them. The requirements provide a rationale for the deployment planning method we propose and serve as basis for identifying weaknesses in related works. The main characteristics of smart item environments are:

- **Heterogeneity of infrastructure:** Infrastructure nodes in the smart item environment can range from resource-constraint embedded system, to conventional personal computers and middleware servers with vast resources. Network links connecting these nodes do also have different capacities.
- **Intermittent connections:** PEIDs are typically connected to the middleware using wireless connections that are not permanently available. This is either due to restrictions in the technology, e.g. mobile phone networks do not have full coverage, or a result of application specifics. For instance, if a PEID in a truck connects to a middleware access point in a depot using wireless LAN, it is unavailable during the time when the truck is not in connection range.
- **Distributed data sources:** Smart item environments are mainly employed to collect and analyse product data, e.g. static product information, the product structure, the operational status of the product, as well as historical records of owners, users, maintenance operations, etc. This data can be provided from local memory of the PEID or read from sensors that are integrated in the product. Other examples for data sources are rule repositories used for data analysis and thresholds, which might be stored on a middleware server. These data sources have a certain location in the infrastructure and send a response of a certain size when they are queried.

A deployment planning method for smart item environments has to take all these characteristics into consideration by fulfilling the following requirements:

1. **Consider cost of demanded resources:** The method shall consider the cost of resource demands at different hosts in the infrastructure. Although there are various resources, the method should at least take CPU, memory, and bitrate into account. These are the resources that are particularly scarce at the edge of the network, e.g. an embedded system has only a small memory, a very limited CPU power, and might only have low-bitrate connectivity, such as GPRS[2] or IEEE 802.15.4[3].
2. **Evaluate the effect of intermittent connections:** Intermittent connections influence the availability of data in the smart item environment. Component deployment plans can lead to better or worse availability. Therefore the method shall evaluate the effects of intermittent connections on the availability.
3. **Explicit modelling of distributed data sources:** Resource consumption depends on the data amounts that have to be transferred between the components and thus between their hosts in the infrastructure. As the traffic originates from the distributed data sources, the method shall provide means to explicitly model the location and message sizes of data sources.

---

[2] General Packet Radio Service, a packet-oriented communication protocol on GSM mobile phone networks.

[3] An IEEE standard for low-rate Wireless Personal Area Network (WPAN) connectivity.

3 Related Work

There is currently no component deployment planning method, which specifically addresses the domain of smart item environments. Hence, we review existing methods from related areas, e.g. mobile applications, grids, and computing clusters.

Mikic-Rakic *et al* present (re-)deployment planning for components in the context of PRISM [10], a middleware for distributed and mobile applications. In this environment, hosts are resource-constrained devices connected with intermittent wireless links. Component redeployment aims to improve the availability of a system. Special focus is put on the evaluation of planning algorithms, e.g. an approximative algorithm based on ordered lists of hosts and components [8], a decentralised algorithm with an auctioning mechanism [9], greedy and clustering algorithms [11]. The input model allows specifying memory constraints, and evaluation of bandwidth constraints through frequency of message exchanges between components and the average message size. The approach is very comprehensive, however, it does neither support the modelling of data sources nor evaluation of CPU utilisation. It also does not consider different costs of resources.

Another approach [4] was proposed for resource-aware deployment planning for component in grid environments based on Artificial Intelligence (AI) methods. For each component the required CPU and bandwidth must be defined to compute a resource-optimal deployment plan, which fulfils a deployment goal specified by the user (such as component $c1$ should run on host $h1$). Additional components for encryption, caching, compression etc. may be added to the deployment plan to adapt the resource demands to the infrastructure's capacities. Although the presented approach is sophisticated, it is not suitable for our purposes, as it does not support heterogeneous infrastructures and modelling of data sources. Also, the effect of intermittent connections is not considered.

Steward *et al* propose automatic deployment for components of a J2EE application running on a cluster of computers [12]. This method aims to find a deployment that maximises the throughput of the distributed application but does not evaluate resource consumption. The method is not applicable for smart item environments as it assumes homogeneity of nodes. Deployment plans are evaluated only in terms of throughput but not for cost or availability. Finally, modelling of data sources is not possible.

Dynamic networks with intermittent connections play a key role in the deployment method for hierarchical components in a heterogeneous distributed system [13]. Unlike other approaches, the deployment plan is not calculated in advance but determined dynamically during the deployment process in a propagative manner. In the context of our elaborated requirements the approach is not applicable, as it only seeks a satisfying solution rather than evaluating different valid deployment plans. Furthermore, it does not support modelling of data sources and different costs for resources in the network.

An allocation algorithm for the placement of complex CORBA components is presented by Wu *et al* [14]. The method supports modelling of resource demands and constraints as well as global weighting of the resources memory, CPU and bandwidth according to their importance in the respective situation. Components are placed in order of their allocation priority, which is derived from the weighted ratio of resource demand and sum of available resource across all containers. However, the method neither considers intermittent connections, nor supports modelling of data sources. It does not allow for assigning different costs for these resources on each host. Finally, the modelling used in this approach is very complex, which is appropriate for CORBA components but less applicable for the simple data processing components in our case.

In summary, existing component deployment methods do not model distributed data sources and are all based on a single evaluation criterion. Resource constraints are considered in some approaches but no cost-based evaluation of resource demands is performed, i.e. the resources are valued the same on all hosts. It can be assumed that the degree of heterogeneity in scenarios addressed by existing methods was low, which made cost-based evaluation unnecessary.

4   Proposed Solution

We propose a solution to the component placement problem that addresses the requirements stated above. Its overall approach is to create and rank deployment plan candidates by evaluating their cost of resource demands and their availability (Figure 1). Expected resource demands are determined, and added as annotation to the composition model. On the basis of a given deployment plan, these demands are mapped to the infrastructure model to relate the demands with the respective cost and capacities. If no resource constraints are violated, the availability of the system and the cost of utilised resources is calculated and compared to the best plans found so far. When all deployment plan candidates have been evaluated or the maximum number of plans to evaluate have been reached, the best ranking deployment plans are presented to the user.

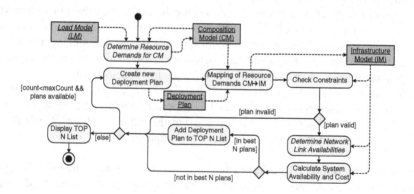

Fig. 1. Solution overview

Details of our solution are presented in the next two sections as follows:

Core Model. The basis of our solution is the core model of the component placement problem, which consists of the following elements:

- *Composition Model (CM)*, which specifies the composition of components, their dependencies, and resource demands. It contains the data sink and data sources.
- *Infrastructure Model (IM)* describing the structure of the network, the resource capacities of each host and network link, and cost per unit for these resources.

- *Mapping function* describing the assignment of components to hosts for mapping resource demands in the CM to resource capacities and costs in the IM.
- *Constraints* to validate deployment plans.
- *Evaluation functions* to calculate quality measures (availability and cost of demanded resources) of valid deployment plans.

Determining Model Parameters for Smart Item Environments. The model requires a number of parameters, which have to be supplied when the model is applied for component deployment in smart item environments. We go beyond estimating these parameters by proposing methods to determine availability as well as the demands for bitrate and CPU based on a load model. As these methods for determining parameters are decoupled from the CPP model, they can easily replaced by other ones when appropriate. Activities related to determining parameters are highlighted with italics in Figure 1.

5   Core Model of the CPP

Composition Model. The composition model is represented as a connected, directed composition graph G, consisting of a set of nodes C and set of dependencies (edges) $D \subseteq C \times C$. The set C consists of a set of nodes C_R that can be relocated and a set C_F of nodes which are fixed to a specific host. The number of relocatable components C and dependencies D is the cardinality of the respective set: $C = |C_R|$ and $D = |D|$.

- *Data Sources and Data Sink* It is characteristic for each component that it receives an input and produces an output of data. Therefore, each component depends on one or more other components. Besides components there are two other node types in the composition graph: First, there can be one or more data sources that only provide output of data. Second, there must be exactly one data sink, which only receives data input. Data sink and data sources represent endpoints in the composition graph and belong to the set C_F as they are fixed to a specific host.
- *Resource Demands* For all components $c \in C$ a resource demand $R_z(c)$, where $z = \{mem, cpu\}$ depends on memory and CPU power. Similarly, for all dependencies $d \in D$ in the composition graph we assign the required bitrate $R_{br}(d)$ for the communication between the respective two components.

Infrastructure Model. The infrastructure onto which components are to be deployed, is modelled using a connected, undirected infrastructure graph I. It consists of a set of hosts $\mathcal{H}$ and a set of network links $\mathcal{L} \subseteq \mathcal{H} \times \mathcal{H}$.

- *Resource Capacities* For each host $h \in \mathcal{H}$ the available capacity $S_z(h)$ of memory and CPU are stored, $z = \{mem, cpu\}$. The same applies to network links, each of which holds a value $S_{br}(l)$ describing its available bitrate of each link $l \in \mathcal{L}$.
- *Cost of Resource Units* As mentioned before, we use a cost-based evaluation of resource demands to address the heterogeneity of hosts and network links in the infrastructure. Thus, we assign the costs $W_z(h)$, $W_{br}(l)$ for a unit of memory and CPU power consumption, and for a required unit of bandwidth, respectively.
- *Network Availability* Each network link l in the infrastructure is assigned a value $0 \le a(l) \le 1$ describing the availability of that link. This measure is important for evaluating the system's availability of a given deployment plan later on.

Assignment of Components to Hosts. For deployment planning, every component c_j is assigned to a host h_i. Such an assignment is called a *component placement*:

$$c_j \rightarrow v(c_j) = h_i.$$

A *deployment plan* $v : \mathcal{C} \rightarrow \mathcal{H}$ is a set of component placements, such that each component of $\mathcal{C}$ is assigned exactly to one host of $\mathcal{H}$. On the opposite, every host can have assigned $0..C$ relocatable components. The *set of all deployment plans* is denoted by $\mathcal{V}$ and has the cardinality $V = |\mathcal{V}| = H^C$.

Constraints

Static Assignments. The subset of nodes C_F in the composition graph are statically assigned to hosts, i.e. these assignments are the same in all deployment plans. *Static assignments* are primarily used for data sources and the data sink as they can not be relocated. Additionally, user-defined static assignments are possible, if a component has to be placed on a specific host.

Resource Constraints. Besides static assignments, we have the requirement that the demand for resources does not exceed the capacity of infrastructure elements. For the hosts this requirement implies that the resource demand does not exceed the capacity

$$\sum_{j,v(c_j)=h_i} R_z(c_j) \leq S_z(h_i).$$

Likewise it is necessary to formulate the constraint for the maximum bitrate demand on network links. This is more complicated as the communication between any pair of components can affect multiple network links in the infrastructure, if the two components are deployed to hosts which are not directly connected with each other. To formulate this constraint, we consider the communication path $\mathcal{P}$ between two components c_i and c_j within the infrastructure at a given deployment plan v. This path is a set of network links connecting the hosts $v(c_i)$ and $v(c_j)$ on which the components reside.

Now the constraint for the maximum bitrate demand on network link l, requires that the sum of all communication between neighbouring components that use this network link to be less than the capacity of this link:

$$\sum_{<i,j>} Q_l(\mathcal{P}(c_i, c_j)) \cdot R_{br}(d(c_i, c_j)) \leq S_{br}(l).$$

Here, we introduced the projection:

$$Q_l(\mathcal{P}(c_i, c_j)) = \begin{cases} 1 & \text{, if link } l \text{ belongs to the path } \mathcal{P}, \\ 0 & \text{, else.} \end{cases}$$

Evaluation functions. If a valid deployment plan was found, both its cost of resource demands and its availability is evaluated. Although both measures can be used independently for evaluating deployment plans, it may be assumed that high availability implies high cost of resource demands.

Cost of demanded resources. The cost of resource demands for a given deployment plan v is the total cost of resource demands, cumulated over all hosts and network links.

$$K(v) = \sum_{i=1}^{H} \sum_{z} Res_z(i) \cdot W_z(i) + \sum_{j=1}^{L} Res_{br}(j) \cdot W_{br}(j) \tag{1}$$

Here, L is the number of network links, H is the number of hosts in the infrastructure and $Res_z(i)$ is the total demand for resource z on host i. Similarly, $Res_{br}(j)$ denotes the total bitrate demand on network link k.

Availability. For the evaluation of a deployment plan's availability, the availabilities $a(l)$ of all individual network links have to be aggregated. Availabilities can be considered as probabilities of success for communication between pairs of components over network links l. The availability of the deployment plan is determined by the product

$$A(v) = \prod_{l=1}^{L} a(l). \tag{2}$$

We note, that the determination of the link availability $a(l)$ is not trivial. We explain the method we have used in section 6.2.

6   Determining Model Parameters for Smart Item Environments

To use the presented core model for deployment planning, it has to be instantiated with actual values for the input parameters. In this section, we explain methods on how resource demands and the availability can be determined. As these methods are decoupled from the core model, it allows for any other way to determine the input parameters.

6.1   Determining Resource Demands

Some resource demands depend on other inputs and have to be calculated before a deployment plan can be evaluated. In principle, we follow an approach proposed by Steward *et al* [12]. It estimates resource demand for components based on "resource profiles", which are created "off-line" by measurements under different workloads.

Load Model. To calculate component-level resource demands, except memory, the load placed on the composition has to be known. Load refers to the number of requests a user issues over a period of time. Generally, the requests over time are POISSON-distributed. As our method only considers static deployment planning, the mean value of this distribution (λ-parameter) is sufficient to characterise the load. This parameter is named *iph* (invocations per hour) and does logically belong to the data sink.

Besides the number of invocations, also the message sizes to be transferred have to be defined in the load model. As the data originates from the data sources, the message sizes are logically assigned to them. Therefore, for each data source the size of the message returned when it is queried has to be specified in the load model.

Bitrate. Bitrate demand $R_{br}(d)$ for the communication between components depends on the message sizes to process and the load. By multiplying the size of the message to process with the invocation per hour iph, we get the incoming bitrate. At each invocation, the incoming data is processed into outgoing data, whereby the size of outgoing data can be different. One approach to model this for simple functional blocks in building automation is used by Plönnigs et al. They use an amplification factor ($gain$) to describe the relation of inputs to outputs in processing devices [15]. We extend this by using a linear function o_c to describe the input/output-relation for each component

$$IORel : o_c(i_c) = e_c \cdot i_c + f_c.$$

Here, o_c is the output of component c, which depends on the input i_c, the amplification factor e_c and the bias f_c. In our model, the input i_c is the sum of all incoming bitrates for a component. Note that e_c and f_c are constant during the calculation.

CPU Power. The CPU demand $R_{cpu}(c)$ is calculated with a method proposed by Steward et al. [12], who used it to plan component distribution in a server cluster for maximum throughput. They describe the CPU demand as linear function, whereby load is the independent variable. The coefficient a_c and the constant g_c were gained by linear regression on a series of CPU utilisation measurements under different loads.

$$R_{cpu} : p_c(i_c) = a_c \cdot i_c + g_c$$

We adopt this method and use the amount of data to be processed by the respective component as load i_c. For each component, such a linear function has to be determined with different data amounts rather than with requests per second. A major difference between our work and the work by Steward et al is the heterogeneity in the infrastructure. While a server cluster consists of identical machines, the CPU power in a smart item environment is diverse. Therefore, we propose to compute the CPU demand function on a reference system, and adjust CPU capacities on each host to reflect its CPU power in relation to the reference system. For example, if an embedded system has only 5% of the CPU power of the reference system, its CPU capacity is set to 5. We recognise that this method allows only for a rough estimation of CPU demands. However, in our view it is a good balance between model complexity and accuracy for our purpose.

6.2 Determining Availability

For the evaluation of the system's availability (Equation (2) in section 5) the availability of all network links in the infrastructure is needed. To characterise intermittent network links, we introduce two parameters: (a) Mean connection duration d_C, and (b) Mean pause duration d_P (see Figure 2). We present three different methods for calculating the availability of a network link, which is understood as probability of success for:

1. Network link availability
2. Immediate successful execution of a request
3. Successful execution of a request within a given time frame

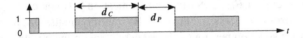

Fig. 2. Parameters to describe an intermittent connection

For simplicity we will denote availability as $a(l)$ for these probabilities and the specific context clarifies the meaning in each case.

(1) The probability of network link availability is the ratio between connection duration d_C and the duration between two connection establishments $(d_C + d_P)$

$$a = \frac{d_C}{d_C + d_P} \tag{3}$$

(2) The probability of immediate successful execution of a request considers the time required to transfer the requested data amount. Based on the data amount msg and the capacity of the network link S_{br}, the required transfer time d_T can be determined by $d_T(l) = \frac{msg}{S_{br}(l)}$. The transfer of the requested data amount is successful, if both the connection is available and the transfer was started before the connection is terminated.

$$a = \frac{d_C}{d_C + d_P} \cdot \frac{d_C - d_T}{d_C} = \frac{d_C - d_T}{d_C + d_P} \tag{4}$$

This only is meaningful if the $d_T < d_C$, otherwise the request will not be successful and the availability of the whole system is set to 0.

(3) For the probability of successful execution of a request within a given time frame, a maximum time d_{max} has to be specified. The calculation is based on probability of the n-fold repetition of the complementary event ("transmission unsuccessful"):

$$a = 1 - (1 - \frac{d_C - d_T}{d_C + d_P})^n \ , \ \text{whereby} \ n = \frac{d_{max}}{d_C + d_P} \mid n \geq 1 . \tag{5}$$

Multiple Uses of Links. All equations defined in this section determine the availability of a network link for a single transmission. As every dependency in the composition graph represents a service invocation (request) and its result (response), the network link is used twice for each dependency mapped to it. Moreover, several dependencies can be assigned to a network link. If a link is used multiple times, its availability is the product of all availabilities for each individual use. For each use, the required transmission time d_T might be different. Therefore, we consider the transmission time d_{Ti} for transmission i to determine availability using Equation (4) for multiple uses by

$$a = \prod_i \left(\frac{d_C - d_{Ti}}{d_C + d_P} \right) .$$

Similarly, the availability can be calculated with Equation (3) and Equation (5). In each case, it can be seen that the availability decreases when the number of network link uses increases.

7 Analysis of the Solution Space

We validate our proposed method by analysing the results of a practical application, which deals with maintenance planning for trucks and was adapted and extended from an earlier publication [5]. It consists of 11 components, which are to be deployed onto an infrastructure with 3 hosts. We show the solution space for all valid deployment plans and identify the location of the best deployment plans in it. Furthermore, the influence of the number of network uses on both cost and availability is analysed.

7.1 Analysis of Competition

The complete solution space for the base scenario is depicted in Figure 3.1. It shows the cost and availability of all valid component deployment plans. The best deployment plans (low cost and high availability) are located in the upper left corner of the diagram. Data points representing the best deployment plans are highlighted with circles and bounded by a rectangle, which marks the area between the two extremal points of lowest cost and highest availability. All deployment plans which are not highlighted can be discarded as they are definitely worse than the highlighted ones. There are 35 deployment plans which were identified as "best". For clarity, we name these "deployment plan candidates".

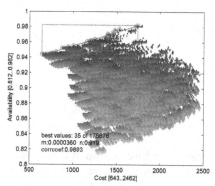

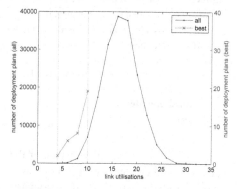

Fig. 3.1 Complete solution space

Fig. 3.2 Distribution of network link uses

7.2 Number of Network Link Uses

We have analysed the effect of the number of network link uses on the quality of deployment plans. As briefly discussed in section 6.2, the availability depends on how many times a network link is used. Furthermore, the cost is also influenced by this measure as the cost for transmission depends on how much bitrate demand from dependencies is mapped to network links. Therefore, it can be assumed that the number of network link uses is an important factor for the quality of a deployment plan.

To verify this hypothesis with our example, the number of network link uses is represented by the colour of data points in Figure 3.1, whereby darker points represent deployment plans with fewer link uses. As it can be seen, there is a tendency that good deployment plans utilise network links fewer times. To further investigate this, we have analysed the position of the best deployment plans in the distribution of link uses.

As Figure 3.2 shows, the deployment plan candidates utilise network links 10 times or less in this example. This is an important finding, which helps to design a heuristic search for good deployment plans in the solution space without complete evaluation of all possible combinations.

8   A Heuristic Algorithm for Finding Deployment Plans

From our findings, we have derived a heuristic algorithm that finds good deployment plans without scanning the whole solution space.

Heuristic Generation of Deployment Plans. As depicted in Figure 1, our method creates a number of deployment plans for evaluation and stores the best found ones. Using the heuristic that a low number of network uses are a characteristic of good deployment plans, our algorithm places neighbouring components only on the same hosts or on neighbouring hosts. Therefore each dependency of the composition model is mapped only to either 0 or 1 network links. The recursive algorithm is initialially invoked with the data sink as argument (see Algorithm 1).

Algorithm 1. placeDependentComp($start$)

1: find host h on which $start$ is placed
2: find all hosts H_n, which are direct neighbours of h
3: find all components K_n, on which $start$ depends
4: **for all** k_j in K_n **do**
5:      randomly select host h_i from $(H_n \cup h)$
6:      place k_j on h_i
7:      **placeDependentComp(k_j)**
8: **end for**

Evaluation. To evaluate the quality of the heuristic, we have compared it to another method, which creates deployment plans based on random placements of components to hosts. Both the heuristic and random assignments were used to evaluate various percentages of all combinatoric possible deployment plans. The quality criterion used is the mean euclidean distance of found deployment plan candidates to the nearest plan found by an exact algorithm, i.e. the optimum.

The results in Figure 4 show that the deployment plan candidates found by the heuristic algorithm are closer to the optimum than almost all random component placements. Furthermore, it shows that good results can achieved without evaluating a large number of deployment plans. However, it can also be seen that the optimum is not reached. The reason for this is that the highest availability is achieved in this scenario by placing all components on the embedded system. This means that there is more than one network link between the data source and the first dependent component. This is prevented by the heuristic algorithm which only allows a maximum distance of one host between any pair of neighbouring components.

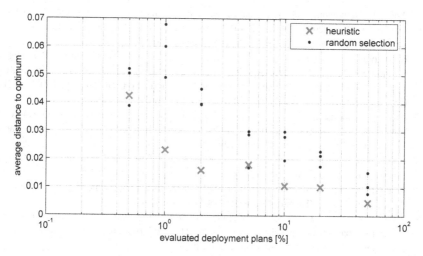

Fig. 4. Evaluation of Heuristic Accuracy

9 Conclusion and Outlook

We have presented a deployment planning method for components that addresses specifically distributed components in smart item environments. These networks are characterised by a high degree of heterogeneity in terms of available hardware resources. The main contribution of this paper is a concept for evaluating deployment plans both in terms of availability and cost of demanded resource. We have shown that these two criteria compete with each other among the deployment plan candidates in the solution space. Furthermore, we have presented a comprehensive model for component deployment, which might serve as basis for other research questions in the domain of smart item environments. Additionally, we have identified the number of network link uses as a key driver for the quality of a deployment plan and derived a heuristic from this finding. As the evaluation showed, the application of this heuristic helps to find very good deployment plans after testing only a small fraction of all possible plans.

In the future, our work will focus on improved heuristic algorithms for creating deployment plans which are likely of high quality. For that, additional characteristics of good deployment plans, such as the average distance of components to the data sinks, are investigated and integrated into the algorithms.

Acknowledgements

The authors would like to thank Mario Neugebauer and Eric Neuber for their valuable comments, and Jürgen Zimmermann for his support with the implementation.

References

1. OSGi Alliance: Open Services Gateway Initiative (2006)
2. SUN Microsystems: Jini Network Technology (2006)

3. Anke, J., Neugebauer, M.: Early data processing in smart item environments using mobile services. In: Proceedings of the 12th IFAC Symposium on Information Control Problems in Manufacturing (INCOM 06) St. Etienne, France (2006)
4. Kichkaylo, T., Karamcheti, V.: Optimal Resource-Aware Deployment Planning for Component-Based Distributed Applications. In: Proceedings of the 13th IEEE International Symposium on High Performance Distributed Computing (HPDC'04), pp. 150–159. IEEE Computer Society, Los Alamitos (2004)
5. Anke, J., Kabitzsch, K.: Cost-based Deployment Planning for Components in Smart Item Environments. 11th IEEE International Conference on Emerging Technologies and Factory Automation, Prague, Czech Republic (2006)
6. Institute of Electrical and Electronics Engineers: IEEE Standard Computer Dictionary: A Compilation of IEEE Standard Computer Glossaries, New York (1990)
7. Wegdam, M.: Dynamic reconfiguration and load distribution in component middleware. PhD thesis, University of Twente, Enschede (2003)
8. Mikic-Rakic, M., Malek, S., Medvidovic, N.: Improving availability in large, distributed component-based systems via redeployment. Third International Working Conference on Component Deployment, Grenoble, France (2005)
9. Malek, S., Mikic-Rakic, M., Medvidovic, N.: A decentralized redeployment algorithm for improving the availability of distributed systems. Third International Working Conference on Component Deployment (2005)
10. Malek, S., Mikic-Rakic, M.: A style-aware architectural middleware for resource-constrained, distributed systems. IEEE Trans. Softw. Eng. 31(3), 256–272 (2005)
11. Mikic-Rakic, M., Malek, S., Beckman, N., Medvidovic, N.: A tailorable environment for assessing the quality of deployment architectures in highly distributed settings. Second International Working Conference on Component Deployment, Edinburgh, UK (2004)
12. Stewart, C., Shen, K., Dwarkadas, S., Scott, M.L., Yin, J.: Profile-driven component placement for cluster-based online services. IEEE Distributed Systems Online 5(10), 1 (2004)
13. Hoareau, D., Mahéo, Y.: Constraint-Based Deployment of Distributed Components in a Dynamic Network. In: Grass, W., Sick, B., Waldschmidt, K. (eds.) ARCS 2006. LNCS, vol. 3894, pp. 450–464. Springer, Heidelberg (2006)
14. Wu, Q., Wu, Z.: Adaptive component allocation in scudware middleware for ubiquitous computing. In: Yang, L.T., Amamiya, M., Liu, Z., Guo, M., Rammig, F.J. (eds.) EUC 2005. LNCS, vol. 3824, pp. 1155–1164. Springer, Heidelberg (2005)
15. Plönnigs, J., Neugebauer, M., Kabitzsch, K.: A traffic model for networked devices in the building automation. In: Proceedings of the 5th IEEE International Workshop on Factory Communication Systems (WFCS 2004) Vienna, Austria, pp. 137–145 (2004)

A Generic Infrastructure for Decentralised Dynamic Loading of Platform-Specific Code

Rüdiger Kapitza[1], Holger Schmidt[2], Udo Bartlang[3], and Franz J. Hauck[2]

[1] Dept. of Comp. Sciences, Informatik 4, University of Erlangen-Nürnberg, Germany
rrkapitz@cs.fau.de
[2] Institute of Distributed Systems, Ulm University, Germany
{holger.schmidt,franz.hauck}@uni-ulm.de
[3] Siemens AG, Corporate Technology, Munich, Germany
udo.bartlang.ext@siemens.com

Abstract. Dynamic loading of code is a crucial and often neglected part of today's distributed systems that face increasing dynamics, complexity and heterogeneity. Ubiquitous computing and mobile computing even strengthen this trend. As the local availability of suitable code cannot be assumed in such environments, we propose a generic, decentralised code loading infrastructure. The whole process of publication, look-up, implementation selection and the final loading of platform-specific code is decentralised and requires only basic peer-to-peer functionality. In contrast to previous work, our infrastructure allows any peer participating in the network to offer and to obtain platform-specific code in a dynamic and heterogeneous environment. By building on our generic concept, we present a JXTA-based service for dynamic code loading, which is realised by extending and improving JXTA-built-in mechanisms for dynamic service integration. Subsequently, we show the practical application of our infrastructure by an integration into our CORBA middleware and an implementation of mobile objects and mobile web services.

Keywords: CORBA, Dynamic Loading of Code, JXTA, Peer-to-Peer, Web Services.

1 Introduction

Distributed applications of any domain face the trend of raising complexity, dynamics and heterogeneity of software and hardware. Two prominent protagonists that emphasise this development are ubiquitous computing [1], targeting distributed applications on small, mostly embedded devices, and planetary-scale execution environments for globally available services such as PlanetLab [2] and Xenoserver [3].

In both cases, applications—especially distributed ones—have the requirement to dynamically load additional code at run-time if that code is not already bound to the local execution environment. There, challenges to dynamic code loading arise if rarely used code has to be loaded on demand or if code to load is not even known in advance. This is a common problem, as distributed applications usually have numerous independently running application parts, which results in some code modules not being

J. Indulska and K. Raymond (Eds.): DAIS 2007, LNCS 4531, pp. 323–336, 2007.

known at compile or even at start-up time. However, it is desirable that newly developed code can be used by already running execution environments. Additionally, for some distributed applications it is not feasible to install and load all code modules at every node of the system. For example, some code modules might only be used by a few of the nodes, and these nodes may not be known in advance or may have resource restrictions.

For addressing these problems, we recently proposed a dynamic loading service that enables the dynamic loading of platform-specific code [4]. However, this work follows a classical client/server-based approach relying on a central component managing metadata of all know implementations and their variants. In contrast to that approach, this paper proposes a generic and decentralised peer-to-peer-based lookup, selection and loading process. This allows multiple parties to independently and non-reliably provide implementations for a certain object or component. Building on this generic concept, a prototype was implemented that uses existing concepts of the JXTA platform [5] to dynamically select and load code based on metadata descriptions called *advertisements*. These advertisements are extended to provide a truly platform-independent support for the dynamic loading of platform-specific code. JXTA is used because of its flexibility: it allows replacing routing mechanisms (e.g., unstructured replaced by structured topology) without having to change the application, i.e. our prototype, itself.

We evaluated the proposed and implemented system by its integration as a common CORBA service to support mobile objects, and ported this approach to a web-service infrastructure. Then, we integrated the infrastructure into our CORBA-compliant middleware Aspectix [6], to extend the support for fragmented objects. Summarising the results of the use cases, the proposed infrastructure meets all demands to dynamically select and load code for CORBA objects, web services, and fragmented objects within heterogeneous execution environments.

In the following section, a platform-independent and decentralised approach to dynamically discovering, selecting and loading platform-specific code is described. Starting from this point, a brief overview of the JXTA peer-to-peer middleware and its facilities for service lookup and integration is given in Section 3. Then, we describe our prototype implementation of a platform-independent peer-to-peer-based loading service. Section 5 outlines two possible use cases of our infrastructure, the integration into the CORBA-compliant middleware Aspectix and the support for the dynamic creation and migration of mobile objects and services. Finally, Section 6 presents related approaches and Section 7 concludes.

2   Generic Decentralised Dynamic Loading of Code

In the following, a generic approach to dynamically loading locally unavailable and platform-specific code is presented. As every functionality might be available in various implementations with different requirements and properties, a generic and decentralised selection process is responsible for identifying the best-fitting one for a certain environment.

2.1   Requirements and Properties for Implementation Selection

We identified three categories of properties and requirements that have to be fulfilled or at least be taken into account during the selection process (cf. Figure 1).

As an interface determines how the application deals with implemented functionality at the programming layer, new and locally unavailable functionality is identified by its *required interface*. Thereby, the interface has to be defined in a generic interface description language, e.g., using the CORBA Interface Definition Language (IDL) or the Web Service Definition Language (WSDL).

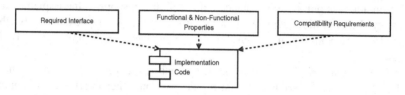

Fig. 1. An approach towards a generic code classification

Functional properties express additional functional aspects beyond the bare provision of an interface, e.g., the supported middleware platform. In general, it is hard to standardise all kinds of functional properties. However, this is a requirement for a generic selection process. Thus, we propose that an infrastructure for dynamic loading should specify well-known functional properties and delegate the evaluation of other ones to the application. Implementations providing the same functionality might also possess *non-functional properties* that specify in general quality-of-service properties, e.g., timing behavior and resource consumption of a certain implementation. In the same way as functional properties, these are hard to be standardised in general and therefore might have to be handled by the application.

Specific *compatibility requirements* for a certain implementation have to be considered as well, e.g., the required programming language and execution environment. Such approach considers the fact that exactly the same functionality can be implemented in various programming languages, e.g. in Java or C++, or for specific run-time environments, e.g. Linux or Windows. Compatibility requirements can be automatically evaluated as there is a limited set of properties (e.g., compiler, processor, operating system), outlined in detail in our former work [4], that determine whether an implementation is executable in the context of a requesting application.

2.2   Basic Infrastructure

For dynamic decentralised loading of code, we propose an infrastructure that is composed of three basic components. A *dynamic loader* provides an interface to the application for requesting locally unavailable functionality. This dynamic loader component is able to discover, to select and to integrate an appropriate implementation into the address space of the requesting application. Thereby, the searching process is supported by a *decentralised implementation repository* that stores information about available code implementations. We favour a repository on the basis of a peer-to-peer overlay network, which only has to provide support for keyword search (e.g., JXTA, Gnutella [7]). The implementation repository itself is updated by multiple *code providers*, i.e., peers, that provide implementation code and publish metadata descriptions specifying requirements and properties.

2.3   Basic Data Structure of the Implementation Repository

Using the set of properties and requirements outlined in Section 2.1 enables the selection of the best-fitting implementation code. Therefore, all data about available implementations is published as metadata descriptions in scope of the implementation repository. For omitting duplicated information and improving extensibility, these descriptions are split up into four kinds of metadata, which are each published separately.

An *interface description* contains the fully-qualified name of the interface and the interface (e.g., IDL or WSDL). Within the description, other interfaces and complex data types are also referenced by their fully-qualified names, which enables a dynamic lookup of unknown interfaces and data types.

For covering all interfaces and complex data types of a module, these are combined and published in a *module description*. There, interfaces are only referenced by name. The combination of module and interface descriptions allows a complete representation of the interface description and can be used for providing a decentralised interface repository.

An *extended functional description* specifies all functional and non-functional implementation-independent properties. These are properties provided by various implementations and therefore are used for selecting equal implementations providing the same interface. As mentioned earlier, it is hard to identify a generic set of functional and non-functional properties that apply to a major number of applications. Therefore, an implementation repository and associated dynamic loaders should provide a flexible interface that enables applications to introduce code for custom evaluation.

An *implementation description* describes a concrete implementation and its compatibility requirements. It includes a reference to the location of the code and a description of the initially accessed implementation element. In context of Java this would in general be a class name of a factory.

2.4   Basic Workflow of Publication, Selection and Loading of Code

Before publishing an implementation, a code provider has to generate appropriate metadata documents, i.e., the interface description, the extended functional description (referencing the interface description) and the implementation description (referencing the extended functional description and the concrete implementation). Then, these metadata documents are published via the decentralised code repository.

When an application requires locally unavailable functionality, it passes the fully-qualified name of the required interface and an optional handler for custom evaluation of extended functional requirements to a dynamic loader entity. This dynamic loader requests the implementation repository to look up the interface description and, if not available, passes an exception to the calling application. Then, the repository is queried for extended functional descriptions supporting the requested interface. If provided, the results are passed to the optional handler, which has to return an ordered list of appropriate extended functional descriptions starting with the best-fitting one. On the basis of this list, the dynamic loader queries the repository for implementation descriptions. These are evaluated depending on a policy, e.g., the first fulfilled implementation description is selected or all are considered and the best-fitting one is selected. After having selected an appropriate implementation description, the code has to be loaded.

3   JXTA and Dynamic Loading of Code

In this section we give a brief introduction to the JXTA platform and present JXTA's facility for dynamic loading of code.

3.1   JXTA Overview

The JXTA project was initiated by Sun Microsystems as an effort to provide a generic and open infrastructure for peer-to-peer computing. For establishing a generic basis for peer-to-peer applications, JXTA standardises fundamental functions by introducing six asynchronous query/response protocols [8].

A JXTA peer-to-peer network consists of *peers* (uniquely identifiable nodes), which syndicate to *peer groups* [9]. These peer groups permit the segmentation of the JXTA overlay and provide a set of services which are represented through *advertisements*, i.e., external programming-language-independent XML metadata representations. In general, the availability of any network resource, e.g., peers and services, is represented through advertisements with a unique identifier, which is published within a certain peer group for a special lifetime [8]. Thus, peers try to discover certain resources by searching for the corresponding advertisements.

JXTA introduces the abstraction of *pipes*, i.e., unidirectional, asynchronous, unreliable and virtual communication channels for peers within the same peer group. The endpoints of a pipe are dynamically bound at run-time, even to different peers. JXTA introduces two different kinds of pipes: a *point-to-point pipe* for unicast communication and a *propagate pipe* for multicast communication.

3.2   Dynamic Lookup and Loading of Services

For structuring and dynamically extending JXTA-based applications the infrastructure offers a generic module framework. *Modules* are managed by the framework and represent distributable units of functionality within a specific peer group that can be initialised, started and stopped by a peer. Thus, modules enable loading and integrating new services into the JXTA platform [10].

For efficiently discovering modules, the definition of a module is divided into three types of advertisements. As JXTA claims to be both language- and platform-neutral, a *module implementation advertisement* enables the differentiation of multiple module implementations, e.g., a module could be implemented in Java or C++. This advertisement specifies implementation-specific details, e.g., the actual code location. For handling different versions of a module, *module specification advertisements* are introduced, which are referenced by corresponding module implementation advertisements. Additionally, a *module class advertisement* announces the pure existence of a unique module class. It provides an abstraction for referring to a module that provides a particular class of functionality (independent from a certain specification or implementation). As multiple module specification advertisements can relate to a certain module class advertisement, references are embedded into the module class advertisement.

Recapitulating the facts, JXTA allows building a decentralised module taxonomy to support the discovery and loading of services. However, class advertisements only announce the availability of a general category of functionality. This gives developers an idea for a certain module specification and supports the selection process at a very high level, but for an automated module selection process at application level, additional conventions have to be established. Therefore, the Java reference implementation of JXTA makes implicit assumptions that a module implementation provides a certain interface for starting and stopping a module, but this is neither specified by the JXTA protocol specification nor declared by advertisements. Additionally, JXTA offers no support for determining and specifying the interface of a module offered to higher layers like an application. This makes it hard to provide multiple implementations supporting the same protocol for the same platform but providing different properties. Furthermore, module implementation advertisements should enable the providing of compatibility information but are not standardised so far. This results in JXTA implementations specifying their own format and parameters, which prevents the use of module implementations in context of different JXTA implementations. Altogether, the JXTA support for dynamic loading and integration of services leads to platform-specific implementations and does not support dynamic loading of arbitrary code.

4 A JXTA-Based Infrastructure for Decentralised Dynamic Loading of Code

Although JXTA's approach for dynamic loading of code seems to be generic and flexible, we outlined its weaknesses and shortcomings. Thus, it cannot be used as a generic and platform-independent infrastructure for dynamic code loading. In this section, we extend this infrastructure based on our generic concept for dynamic code loading, which in general only relies on support for keyword search within a peer-to-peer infrastructure (cf. Section 2).

4.1 Extended Advertisements

We extended the advertisements conforming to our specified requirements in Section 2.3 to provide an own code loading infrastructure on top of JXTA. Figure 2 shows required advertisement types and their relations. In our approach a *module class advertisement* represents the implementation interface. We define that the *name* field of the advertisement specifies the fully-qualified name of the described functionality's most-derived interface. The advertisement's *description* field is used for representing

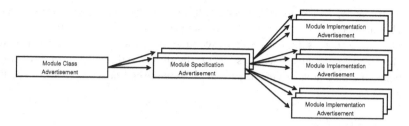

Fig. 2. Relations of extended advertisements

the interface description. As the name field of the class advertisement is indexed in the JXTA network, an interface can easily be searched by its name.

The *module specification advertisement* is mapped to an extended functional description, considering non-functional properties as well (e.g., code-versioning). We consider the protocol specification as a functional property that declares if and how a functionality is network-dependent. Additional functional and non-functional requirements are encoded into the *description* field. If the specified functionality is offered by a JXTA service, there is a pipe advertisement for addressing; otherwise the dependent field is left open.

Finally, the *module implementation advertisement* is extended using standardised compatibility requirements that we defined in previous work [4], e.g., system parameters as the used run-time environment. These requirements are stored in the *comp* field. In addition to our former work, we add platform-dependent interfaces to the compatibility requirements. This explicitly allows to specify an integration of certain functionality at platform level. In contrast to the Java JXTA reference implementation that only allows loading a JAR-file from a web server specified within a *puri* field, we provide extended facilities to reference and to transfer a code archive from an arbitrary code provider. Therefore, we embed a module specification advertisement in the *puri* element, enabling the specification of necessary functionality to communicate with a certain code provider. This enables the flexible integration of arbitrary services for the dynamic code transfer as there is no predetermined transfer protocol. A requesting peer is able to dynamically fetch a code transfer service over the peer-to-peer network. For instantiating the service, the main class is specified within the *code* element.

Such code transfer handler should either be offered via the HTTP-based code transfer support provided by JXTA or by the implementation of the basic JXTA transfer service that is described in Section 4.3. Thus, in general we assume at most one level of indirection.

4.2   Decentralised Implementation Repository

Section 3.1 introduced peer groups as a mechanism for grouping users with similar interest. In context of our prototype implementation we use a dedicated peer group (*Code Peer Group*) for publishing and discovering implementations. A *code provider*, which is described in the following subsection, publishes advertisements related to offered implementations within this peer group.

Unfortunately, JXTA binds module specification advertisements to a pipe that is again bound to a certain peer group. The consequence is that this peer group is also used as the group to address the services for execution. If this is not feasible, the dependent module specification advertisements have to be discovered, modified by providing a group-specific pipe advertisement, and finally republished in scope of the Code Peer Group.

4.3   Code Provider

As described before, JXTA provides only restricted mechanisms for code transfer and sharing. Therefore, we developed an own code provider service, which enables code sharing and transfer via the JXTA network.

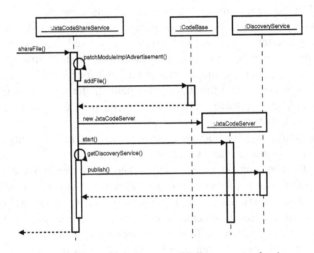

Fig. 3. Code sharing process (UML sequence chart)

Before publishing an implementation and its dependent code archive, associated advertisements have to be generated, if not already available. Therefore, a local JxtaCodeShareService object offers the core functionality to publish and to share implementations. Thereby, a code archive together with the three advertisements is passed to the JxtaCodeShareService via the shareFile() method. Then, the service contacts two other objects as shown in Figure 3. First, the JxtaCodeShareService adds its pipe advertisement for code transfer to the module specification advertisement, then it passes the archive to the CodeBase. This object administrates the locally offered code archives. Then, an instance of the autonomously working class JxtaCodeServer is created, which provides a multi-threaded server that is responsible for the file transfer via a simple JXTA-based protocol. In the last step, advertisements are published via the standard JXTA discovery service.

4.4   Dynamic Loader

The dynamic loader builds the core of our prototype. Figure 4 illustrates the collaboration between its important components. JxtaCodeHandler is the central

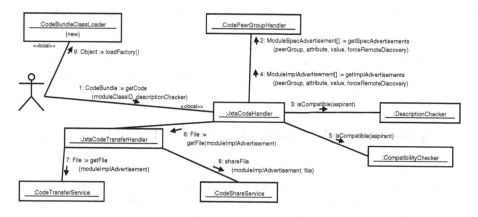

Fig. 4. Collaboration of central system components

entity during the whole dynamic loading process. It is responsible for coordination and finally initiates the code transfer.

The dynamic loader expects only a module class ID to determine the basic interface and additionally the information of a module specification advertisement to determine appropriate functionality. The module class ID can be determined by the application using the fully-qualified name of the most derived interface of the required functionality. The method `getCode()` of the `JxtaCodeHandler` enables searching for a certain module specification advertisement. Therefore, it allows key identifiers as a module class ID, name, version or a generic description within the *desc* element. The latter is achieved by passing an object that implements a `DescriptionChecker` interface that is able to perform a validity test for the concrete use case (1). For selecting a specific implementation code instance, the dynamic loader uses the module class ID for discovering corresponding module specification advertisements within the code peer group (2). Based on the module specification advertisement and the generic `DescriptionChecker`, the discovered specification advertisements can be filtered for a suitable one (3). It might be necessary to start multiple requests to the JXTA network if no suited specification advertisement is available yet. Based on the extracted module specification ID, a search for corresponding implementation advertisements can start (4). The dynamic loader compares received implementation advertisements to requirements of the local execution environment (5): An advertisement is chosen by using an object that implements a `CompatibilityChecker` interface, which is able to validate the suitability for the current execution environment. If a suited module implementation advertisement is found, the `JxtaCodeHandler` is able to initiate the code transfer, if an appropriate transfer handler is locally available (6) (Otherwise, a suited transfer handler has to be fetched recursively). This operation is transparently processed by the `JxtaCodeTransferHandler` (7). Thereby, the `JxtaCodeTransferHandler` encapsulates the whole transfer process by offering a method `getFile()` that only takes a module implementation advertisement as parameter. If the code transfer to specific provider fails, another code provider could be chosen if available. Exemplarily, a code transfer service supporting file transfer using the JXTA network is realised within our prototype implementation. If the code transfer succeeded, the code can be offered by the requesting peer for supporting the scaling of the whole peer-to-peer system (8). Additionally, persistent caching of the code avoids further remote transfers of identical code resulting from future requests. As a last step, an object-specific factory is used to dynamically integrate the fetched code bundle into the running system (9).

5   Applications of the Generic Decentralised Dynamic Loading Infrastructure

In this section, we present two exemplary applications using our proposed loading infrastructure: integration into a CORBA middleware to support mobile objects/services and support for fragmented objects.

5.1   Supporting Dynamic Loading of Code for Mobile Objects and Services

Recently, we proposed a platform-independent object migration service based on the CORBA Life-Cycle Service (LCS) [11]. The LCS specifies several interfaces for supporting object migration. The migration process is shown in Figure 5. A migratable object has to support the `LifeCycleObject` interface that includes a `move()` method for initiating the migration. Within this method, a target location has to be determined. Such location is represented by a *generic factory*, which enables the creation of objects on remote machines. The selection process of an appropriate generic factory is supported by a *factory finder*.

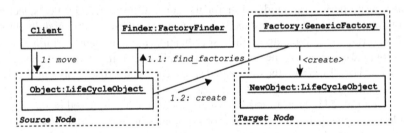

Fig. 5. Object migration based on the CORBA Life Cycle Service

For migrating an object from a source node to a target location, current state and code have to be transferred, as local existence of arbitrary code cannot be assumed. For transferring the state of an object, we use CORBA value types. For code provision, we use our decentralised dynamic loading infrastructure as a CORBA service. Thus, it can be accessed by the generic factory or any other local CORBA application. During the initialisation phase of the ORB, the local JXTA runtime platform is configured and connected to the peer-to-peer network, which enables the service immediately after the ORB's initialisation. The service interface is equal to the interface of the Dynamic Loading Service (DLS) [4] that offers one central method `getFactory()`

for requesting new functionality that is provided by an object implementing the factory pattern. Additionally, our decentralised dynamic loading service offers the opportunity to pass a custom handler for supporting the selection process. The generic factory's create() method for object creation expects a parameter with the required interface's fully-qualified name and optionally a selection handler. Thus, the generic factory is able to request platform- and object-specific factories using the getFactory() method offered by our service. Figure 6 outlines the core sequence of the loading process performed by the service. First, the JxtaDynamicLoader class is invoked for requesting a new implementation and passing a custom object for selecting an appropriate implementation. On success, a CodeBundle reference is passed to our custom class loader instance, which offers a method for creating and initialising a requested object implementation, i.e., in case of the generic factory a specific factory that is able to instantiate the demanded object.

```
public Object getFactory (String moduleClassID,
    DescriptionChecker desc){
  try {
    CodeBundle codeBundle = JxtaDynamicLoader.getCodeHandler().
        getCode(moduleClassID, desc);
    CodeBundleClassLoader loader = new CodeBundleClassLoader(
        codeBundle);
  } catch (NoCodeAvailableException e1) { ... }
    catch (MalformedURLException e2) { ... }
  return loader.loadFactory();
}
```

Fig. 6. Dynamic loading of a previously unknown object within the getFactory() method

Additionally, we implemented a prototype for migrating a web service. Therefor, we transferred the LCS concept to web services, which results in the factory finder and the generic factory being implemented as web services. The generic factory web service offers a create() method, to which the required web service interface is passed (as WSDL). Based on this WSDL description, the generic factory is able to determine the required interface and implementation. In this scenario, the factory directly interacts with our decentralised dynamic loader infrastructure. By using the getCode() method, a service-specific factory can be loaded and created. This service-specific factory is able to deploy a platform-specific instance of the required web service at the target location with setting the correct state (transferred from the original web service).

5.2 Enabling Dynamic Binding of Fragmented Objects

The Aspectix middleware provides a CORBA-compliant but more flexible and extensible Object Request Broker (ORB) implementation compared to standard CORBA by building on a modularisation of the handling of object references (IORs). A *generic reference manager* uses *portable profile managers*, which encapsulate all tasks related to reference handling, i.e., reference creation, reference marshalling and unmarshalling, external representation of references as strings, and type casting of representatives of remote objects [6]. Currently, Aspectix provides profile managers for standard CORBA and additionally offers support for the fragmented object model and other non-CORBA middleware platforms, such as Jini or Java RMI.

On the one hand, a fragmented object offers a standard object interface to the outside, on the other hand, a fragmented object can be composed of several fragments and could be distributed with arbitrary internal architecture. This offers a high degree of freedom and flexibility. For interaction with a fragmented object, a corresponding local fragment has to be created that either acts as a simple stub for the fragmented object or as a more intelligent stub that includes parts of the fragmented object's functionality (implicit binding). Furthermore, such infrastructure enables the exchange of a fragment implementation at run-time and leaves the implementation of the internal communication and structure open to the developer. Binding to a fragmented object in general requires dynamic loading of fragment-specific code as it is not predictable if and when a certain fragment implementation is needed. Therefore dynamic loading of code is an essential service to support fragmented objects at their full flexibility.

We extended the fragmented-object-supporting profile manager by using the dynamic loading service outlined in the previous section. The profile of a fragmented object references the initial fragment implementation, either directly by specifying a class name or indirectly by providing a code reference to the standard DLS. Depending on a tag, either the implementation is directly loaded or one of the two code loading services is used (standard or decentralised). In case of the decentralised loading service, the profile includes a module class ID. This enables loading the code of a certain fragment implementation using the JXTA-based dynamic loading infrastructure as described in Section 4.4. After having loaded the code, the fragment implementation has to be instantiated and initialised. As this is a fragment-specific task, every fragment implementation has a standardised constructor that is executed by the profile manager.

The fragmented object model allows an easy integration of arbitrary internal communication patterns. Thus, by building on our dynamic loading infrastructure, we also created a prototype for dynamic selection, loading and integration of peer-to-peer services into a standard-CORBA-compliant middleware [12]. Therefore, based on the support for fragmented objects, we provide a special JXTA IOR profile that contains a module specification advertisement, which contains the service description and the supported protocol. This enables loading the fragment implementations, which are actually represented by JXTA service instances, using our presented decentralised loading service. Such fragmented objects provide a standard CORBA interface to the outside while internally interacting in a peer-to-peer fashion. Through this, the gap between standard client/server-based middleware and the JXTA peer-to-peer infrastructure can be closed.

6   Related Work

In previous work [4], we presented the Dynamic Loading Service (DLS), a CORBA service for dynamic code loading. Similarly to the realised loading service of this work, the DLS permits to load remote code with consideration of the current runtime environment and other requirements. However, the DLS follows the client/server paradigm and uses dedicated servers to host the program code and to offer specific information about available code. In contrast, our current work builds on a JXTA-based peer-to-peer-network.

Another interesting system is Java Web Start [13]. This software deployment system uses the Java Network Launching Protocol and describes the code and the requirements of a Java application in a special XML format. This results in applications that can be installed over the net via a special Java Web Start client (even system-dependent native libraries can be selected and installed). However, the format is highly Java-specific, aims at installing and updating software and the current release lacks the support for dependent resources and for locally executed compatibility tests.

The OSGi service platform [14] defines an open run-time environment, enabling dynamic service integration. For the bundled representation of a service's functionality, the concept of an OSGi bundle is defined. A special characteristic of such a bundle is the possibility to be dynamically added and removed from the run-time environment. Compared to this work, a bundle offers extended possibilities, in order to specify dependencies of other services. However, the OSGi approach misses sophisticated mechanisms for describing, remotely discovering and selecting code portions as outlined in this work. Furthermore, OSGi primarily targets at code loading and sharing for the Java programming language, whereas our approach is generic and can be applied to other programming languages as well.

Paal et al. proposed a distributed code loading infrastructure based on multiple application repositories that can be dynamically queried by a custom application loader [15]. In contrast to our approach, this system offers fine-grained code loading based on *class collections*, which are represented by class subsets of a Java archive. However, the system is limited to the Java programming language and application repositories have to be preconfigured at initial deployment time for enabling code loading.

A peer-to-peer-based architecture for remote loading of Java classes is described in [16]. This approach shows an alternative way to the standard Java class loader mechanism and is exemplarily realised using JXTA. Compared to our solution, it lacks flexibility to describe and to search for suitable program code. Thus, the architecture neither permits a representation of loadable code with the JXTA concepts of module advertisements nor offers support for a custom transfer protocol.

7 Conclusion and Future Work

We presented a generic and decentralised approach to dynamically discover, select, load and integrate platform-specific code. According to the common peer-to-peer idea, every peer within our infrastructure is able to load code and, additionally, to provide this code on demand. Our prototype implementation extends and improves the mechanisms for dynamic service integration of JXTA. However, the proposed generic concept can be applied to any peer-to-peer infrastructure that at least supports keyword-search. For evaluating the dynamic loading infrastructure, we presented exemplary applications.

Security issues are beyond the scope of this paper. Dynamic loading of code always involves security considerations, and we assume that standard security mechanisms such as code signing and a public-key infrastructure can be used for securing our peer-to-peer-based dynamic loading service. Additionally, JXTA enables restricted groups, in which only authorised peers are able to participate. Thus, a general trust between users can be achieved using such mechanism. However, our implementation does not yet make direct use of such techniques.

Even though our prototype supports the precise selection of platform-specific code, we currently assume that a concrete implementation is more or less self-contained. This means, that either necessary libraries are at the target platform, as described by the compatibility requirements, or included in the dynamically loaded code archive. We therefore would like to provide support for implementations that reference other interfaces or implementations that should be loaded dynamically.

References

1. Weiser, M.: The Computer for the Twenty-First Century. Scientific American, vol. 265(3) (1991)
2. Peterson, L., Anderson, T., Culler, D., Roscoe, T.: A blueprint for introducing disruptive technology into the Internet. SIGCOMM Comput. Commun. Rev. 33(1), 59–64 (2003)
3. Kotsovinos, E., Moreton, T., Pratt, I., Ross, R., Fraser, K., Hand, S., Harris, T.: Global-Scale Service Deployment in the XenoServer Platform. In: 1st Works. on Real, Large Distrib. Sys.—WORLDS'04, San Francisco, CA (December 2004)
4. Kapitza, R., Hauck, F.J.: DLS: a CORBA service for dynamic loading of code. In: OTM Confederated Int. Conf., Sicily, Italy (2003)
5. Gong, L.: JXTA: A Network Programming Environment. IEEE Internet Computing, vol. 5(3) (2001)
6. Hauck, F.J., Kapitza, R., Reiser, H.P., Schmied, A.I.: A Flexible and Extensible Object Middleware: CORBA and beyond. In: 5th Int. Works. on Softw. Eng. and Middlew. ACM Digital Library (2005)
7. Klingberg, T., Manfredi, R.: Gnutella 0.6. Technical report (2002)
8. The Internet Society. Jxta v2.0 protocols specification. Technical report, Sun Microsystems (2001)
9. Sun Microsystems. Jxta v2.3.x: Java programmer's guide. Technical report (2005)
10. Wilson, B.J.: JXTA. New Riders (2002)
11. Kapitza, R., Schmidt, H., Hauck, F.J.: Platform-Independent Object Migration in CORBA. In: OTM Confederated Int. Conf. LNCS, vol. 3760, pp. 900–917. Springer, Heidelberg (2005)
12. Kapitza, R., Bartlang, U., Schmidt, H., Hauck, F.J.: Dynamic integration of peer-to-peer services into a CORBA-compliant middleware. In: OTM 2006 Workshops, Springer, Heidelberg (2006)
13. Sun Microsystems. Java Web Start Overview. White paper (2005)
14. The OSGi Alliance. OSGi service platform: Core specification, release 4. Technical report (2005)
15. Paal, S., Kammüller, R., Freisleben, B.: Dynamic Software Deployment with Distributed Application Repositories. In: 14. Fachtagung Kommunikation in Verteilten Systemen (KiVS), Springer, Heidelberg (2005)
16. Parker, D., Cleary, D.: A p2p approach to classloading in java. In: 2nd Int. Works. on Agents and P2P Comp.—AP2PC'03 (2003)

Author Index

Lecture Notes in Computer Science

For information about Vols. 1–4411

please contact your bookseller or Springer

Vol. 4476: V. Gorodetsky, C. Zhang, V.A. Skormin, L. Cao (Eds.), Autonomous Intelligent Systems: Multi-Agents and Data Mining. XIII, 323 pages. 2007. (Sublibrary LNAI).

Vol. 4475: P. Crescenzi, G. Prencipe, G. Pucci (Eds.), Fun with Algorithms. X, 273 pages. 2007.

Vol. 4472: M. Haindl, J. Kittler, F. Roli (Eds.), Multiple Classifier Systems. XI, 524 pages. 2007.

Vol. 4471: P. Cesar, K. Chorianopoulos, J.F. Jensen (Eds.), Interactive TV: a Shared Experience. XIII, 236 pages. 2007.

Vol. 4470: Q. Wang, D. Pfahl, D.M. Raffo (Eds.), Software Process Dynamics and Agility. XI, 346 pages. 2007.

Vol. 4465: T. Chahed, B. Tuffin (Eds.), Network Control and Optimization. XIII, 305 pages. 2007.

Vol. 4464: E. Dawson, D.S. Wong (Eds.), Information Security Practice and Experience. XIII, 361 pages. 2007.

Vol. 4463: I. Măndoiu, A. Zelikovsky (Eds.), Bioinformatics Research and Applications. XV, 653 pages. 2007. (Sublibrary LNBI).

Vol. 4462: D. Sauveron, K. Markantonakis, A. Bilas, J.-J. Quisquater (Eds.), Information Security Theory and Practices. XII, 255 pages. 2007.

Vol. 4459: C. Cérin, K.-C. Li (Eds.), Advances in Grid and Pervasive Computing. XVI, 759 pages. 2007.

Vol. 4453: T. Speed, H. Huang (Eds.), Research in Computational Molecular Biology. XVI, 550 pages. 2007. (Sublibrary LNBI).

Vol. 4452: M. Fasli, O. Shehory (Eds.), Agent-Mediated Electronic Commerce. VIII, 249 pages. 2007. (Sublibrary LNAI).

Vol. 4451: T.S. Huang, A. Nijholt, M. Pantic, A. Pentland (Eds.), Artifical Intelligence for Human Computing. XVI, 359 pages. 2007. (Sublibrary LNAI).

Vol. 4450: T. Okamoto, X. Wang (Eds.), Public Key Cryptography – PKC 2007. XIII, 491 pages. 2007.

Vol. 4448: M. Giacobini et al. (Ed.), Applications of Evolutionary Computing. XXIII, 755 pages. 2007.

Vol. 4447: E. Marchiori, J.H. Moore, J.C. Rajapakse (Eds.), Evolutionary Computation, Machine Learning and Data Mining in Bioinformatics. XI, 302 pages. 2007.

Vol. 4446: C. Cotta, J. van Hemert (Eds.), Evolutionary Computation in Combinatorial Optimization. XII, 241 pages. 2007.

Vol. 4445: M. Ebner, M. O'Neill, A. Ekárt, L. Vanneschi, A.I. Esparcia-Alcázar (Eds.), Genetic Programming. XI, 382 pages. 2007.

Vol. 4444: T. Reps, M. Sagiv, J. Bauer (Eds.), Program Analysis and Compilation, Theory and Practice. X, 361 pages. 2007.

Vol. 4443: R. Kotagiri, P.R. Krishna, M. Mohania, E. Nantajeewarawat (Eds.), Advances in Databases: Concepts, Systems and Applications. XXI, 1126 pages. 2007.

Vol. 4440: B. Liblit, Cooperative Bug Isolation. XV, 101 pages. 2007.

Vol. 4439: W. Abramowicz (Ed.), Business Information Systems. XV, 654 pages. 2007.

Vol. 4438: L. Maicher, A. Sigel, L.M. Garshol (Eds.), Leveraging the Semantics of Topic Maps. X, 257 pages. 2007. (Sublibrary LNAI).

Vol. 4433: E. Şahin, W.M. Spears, A.F.T. Winfield (Eds.), Swarm Robotics. XII, 221 pages. 2007.

Vol. 4432: B. Beliczynski, A. Dzielinski, M. Iwanowski, B. Ribeiro (Eds.), Adaptive and Natural Computing Algorithms, Part II. XXVI, 761 pages. 2007.

Vol. 4431: B. Beliczynski, A. Dzielinski, M. Iwanowski, B. Ribeiro (Eds.), Adaptive and Natural Computing Algorithms, Part I. XXV, 851 pages. 2007.

Vol. 4430: C.C. Yang, D. Zeng, M. Chau, K. Chang, Q. Yang, X. Cheng, J. Wang, F.-Y. Wang, H. Chen (Eds.), Intelligence and Security Informatics. XII, 330 pages. 2007.

Vol. 4429: R. Lu, J.H. Siekmann, C. Ullrich (Eds.), Cognitive Systems. X, 161 pages. 2007. (Sublibrary LNAI).

Vol. 4427: S. Uhlig, K. Papagiannaki, O. Bonaventure (Eds.), Passive and Active Network Measurement. XI, 274 pages. 2007.

Vol. 4426: Z.-H. Zhou, H. Li, Q. Yang (Eds.), Advances in Knowledge Discovery and Data Mining. XXV, 1161 pages. 2007. (Sublibrary LNAI).

Vol. 4425: G. Amati, C. Carpineto, G. Romano (Eds.), Advances in Information Retrieval. XIX, 759 pages. 2007.

Vol. 4424: O. Grumberg, M. Huth (Eds.), Tools and Algorithms for the Construction and Analysis of Systems. XX, 738 pages. 2007.

Vol. 4423: H. Seidl (Ed.), Foundations of Software Science and Computational Structures. XVI, 379 pages. 2007.

Vol. 4422: M.B. Dwyer, A. Lopes (Eds.), Fundamental Approaches to Software Engineering. XV, 440 pages. 2007.

Vol. 4421: R. De Nicola (Ed.), Programming Languages and Systems. XVII, 538 pages. 2007.

Vol. 4420: S. Krishnamurthi, M. Odersky (Eds.), Compiler Construction. XIV, 233 pages. 2007.

Vol. 4419: P.C. Diniz, E. Marques, K. Bertels, M.M. Fernandes, J.M.P. Cardoso (Eds.), Reconfigurable Computing: Architectures, Tools and Applications. XIV, 391 pages. 2007.

Vol. 4418: A. Gagalowicz, W. Philips (Eds.), Computer Vision/Computer Graphics Collaboration Techniques. XV, 620 pages. 2007.

Vol. 4416: A. Bemporad, A. Bicchi, G. Buttazzo (Eds.), Hybrid Systems: Computation and Control. XVII, 797 pages. 2007.

Vol. 4415: P. Lukowicz, L. Thiele, G. Tröster (Eds.), Architecture of Computing Systems - ARCS 2007. X, 297 pages. 2007.

Vol. 4414: S. Hochreiter, R. Wagner (Eds.), Bioinformatics Research and Development. XVI, 482 pages. 2007. (Sublibrary LNBI).

Vol. 4412: F. Stajano, H.J. Kim, J.-S. Chae, S.-D. Kim (Eds.), Ubiquitous Convergence Technology. XI, 302 pages. 2007.